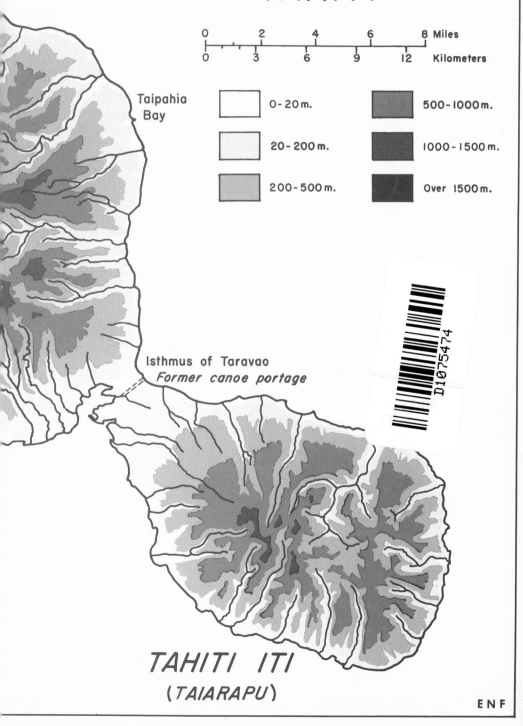

A RELIEF MAP OF

TAHITI

| 0 | 2 | 4 | 6 | 8 Miles |
| 0 | 3 | 6 | 9 | 12 Kilometers |

Taipahia
Bay

0 - 20 m.

20 - 200 m.

200 - 500 m.

500 - 1000 m.

1000 - 1500 m.

Over 1500 m.

Isthmus of Taravao
Former canoe portage

TAHITI ITI
(*TAIARAPU*)

ENF

EARLY TAHITI

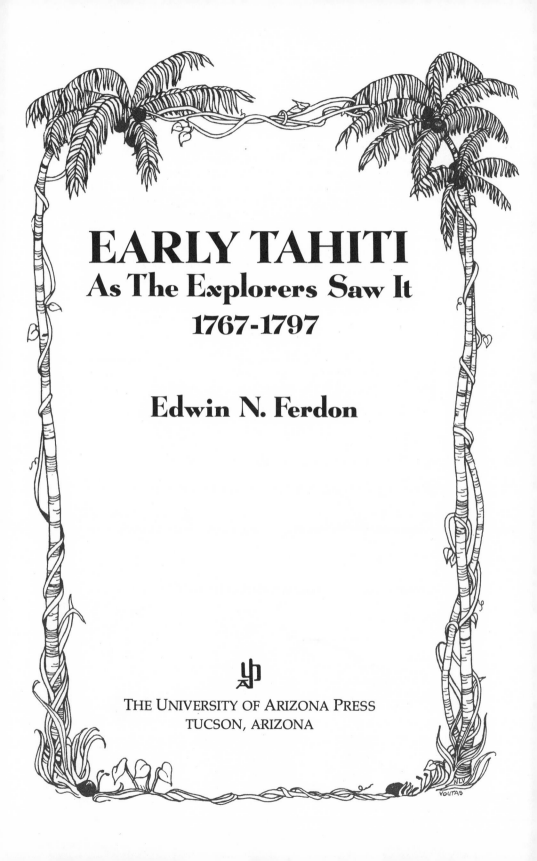

EARLY TAHITI
As The Explorers Saw It
1767-1797

Edwin N. Ferdon

THE UNIVERSITY OF ARIZONA PRESS
TUCSON, ARIZONA

About the Author ...

EDWIN N. FERDON first became interested in early Polynesia in 1955 while serving as an archaeologist on Thor Heyerdahl's Norwegian Archaeological Expedition to Easter Island and the East Pacific. Since then he has published numerous papers and a popular book, *One Man's Log,* on Polynesia's archaeology, ethnography, and geography. During twenty-four years of association with the Museum of New Mexico and School of American Research in Santa Fe and the Arizona State Museum in Tucson, he conducted archaeological surveys and excavations in Mesoamerica, South America, the southwestern United States, and Polynesia. From 1961 to 1978 he was associate director of the Arizona State Museum.

THE UNIVERSITY OF ARIZONA PRESS

This book was set in 11/13 Palatino on a V-I-P Phototypesetter.

Library of Congress Cataloging in Publication Data

Ferdon, Edwin N. 1913–
    Early Tahiti as the explorers saw it, 1767–1797.

    Bibliography: p.
    Includes index.
    1. Ethnology—Society Islands—Tahiti. 2. Tahiti—
Social life and customs. I. Title.
GN671.S55F47   996'.211   80-26469

ISBN 0-8165-0708-2
ISBN 0-8165-0720-1 (pbk.)

To my three children, who
have given me so many years
of happiness and so few moments
of complete obfuscation

Contents

List of Illustrations   xi

A Word From the Author   xiii

The Early Observers   1

Landfall Tahiti   15
   The Tahitians   19
   Dress and Ornament   22

Law and Order   26
   Government by the Chiefly Class   28
   Position of the Paramount Chief   35
   The Lower Classes   44
   Crime and Punishment   47

The Supernatural World   50
   Marae: The Places of Worship   52
   Priests   60
   Red Feathers and Deity   63
   Human Sacrifice   65

Daily Life   71

Houses and Their Furnishings   72
Rahui   83
Division of Labor   84
Meals and Their Preparation   84
Music   99
Records and the Calendar   100
Greetings   103

Tapa: The Gift of Value   108

Materials and Manufacture   109
Techniques of Decoration   118

Recreation   123

Wrestling and Boxing   124
Archery   127
The Performing Arts   129
The 'Arioi Society   138

From Birth to Death   142

Infanticide   142
Birth and Removal of Taboos   144
Growing Up in Tahiti   147
Marriage, Divorce, and Concubinage   152
Illnesses and the Healing Arts   156
Death and Mourning   159

Food From the Land   176

Domesticated Crops   179
Preservation of Breadfruit   190
Animal Husbandry   194

Food From the Sea   199

Fishing With Spear and Net   204
Line-Fishing   211

Trade and Transportation   219

   Methods of Acquiring Goods   221
   Transportation   227
   Types of Canoes   230
   Canoe Construction   240
   Navigational Limits of the Tahitians   245

Warfare   254

   Tahitian Naval Battles   257
   Effects of Defeat   269

To Accept or Reject   274

   Effects of European Trade Goods   275
   Introduction of Foreign Crops   287
   Introduction of Foreign Livestock   295
   Further Effects of European Contact   302

Glossary   315

Notes to the Chapters   319

Bibliography   359

Index   365

Illustrations

Coastal Plain of Tahiti	17
Marae Mahaiatea	53
Features of a Typical Marae	54
Human Sacrifice	67
Coast of the Taiarapu Peninsula	73
Dwelling Complex of a Chief	77
Tools and Household Implements	85
Young Woman Bringing Gift of Tapa	106
Women Beating Out Tapa	115
Heiva Performance	131
Dancing Girls	133
The "Wry Mouth"	135
Tattoo Designs	149
Desiccation of a Chief's Remains	161
Chief Mourner's Costume and Mask	168
Variation of Chief Mourner's Costume	169
Coastal Plain With Breadfruit Tree and Taro Plants	181
Breadfruit	188
Fishing Implements	212
Fishing Crane	215
Va'a-type Canoe	231
Pahi-type Canoe	233
War Canoes	263
Helmet and Gorget	265
Paramount Chief Ceding Land to the Missionaries	313

Maps

Tahiti and Its Location
   Within the Society Islands   29
The Extent of Tahitian Voyaging
   in the Eastern Pacific   250

Sources of Illustrations
(by page number)

By Permission of the British Library

17 (Add. MS 23921, f. 7)
67 (Add. MS 15513, No. 16)
73 (Add. MS 15513, No. 13)
77 (Add. MS 23921, f. 10)
106 (Add. MS 15513, No. 17)
115 (Add. MS 23921, f. 50*b*)
131 (Add. MS 15513, No. 19)
133 (Add. MS 23921, f. 38)

135 (Add. MS 23921, f. 51*a* and *b*)
149 (Add. MS 23921, f. 51*v*)
168 (Add. MS 23921, f. 32)
169 (Add. MS 15513, No. 18)
181 (Add. MS 23921, f. 9)
231 (Add. MS 23921, f. 17)
233 (Add. MS 23921, f. 20)
263 (Add. MS 15743, No. 8)

Reprints From Old Books

53. James Wilson, *A Missionary Voyage to the Southern Pacific Ocean, Performed in the Years 1796, 1797, 1798 in the Ship Duff* ... (London, 1799).

85, 188. John Hawkesworth, *Cook's First Voyage*, vol. II in *An Account of the Voyages Undertaken ... for Making Discoveries in the Southern Hemisphere* ... (London, 1773).

161. James Cook, *A Voyage to the Pacific Ocean Undertaken ... for Making Discoveries in the Northern Hemisphere* ... (London, 1784).

215. William Ellis, *Polynesian Researches, During a Residence of Nearly Six Years in the South Sea Islands* ... , vol. II (London, 1829).

265. Reproduced by permission of the Bernice P. Bishop Museum, Honolulu.

313. William Ellis, *Polynesian Researches, During a Residence of Nearly Six Years in the South Sea Islands* ... , vol. I (London, 1829).

A Word From the Author

The sudden shudder that ran through the hull of the stretched-out DC-8 clearly signaled the lowering of wing flaps and wheels as the huge plane made its final approach to Tahiti's international airport in the fall of 1976. A brief screech of black rubber on the runway abruptly announced the arrival of yet another planeload of tourists to be disgorged onto the lush green coastland of Tahiti.

Accommodating myself to the teeming movement of crowds at the busy air terminal, I reflected that only twenty years had passed since Captain Arne Hartmark had gently eased Thor Heyerdahl's Norwegian Expedition ship alongside the quay at Papeete. Then, there had been several hundred brown-skinned men and women assembled on the wharf to stare with open curiosity at us foreigners and our little Greenland trawler. But gone was that day. The seemingly inherent native curiosity about visitors to Tahiti had long since been diluted by the ever-increasing flood of tourism to this island world.

In the latter half of the eighteenth century, when the first Europeans arrived in the Pacific, Polynesian life was still pristine. The purpose of this volume is to reconstruct the culture of early Tahiti, as it was before the irreversible influences of the Europeans altered it for all time.

The book itself is the delayed result of my participation in Heyerdahl's Norwegian Archaeological Expedition to Easter Island and the East Pacific during 1955–56. Having never before worked in Polynesia, I soon found that it is one thing to excavate the remains of prehistoric Polynesians and quite another to re-create the life that originally made the shell and bone artifacts, built the ceremonial structures of stone, and occasionally carved statues out of native rock. One way to accomplish this task might be to examine the living patterns of today's residents, an approach used by my former mentor, Edgar L. Hewett, in studying the Indians of the southwestern United States during the 1930s. By observing their customs and lifeways, and by winnowing out that which had been acquired from the Spanish and later the Anglos, he could acquire a reasonable idea of how their prehistoric ancestors might have lived. This concept of living archaeology is as valid in the 1980s as it was some forty-five years ago when Hewett patiently tried to drill the idea into the minds of his young students.

However, most of Polynesia is different. European and American acculturative forces have, in somewhat more than one hundred and fifty years, effectively destroyed—to a degree much greater than in the southwestern United States—the unifying strength of native governments, social organization, and religion, while foreign goods and materials have largely replaced the material manifestations of Polynesian life. Thus, if valid living archaeology no longer exists in that island world, or is watered down by contaminated legends and orally transmitted memories of how things were thought to have been, then one must look elsewhere.

The first Europeans to explore the Pacific had seen pristine Polynesian life and had written down what they saw. The observations they recorded provide an indirect means of reaching back through history to the living archaeology that they had been privileged to witness. The officers and naturalists of these earliest voyages were not trained anthropologists, although John Forster, a naturalist on Captain Cook's second voyage, could have passed himself off as one, but they were intelligent, inquisitive men and, being sailors and naturalists, had an observational ability that was a mark of their trade. However, there is a vast area of culture which is not easily discernible to the eye and must be acquired through verbal communication. With a few notable exceptions, this aspect of Polynesian culture remained unavailable to the earliest explorers, for they were poor linguists, and the Polynesians made little effort to learn the languages of their visitors.

It was not until the early 1800s that missionaries broke the language barrier and, largely through the use of informants, attempted to reconstruct the life of the past. However, by then much had already been lost, and the memories of things past had become both vague and confusing. Thus, while incomplete at best, the pre-missionary accounts of the earliest explorers must stand as the most accurate records of pristine Tahiti. While their personal interpretations, and there are not many, may be faulty, their descriptions of things seen should be reasonably precise, just as the missionary records of things observed are probably correct for their time. Therefore, it was the early exploration record that I came to use in attempting to re-create pre-missionary Tahitian life. It is through the eyes of these early explorers that I have described the life of Tahiti in the latter half of the eighteenth century, using later missionary observational accounts only to fill occasional gaps or to illustrate historical changes through time.

While early voyagers endeavored to record many of the Tahitian words, what each one heard and how he wrote it down was anything but systematic. To bring consistency to the spelling of such words I have used the work of Edmund Andrews and Irene D. Andrews, *A Comparative Dictionary of the Tahitian Language,* as my principal reference.

I happily confess my indebtedness to various friends and colleagues who helped me during the seven years of intermittent research that it took to bring forth this final study. Initially, there was my friend Raymond H. Thompson, director of the Arizona State Museum of the University of Arizona, who encouraged me to undertake this investigation and aided me in successfully applying for an NSF Institutional Grant, and a research stipend from the University of Arizona's Graduate College Committee for

Faculty Research Support. To him, and to those members of the committees who so generously saw to the financial assistance of my research, I express my sincere gratitude. For their active interest and competence in acquiring the documents that made this study possible, I am profoundly grateful to the library staff of the University of Arizona in general, and most particularly to Hans R. Bart, later with the library of the Arizona State Museum, and Andrew L. Makuch. The cooperation and interest they have shown to researchers set a fine example of librarianship. To the secretaries of the Arizona State Museum and the University of Arizona Department of Anthropology, Barbara Fregoso, Suzie Horning, and the late Mildred Ogg, I am indebted for the hours they spent typing early drafts of the manuscript. Thanks are due to the University of Arizona Press for bringing about publication, especially to Kim Vivier and Francis Morgan, for their personal attention to editorial and production refinements, and to Nora Voutas, for her title-page and chapter-title decorations.

Finally, while I accept full responsibility for any weaknesses of interpretation in this book, I am certain that it would not have fared as well as it has without the critical review and commentary given each chapter by Jane Underwood, of the Department of Anthropology at the University of Arizona, and the painstaking editing and final typing by my most patient wife, Vearl. For this, as well as for their constant encouragement, I offer my heartfelt thanks.

EDWIN N. FERDON

The Early Observers

To a certain extent it was Captain James Cook and his voyagers who inadvertently started the whole business of tourism in Tahiti. Although Samuel Wallis discovered the island for Europeans, it was Cook and other eighteenth-century explorers whose written and garrulous accounts of the Pacific led Europeans and Englishmen alike into euphoric dreams of Tahiti as nature's human paradise. With life as it was for the lower classes in the squalid, burgeoning cities of the Industrial Revolution of eighteenth-century Europe, there can be little wonder that only the pleasant and desirable in these accounts maintained a hold on the imagination, all else being forgotten or pushed aside.

For those of a religious bent, paradise gained became paradise lost, for the early accounts were soon followed by a series of sobering nineteenth-century reports from the London Missionary Society's devout and strong-willed field men. These proselytizers sent back what appeared to be more realistic accounts of the Tahitian lifestyle. In their eyes, the dreamed-of paradise in the Pacific, if it had ever existed at all, had been lost long before Europeans set foot on the sandy shores of these miniature islands. Besides the horror of false, heathen gods, it was found that the chiefs were autocratic crushers of the common man, that mass death and destruction marked a seemingly endless series of wars for conquest, and that between battles time was spent in orgies of lewd dancing and indiscriminate bed-hopping by both sexes. As if this were not enough to prove the need for ecclesiastical interference and the money to undertake the endeavor, it had been revealed that children born out of wedlock were killed at the moment of birth. Thus, for a brief period, Europeans thought that they had discovered a paradise on earth, only to find that it had never existed.

While missionary accounts became the mainstay of anthropologists, the idyllic dreams created by the accounts of Cook and his eighteenth-century cohorts took hold in the imagination of the general public. Two hundred years after Europeans discovered the island, its attraction was even greater than before: with the speeding jets of the 1970s the young eagerly searched out the Tahitian paradise, while the elderly and retired satisfied themselves with a leisurely cruise to "the island of love."

There is little doubt that the years they spent in Tahiti and the other Society Islands gave the missionaries ample time to observe and study the Polynesian people. However, their tight moralistic confines biased their views of any behavior that did not meet their approval. That which did not conform was considered the work of the devil and loomed large in their eyes and in their writing. Nonetheless, where the devil was not involved, and direct observation was employed, their written records are sound enough. That is to say, they are sound for the time in which they were written. Unfortunately, changing culture waits for no one, not even a missionary, and thirty years had passed between the discovery of Tahiti in 1767 and the arrival of the first missionaries in 1797. Minor, but significant, changes had already altered Tahitian life, and in no time at all the hard-driving missionaries succeeded in modifying the culture still further. Thus, except for the original reports of the first missionaries from the ship *Duff*, these records present a Tahitian culture already affected by Christian mores. In fact, some informant-derived accounts include obvious, intentional berating of their own "savage" past so that contemporary Tahitians might now appear more "civilized" in the eyes of their culture-probing missionary friends. As for those lost thirty years, the missionaries valiantly employed a technique, still dear to Pacific anthropologists, of querying the elderly as to how it was "in the old days." The results are exactly what one might expect from an elderly mind: there are spots of brilliantly lit memories of the past, but there are also vast areas of dim recollection in which the past, present, and imagination have become inextricably mixed and confused.

While the self-righteous missionaries tended to look down on the Tahitians as pitifully simple, savage souls, the less-than-righteous early explorers saw them in a different light. Their view was that people were people the world over, and if the Pacific was to be known and the crews fed, the Polynesians had to be dealt with in the same manner as any other nation. Caution, force — including that of superior arms when needed — and beguiling — through trade and participation in the customs of the island — all played a part. Most came to Tahiti as voyagers bent on refurbishing their sea stores and giving their men a well-earned rest. They were explorers at heart, and as such they recorded their observations, with no more biases than anyone takes with him into a field of strangers. Some, such as the naturalists, Joseph Banks, John Forster, and George Forster, and the Swede, Anders Sparrman, were highly educated in a formal sense. Others were self-taught in the rugged school of experience. None, not even William Bligh, allowed himself the superior, overlording attitude that is so blatantly visible in the writings of the missionaries. They were, in summation, men trying to do their job, and do it they did.

It is the accounts of these voyagers, from 1767 to, and including, the first missionary arrivals in 1797, that constitute the best extant record of Tahitian life before the onset of forced "civilizing" which sharply skewed the direction of Tahitian culture change. While masses of trade goods and gifts, especially iron, changed certain aspects of material culture during this period, the general lifestyle, the manner of growing up and of doing things both secular and religious, was altered but slightly, if at all. The explorers made no overt effort, unlike the missionaries, to force the Tahitians to abandon their ways. They were essentially free to pick and choose from the goods offered them, and to copy at will the European customs they heard about and saw practiced by sailors, officers, and naturalists alike. While such change was going on at the Tahitians' discretion, the voyagers avidly recorded their own daily lives on the island, punctuated here and there with detailed descriptions of those aspects of Tahitian life that interested them. Although the entire record of such logs and journals over this thirty-year period has yet to be published, many of them have been, and it is from these that the following account has been gleaned. It is not a record of one or another explorer, but rather a composite of many different accounts. Since language was always a problem, except for the Spanish interpreter Máximo Rodríguez, observable patterns of culture are the rule. Such as it is, the record is a vivid picture of Tahitian life. Although it falls short of that euphoric paradise that Europeans dreamed of, it must be looked upon as a rather pleasant, unassuming existence.

The Expeditions

1767   Captain Samuel Wallis, commander of the British ship *Dolphin*, sighted Tahiti, a new discovery, on June 19, 1767, and dropped anchor in Matavai Bay five days later on June 24. He left Tahiti on July 27 of the same year after a stay of thirty-two days.

  The published journal of Wallis and the diary of the ship's master, George Robertson, contain remarkably fine ethnographic descriptions, though the former must be used with caution because of Wallis's illness at the time and his admission that, because of it, his record regarding Tahiti may not be accurate.

1768   Louis Antoine de Bougainville, commander of the French expedition ship *La Boudeuse* and the store ship *L'Etoile*, sighted Tahiti on April 2, 1768, and dropped anchor in Taipahia Bay on the northeastern coast of the island on April 6. He remained only eight days, leaving his anchorage on April 15, 1768.

Bougainville's brief observations of Tahitian life published in the journal of his voyage are extremely limited because of his short stay.

1769   Captain James Cook, commander of the British ship *Endeavour*, making the first of his three voyages of discovery, anchored in Matavai Bay, Tahiti, on April 13, 1769. After a lengthy stay of three months he continued his voyage, leaving Tahiti on July 13 of the same year.

Like Cook's later two voyages, this one resulted in the publication of extremely valuable ethnographic observations. Besides the data in his own journal, there are the youthfully inquisitive observations of that renowned and financially independent naturalist, Sir Joseph Banks. Banks, only twenty-five years of age at the time, not only shipped out with Cook but supplied his own entourage of scientific staff to help him in his studies. Among these men was the botanical draftsman Sydney Parkinson, one year younger than Banks, whose writings, published after his death, include a valuable record of the various plants of Tahiti and their uses. His paintings and sketches made during the expedition have also served as sources of valuable information. In addition to these prime sources is the record of the voyage published by an anonymous author and member of the expedition.

1772   Don Domingo Boenechea, commander of the Spanish vessel *Santa María Magdalena,* also called *Aguila,* out of Callao, Peru, dropped anchor in the small bay immediately west of Tautira on the north side of the Taiarapu Peninsula of Tahiti on November 19, 1772. After a stay of thirty days he departed for South America on December 20, taking with him four Tahitian men, two of whom lived to return to their island on the second voyage of the *Aguila* in 1774.

Boenechea's published observations of Tahitian culture, along with those of Ensign Raimundo Bonacorsi and Fr. José Amich, although limited to the area around Tautira, are nonetheless of considerable value. Of additional worth is the published information gathered by Juan Hervé, master of the *Aguila*, who obtained his data through direct questioning of the Tahitians taken to Lima, Peru.

1773–74 Captain James Cook, commanding his second expedition into the Pacific with the ships *Resolution* and *Adventure*, visited Tahiti twice in the course of this voyage of discovery. His first contact almost resulted in shipwreck when he attempted to enter the bay west of Tautira where the Spanish vessel *Aguila* had lain the year before. After finally making a landing on August 18, 1773, he spent only five days at this location and on August 24 set sail for his previous anchorage at Matavai Bay, arriving there on August 26. Here he stayed another five days, setting sail again on September 1. Returning from his Antarctic explorations, Cook again put in to Tahiti, dropping anchor in Matavai Bay on April 4, 1774. After twenty-one days of recuperation and taking on supplies, he again set sail on May 14.

While the total number of days Cook spent on the island of Tahiti was considerably less than during his first visit in 1769, the published ethnographic records from his journal, and those of the naturalist team of John R. Forster and his son George, are excellent in corroborating some of the earlier observations as well as adding considerable new data. Anders Sparrman, the Swedish naturalist whom the Forsters discovered working at the Cape of Good Hope and insisted be allowed to join the expedition, eventually published his own journal of the voyage. Although containing some ethnographic observations of value, it offers considerably less than one might have expected, or at least hoped for, from such a man. As for the published account of the voyage by gunner's mate John Marra, the work does not appear to be too solid, although here and there one finds bits of data which, taken with the above documents, are of some value.

1774–75 Don Domingo Boenechea made his second voyage to Tahiti as commander of the *Aguila,* which served as an escort for the store ship *Jupiter,* owned and commanded by Don José de Andia y Varela. Both vessels anchored in the bay west of Tautira on November 27, 1774. Here they stayed, except for a brief trip to the island of Raiatea west of Tahiti, during the period from January 7 to 20, 1775. It was on January 26, after their return to their old anchorage of Tautira, that Commander Boenechea died and his position was taken by the Lieutenant-Commander Tomás Gayangos. The ships sailed for Peru on January 28, 1775.

The primary, overt purpose of this voyage was to install two Catholic priests, Fr. Geronimo Clota and Fr. Narciso González, on the island for the purpose of bringing Christianity to the natives of Tahiti. They arrived fully equipped with a house, tools, garden seeds, and trade goods, as well as a servant of sorts and, more important to this study, an interpreter by the name of Máximo Rodríguez. Rodríguez had learned the language of the island from those Tahitians who had survived the trip to Lima.

As for the priests, it is doubtful if two more ill-prepared missionaries could have been sent to Tahiti. Barely able to take care of themselves, they looked askance at much that was Tahitian and seem to have spent most of their time concerned with their living conditions and in fear of their personal safety. However, it was quite the opposite with their interpreter, whose fluency in Tahitian and apparent willingness to adapt to the local culture immediately placed him under the friendly protection of the chiefly class.

During the nine and one-half months he spent on Tahiti, from January 28 to November 12, 1775, Rodríguez freely roamed the entire island and was treated as a member of the chiefly class. With such freedom of movement and no language barrier, it is little wonder that his diary contains some of the most authentic data available for this early period. While it seems that he lacked the investigative curiosity of Joseph Banks or George Forster, this may be a premature assessment, since he referred in his diary to a special document he prepared which seems to have been directly concerned with various aspects of Tahitian culture. Unfortunately, this document has yet to come to light. As for the reports of the two missionaries, they are of somewhat limited ethnographic value considering their length of stay. Of more importance are the published reports of the two commanders who brought them to the island, Andia y Varela and Gayangos.

With the third voyage of the *Aguila*, which arrived in Tahiti November 2, 1775, to pick up the missionary entourage and left on November 12, active Spanish interest in Tahiti ceased to exist.

1777   Captain James Cook, commanding his third expedition into the Pacific with the ships *Resolution* and

Discovery, put in to Tahiti for the shortest stay of his three voyages. First anchoring in the bay off Tautira on August 13, 1777, he obtained a few supplies and gathered what information he could regarding the Spanish visits. Completing his business, he transferred his vessels to Matavai Bay on August 23 and, on August 29, set sail for Raiatea.

This was the last of the great voyages of Captain Cook, who lost his life at Kealakekua Bay, Hawaii, on February 14, 1779. Cook's published journal of his last voyage and the splendidly useful published extracts of ethnographic observations by others of the expedition so thoughtfully included in the J. C. Beaglehole edition of his voyages have been of immense value. These include observations by such men as Charles Clerke, second in command of the expedition and commander of the *Discovery* until Cook's death, when he assumed command of the *Resolution* until his own demise; James King, originally second lieutenant of the *Resolution,* then promoted to first lieutenant and, on August 22, 1779, to commander of the *Discovery;* David Samwell, surgeon's first mate on the *Resolution* and later surgeon on the *Discovery;* and William Anderson, surgeon on the *Resolution* until his death. In addition to these sources, the published journal of the American from Groton, Connecticut, John Ledyard, who became corporal of marines aboard the *Resolution* after Cook's death, has been most helpful, while the journal of John Rickman, second lieutenant on the *Discovery,* has been of only marginal aid. A rather large number of unpublished logs and journals that accrued from Cook's three voyages are located in the Public Record Office in London, while others are in the Mitchell and Dixson libraries in Sydney, Australia, and the Alexander Turnbull Library in Wellington, New Zealand.

1788–89 Lieutenant William Bligh, who at twenty-two years of age had been master of the *Resolution* on Captain Cook's last voyage, was placed in command of the ship *Bounty* for the purpose of sailing to Tahiti to collect breadfruit plants for transferral to the West Indies. Arriving at his destination, he anchored in Matavai Bay on October 26, 1788. After a stay of somewhat more than five months, his collecting completed, he left the island on April 4, 1789. It was during the latter part of this voyage, after the *Bounty* left the Tongan Islands, that the famous mutiny occurred, and he and a few loyal crew members made the remarkable open-boat voyage through the uncharted waters of the Fiji Islands and on to Timor, a distance of about 4,000 miles.

Not only had Bligh learned something of the Tahitian language during his brief stay on the island during Cook's third voyage, but he appears to have continued his study by way of word lists and native informants from the chiefly class during this particular visit. Regardless of how he may have treated his crew, his journal reflects a kindly concern for the Tahitians and a keen interest in their cultural activities. While collecting breadfruit plants may have been his prime mission, his lengthy stay allowed him to leave us some excellent ethnohistoric records published in his journal of the voyage.

1789   John Henry Cox, commanding the British brig *Mercury*, landed in Tahiti on August 9, 1789, only about four months after Bligh had departed. He stayed on the island less than one month, departing September 2, 1789.

What makes Cox's visit to the island of some help to this study are the observations made by his lieutenant of marines, George Mortimer, who published a journal of this voyage.

1791   Captain Edward Edwards, commanding the frigate *Pandora*, was sent into the Pacific to track down and return the mutineers of the *Bounty*. He reached Tahiti and anchored in Matavai Bay on March 23, 1791, and left there two weeks later on April 8.

Edwards was clearly in the Pacific for one purpose only, all else being of secondary importance. However, his published record, as well as that of his surgeon, George Hamilton, have added to our composite picture of Tahitian culture in spite of the *Pandora's* short stay at the island.

1791–92 George Vancouver, commanding an expedition of two British naval vessels, the *Discovery* and the *Chatham* (the latter commanded by William Robert Broughton), reached Tahiti on December 30, 1791, and happily found the *Chatham* already anchored in Matavai Bay. The two ships had become separated when off southern New Zealand and, while both vessels had made new discoveries in their separate runs, the *Chatham* had reached their Tahiti rendezvous three days earlier on December 27. Both vessels sailed for the Hawaiian Islands on January 24, 1792.

Tahiti was not new to Vancouver who, as a midshipman, had sailed with Captain Cook on his third voyage. However, on this somewhat brief visit fourteen years later, he found himself concerned about what he saw as a Tahitian dependence upon European trade goods, resulting in a loss of traditional native items and the knowledge of their manufacture. Such insight is typical of his observations, and one wishes that he had stayed longer to add to his record of the culture change that was taking place. In one respect, this year of 1792 was historic for Tahitians in presaging the coming economic forces which were to eventually accelerate these cultural changes. It was only the following month after the *Discovery* and *Chatham* had left Matavai that the first whaling ship, the *Matilda*, anchored briefly in the bay. Other European ships bent on economic gain were soon to follow in increasing numbers.

1792   Captain William Bligh, commanding a return expedition to collect breadfruit plants, anchored his two ships, the *Providence* and the smaller vessel *Assistance* (the latter commanded by Nathaniel Portlock), in Matavai Bay on April 10, 1792. This time the mission took only slightly more than three months, and he sailed from Tahiti on July 20 of the same year.

The full journal of Bligh's second voyage has not been published, but Ida Lee has faithfully extracted and published his observations of a historic and ethnographic value in her book on his second voyage. Bligh not only recorded the cultural scene but specifically requested his hosts to allow him to view practices which he had failed to observe on his previous voyage. His notes have been well worth the reading.

1795   William Robert Broughton, commanding the British sloop *Providence* and her tender, reached Tahiti and anchored in Matavai Bay on November 29, 1795. His was a brief stay of less than two weeks, for he set sail on December 11 of the same year, bound for Hawaii and Japan.

Broughton's visit was so brief that the published account of his voyage has been of only marginal importance to this study.

1797   Captain James Wilson, commanding the British missionary vessel *Duff*, first anchored in Matavai Bay, Tahiti, on March 6, 1797. After arrangements had been made and cargo unloaded for the settlement of a small missionary party brought out from England, Wilson set sail on March 26 to establish still other missionaries on Tongatapu and the Marquesas Islands. Returning to Tahiti on July 6 of the same year to ascertain the welfare of the missionaries and to make final allocations of cargo for their use, he set sail for Tongatapu and England on August 4, 1797.

While Wilson's published journal contains many useful ethnographic observations, one of his most significant contributions was the survey he made around the perimeter of Tahiti to determine the probable population of the island. While the figure that he arrived at may be questioned because of the technique employed, the additional information recorded in the process, such as his notes on land divisions and use, is of inestimable value for this early period. In addition, his Appendix, which appears to constitute a summation not only of his observations but also of those of the missionaries who had remained on the island for more than three months during his absence on Tongatapu and the Marquesas, constitutes an excellent, organized source of cultural and natural history data.

One might take the view that the above voyages represented nothing more than relatively brief visitations during which little data of ethnographic value could be gained. However, summation of the days spent on Tahiti by all of the above, including those few who were left on the island for varying periods of time, is startling. It amounts to no less than 1,014 days, or about two and three-quarters years. If we should go so far as to determine the man-days on the island, including only those whose published journals and records have been used in this study, that figure would be more than doubled. This is not to suggest that even one quarter of each man's time was spent in actively observing and recording cultural data, but rather to make the point that such observations as they did make, when considered temporally, represent an important amount of time devoted to such studies.

Landfall Tahiti

"The country has the most delightful and romantic appearance that can be imagined..." wrote Englishman Samuel Wallis of his discovery of Tahiti in 1767.[1] The fact that his men were sick and in need of fresh fruit and greens no doubt added to the beauty of the vision, just as it must have done for the first settlers of the Society Islands, of which Tahiti is a part. Like Wallis, those first human migrants were part of a biological chance dispersal trend that had been going on in the Pacific Ocean for thousands of years. However, there was one significant difference between the late arrival of these human populations and their earlier plant and animal counterparts that had also found their way onto this bold speck of land. The former had arrived by means of a transport system of their own independent devising, while the latter had not. Culture, that uniquely human, extrabiological trait, created the craft that brought people there and, in a more complex and less understood manner, initially caused them to be set adrift, or to purposely face the unknown seas in voyages of discovery.

Tahiti had not always presented itself in the pleasingly seductive manner described by Wallis. It had taken centuries of unnoticed volcanic activity to build its underwater cone from the ocean floor upwards some ten or fifteen thousand feet until the pressure of the overlying sea could no longer contain the eruptive forces. When that point was reached,

Tahiti rose through the troubled waters and, roaring with fiery anger, commenced to build its island world. For numerous years it continued to tap its wellspring of extended youth by periodically pouring forth lava and volcanic debris so that its older, weathered skin was covered anew. However, death comes even to volcanoes, and, long before the arrival of the first humans, Tahiti had quitted the noisy scene of its youthful virulence.

Silently, and ever so slowly, living, reproducing life came to settle on the initially barren rocky mass. Some of it must have arrived while the volcano was still building, while other forms touched down, or drifted in, after the paroxysms of violent growth had ceased, and peace had come to the land.

The passing of ten or twenty thousand years between each new, and successful, transplant of life is not unlikely, since one of the great barriers to natural dispersion, the living ocean, surrounds Tahiti and its neighboring islands. To cross this watery waste by natural methods meant floating, rafting, or spinning aloft in the violent winds of some tropical storm, and gently gliding down again a thousand miles from home. Just as likely was the accidental hitching of a ride in the downy feathers of some sea-searching bird. Or perhaps a seed, surviving a trip through a bird's stomach, was dropped in a nest or a crack in a rock on some distant island. Under such conditions a successful landing and colonization on a miniature earthy spot in the middle of the southern Pacific represented a minor miracle. Nonetheless, we know that it happened, not just once but many times, as the native fauna and flora of the Polynesian Islands prove. However, nature provided a series of dispersal filters which restrained some would-be migrants, while allowing others to pass through. Distance, available transport mechanisms, and, in some cases, the need for bisexuality in reproduction, represented some of these filters, which worked separately or in unison. Their result is well illustrated by the limited range of native plants and animals present in the Pacific island world.

Human migrations into the mighty Pacific were no exceptions in being regulated by dispersal filters. However, in

View of the narrow coastal plain of Tahiti with a pandanus tree in the foreground. Unsigned wash drawing by Sydney Parkinson.

this case the filters that restrained some and yet let others pass through were often of mankind's own making. Thus, there were those who were land-based and by tradition turned their backs to the sea; but there were others who looked outward toward the vast ocean, and descendants of these latter can be found scattered around the entire rim of the Pacific. For them, the basic obstacle of land orientation had been overcome. Why, then, did some move outward into the deep blue water in search of who knows what, while others contented themselves with coasting? Cultural orientation, technology, and history all play a part in the ultimate answers. However, to these we must add the factor of chance, for in any seafaring there is always the risk of storms and losing one's course, sometimes resulting in an accidental voyage to the farthest reaches of the sea.

Thus it would seem that the human populating of Polynesia may have been due partially to intentional searching by early deep-water sailors, and partially to the same naturally induced dispersal methods which furnished the islands with plants and animals. In this latter case, however, the transport mechanism would have been an accidental voyage.

Certainly by historic times the great majority of the islands were populated. The presence of certain dominant economic plants and the Malayo-Polynesian language indicates that a major component of the inhabitants came from the general area of tropical east Asia. This is not to say that other circum-Pacific seafaring cultures had not passed this way and contributed to the cultural melange found on various Polynesian islands. Many groups were fully capable of deep-water sailing, and some may have even settled certain of the islands before they were culturally overwhelmed and submerged by later arrivals. With time, patience, and effort scholars may eventually reveal the picture of human dispersals into the Pacific. In the meantime, let us simply proceed to bring our settlers of Tahiti sailing, or perhaps drifting, across the Pacific from an as-yet-unknown homeland. Raising an island suitable to their needs, they settled it and, in the course of time, came to refer to it as Tahiti.

How fared these first migrants to Tahiti, and how managed the other voyagers that must have followed them in the intervening years before European discovery? These questions remained unanswered at the time of this writing, for in 1980 the archaeological investigation of the Society Islands was still in its infancy. That many, if not most, successfully survived the landing and adapted to the island's environmental riches is amply demonstrated by the historical records from which this volume derives.

The Tahitians

Though the populations of Europe were characterized by a rather limited range of skin colors, the early explorers found the Tahitians well within their tolerances of racial acceptability. A few were actually described as being white, while other writers hedged a little and described these fairer people as being "almost" like Europeans. In fact, there were two reports of true blondism, two women being described as having white skin and blue eyes, and at least one of these having reddish curly hair. However, the bulk of the population was described as having some tint of brown in their skin. The lighter shades were described in such terms as clear olive, pale mahogany, light brown, or tawny. The darker ones received such descriptive terms as red, dark copper, and very dark brown. These deeper tones were said to be found principally among fishermen and the working classes, and thus were thought to be attributable to the burning of the sun's rays. Certainly tanning from outdoor activity would account for a degree of darkening of the skin. However, it must also be kept in mind that high chief Tu, who was hardly a laborer, was described as being of swarthy, or dark, complexion.

Tahitian men could never have been described as little people. Europeans found them to be about their own average height, or a little greater, while Wallis was a bit more specific, giving an average range of between five feet seven inches and five feet ten inches, a few being somewhat taller or shorter. The taller individuals apparently belonged to the well-fed chiefly class, the missionaries claiming that few chiefs were under six feet in height. High chief Tu was said to be one of the tallest men on the island and measured six feet three inches, and his son Tinah was said to measure six feet four inches. As for the Tahitian women, they measured between five feet and five feet five inches, though the wives of some of the chiefs were described as being tall. However, women of the common class were pictured as being rather small. Because the women of the lower Tahitian ranks were the most accommodating to the sailors, their smaller build was thought by some to be the result of stunted growth due to too much early sexual activity! Why a similar effect was not in evidence on their equally young and fervent Tahitian male companions seems never to have been put to the question.

To the European voyagers the Tahitian face represented a pleasantly handsome countenance enhanced by sparkling, brilliant black eyes. Apparently Tahitian lips were more prominent than those of their European visitors but were not regarded as being disagreeably so. However, it was the Tahitian nose which was most disappointing, because it tended to be short and flat. This latter characteristic seems to have been an artifically induced feature which the Tahitians apparently thought improved their looks. The process of depressing the nose was begun by the midwife immediately upon the birth of a child and continued during its early years. The formation of this shape may have been at the will of the child's parents, for it was not universal among the population. Thus, it is stated that the high chief Tu had an aquiline nose, while another chief, Tai, had a nose described as being well proportioned. The fact that both of these men held chiefly status suggests that flattened noses were a mark of beauty only for those of lower rank.

There is little question that the dominant hair color among Tahitians was black, though there were reports of shades of brown, and even blond. Although some Tahitians' hair was tightly curled and others' was slightly less so, that of the majority hung in smooth, straight strands.[2] In the case of women, and the men who worked at fishing, it was cropped short around the head. The hair of other men, especially those of higher rank, was allowed to grow long, and was then either tied on top of the head or allowed to fall loosely down the neck and over the shoulders. If the hair was coarse and tightly curled, as with the high chief Tu and his brothers, it simply stood out as one large puff surrounding the head. Members of the upper classes strewed their hair with the male flowers of the *fara*, or pandanus, to give it a pleasant odor. Scented coconut oil, as will be described later, was also employed for this purpose.

All the men appear to have grown beards, but they seem to have extended from the chin downwards, the upper lip and cheeks usually, though not always, being cleared of hair. This was accomplished by plucking, cutting it with a sharpened shell, or shaving the area with a shark's tooth conveniently fitted to a rough piece of shell. Eradication of hair from under the armpits was also deemed essential for both sexes for the sake of cleanliness, the lack of which practice among Europeans furthered the Tahitians' view that the foreigners were rather unclean.[3]

Finally, as far as the natural body beautiful was concerned, certain of the higher chiefs, as well as the dancing girls who came from the upper social ranks, allowed their fingernails to grow long as a symbol of their nonworking status.[4] John Forster was immediately struck by the similarity of this custom to that reported for China and Java, and he further noted that lengthened thumbnails were common among certain people in Mindanao in the Philippines.[5] The isolated occurrences of this seemingly Asiatic trait in the middle of the Pacific present an intriguing question: Did some mainland junk once touch briefly in Tahitian waters and leave this status symbol as evidence of its visit? The native chief, priest, and island geographer, Tupaia, in 1769 was said to have reported that in the lifetime of his great-grandfather a hostile ship had reached the Society Islands.[6] John Forster reasoned, with the help of Alexander Dalrymple, that such a vessel must have been that of Pedro Fernández de Quiros in 1606, but evidence does not support this assumption. In 1722 Jacob Roggeveen's ships did pass within distant sight of Borabora and Maupiti but made no attempt to move into the Society group.[7] Did all exploration of Polynesia have to originate in Europe, or be conducted by

Europeans living on the western shores of the Americas? I think not; however, long fingernails as a fashionable device have appeared independently elsewhere in the world, and thus the Tahitian custom probably had a similar local origin. Regardless, there is no reason to completely rule out voyages of exploration into the central Pacific by other than Polynesians and Caucasians. But however the custom of growing long fingernails in Tahiti began, it does not seem to have been deeply ingrained in the island's cultural traditions. First noted and recorded during Cook's second voyage to Tahiti, the custom was never again mentioned in later literature and thus would appear to have been discontinued as a feature of high society soon after 1774.

Dress and Ornament

While noses could be flattened and hair could be trimmed, the greatest medium for artistic bodily expression in Tahiti was the skin itself. Tattooing was virtually mandatory for both males and females. It seems to have served a variety of purposes, such as noting the arrival of puberty or membership in particular family lines, and there were even special small punctures which permanently indicated that a person had gone through certain important childhood rituals. However, it would also appear that some of the tattooed designs, such as birds, dogs, and varieties of circles and crescents, had no purpose other than to beautify the body. However, such beautification came at a price, and that price was pain.

The tattooing instrument, which looked like a miniature rectangular comb, was made of a flat piece of bone or shell. Across one narrow end a series of fine, sharp needles, perhaps as many as fifteen to the inch, was carved out of the material. This working edge varied from one-quarter of an inch in width to as much as two inches, the different sizes serving, like artists' brushes, to create certain types of decorative design. This tattooing comb, as it has come to be called, was fastened crosswise to the end of a sticklike handle, the needled edge pointing downward. To make a tattoo, the tips of the needles were dipped into a solution of water and fine carbon derived from the smoke of candle nuts. The needled edge was then placed against the skin and its wooden handle smartly tapped with another stick. This drove the blackened points into the flesh sufficiently that with each blow small droplets of blood appeared where the needles had penetrated. This dipping and tapping continued until either the design was completed or the victim's patience was exhausted. Joseph Banks witnessed a young girl of twelve having one side of her bottom blackened in this manner as an indicator of puberty. She held up well for the first fifteen minutes, but from then on each tap of the comb brought howls of anguish from the unwilling patient and words of coaxing and scolding from the two women who forcibly held the girl down while the artist rendered his masterpiece.[8] No doubt for the young, tattoo designs were not always completed in one session, the pain of the procedure and the postoperative discomfort keeping the recipient at a safe distance from the practitioner until courage and morale could again be built up to complete the ordeal.

In the Tahitian world of the warm, damp tropics, clothing was less a necessity than a form of personal enhancement, though somewhat cooler evening and early morning temperatures made the wearing of at least some clothing a distinct comfort. However, there never seems to have been a moral commitment to hide one's body from the view of others. That is to say, there was no such commitment except, it would appear, where a man's genitalia were involved. Women could, and did, expose themselves completely in various public situations, but there is no record of a male ever appearing without his breechclout. This *maro*, or breechclout, could be made of bark cloth or fine matting and had the appearance of a long sash. It was brought up between the legs and securely wrapped around the waist and then fastened to itself with a half hitch knot. Perhaps its vital importance to male genitalian dignity is best exemplified by the fact that a new high chief was invested not with a headgear, a flowing robe, or perhaps a spear signifying authority, but rather with a beautifully wrought feathered and sacred maro, called the *maro 'ura*.[9]

For women the common basic garment was a wraparound skirt reaching from the waist to below the knees.

Like the men, who frequently went around dressed in nothing more than a maro, the women, at least those of the lower social ranks, commonly did their daily chores dressed only in this skirt. Although there are three time-scattered references to women who wore breechclouts, these reports are so discrete that I would hazard the suggestion that such a loincloth was only used during a woman's menstrual period, rather than as a part of her everyday apparel.

Except for the ever-present breechclout of the men, the clothing for both sexes was of the same cut. Men, too, wore a wraparound skirt, or *pareu,* while both sexes covered their shoulders and torsos with a *tiputa,* or poncho. This latter was a piece of bark cloth six to eight feet long and slightly wider than a person's shoulders. A lengthwise slit in the middle served as a neck opening so that the garment fell in front and behind, leaving the sides open to allow free movement of air. This particular class of garment was indeed handy, several being stacked one on top of the other for greater warmth and then fastened around the waist with a bark cloth sash.

While the wraparound skirt and poncho were common to all Tahitians, it remained for the upper social classes to add a flair by using nothing more than a large rectangular mantle, which occasionally reached the size of a bedsheet. Simple as this outer garment was, the socially elite Tahitians made it a classic of apparel by dyeing or staining it and then draping it over their shoulders or around their bodies in a multiplicity of patterns and styles. For those of somewhat lower rank who could still afford a mantle, such a cloth was conservatively wrapped around the body just below the arms. Obviously, high fashion was only for the elite.

Tahitians made occasional use of a variety of headgear. Often a hat consisted of nothing more than a turbanlike draping of a piece of bark cloth around the head, though a conical cap was mentioned by Sydney Parkinson, and other writers referred to small bonnets. These latter were usually made up quickly from palm leaves, though Captain James Cook also noted others constructed of fine matting.

While turbans and bonnets were basically designed to protect the wearers from the strong rays of a tropical sun, the purely decorative potential of the head and ears was also realized by the Tahitians. Gaily colored flowers were stuck in the hair, or a fillet of "Indians peas," little red seeds with black dots on them, was woven into the hair. Even the thinly transparent spathe of the coconut flower was twisted into different shapes and used to decorate the head. Both men and women had their ears pierced so that flowers might be stuck in them, or lacking anything better, a small stick or even a fish bone could be inserted. Eardrops were also used, the decorative elements being drilled and strung on finely plaited strands of human hair. The simpler of these consisted of shells, berries, seeds, and even bits of rock, while another type, cut from pearl shell, was shaped into a variety of figures. Although pearls were reported in the lagoons of Raiatea to the west, they appear to have been rare in Tahitian waters, and thus constituted the most valuable form of eardrops. As might be expected, they were limited to men and women of the higher social ranks. Indeed, so rare were pearls that no more than two or three were strung on each eardrop. Although clumsily drilled and therefore of little commercial value to Europeans, most of these seem to have been picked up by the earlier explorers, for they were not mentioned in the literature after about 1775. In fact, most of the locally produced ear decorations must have quickly given way to European baubles, for by the time Cook first reached the island in 1769, foreign beads and buttons were already in use. [10]

All in all, Tahitians left a pleasant impression on early European travelers. Not only were they pleasing in mien and generally outgoing in personality, but their chiefs were cooperative and generous. Although these latter traits were sometimes spontaneous, they were just as often calculated. However, the end result for the Europeans was the same, and so Tahiti, like equally friendly Tonga, quickly became a routine port of call.

Law and Order

The social nature of mankind has always caused groups of people throughout the world to organize themselves. Such social organizations do not stay crystallized in any given pattern for long. They change with time as natural and human forces from within and without the pattern exert modifying pressures or create chain reactions that lead to new forms of crystallization. Tahitians were no exception in this respect, and thus the pieced-together descriptions of their forms of government and social organization recorded by European explorers are like momentary glimpses in time showing no movement or change. Actually, the very coming of these Europeans, and the introduction of their arms and ammunition, precipitated a chain reaction of war and greed for imperial power that substantially reshaped the earlier pattern of Tahitian human organization.

Our view of the old Tahitian order of things lacks the refinement of an in-depth study. After all, none of the early voyagers was on the island a sufficient length of time to recognize the more delicate nuances of social ranking and authority which must have existed. Furthermore, many of them were forced to rely upon direct observations for their cultural descriptions. Most had but a limited knowledge of the Tahitian language and thus could not use this better source of information to its fullest capacity. Unfortunately for us, Tahitians had a rather narrow range of overt symbols and expressions of governmental order and status to help the Europeans deduce information about their social patterns. Nonetheless, despite these limitations, the men that sailed the seas to Tahitian beaches succeeded in leaving us sufficient data for a reconstruction of the major aspects of Tahitian society between 1767 and 1797.

The early records indicate that Tahiti was divided geographically into two distinct governmental units. The main portion of the island, called *Tahiti nui*, or "big Tahiti," constituted one of these, while the smaller, pear-shaped peninsula, extending southeastward from the main island mass, formed a second independently governed society.[1] This latter is referred to in the early reports as either *Taiarapu* or *Tahiti iti*, that is, "little Tahiti." Since these discrete governmental units shared certain basic features of political organization, one might conclude that they represented nothing more than a factional split from a former single, island-wide governmental organization. However, this is not necessarily the case. As will be noted in later chapters, Taiarapu possessed a number of traits that seem not to have been shared by Tahiti nui. Such segregated cultural differences on a relatively small island present the intriguing possibility that the people of Taiarapu may have been the descendants of a group of migrants who came to Tahiti before, or after, the arrival of the controlling chiefly class that occupied Tahiti nui. If they were the earlier of the migrants, they may have been driven into their less desirable peninsular domain by the arrival of a superior force. However, if they were late arrivals in search of land, they may have been allowed to reside on the peninsula at a time when it had not yet been settled. In either event, the fact that the basic political system of Taiarapu was essentially like that of Tahiti nui suggests that their original homeland was not too distant from that of the dominating group of Tahiti nui. Be that as it may, the two societies remained distinct until about 1791 when Tahiti nui gained control of Taiarapu and thus unified the island's government.[2]

The social organization of both governments was divided into three major categories. Most prominent was the chiefly, or governing, rank, followed by a large group of freeholders who owned and worked their personal land but

held no chiefly status, while at the bottom of the social regis-
ter was an equally large, if not larger, class of landless
laborers and servants. Although incomplete and spotty, the
records indicate that there were graded social rankings within
each of these three basic categories. As for upward mobility,
there is some indication that it may have been allowed
within categories but not between them. Thus a Tahitian was
born into a given social category and lived and died in it.
Such restricted mobility, however, does not seem to have
resulted in the development of snobbery between major
ranks, for socializing, except during certain ceremonial occasions, was common among people of differing status.
Nonetheless, marriage between people of unlike categories
was forbidden, and children resulting from casual affairs between members of differing major social ranks were killed
immediately upon birth.[3]

Government by the Chiefly Class

Of the three major social ranks found in Tahiti, political
authority rested in the highest, or chiefly, category.[4] Here
status and, to some extent, governmental position depended
upon one's degree of relationship to certain important family
lines, which quite possibly reflected the original authoritar-
ian position of each family of the migratory founding group.

The precise ranking system for the various family lines
cannot be determined from the eighteenth-century records.
What is known is that in each of the two governmental areas
there was a socioreligious head, or paramount chief. In
Tahiti nui this god-given position rested in the Tu family,[5]
while in Taiarapu it remained in the Vehiatua line.[6] Below
this highest of governmental ranks there was a series of
chiefs whose social position did not necessarily coincide with
their political power or degree of religious or governmental
authority. The most obvious of these were the more important landed chiefs whose titles and territories were inherited.[7] Not only was the area they controlled a reflection of
their economic and political strength, but the number of
commoners and administrating chiefs under their jurisdiction was a further indication of their relative power.

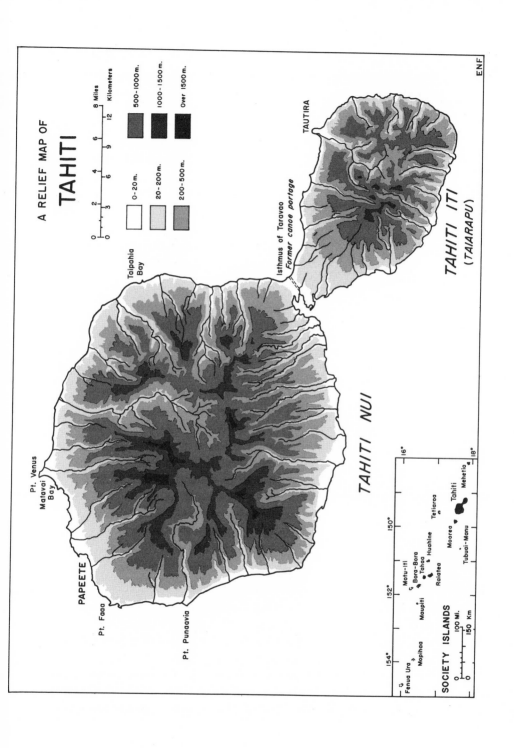

A RELIEF MAP OF
TAHITI

0   2   4   6   8 Miles
0 3 6   9   12 Kilometers

0 - 20 m.   500 - 1000 m.
20 - 200 m.   1000 - 1500 m.
200 - 500 m.   Over 1500 m.

Pt. Venus
Matavai Bay

Taipahia Bay

PAPEETE

Pt. Faaa

Pt. Punaavia

TAHITI NUI

Isthmus of Taravao
Former canoe portage

TAUTIRA

TAHITI ITI
(TAIARAPU)

ENF

SOCIETY ISLANDS

154°   152°   150°

Fenua Ura
Mopihaa
Maupiti
Motu-Iti
Bora-Bora
Tahaa
Huahine
Raiatea

16°

Tetiaroa

Moorea
Tahiti
Tubuai-Manu
Mehetia

18°

0   100 Mi.
0   150 Km.

William Bligh determined that Tahiti nui was divided into at least two, and possibly three, major areas, which he called "princedoms," each governed by a powerful chief. These, in turn, were subdivided, although not equally, into a total of twelve or thirteen lesser divisions, which he termed "counties" or "governments," each of which was presumably controlled by a lesser chief. Finally, each "county" was still further divided into what Bligh termed a "district" or "chiefdom." Here it is interesting to note that while Tahiti nui was divided into three "princedoms," the total being subdivided into twelve or thirteen "counties," the smaller Tahiti iti, or Taiarapu, differed in constituting a single "princedom," the whole of which was divided into no fewer than twelve "counties."[8]

In later years, James Wilson and the missionaries made no mention of the two or three major land divisions, or "princedoms," of Bligh. However, Wilson's map of Tahiti showed the two most important of those mentioned by Bligh clearly lettered into his drawing, indicating that at least these two were recognized by him, though not discussed. Also, though Wilson made no mention of any land division comparable to Bligh's "counties," he did report that several districts were governed by one chief with subordinate chiefs in charge of each individual district.[9] Thus it is possible that these plural holdings represented what Bligh chose to call "counties." Although Wilson designated each land element within such a multiple holding a "district," the missionaries came to use the Tahitian term *patu*, or parish, for subdivisions of a particularly large district, each patu being ruled over by a lesser chief. Within Wilson's districts were smaller subdivisions called *mata'eina'a*, themselves divided into units called *ti'i*.[10]

Although district chiefs owned large tracts of what was undoubtedly the best agricultural land in their territories, there were other plots within their governmental boundaries which were owned by commoners, occasionally by other district chiefs, and even by the paramount chief.[11] However, governmental power over the political division rested with the district chief, just as religious power over the total domain rested with the paramount chief.[12] The district chief could requisition labor as needed, levy taxes in the form of foods and goods, raise a military force, and place a *rahui* on the land and adjacent lagoon.[13] This latter was a special taboo which might be placed against the harvesting of certain crops, the killing of domestic animals, or even the fishing activity in the waters of the district. The rahui initially functioned as a very sound device to assure ample food for a forthcoming feast or to guard against resource depletion. Its use was not just limited to district chiefs, since a paramount chief could employ it to control production on his entire governmental domain, and the smallest landholder could do the same for his own property or fishing area if he thought such was desirable.[14] However, with the arrival of Europeans the chiefs quickly realized that they could also use the rahui as a lever against their foreign visitors, who were dependent upon them for food.[15]

Since it would be difficult for a district chief to handle all of the administrative needs of his entire domain, he maintained a number of subordinates of chiefly status, called *to'ofa*, to carry out his wishes. These men, who might be younger brothers, other near relatives, or even formalized friends of the district chief, were occasionally referred to as "captains" in the literature and thus may have served as warriors in times of need. These subordinate chiefs were placed in direct political authority over a varying number of landholding commoners and, presumably as recompense, possessed larger agricultural tracts than those they governed. However, at least in Taiarapu, a to'ofa apparently did not inherit full title to his land, for he could lose it and be banished if he did not follow his chief's instructions.[16] Since Bligh defined a mata'eina'a as a set of people belonging to and governed by a chief, and the to'ofa was a lesser chief, it seems likely that these smaller subdivisions of a district were the mata'eina'a mentioned by Wilson, and represented the units controlled by the to'ofa. This arrangement would then make the still smaller ti'i, also mentioned by Wilson, represent the individual landholdings of the various commoners within each mata'eina'a.[17]

Since both the paramount chief and various of the district chiefs maintained property in several districts, yet another type of subchief was needed. This was the *metua*, who represented the absentee owner and was usually his relative. As payment for his caretaking duties he was given the use and products of the land, but he also had to supply the chiefly owner upon demand.[18]

Above and beyond these economically important political positions, there were other stations to be filled from the chiefly ranks. There was, for example, a series of *tahu'a* generally referred to by Europeans as "priests," who were directly connected with religious activities and who are described in the following chapter.

While the priests took care of the spiritual needs of the people and managed the government's more formalized aspects of education and religion, there still remained ample need for administrative assistants to the paramount chief. These latter were formed into two groups, the *hova* and the *fana*, the former being rated administratively at a somewhat higher order of importance than the latter. There appear to have been twelve hova and an undisclosed number of fana who served the paramount chief on a rotating basis, several always being in attendance. Cook suggested that they were usually, if not always, relatives of the paramount chief. Since they stood in the same administrative position relative to the paramount chief as the to'ofa did to a district chief, and since family members occupied this latter post, it seems a logical conclusion that relatives were also employed to fill the hova and fana positions. Be that as it may, the two positions apparently represented a symbolic extension of the paramount chief himself. As such, their members not only ate with their chief, but were not required to bare their shoulders as a sign of respect when on duty and in the presence of their paramount chief. Although the duties varied, their more important activities appear to have been acting as official messengers and seeing to it that the paramount chief's wishes, such as those regarding collection of goods or requests for services from any of the districts under his jurisdiction, were properly carried out. When conducting such official business the hova or fana carried with him a branch of the *roava* tree to indicate that he represented the paramount chief and spoke for him, thus assuring that the people would listen to him with the same respect shown the actual paramount chief. Although the wood of the roava was used for various secular construction, the tree was also planted in their sacred structures where its leaves were sometimes used in religious ceremonies.[19] Thus, its use by the hova and fana gave their voices both political and religious sanction.

A more obvious, and occasionally more active, role for these men was that of controlling crowds at official functions. In this capacity they were supplied with long bamboo poles, and if inquisitive onlookers pushed forward too closely it was the business of these officers to lash out with their sticks and beat the offenders back to a more appropriate distance. However, they occasionally were given more mundane jobs as, for example, when the paramount chief of Tahiti nui was presented with a European dog, which he valued most highly. The beast was immediately turned over to an unfortunate hova, whose job from then on was to carry the dog wherever the chief might choose to go.

There was little evidence, if any, to indicate that the duties of the hova and fana differed from one another, even though the former was said to outrank the latter. It is possible that the higher status of the hova was significant only in situations of special protocol or urgency. Thus, at any particular time when a somewhat higher ranking chiefly assistant seemed necessary to add importance to a message or request from the paramount chief, a hova was dispatched rather than a fana.[20]

Besides the assistants to the paramount chief, there were at least two other permanent governmental positions mentioned in the literature, although others of less prominence may well have existed. One of these was referred to as the "spokesman" for the paramount chief and may well have been the equivalent of the so-called talking chiefs of Samoa. The spokesman, or *ta'ata 'orero*, was employed on formal occasions which required lengthy speeches enumerating, as far as can be gathered, the gods of the paramount chief and his descent line, as well as certain historical happenings on the island. Since there was no method to record such factual material, the ta'ata 'orero served as the paramount chief's memory bank to be brought out and put into play whenever the occasion demanded. He also had other, more important functions, for, when the Spaniards appeared to have become annoyed with Vehiatua of Taiarapu, the latter made a formal call on them and brought with him his spokesman. While the youthful Vehiatua said not a word, his aged spokesman put forth a series of questions to the Spaniards asking, in effect, their reasons for being annoyed. Once the formalized questioning and answering had been completed to the satisfaction of both parties, Vehiatua dismissed his spokesman so that he might settle down and have a pleasant chat with his foreign visitors.[21]

The remaining position, ascribed to Taiarapu but never mentioned as existing in Tahiti nui, was that of the 'iatoai.[22] The single reference to this post suggested that the office was nothing more than that of a substitute judge who tried cases in the absence of the paramount chief, who normally undertook this function. However, his position may well have been considerably more powerful, since he was also described as a "governor-general." As such, he may well have acted in a ruling capacity during any extended absence of the paramount chief.

While the official positions described above covered the day-to-day operations of the government, the infrequent need for policy decisions was undertaken through councils made up of the chiefly class. Vehiatua, paramount chief of Taiarapu, had three men who acted as his principal counselors, and Captain Cook mentioned finding the regent Tuteha apparently in council with a small group of old men. However, counseling was not always limited to these smaller groups when it came to matters of great concern affecting a district or much of the island. On such occasions it was necessary to bring together all of the pertinent people of note within, presumably, the chiefly class. On such occasions the people formed a large circle in, or near, the center of which the chief sat as presiding officer. Whoever wished to counsel the chief arose from his place in the ring and entered the circle to make his presentation. George Forster described a specialized rectangular area for such large council meetings which measured sixty by ninety feet and was surrounded by a sixteen-inch-high reed fence. Such meetings do not appear to have occurred on a regular basis, but rather were called only when important decisions had to be made, either at the district or national level. [23]

Position of the Paramount Chief

There was yet another source of power in the chiefly ranks, and that had to do with deity. While divinity pervaded almost every aspect of chiefly government and deities were called upon for aid at critical times, the importance of sanctity reached a zenith in the person of the paramount chief of Tahiti nui. It was this aspect more than any other that set apart the government of Tahiti nui from that of Taiarapu. [24]

There has been a prolonged misconception, apparently started by misinformation obtained by the missionary William Ellis, that the paramount chief of Tahiti nui was so sacred and filled with spiritual power that throughout his entire lifetime he was carried about. This was the result of the belief that anything he touched, be it land, buildings, or even a tree, became his property and was henceforth too sacred for the use of anyone else. [25] That he was carried during the early years of his life, and for these very reasons of sanctity, appears to be correct, but such extreme sanctity did not carry through into middle and old age. However, before looking at the eighteenth-century record in this regard, it would be best to review what was recorded of the mode of chiefly succession.

Under what might be termed a normal family situation, the firstborn son of a Tahitian family became the head of that family. Should the father be the paramount chief, or have any other title, the son succeeded to his father's name and title. The switch in name was necessary since apparently only the senior member of a Tahitian family bore the family name (in contrast to the multinomial system of identifying European and American family members in which the last name of each individual identifies his or her male family line). While the title of paramount or district chief was immediately transferred to the young child, the administrative powers that normally accompanied the title remained with the father, who thus became his son's regent until the child came of age. However, in the event of the father's untimely death, his widow took over the duties of regent until her son was ready to accept the reins of government.

While the above represented the normal course of events, the vicissitudes of nature are such that the abnormal situation had also to be taken into account when it came to rightful succession. Thus, it was reported that if the firstborn son died without issue, his brother, presumably the next oldest, became the rightful successor. Since there is no record of a daughter ever inheriting the title of her chiefly father, it is probable that the Europeans' use of the term "issue" actually referred to male issue. At least we do know that upon the death of young Vehiatua, his brother became paramount chief of Taiarapu. There is also the interesting record of Charles Churchill, one of the mutineers of the *Bounty,* who succeeded to the position of district chief because he had become a *taio,* or formally adopted friend, of a district chief who passed away. In this event, it seems likely that the old chief had no son or brother to succeed him.

While women seem not to have inherited chieftainship through their own family line, they were not totally excluded from the rights of succession. For example, if a district chief should die without male issue and had no brother or taio to succeed him, his wife became district chief. Should such a widow remarry, her second husband, by virtue of being married to her, served as chief of the district. However, his was a fragile position for it depended upon the good health of his wife. Should she die, he would no longer have any legal right to the post and would be forced to return to whatever position he had held prior to the marriage. This practice suggests that upon the death of a female district chief, whether she had remarried or not, the title and command of her first husband reverted to some male member of his extended family.[26]

It was in the normal successional events of the earlier part of the paramount chief's life cycle in Tahiti nui that he was forced to be carried because of his great sanctity. However, this seems to have lasted only up through the teenage years, while he held the title of paramount chief but his father operated as his regent. Sometime between the ages of nineteen and twenty-four the paramount chief took over the full power of his position, the regent no longer being needed. At the same time he became sufficiently profaned that he could walk among his people, enter European ships, and act like a normal man without sancitifying everything he touched. Thus, in 1773 and 1774 when Tahiti nui's paramount chief, Tu, was estimated to be twenty-four or twenty-five years old, there was no mention of his being carried, and he had no compunction about coming on board Cook's vessels and dining there. The same was true in 1777 when Cook again returned to Tahiti. However, in 1781 or 1782, a son was born to Tu and, since the son inherited his father's name, the father took on the name of Tinah and later that of Pomare. When Bligh arrived on the island in 1788, not only was the young Tu being carried about on men's shoulders, but his father, the regent, was under a restrictive taboo which did not allow him to feed himself. This same set of restrictive taboos involving the young Tu's being carried and the regent's being fed by another person continued at least until 1797 when Tu's age was reckoned between sixteen and seventeen years. It may also have been in effect in 1802 when John Turnbull first dropped anchor off the island, since the young paramount chief, then twenty-one or twenty-two years of age, cruised his outrigger around the ship but refused to come aboard. However, the following year, Turnbull found the chief walking about and sat and conversed with him. Obviously, something had happened, because the restrictive taboos were no longer in effect.

What had happened was that a special ceremony, known as *amo'a*, had been carried out to profane the youthful paramount chief to the extent that he could finally eat with his father, who also could now feed himself, and govern his lands with, so to speak, a firm footing. Actually, as will be described in a later chapter, all children, with the possible exception of certain servant classes, were born with a high degree of sanctity and thus were surrounded by innumerable taboos. These, however, were gradually reduced by a series of amo'a ceremonies designed to profane the youngsters enough that they could eat with their parents and enjoy life in general without fear of religious contamination. The difference between a commoner's child and a young paramount chief was in the length of time during which these religious taboos were in effect. Although we do not have the precise age for the final amo'a ceremony for the child of a commoner, it would appear to have been rather early in his life. For a paramount chief, however, it seems to have ranged between his nineteenth and twenty-fourth birthdays. The fact that neither George Vancouver nor Bligh, both of whom made special efforts to investigate this matter, could get a precise time for this ceremony suggests that the date was fixed on the basis of the father's judgment, as regent, of when his son was sufficiently trained to take over the administrative duties of government.

The period of taboos for a young paramount chief and his father was certainly not designed to bring them together nor, for that matter, to bring the tabooed paramount chief into close contact with his subjects. The young man's father could approach no closer than thirty feet from his son when speaking to him, while his mother was allowed only to nurse him, the young paramount chief's other needs being taken care of by a male attendant.

As long as the young chief was at home on his own property, he was free to run about like other children. However, when he wished to go beyond these limits, he had to be carried, since, theoretically, any piece of ground that his foot might touch became not only sacred, but his personal property as well. While the job of carrying the paramount chief during his period of taboo represented no great exertion during his early years, it must have become quite a chore as he began to grow and put on weight. Bligh reported that there were between twenty and thirty male attendants who took turns carrying the chief on his various expeditions into the countryside. Instead of highborn people, Vancouver found that these attendants were of the lowest social ranks. Should the paramount chief marry while still under restrictive taboos, his wife was also carried on men's shoulders; George

Vason described how Tu's wife directed her bearer to turn, slow down, or speed up by using a stick.

While the taboos of a paramount chief during his restricted years were generally followed, they could be broken from time to time without the prescribed condemnations being put into effect. In 1769, when Cook's men were first confronted by a young boy carried on the shoulders of a man and introduced as the paramount chief of the island, they knew nothing of the restrictive taboos, and so Daniel Carl Solander courteously led the young boy into one of the tents. Although, under the restrictive taboos then in force, this would have meant that no other native could again enter that tent, in this case the Tahitians merely forced the young man to leave the abode and then continued with their business at hand. In 1797, when the missionaries unfolded a dress meant as a gift for the young Tu's wife, the couple became so excited that they immediately dismounted from their carriers so that she could try on the dress, while the surrounding populace looked on approvingly. Here again there is no record of the ground being henceforth considered sacred. A little later during the same year the missionaries, hearing of an impending human sacrifice, remonstrated with Tu and his wife so forcefully that the couple became frightened, leaped to the ground, and started running home along the beach, yet the beach seems never to have been tabooed to future users. However, these were all spontaneous occurrences involving outsiders, rather than calculated taboo-breaking, and apparently could thus be overlooked. Under normal circumstances, the taboos seem to have been carefully maintained. Vancouver discovered this when he desired to offer the young Tu a glass of wine and was told that if he did so the glass would have to be broken afterwards. Not wishing to have his table setting gradually destroyed, Vancouver came up with the idea of using a coconut shell container. After Tu had consumed the contents the shell was immediately broken and thrown into the sea. Again, when the missionaries showed an umbrella to Tu and his wife and opened it to demonstrate its use, they were immediately warned not to put it over the heads of the young couple. To do so would, in effect, have forced them to give the umbrella to the chief and his wife, for it would have become sacred to their use.

It was in this matter of lengthy ceremonial restrictions that the paramount chief of Tahiti nui differed from that of Taiarapu. Although quite probably the paramount chief of the latter region went through the same amo'a ceremonies that most of the young people did in Tahiti generally, it was specifically stated by José de Andia y Varela that the restrictive taboos causing an object to be made sacred if the paramount chief touched it and requiring the feeding of a regent pertained to Tahiti nui and not Taiarapu. It was only after the regent of Tahiti nui took over control of Taiarapu, placed his younger brother in the paramount chief position, and appropriately changed his name to the titular one of Vehiatua that carrying the youthful chief in that area of Tahiti suddenly became the practice. It represented nothing more than a transfer of Tahiti nui governmental tradition to the newly acquired territory of Taiarapu. Before this happened, however, it is interesting to note that the Tahiti nui regent, normally under the taboo of having to be fed when in his own country, did not have to honor that sanction when visiting Taiarapu.[27]

Once the highly restrictive taboos had been removed from the Tahiti nui paramount chief, he and his property retained certain powers of sanctity which were also held by the paramount chief of Taiarapu. These were best illustrated by Rodríguez, who described the difficulty he had getting Tahitians to move a dwelling that had once belonged to their paramount chief. On another occasion, his canoe, which had been given to him by Vehiatua, paramount chief of Taiarapu, was in need of a portable cabin. Unfortunately, the only readily available one belonged to a commoner who would not loan it because a commoner's shelter should never be placed on a canoe once owned by a chief. It was only after Rodríguez had found a to'ofa, or subchief, who had such a cabin that he was able to borrow the structure and place it on his own canoe. Whereas goods from different chiefly levels apparently could be mixed, that of a commoner could not be elevated by placing it with chiefly paraphernalia. By the same token, Cook learned that if one wished to send a man to discuss a problem with a chief, that man also should be a chief. However, there were restrictions within the chiefly category as well, for Rodríguez explained that Tu's own parents were not allowed to enter their son's sleeping compartment.[28]

A paramount chief, whether under his early restrictive taboos or not, was always shown the Tahitian's sign of infinite respect. This took the form of uncovering one's shoulders and chest down to the waist whenever one was in his presence. The practice was also required of his wife and brothers and sisters, and was a necessary procedure, at least on Tahiti nui, while passing one of the paramount chief's properties. Since both men and women were involved in this ritual of respect, the normally staid naturalist George Forster could not resist noting in his journal that the practice afforded the women "numberless opportunities of displaying an elegant figure to the greatest advantage."[29] As for the respect shown to the regent or to the various district chiefs, the consensus would seem to be that only women uncovered their shoulders, although the paramount chief's immediate family was understandably exempted from this practice.

The introduction of European longsleeved coats and shirts, gradually adopted by a majority of Tahitians, brought about a change in this etiquette pattern, however. The first indication of an adjustment in the procedure of uncovering one's shoulders in the presence of a paramount chief occurred in 1773. It was then that Anders Sparrman laughingly described the predicament that one native encountered when, suddenly confronted by his paramount chief, he tried to slip a British seaman's coat down off his shoulders. By 1788 a telltale change was obviously in the making when the regent Tinah requested Bligh to take off the clothes above his waist when he approached the young paramount chief. Bligh, refusing to submit to this traditional custom, found his hat removed and a tapa mantle draped over his shoulders, allowing him to remove at least this item of clothing from his shoulders when presented before the youthful chief. Finally, by 1797, the change was so complete that the Tahitians related to the missionaries that, because of the introduction of European coats and shirts, they now simply covered their European dress with a tapa cloth and removed only that item from their shoulders when in the presence of the paramount chief. From such small things does culture make its adjustments.[30]

Although we have no eyewitness account of the ceremony that admitted the Tahiti nui paramount chief into the field of direct administration and at the same time profaned him to the extent that he might walk among his subjects, there is at least a secondhand account of his being invested with the sacred maro, or loincloth, of his high position. This investiture ceremony must have taken place at a rather early age, since young Tu had already gone through the ritual by 1792 when Bligh watched him perform at a sacrificial ceremony which was given for him as an atonement for someone's wrongdoing. By Vancouver's estimate, he was then only nine or ten years of age.[31]

Unlike the crowning of European royalty, the making of a paramount chief was witnessed by a very limited audience. This particular investiture took place at the great *marae,* or open-air religious structure, at Pare. First the sacred insignia of office, the maro'ura, or special loincloth, was unwrapped from its tapa cloth container and placed on the *ahu,* or platform, of the marae. Cook described this piece of ceremonial dress as consisting of a band some fifteen feet long and fifteen inches wide decorated with red and yellow feathers, of which the latter predominated. These were pasted, or otherwise fixed, to a piece of tapa cloth so that the pattern formed a series of squares laid out in two rows, the whole being sewn to the upper end of a red English pennant which had been left on the island by Wallis, the first European to set foot on Tahiti. One end of the maro was edged with a series of eight horseshoe-shaped elements fringed with black pigeon feathers, while the opposite end was said to be forked, with one prong of the fork longer than the other.[32]

With the unveiling of the maro completed, the ta'ata 'orero, or spokesman, of Tahiti nui began his oration, which consisted of setting forth all of the pertinent data support-

ing the young man's right to the maro 'ura and the position
of paramount chief which came with it. The youthful chief
was then invested with the ceremonial rainment which, considering its length, and the probable small size of the boy,
must have been a symbolic gesture at best. This completed, it
was now time for each of the districts under the government
of Tahiti nui to present their homage to the new paramount
chief. As the young chief sat astride his human carrier, each
district chief in turn brought forward one or two human
sacrifices, always male, from his district. With the presentation of each body, the priest bent over and, scooping an
eyeball out of a now-dead socket, placed it on the leaf from a
young banana plant and, after a lengthy speech, presented it
to the young paramount chief as if to be eaten. The chief
then obligingly opened his mouth as if to accept the offering,
but he always fell short of actually touching it. With the
completion of each eye-extracting ceremony, the body of the
sacrificial victim was taken away to be buried within the
precincts of the marae. The ceremonial significance of this
part of the ritual was based on the belief that the head was
the sacred part of an individual and the eyes the most important parts of this element. Thus, in presenting the eye of a
sacrificial victim, each district was symbolically offering its
most precious item to the paramount chief. Beyond this, the
pretended eating of the eye symbolized the paramount
chief's reception of additional wisdom from each district.[33]

With the sacrificial part of the ceremony over, large
quantities of tapa cloth were presented to the young chief as
gifts, along with innumerable hogs, which were immediately
strangled for the feast to follow. After removing the maro
'ura, the assembled chiefs and their new paramount chief
retired to the sacred grounds of the marae to sate their appetites on large quantities of pig, turtle, chicken, and fish, not
to mention an array of vegetables in different forms. It was
further added that feasting in general, accompanied by entertainment, continued for a period of some two months.[34]

While human sacrifice was a distinctive feature of the
investiture ceremonies of Tahiti nui, it seems to have played
no part at all in similar ceremonies in Taiarapu. While large
numbers of people assembled from the various districts of

the peninsula, the district chiefs each paid homage to the young boy who was about to become their paramount chief by presenting him with quantities of hogs and rolls of tapa cloth. On the day of the actual ceremony the chiefs were brought together in a large dwelling in which the young man was seated. Here various speeches were delivered, after which the entire assembly moved on to a large marae where a tahu'a, or priest, offered prayers. At the conclusion of this latter ceremony, a large feast was held which, according to the Spanish onlookers, ended in near riot when the twelve roasted hogs and other foods were not passed out with sufficient speed to satisfy the multitude.[35] Unfortunately, the Spaniards were too fearful that their home would be raided to participate as viewers at these ceremonies. However, had there been reports of any human sacrifices at this time they surely would have mentioned it, for they had taken pains to report such sacrifices when the previous paramount chief was in the throes of his final illness.

The Lower Classes

While the life of the chiefly class was rather well documented by European observers, the meaningful core of the island's wealth and muscle was given but half a glance. These were the people of the lower social categories, some of whom owned and worked their land, while others were employed as day laborers, specialists, and servants of the chiefs. And as with other nations of the world, there were also a few unemployed drifters who somehow survived.[36]

The published records from Cook's first two voyages to Tahiti concerned themselves primarily with Tahiti nui, and here they were explicit in describing three categories of people. There were the *ari'i*, or chiefly class; the *manahune*, who were not chiefs but owned and inherited their lands; and the *teuteu*, who represented the lowest class of people and included both skilled and unskilled laborers as well as servants.[37] While the manahune were defined as farmers who worked their own land and paid their chiefly taxes in goods, the teuteu were described as offering a wide variety of services. Some obviously worked as servants preparing food and running errands for the particular chiefly family to which they were attached. In fact, according to John Forster, they also served as expert thieves, stealing from the Europeans and turning over their gains to the head of the household, or sometimes sharing them. There were others who tilled the chiefly land and took care of its stock. Finally, there appear to have been certain teuteu who were specialists in building houses and canoes, fishing, or fabricating bark cloth for the chiefly families. Those who actually worked for chiefs, not all of them being so attached, were paid in vegetables and fish and used either the women's eating house or some kind of a shelter nearby for their evening quarters. Basically teuteu were subdivided into skilled workers, common laborers or farmers, and servants, of which only the latter two appear to have been specifically attached to chiefly families. There is no indication that the skilled workers of the teuteu class were ever specifically attached to any particular chief, although they most certainly must have been available when needed. Fishermen, for example, traded their catch with their neighbors for such things as vegetables, hogs, cloth, and even canoes.[38]

While Tahiti nui, at least through 1773, used the term *manahune* for landowning people below chiefly status, the government of Taiarapu in 1774 termed this class of people in their society *ra'atira*.[39] However, by 1797 the term *manahune* apparently had come to be used to refer to the landless laborers and cultivators of the soil, while *teuteu* had been reduced to referring to only the servant class. In fact, a new term, *tuti*, had been added to refer to servants who waited only on women.

How did this shift in terminology come about? For shift it must have been, since there is no reason to believe that Cook and the Forsters, who first described the Tahitian's social classes, were any more or less capable of recording information than were the later missionaries. I suggest that this seemingly unwarranted alteration of class terms took place as part of the great language change that the regent Pomare initiated and enforced when his son Tu was invested with the sacred maro and became the new paramount chief.

This must, then, have taken place sometime between 1781 or 1782, when the child was born, and 1792, when it is known that he had already been invested with the maro. Since the first English missionaries recounted how numerous Tahitians sought refuge in the homes of the *Bounty* mutineers to keep from being sacrificed during Tu's investiture, the year may well have been 1789, the year after the mutiny but before the *Pandora* came in 1791 to arrest the mutineers.

Why Pomare decided to alter innumerable common terms in the language of Tahiti is a question that probably cannot be answered without further research. Ellis, writing in the early part of the nineteenth century when considerable culture change had already taken place on Tahiti as a result of European intervention, generally followed the 1797 missionary accounts of class structure; however, by then he found it necessary to place the skilled workers in an unnamed transitional category between the ra'atira, which, at one point, he described as constituting a class of secondary chiefs but elsewhere as land-owning gentry and farmers, and the manahune, or commoners. In addition to the teuteu, or servant, class he listed a new group referred to as *titi*. These latter he described as people who had "lost their liberty" through warfare. That the use of the defeated in this manner was a new concept in Tahiti in the nineteenth century suggests that it was introduced by Europeans, who were accustomed to the sale and capture of slaves in various colonial settlements. The early accounts, in describing the life of at least the servants in the teuteu class, seemed to portray a situation of benign vassalage in which a chief might occasionally offer one of his servants to another chief or to a guest. When Cook brought two Maori boys from New Zealand to Tahiti on his second voyage, one of them was given a young servant as a gesture of kindliness. Though Ellis reported only what he saw and heard at the time of his missionary endeavors, with little attempt at historic analysis, more recent anthropologists have, with unclear reasoning, further confused the class structuring. For example, in one case, the ra'atira have been elevated to the level of subchiefs, and skilled workers have been reduced to the level of slaves.[40]

What is probably the most intriguing facet of the teuteu problem was suggested by that protoanthropologist and naturalist on Cook's second expedition, John Forster. Noting that teuteu were generally of darker complexion than the landowning gentry and the chiefly class, he wondered if they were descendants of Melanesians who may have been the first inhabitants of Tahiti, but who were later conquered by more powerful Polynesians and ended up as the land-less servants and laborers of their conquerors.[41] Tending to support Forster's hypothesis is the interesting point that in 1797 the missionaries found that among the laboring class, or teuteu, were some *ra'a,* or sacred, while others were re-garded as unclean. Those who were ra'a could partake of food when the landed gentry had feasts at their marae, but if one was unclean and feigned being ra'a for the sake of the food, he could be killed for the offense.[42] Were the unclean individuals those who traced their ancestry back to the first immigrants, who were later conquered? Although it is doubtful that the teuteu's appearance reflected the Melane-sian physical type of the twentieth century, Forster's suggested homeland of the earliest immigrants to Central Polynesia may not have been too far amiss. Archaeological and linguistic evidence presented in 1967 suggests the theory of an eastern Melanesian source for such early migrants.[43]

Crime and Punishment

There were those among the Tahitians who broke with traditional rules of behavior, and thus a deterring type of punishment had to be meted out from time to time. For example, when it came to murder, that is, any killing outside of warfare, socially demanded infanticide, or the religious requirements for human sacrifices, death for the murderer, with his body offered as a sacrifice at some marae, appears to have been the custom. So far did this concept go that the regent Tinah once sent Bligh a dog, said to have killed one of Bligh's sheep, with the suggestion that he kill the animal because of his unsocial action! However, the taking of another's life seems to have been quite low on the scale of Tahitian crimes against society. In fact, John Forster could learn nothing of it and concluded that murder was unknown. He seems to have felt that at least part of this situation stemmed from the observed fact that personal fights between individuals were almost immediately broken up by bystanders. In such cases, each antagonist was given the opportunity to exhibit strong personal resentment for whatever indiscretion had caused the commotion, after which the two quickly came to a reconciliation. Obviously the advantages of saving face were well recognized in Tahiti.

If murder was not a dominant crime on the island, thievery between Tahitians certainly was. Here a wide variety of punishments was available, depending not only upon the value of the item stolen, but whom it was stolen from. If it was a trifling matter, the thief might have his hands tightly bound and his beard and body hair burned off. Should the theft be of somewhat greater importance, personal banishment from the district the thief lived in might be in order. However, stealing of economically important items, such as tapa cloaks or canoes, was punishable by death. While hanging was mentioned as one means of carrying out the death sentence, drowning the thief or killing him by other means and then offering up his eye at a marae and burying the body in the lagoon, appears to have been more common. Drowning was accomplished most efficiently by tying the thief's hands and feet together, or by trussing them up to his neck, after which heavy stones were fastened to the body and the unfortunate soul taken out in a canoe and unceremoniously dumped in the ocean. As for stealing from a paramount chief, the one case reported described how the thief was immediately killed and the body buried opposite the great marae of Taputapuatea. However, while the punishment for stealing could be quite extreme, a thief may have had a pretty good chance of survival, since custom dictated that if he was not actually caught in the act of stealing, no punishment could be meted out.

Unfortunately, the range of social abuses for which punishment was the controlling factor was not well clarified in the early literature. We do know that in one case in which a district chief was thought to have committed treachery against his paramount chief, he was not only stripped of all power, but lost his district as well. What other crimes existed were not recorded. However, other forms of criminal punishment were mentioned. These ranged from tying a person up and beating his stomach with a stick, to cutting off his head and offering one of his eyes to the paramount chief. Since the island of Mehetia was under the domain of Vehiatua of Taiarapu, that high chief occasionally banished criminals to its rocky shores for greater security.

In all of these cases, justice was obtained not through trial or council, but through the decision of a district or paramount chief. It would appear that in the case of a district chief's judgment, the right of appeal to the paramount chief was available for the asking. However, the Tahitians had yet another, though less formal, method of dealing with the socially undesirable. This was through the technique of marking them, so to speak, for human sacrifices whenever such became needed for particular ceremonies. However, a chance for survival was still possible for these individuals, for, whenever a ceremony requiring such victims was about to take place, they could protect themselves by getting to any sacred ground, usually around a marae, where tradition forbade their being killed. That social misfits were aware of their potential danger at such times was well confirmed when many of them fled to the homes of the *Bounty* mutineers, whose dwellings had been made sacred at the time of Tu's investiture ceremonies.[44]

Thus did the chiefly government of Tahiti operate. The checks and balances of inherited power in the ruling class and the productive, economic strength among the lower order of people made for an equilibrium in lifestyles in which excesses affecting the society as a whole were difficult, if not impossible, to maintain. Much of this well-balanced structure was soon to fall, as European concepts of power and conquest, helped no little by guns, ammunition, and the people to work them, brought forth latent greed and the tools and techniques to satisfy it.

The Supernatural World

So numerous were the gods of Tahiti that the early missionaries came to the conclusion that there were almost as many of these immortal souls as there were people on the island.[1] The existence of such a teeming conglomeration of deities can best be explained by the Tahitians' practical-minded approach to dealing with the unknown. There was, in their minds, one supreme god by the name of Tane, and somewhat below him, but still abundantly powerful, was the deity Oro. According to the missionaries, there was yet another god slightly below Oro who was named Ta'aroa, or Tangaroa. Since this latter deity does not appear in the literature before 1797, there is a possibility that his arrival on the scene may have been the result of a historic transfer from the west, perhaps from Tongatapu where European ships often put in on their way to Tahiti. Still another god, closely linked to natural phenomena, was Maui. Lewis de Bougainville mentioned a god of the sun, or light, which was probably a reference to Tane, while Máximo Rodríquez noted that priests of Tahiti iti prayed to a deity by the name of Opunua.[2] All of these represented the upper echelon of Tahitian gods.

The Tahitians reasoned that such gods could not be bothered with the mundane problems of the individual. They should, therefore, only be called upon by the chiefly class in times of disaster, national emergency, or for the welfare of the state.[3] To provide for the less important, day-to-day needs of individual Tahitians, there appears to have been a long string of subordinate deities, a deific bureaucracy as it were. These, like the great gods above them, were placated with gifts appropriate to their station to insure that the desired service would be rendered. Finally, at the very bottom, or family, level, there were guardian spirits who were nothing more than long-departed relatives whose excellence of behavior during their lives on earth had occasioned their families to deify them. Like shadowy patriarchs, they watched over their broods and, like many living patriarchs, could cause trouble if not shown proper respect.[4]

While the greatness of the supreme god Tane was such that it forbade conceptualization in material form,[5] this rule did not hold for Oro, whose autocratic level was somewhat less than that of the supreme being. However, even in this case the symbol was less than personified since it consisted of what appeared to be a wrapped package. The form and nature of this parcel appears to have changed with time. In 1777 it was described as looking like a sailor's fid, being an elongated cone with rounded ends and made of the twisted fibers from coconut husk. However, in 1797 James Wilson found it composed of two parts with the appearance of a lashed-up sailor's hammock. And it is possible that the three- or four-foot-long wickerwork cylinder covered with black feathers, which Bougainville saw in 1768, also pertained to Oro. Unfortunately, no eighteenth-century European seems to have ever been allowed to see what these packages contained other than red, and at other times both red and yellow, feathers.[6]

Basketry or wickerwork was used to create the material representation of at least one of the higher-ranking gods. This was Maui, whose legendary size and acts of incredible strength made him a Polynesian version of that equally legendary character Paul Bunyan. As such he appears to have been a culture hero who eventually became deified. It was Maui who stuck the stars in the heavens, created earthquakes with his mighty shaking, and harnessed the sun with a rope so that it could not move faster than he desired. By one account, it would even appear that this same colossus created Tahiti and the other islands by drawing a continental land mass through the Pacific, bits and pieces of which broke off and formed the present islands. The fact that this original large land mass of Maui's was known to lie at a great distance to the east suggests an early Tahitian knowledge, albeit vague, of the South American continent.[7]

Maui's feats were fittingly matched by his basketwork figure. This was a humanoid creation some seven feet high and proportionately wide. It was neatly covered with feathers, white ones representing skin and black ones indicating hair and tattoo decoration. The head was not strictly lifelike, having three knoblike protrusions across the front and another on the back. The hips were engulfed in a loincloth, but Captain Cook must have taken a quick peek beneath it, for he pronounced the figure to be obviously that of a male! The use of this figure, said to be the only one of its kind on the island, was explained to Cook and Joseph Banks, but their language deficiency did not allow them a full understanding. Cook, however, came up with the notion that the figure was used in certain performances, possibly like Punch in a puppet show.[8] He may not have been far off in his judgment, since grotesque plaited masks were reported to have been worn on occasion on the Taiarapu peninsula, and thus it is conceivable that this figure of Maui was employed in a similar manner.[9]

While the wickerwork figure was clearly identified as a personification of Maui, there was a variety of other figures, mostly of wood, whose clear identification was never learned. A few of these were portable and found in houses, but the great majority, consisting of posts and carved-out flat boards, were in and around the sacred formalized areas known as marae.

Marae: The Places of Worship

Marae were open-air religious structures used for formal worship. As such, they ranged from what might be called a small altar, such as that described by William Bligh, which

Marae Mahaiatea, whose ahu, or stepped platform, was the largest ever built in Tahiti. Engraving based on a sketch by W. Wilson.

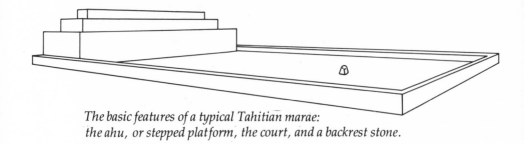

The basic features of a typical Tahitian marae:
the ahu, or stepped platform, the court, and a backrest stone.

consisted of a few stones made into a square,[10] to the
greatest of all Tahitian marae, known by the name of
Mahaiatea, whose court alone measured 360 by 354 feet.[11]
However, had European voyagers been more architecturally
oriented, they probably would have found that Tahitians
had descriptive or classificatory terms for their rather limited
range of religious buildings. What we do know, thanks to
Kenneth Emory's excellent archaeological study of stone remains in the Society Islands, is that there was one basic
marae design which dominated all others.[12] Like Catholic
churches that range from noble cathedrals to the humblest
family chapel, there were certain constant features which
might, or might not, be elaborated upon. Other less important architectural elements, however, could be included or
avoided, depending upon the builder and, in the case of
Tahiti, the deity involved.

In its simplest form, this basic Tahitian marae consisted
of an *ahu* and a court. The ahu was a raised mass of stone,
flat on top, and made into an elongated rectangle faced with
dry-laid masonry which, in larger marae, was often shaped
and fitted. In smaller marae the ahu was frequently nothing
more than a single, vertically faced rectangular platform.
However, a two- or three-step platform seems to have been
more common, each step usually running completely
around the ahu. In the truly large marae the ahu contained
as many as eight, ten, or even eleven such steps, giving the
appearance of a great rectangular stepped platform. During
Emory's archaeological survey on Tahiti he found a number
of small marae in which the ahu was a single platform
measuring no more than three by eight feet and with a

height of less than one foot. From this humble level, ahu increased in size and stepped height, the largest ever known having a base length of 267 feet, a width of 87 feet, and a total height of no less than 44 feet. However, this latter structure is a uniquely large example, other chiefly ahu ranging closer to about one third of this size.

Although there were cases of an ahu standing alone, the great majority stood at one narrow end of a rectangular court, one of the longer sides occasionally filling that end of the enclosure.[13] Such courts were usually outlined by a low wall, sometimes constructed of fitted stone, and the interior was often paved with flagstone or waterworn cobbles. In the larger marae such pavement might not cover the entire area, a rectangular space covered with pebbles being left to mark the location where the bones of chiefs had been buried. Another feature of the court was a series of upright stones. These marked where a chief and one of his brothers, probably the next oldest, sat during ceremonies, and where the priests sat as well. The larger of these stones probably had the added advantage of serving as backrests. José de Andia y Varela claimed that some of these were also placed on the ahu and served a similar purpose. He also stated that such seating stones belonged to individuals, and when they died the stones remained in the marae but could not be used by anyone else.[14]

A final constant feature of this kind of marae was an offertory, usually referred to in the early literature as an altar. These were essentially large tables which were sometimes decorated, stood from eight to twelve feet above the ground, and rested on solid wooden posts. Such offertories could be found within the court but just as often were located on the sacred ground surrounding the marae. Here offerings of food were left for the deity to eat. Fish, dog, turtle, and pig were found on them, the latter predominating, along with such plant foods as bananas, coconuts, and breadfruit. None of the important starchy root crops or chicken were ever offered up to the gods. Were they too ordinary for godly appetites? Or did they represent foods of an earlier island population who were subdued, whereupon their food became unacceptable for the gods of the conquerors? In any case, since the gods did not physically eat the proffered food, the odor of rotting flesh tended to permeate the marae.[15]

Being open-air structures, marae were frequently shaded by trees growing within the enclosure. Two of these, the tamanu and miru, were specifically dedicated to the god Tane, though at least two other shade trees were employed, and occasionally coconut palms and even a few banana plants were found within the enclosure.[16] Some of the more important and larger marae contained small houses and sheds within their courts, while the particular marae that contained the symbol of Oro also had a miniature thatched structure where the god symbol "rested."[17] Finally, at no great distance from the marae, and well within the sacred grounds surrounding the structure, were the homes of priests who stood guard over the establishment, allowing no one to enter who did not have a right to do so. It was this hallowed ground surrounding the larger marae that was most useful to thieves and other miscreants who, if they reached such sacred ground without being caught, avoided punishment because of its sanctity. It also proved to be a much sought-after location during the time of special ceremonies requiring human sacrificial victims.[18]

The larger chiefly marae were usually built close to the sea, often on promontories, though a few were scattered inland along the coastal plain and lower valleys.[19] The ceremonies held in the marae were prime examples of religious segregation, since commoners were never allowed within their walls, and women, even those of the chiefly class, were not permitted to enter them except during one special ritual whose purpose was never reported.[20] All of this, however, did not mean that the lower-ranked citizens were excluded from worship. On the contrary, each district seems to have maintained a public marae for those living within its boundaries. Domingo Boenechea reported that each of the four Tahitians whom he took back to Lima with him in 1772 independently claimed that each district had a marae where both men and women of the district assembled for a special ceremony once every six moons, or about every six months. On these occasions the men, as was the custom in all marae, wore only their breechclouts. The women and priests, however, wore large sheets of tapa cloth, the women fastening them around their waists, the priests around their necks. The simple ceremony described by the four Tahitians seems to have been one of prayer and reaffirmation to deity, though which god was involved was not stated. When all from the district had assembled, one of the priests began the ceremony with a long prayer, after which a live pig was symbolically offered up, and the crowd, lifting their eyes heavenward, loudly proclaimed what was probably a prayer or chant. This simple exercise in devotion completed, the pig was killed and set to cooking while the multitude retreated to a stream to bathe. Thus cleansed, the worshipers returned to the marae where the pig was now thoroughly cooked. After again offering the pig to the deity, it was torn apart and a small piece given to every individual, the district chief getting the largest portion, as befitted his civil and religious position.[21]

While each district had its marae for commoners, it would also appear that each parish, or patu, had its own marae dedicated to the more limited use of the people living in the various land divisions, or *mata'eina'a,* that made up the parish. This was suggested indirectly by Wilson, who was told that the head of each patu had the right to set up his *ti'i,* a carved board or figure, on the marae. This, by extension, allowed the landholders under him also to worship at that marae.[22] While the marae involved was not identified, the inference that it was a parish religious structure was based upon the fact that a district marae is known to have existed and, as we shall see, a marae for a still smaller landholding, probably a mata'eina'a, and even a family marae appear to have been maintained. It thus seems probable that each of the increasing land divisions, from family to mata'eina'a and on to patu and district, had a particular structure for religious ceremonies for those living within each prescribed area.

The existence of what was possibly a mata'eina'a was noted by the missionaries of 1797. In their report they mentioned a feast held at what they called the ra'atira's, or commoner's, marae, where men met in small companies, the women having been excluded. That this may have been the marae of a mata'eina'a land division is strongly suggested by the fact that the chief of the patu, of which a mata'eina'a was a part, was always invited, along with the priests. This particular ceremony was indeed a simple one, as might be expected in this small land division. A pig was baked, after which a priest offered up a prayer. After small portions of all the foods brought were placed on an offertory along with a bit of kava root, everyone pitched in, drinking plenty of kava and eating a great deal. If a stranger passed by during the feast, he was invited to partake, providing he was ra'a, or clean. However, anything left over had to remain at the marae and be eaten there on the following day. Should the chief of the patu fail to arrive, the portion which had been saved for him was given to the attending priests.[23]

Thus it would seem that some kind of formal religious structure existed for all levels of society, beginning with the paramount chief and extending to the district chiefs and on down, in ever-decreasing population and land units, to the individual family. We know but little of the family marae except that it must have been a rather diminutive affair which lacked an ahu but did have a small offertory, or altar, upon which food was placed from time to time, and where a pig was offered up on the occasion of the birth of a child. It must have been located quite close to the dwelling, for during part of the ceremonial procedure after a birth in the family the child was said to have been moved into a temporary hut built on sacred ground near the dwelling.[24] It was in this area around the offertory that a pleasantly bitter-smelling shrub sacred to Tane was said to be planted.[25]

All marae must have had certain restrictions aimed at maintaining the degree of sanctity appropriate to the socioreligious level of each structure. What these were for the lesser marae was not reported in the early literature, since Europeans tended to deal only with the chiefly class, whose religious structures were the most imposing and, at the same time, the most segregated. Such marae, and probably others, were said to have been built by the priests,[26] but it is most likely that, like the building of a sacred canoe, the backbreaking work was done by commoners, while the priests served as architects and foremen who dutifully sanctified each stage of the construction.

Once a marae was built, it was not always maintained in pristine condition, grass and weeds being allowed to grow in the courts between periods of religious ceremony.[27] In fact, this very characteristic got the Spanish in trouble for, without knowing that there was an interdiction against removing anything from a marae, they sent their sailors into one of these sacred courts to cut the lush green grass for their animals.[28] Rodríguez later intentionally raided a marae to gather purslane, a weed very much enjoyed by the Europeans of the time as a salad green. However, the local Tahitian priests saw to it that this did not happen again. They quietly went into the marae and removed all of the purslane, thus forcing Rodríguez to go much farther afield to obtain the makings for his salad.[29] So great was the fear of this taboo, which if broken brought down the wrath of the god of the marae, that at one point William Bligh had to have a chief remove the sanctity of a branch of a candlenut tree which had been plucked on sacred ground. The offending stem had been brought into one of Bligh's houses, whereupon all the natives had gotten up and left the building. To make matters worse, the crew member who caused the trouble had hung the twig on one of the houseposts, thus effectively tabooing the place to all Tahitians. It took a trip to the marae by a priest with a plantain stem peace offering and a prayer to the deity to remove the taboo so that the natives could again enter the building.[30] The same taboo applied to the removal of stones. Thus, when the Spanish robbed a nearby marae of some neatly wrought masonry for use as steps to their house, the high chief Vehiatua, a friend and frequent guest, refused to visit them because of this sacrilege.[31] Even Cook's men got into a bit of trouble when they raided a marae to collect stones for more ballast for their ship. Oddly enough, while the natives objected to the removal of the stones from this particular marae, they graciously showed the sailors another whose stones were, apparently, available for the asking! Could marae be desanctified, or did they lose their sacredness upon the death of an owner who left no male offspring? Cook did not bother to investigate the matter, but cautiously ordered his men to get their ballast from a nearby river bed.[32]

There seems little doubt that at least these larger marae were fearful places for the uninitiated. They were not the type of holy ground where one might go to contemplate and come to feel as one with the deity. Tahitian gods were jealous of their property and the respect that was due it. Normally, Tahitians kept at a distance from the structure for fear of supernatural retribution.[33] In fact, it was necessary for those living at no great distance from one of the greater marae to sleep with their heads toward the sacred structure. To do otherwise was an act of irreverence.[34]

Priests

The secrets of dealing with deity were centered in the chiefly class and were manipulated by a rather large and widespread group of priests known as *tahu'a*, or masters. However, they were not the only ones to deal with the gods, for chiefs were also called upon on certain occasions to perform priestly functions. In fact, the higher ranking chiefs may have had as much ritualistic knowledge as their priests, since Manne Manne, the exiled paramount chief of Raiatea, became high tahu'a of Tahiti. Thus, chiefs who lost their command sometimes merely moved over to equally prestigious positions as priests.

With a wide range of marae extending, as they did, from the most chiefly structures down through the ranks to the smaller sacred areas of the common people, it is not surprising that there was also a religious ranking among the tahu'a. However, it would appear that while those who ministered to the commoners conducted essentially the same kind of rituals as those at the great marae, they seem to have been less well trained and, perhaps, a bit more specialized. The missionaries found that the lower order of priests worked their ceremonies in accordance with their "craft and abilities."[35] What is most interesting, considering the near total exclusion of women in the higher chiefly marae, was the existence of female tahu'a at these lower religious levels. They appear to have shared with male priests the sacred rituals pertinent to their own sex.[36]

Tahu'a had a variety of duties, all of which were connected in one way or another with the gods. Their most obvious function was conducting the ritualistic ceremonies at the marae where gods were to be appeased and supernatural help implored, all accompanied by appropriate offerings of food and, when necessary, of humans as well. So ingrained was this concept of appeasing one's god by food offerings that at one time, after Bligh had completed Sunday devotions for his Christian crew, he was asked by the perplexed Tahitian onlookers if he was not now going to offer up food to his god so that he might eat.[37] Besides these more usual ministrations, there were auguries to be made and thanks to be given for successful campaigns of war. Beyond this, the tahu'a served as the ultimate physician in case of illness, since poor health was thought to have been inflicted by an offended deity. In this capacity the priest was employed to intervene with the gods and persuade them, through prayers and offerings, furnished by the ill one's family, to return the patient's health.[38] Should the gods fail to respond, the priestly physician conducted prayers at the marae for the soul of his lost patient. Since there is ample evidence that the priests prayed at the marae upon the demise of a chiefly person, the missionaries' claim that no such prayers were offered up except when death was thought to have occurred from an infectious disease may refer only to commoners. In this latter case, the prayer was not directed toward the welfare of the deceased in afterlife, but rather toward the welfare of the living: the dead person was asked to bury his disease with him and not bring it back when he returned as a spirit.[39]

Beyond these clearly religious functions, the more knowledgeable tahu'a served as sources for the traditional history of the people. As such they spread the island's history, both factual and legendary, in formal recitations in the homes of chiefs and commoners alike, and occasionally at large outdoor gatherings.[40] Finally, with such power and knowledge in their hands, it is not surprising that tahu'a were thought to have great powers of sorcery to kill or cripple their fellow human beings.[41]

The priests who carried out the day-to-day tasks of prayer and ritual were the real rulers of the religious life of the island. However, there was another class of tahu'a who may be referred to as inspirational priests. These were the very few people who claimed to belong to certain deities and, from time to time, were possessed by them, the particular god entering their bodies and thus inspiring them. Some were possessed by only one god, but there were others who claimed possession by as many as three of the superior deities. These latter received the utmost in reverential treatment by the people of the island. Such priests could, upon request, call down their god for oracular comment, but it seems that just as often the god dropped in quite unexpectedly. When he did, the priest was apt to go into a wild, and sometimes dangerous, demonstration of force. On such occasions it must be said that he had everything in his favor, since it was believed that anything he did was for the good because it was inspired by the god within him. To oppose him would almost certainly result in death or serious illness. While under such possession, a priest might offer some oracular words of advice, but apparently it was more common for him to request all manner of good things, either for himself or for the deity within him. Since to negate him was to expose oneself to potential supernatural danger, he usually got what he asked for. But not all gods dropped in unannounced, for at times the priests had enough forewarning to dress in a manner certain to call attention to themselves. Cook reported one such inspired priest as wearing nothing more than a large quantity of banana leaves around his waist, while some years later another inspired tahu'a showed up in a blue coat trimmed with red and wearing a mass of feathers which completely hid his face. In this latter instance the god left the inspired priest in remarkable haste when an irate missionary dispossessed the inspired body of the club it was wielding and revealed the man as a known thief. Even then, the crowd of natives interceded on his behalf, and he quickly disappeared into the multitude.

A requested possession by a god of an inspirational priest was far less dangerous to the public at large than the unexpected visits of deities. When asked to consult his god, the priest dressed himself in a costume of black and red feathers said to be pleasing to the deities. He then called for his special god, and that deity, as so often happened at marae ceremonies, descended in the form of one of the sacred birds, the kingfisher or the heron, which frequented marae and ate well from the decaying offerings. As soon as one of these birds alighted in the marae it was the signal for the priest to begin. He started with a yawn, and then his stomach became distended, his eyes contorted, and in no time at all his body was shaking convulsively. His first speech was squeaky and difficult to understand, squeaky voices always being associated with the voice of deity, but then he lapsed into more normal speech and presented his oracular message. Not surprisingly, this also included a request for gifts which his assistant carefully noted. According to the missionaries, who might have been slightly prejudiced, the timing of his performance was perfect, for the trance lasted until one of the sacred birds left the marae, presumably carrying the god homeward. At this moment a final convulsion struck the priest, after which he fell limp with exhaustion and concluded the performance with a mighty shout as he awakened to the real world about him.[42]

Red Feathers and Deity

While masonry-built marae and effigies of wood, basketry, and even a few of stone[43] were the solid manifestations of Tahitian religion, there was one beautifully delicate symbol of deity that surpassed all others in value. This was the red feather, or 'ura, which came from the head of a Tahitian parrot.[44] However, the species source was less important than the brilliance and naturalness of the color. Some shrewd observer on Cook's first voyage must have recognized the bargaining power of these red feathers, for when Cook reached Tahiti the first time on his second voyage, his ships appear to have carried a small cargo of cock feathers suitably dyed to the proper red.To the amazement and chagrin of these would-be profiteers, the Tahitians immediately recognized the fakery and, while politely accepting the proffered feathers, firmly refused to give anything in return. Thus it is difficult to believe John Forster's bland statement that when the ships reached Tongatapu they "accidentally" procured a large quantity of natural red feathers which Tongans enjoyed using to decorate a wide variety of objects. Numerous examples of these particular artifacts were picked up and brought back to Tahiti, some being traded intact, while others were broken apart and disposed of piecemeal.[45]

Although the investment in English cock feathers had been a total loss, the Tongan feather trade more than made up for the original minor debacle. Anything could be purchased for the bright, naturally red feathers. A bit of feathered-covered Tongan tapa cloth measuring only two inches square would easily purchase a hog, and even the famous mourning costumes with their shell masks, which Cook's men had tried but failed to obtain on their first voyage, appear to have been offered with little hesitation, as long as the Tongan red feathers were the items of exchange. Finally, to John Forster's everlasting horror, one of his friends among the Tahitian chiefs offered to prostitute his own wife for a package of the feathers.[46]

The cause of all of this zestful trading was deity itself. Red feathers made up at least part of that symbolic package that represented the god Oro and must have served as deific protection when they formed part of the tassels worn by warriors. As a highly portable symbol of divinity, they were grouped together, eight or ten being fixed in a bunch on the end of a tightly twisted string made from coconut husk. As such, like the handheld cross of a Christian, they were held by priests and chiefs during prayers. The strength of deity could be further increased by holding still a few more red feathers between the thumb and forefinger. They must have been a constant source of divine aid and security, Anders

Sparrman having once witnessed a distraught chief bring out his bundle of red feathers and say a little prayer to them. And if red feathers were held in a person's hands while making a vow, it was considered a sacred promise that would not be broken.[47]

Human Sacrifice

There are remarkably few descriptions of the ceremonies held in the marae, possibly because Tahitians were not eager to have Europeans meddling in things religious, especially since the gods might take umbrage at such foreign interference. There is also the probability that for Europeans such ceremonies were boring affairs consisting of innumerable prayers whose content could seldom be understood. Most attention was paid to ceremonies involving human sacrifice, for that very act was so antithetical to European mores that it had to be observed to be believed. The paramount chief's investiture ceremony with its numerous human sacrifices has already been described, but there were other occasions as well when such sacrifices were appropriate.

Though it was up to the tahu'a to decide how many sacrificial victims were needed in certain cases, such as during what proved to be the terminal illness of Tahiti iti's high chief Vehiatua, the early missionaries described the choice of victims as a cold-blooded affair determined by a council of chiefs and landowners. The Spanish, however, who lived through the final demise of this young chief, and who attempted by their own crude medicines to save his life, recounted a series of events that suggests a quite different approach to the matter. Various of Vehiatua's men, probably all belonging to the chiefly class, were sent out to search for human sacrifices. One victim was killed in the very canyon whose use rights had been given to Rodríguez, but when all the families headed for the hills in fear of their lives, a group from another district proceeded to search their own area. Here they managed to catch up with a twelve-year-old boy; when his father went to his aid, he was also killed as a sacrificial victim. Finally, a fourth victim was obtained from yet another province. That the whole affair was not too well organized or controlled, at least on this particular calamitous occasion, was demonstrated by the fact that one of Vehiatua's men showed up in the Spaniards' dwelling with a bad cut on his head. He had proceeded on his own initiative to search for a sacrificial victim to help save the life of his chief, but he had picked a man who had a strong desire to live and showed it by nearly destroying his would-be assassin.

The impending death of a youthful high chief like Vehiatua was, from the Spanish accounts of the uproar, a very serious and frightening occasion, and any means of appeasing the gods was grabbed at in a near hysterical fashion. It thus seems probable that under less calamitous conditions the search for human victims was a more deliberate undertaking in which, as the missionaries claim, undesirable local characters were searched out and destroyed for what must have been regarded as a highly worthy cause.

Human sacrificial victims were never killed by a knife or by spearing, a stone being the preferred instrument and the nape of the neck the proper point for the lethal blow. This was due to the desirability of having a victim who had no broken bones and who was not disfigured. Women were never chosen as sacrificial material and, again according to the missionaries, any man who had been bitten or otherwise scarred by a woman was not suitable as a proper offering (though how the source of a man's scars was determined is a little difficult to figure).[48]

As far as can be determined, all human sacrificial victims were taken to a marae known in the literature as Taputapuatea.[49] In Rodríguez's time this was located in Punaauia in the district of Atahuru on the west coast of Tahiti nui.[50] It was here that the sacred feather maro, or loincloth, was kept, as was the symbolic parcel representative of the god Oro. However, in 1792 Bligh found the maro and the symbol of Oro at Tu's marae in Pare up on the north coast, the result of this chief's having conducted a successful war against the people of Atehuru. What is interesting here is Bligh's statement that, upon completion of this conquest, Tu brought the maro, the symbol of Oro, and the "Tebbootaboo," or *taputapu*, back to Pare with him. The taputapu were lattice-like, cut-through boards, some

Captain James Cook viewing a human sacrificial ceremony in a Tahitian marae. A food offertory set on carved posts may be seen in the right middle foreground while in the background taputapu carved boards decorate the top of the low ahu. Painting by John Webber.

vaguely suggesting a man and others decorated with a bird motif. When grouped together on top of the ahu of a marae they were, according to Bligh, given the name "tebbootaboo-ataiah," or *taputapuatea.* Furthermore, when the symbol of Oro was housed in the same marae where the taputapu boards stood, the entire structure, or marae, was given the name of taputapuatea, meaning "the principle place of worship."[51] As such it also became the marae where the sacred maro was kept and human sacrifices to Oro were brought. However, this distinction lasted only as long as the symbolic items remained at that particular structure. (This special function could even apply to a sacred canoe when it carried the taputapu boards and the symbol of Oro, as shown in a sketch of such a canoe attributed to Bligh. Here a raised, slightly troughed platform carrying taputapu boards and the Oro symbol is identified on the drawing as "The Morai Tebbootabooataiah," or marae of taputapuatea.[52]) An excellent illustration of such a highly sacred marae, complete with a human sacrifice and taputapu boards standing on an ahu, was made by John Webber, artist on Cook's third voyage. By the first quarter of the nineteenth century the unique significance of the taputapu boards was no longer fully understood and their name had been changed to that of *unu.*[53]

The sacrificial bodies, laid out in extended position, were wrapped in a plaited basket cover of palm fronds and then slung from a long pole. In this manner they were transported to the sacrificial marae by means of a sacred canoe.[54] The only extant illustrations of such a canoe show it to be double hulled, each hull having a raised stern and a long, horizontal board forming the prow. Over the forward hatch of at least one of the hulls was a troughed platform raised on three broad arched supports, on the top of which was placed the symbol of Oro. On this same platform stood a series of upright trestle-like geometric constructions identified by Bligh as taputapuatea, at least one of which was surmounted by a carved bird. In the other hull was the little shed, or god house, for the Oro symbol, while in the rear of each hull rested a vertical-type sacred drum, and on the forward extending prow boards were animal offerings.[55] It was at this latter location that the human sacrificial victim was placed for its trip to the sacrificial marae, the brief voyage being made at a slow pace with the drums sounding out a somber beat.[56]

Such sacred canoes were the objects of considerable ceremony during their construction. It required at least a district chief to order the building of such a craft. He issued instructions to his subchiefs, or to'ofa, who in turn passed the word down to the landholding gentry, who were then required to furnish food and such gifts as tapa cloth and oil to the carpenters. These latter first scoured the hills for the proper trees, and when these were found it was up to the owner of the property on which they grew to have them cut down and roughed out under the watchful direction of the carpenters. This activity, done in place, saved considerable labor in snaking the material down the hills to the building shed on the coast. Virtually every act of constructing a canoe was given assurance of sacred sanction with feasts and prayer. There was a ceremony before cutting the timber, another upon assembling all of the required materials, and others at every step of construction until the vessel was complete. At that point the canoe was splendidly decorated with, among other things, red feathers. A final feast and human sacrifice firmly committed the canoe to its sacred function.[57]

There is little doubt that human sacrifices for a variety of religious reasons were a fairly common occurrence in Tahiti. While they were usually offered as a direct sacrifice to gods, in which case the bodies were buried in the marae, sacrificial victims were occasionally sent to a paramount chief as a form of atonement for some offense and as a pledge of future good faith. In cases such as this, however, the victim served a secular need, and thus the body, rather than being buried in sacred ground, was taken out to the barrier reef and laid to rest in a watery grave beneath the coral rocks.[58] However, not all marae ceremonies were grisly, and, while Tahitians may have lived in awe of their deities, it is doubtful that they felt constantly threatened by the possibility of being sacrificed to their gods.

Religion involving the supernatural is a prime source for dealing with and explaining the unknown, and so it was, in part, for the Tahitians. Unknown illnesses were considered god-inflicted and could only be cured by appeasement and prayer. Unexplainable natural phenomena were thought to be god-induced, even if it took a giant of a god, like Maui, to do it, while shooting stars and what may have been heat lightning were explained to Rodríguez as deity itself.[59] But religion in Tahiti went further than this. The paramount chief, though earthly born, was created by the gods and ruled by their will,[60] thus giving him deific strength in his capacity as the prime center of government. Success in war was god-given, while defeat was attributed to human error, or, where this was not clearly the case, to some disgruntled deity. The Tahitian gods were an unforgiving, fearsome lot unless properly propitiated and well fed, and even then they were capable of turning their backs. As an overriding force for social control, they were better than a thousand laws, since the punishment for infractions was not clearly defined in the supernatural world, and one could never be sure that the divine punishment would necessarily fit the earthly crime.

Daily Life

The first faint graying of the sky announced the dawn in pristine Tahiti, just as it did on countless other islands in the tropical Pacific. From high in the mountains damp air, made cool by nighttime temperatures, flowed in invisible currents down the mountainsides and into the valleys leading to the coast. The broad leaves of numerous banana plants fluttered, and as the breezes spread out over the coastal plain, their movement set acres of dark green taro leaves to shimmering in the first light of day. In groves of trees and protective bushes, small birds began their daily fidgeting from branch to branch, while out on the mud flats long-legged heron yawningly stretched their wings preparatory to seeking their morning refreshment. No sudden noises broke the stillness of the dawning light, for the rippling of mountain streams, the lunging roar of waterfalls, and the steady rush of rhythmic waves formed only a soothing background of alternating tones to an otherwise quietly emerging day.

As silently as the new dawn began, so the Tahitians commenced their daily routine of life's activities. There was work to be done, but unless there was a catastrophe or the district chief had called upon them for an immediate service, their lives were a pleasant mixture of work and relaxation, with occasional entertainment supplied by the chiefs and *arioi*, or entertainers', society. Rising with the sun, each member of the family clothed himself in the very garments used to cover him in the night, for dress and bed linen were essentially one and the same in Tahiti.[1] Glorified by their European visitors as the cleanest people in the Pacific,[2] and certainly cleaner than Europeans of that day, they proceeded to the nearest freshwater stream or spring and, using a broad leaf to cover the most critical aspects of their nakedness when once in the water, proceeded to take their morning baths.[3] This may have been followed by a small bite of breakfast. However, the record is not clear on this matter, for the earliest reports mentioned only two meals a day. On the main part of the island these consisted of a principal meal at noon and a smaller repast in the evening, while on the Taiarapu peninsula a morning and evening meal may have been the custom. It was only later, in 1797, that the practice of three meals a day, including breakfast, was mentioned.[4] Here one must wonder if perhaps this later custom developed from an appreciation of the eating patterns of their European visitors.

Had Tahitians lived in towns or villages, this habit of morning bathing could have created quite a spectacle. However, this was not the case for, in keeping with their dispersed agricultural practices, their homes and public buildings were scattered throughout the plain and up the meandering floors of the wider valleys. This dispersed settlement pattern, as it is called by geographers, showed no sign of even the slightest trend toward agglutination of buildings around ceremonial centers except, perhaps, for the fact that a chief's home was sometimes near his family marae. Only on the Taiarapu Peninsula, where coastal plains were narrow or nonexistent, was there a clustering of houses at the mouths of valleys, which invited a few Europeans to use the term "village" in describing them.[5]

Houses and Their Furnishings

The great majority of dwellings, as well as public buildings, varied enormously in size but were consistent in having their long sides parallel and their ends rounded.[6] However, there were two intriguing references to round houses, and one reference to a few large dwellings occupied by chiefs on the Taiarapu Peninsula which had the distinction of having high arched, or vaulted, roofs.[7] The fact that these two forms were overlooked in the records of the majority of early

View of the mouth of the Vaitepiha River on the windward side of the Taiarapu Peninsula show-ing a clustering of houses where the river breaks out of its canyon. Drawing by John Webber.

European observers suggests that they were uncharacteristic of the island's architecture and encountered infrequently enough as not to be mentioned. John Forster described the round houses as being small affairs, but the one in which the youthful high chief Tu was living when Domingo Boenechea visited him in 1772 was described as being more capacious than other dwellings of the area.[8] The presence of these seemingly anomalous house forms suggests that one or the other may represent the remnant of an earlier traditional dwelling type, perhaps even that of the original founding population. On the other hand, either or both could represent the physical manifestation of infrequent later incursions of people who had quite different building traditions than the one common to Tahiti. After all, historical records of round houses in Polynesia are not as rare as once was thought, masonry-walled ones being found even on lonely Easter Island and an oblate form occurring in Samoa near the western extremity of Polynesia.[9] However, circular dwellings are also known to have occurred farther west in Melanesia.[10] As for arch-roofed houses, their common occurrence in Polynesia was far to the west of Tahiti in Tonga and Samoa,[11] and, like the round dwellings, their use extended into Melanesia. Unfortunately, there is no constructional data on the Tahitian round and arch-roofed dwellings.

The belief that Tahitians occupied rectangular houses in prehistoric times[12] is not supported by the pre-1800 European accounts or by archaeological investigations. Further research in the Society Islands may, of course, reveal their pre-contact presence within this island group. However, the first historic record of such a native house style appears to have been made by William Ellis in the early 1800s, well after missionaries and various sailors had settled on the island and built their homes in traditional European form. In fact, Ellis may not have been too far amiss when he described nineteenth-century Tahitian rectangular houses as resembling English dwellings.[13] They were, quite probably, native attempts to copy the buildings of their foreign visitors, rather than some resurgent effort to reproduce a traditional house type of a bygone prehistoric era.

A Tahitian's house tended to reflect his economic status as well as his station in life. That is to say, whether he had a small, poorly constructed dwelling or a large one with polished beams and neatly laid thatch tended to indicate his position in society. There was no multiplicity of house styles to choose from, and the interior furnishings were so limited that the mere presence of an elongated stool and a few fine mats clearly separated the higher classes from the lower.

A common house, such as one belonging to a teuteu or perhaps one of the poorer farmers, measured from twelve to twenty feet in length, ten to fifteen feet in width, and had a central roof height of from eight to nine feet. The roof sloped down to a height of five or six feet around the edge of the dwelling, and continued downwards beyond the limits of the house as a very effective eave. Captain Cook described what he regarded as a medium-sized dwelling: it had a length of about twenty-four feet, a width of twelve, and a central roof height of from eight to nine feet, with eaves dropping down to within three and a half or four feet of the ground. Others, somewhat narrower, had a length of thirty feet and a width of only ten feet.[14]

Chiefs seem to have had a variety of dwellings, some being no larger than those already mentioned. As might be expected, however, their construction exhibited superior workmanship. Sometimes a chief maintained a shelter on his canoe, consisting of a small deck house with walls and roof of coconut palm thatching, or just a slightly raised, gabled roof or awning. These were secured in a fore-and-aft position on the platform connecting the two hulls of a double canoe or were occasionally set crosswise over the flattened horizontal prows of the hulls. Many of these were so designed that, should the chief decide not to sleep aboard his craft, the shelter could be lifted bodily by a few stout men and set ashore wherever the chief pleased.[15] However, there was always at least one very large and handsome structure which represented the formal dwelling of the chief and served for a variety of chiefly functions. These were large, impressive affairs ranging from 80 to over 300 feet in length and proportionately wide and high. For example, Wallis measured the chiefess Purea's house and found it 327 feet long, 42 feet wide, with a ridgepole resting 30 feet above the floor. The ridgepole was supported by fourteen massive posts, while thirty-nine posts supported the eaves of the roof.[16]

Large or small, all of these flattened oval houses were constructed along fundamentally similar lines (except, perhaps, those unique arch-roofed dwellings of some of the chiefs on the Taiarapu Peninsula). Basically, they consisted of a framework set upon three rows of upright posts, the center row being the tallest and supporting the long ridgepole. In the better homes these posts were made of the yellowish wood of the breadfruit tree, which was said to resist the onslaught of worms. Less desirable were posts of hibiscus logs.[17] The two outer rows of posts were considerably lower than the central ones which carried the ridgepole. These lower posts effectively served to outline the two longer sides of the house. They were connected across their tops by long beams, or wall plates. Occasionally, and quite probably in the larger buildings, these side posts rested on long, horizontal foot plates which lay directly on the ground and seem to have served to disperse the otherwise concentrated weight of each upright.[18]

Rafters were formed of long, thin poles of hibiscus, previously prepared by peeling and soaking the wood in water for several days to extract the sap because it was thought to attract insects. These stretched down from the ridgepole to the lower side beams and extended beyond to form a deep, protective eave.[19] None of the early reports explained the roof construction needed to cover the rounded ends of these dwellings. However, later studies indicated that these were covered by rafters radiating from points just below the ends of the ridgepole.[20] Although Ellis referred to the use of such carpentry techniques as grooving, beveling, and mortise-and-tenon joining in describing early nineteenth-century Tahitian construction, it seems possible that such refined craftsmanship represented either a European introduction by example or a result of the use of European metal tools, which, because they were sharper than the Tahitian ones of

The dwelling complex of a Tahitian chief. Pen-and-wash drawing by Sydney Parkinson.

stone, bone, and shell, made such carpentry easier to accomplish. Quite probably the supple vines of the *'ie'ie* plant
were used to lash the entire structure together, just as they
were still used to lash the rafters in place in the early
nineteenth century.[21]

The preparation of prefabricated roof thatching elements must have taken considerable time and effort. First,
several thousand of the long, narrow leaves of the pandanus
had to be picked and then soaked in water for several days.
This was followed by coiling each separate leaf around a
stick in such a manner that its concave side was outermost.
Dried in this manner, the leaf lay flat and even when un-
coiled. The next step was to obtain bundles of reeds that
grew in such abundance on the lower hills that it was frequently necessary to burn them off.[22] These were cut to a
predetermined length, and then the prepared pandanus
leaves were folded once around and over each reed near the
base of the leaves so that their points hung down in an even
line. Fastening the folded base of each leaf was accomplished
by sewing it with the stem of a coconut leaf, the thatching
needle being nothing more than the sharpened rib of a pig.
Once sufficient thatching elements had been completed,
they were lashed onto the rafters starting at the bottom, or
eave, and working upwards towards the ridgepole in deeply
overlapping rows.

As with most thatch-roofed dwellings, the ridge line,
where the thatching elements from both sides came together, required a special closure technique. In Tahiti this
was accomplished by first covering the long, thin ridge crack
with coconut or fern leaves, over which was fastened a
woven or braided mass of long grass. The technique was
not simple, for Ellis pointed out that anyone was capable
of laying on the thatching elements, but only specialists
knew the precise technique for successfully covering the
ridge crest.[23]

Once the roof was in place and thatched and the earthen
floor treaded down into a firm, even surface, the basic house
structure was complete.[24] No fireplace or pit oven was
placed within the dwelling, for cooking was done out-of-

doors, and heating was not exactly desirable in a tropical climate. However, there was a variety of minor additions that could be made. One of these was an apron of pebbles or cobblestones around, or along one side of, the house. This served as a well-drained work, rest, and eating area.[25] Another was a wall or fence around the perimeter of the dwelling, with an opening on one side for a door and made of a series of small, spaced bamboo poles or reeds held in place by horizontally lashed wooden sticks. According to some of the Europeans, the overall appearance of this construction was that of an enlarged birdcage. Only rarely were these walls thatched, perhaps only partially, to serve as a windbreak. Apparently on the Taiarapu Peninsula some householders quickly fabricated temporary palm mats to hang on the windward side of their dwellings during periods of heavy gusting storms.[26] It may have been the use of these temporary, disposable mats that many years later gave rise to the mistaken notion that Tahitian homes were fitted with permanently movable screens like those employed in Samoan dwellings.

Although the majority of house interiors were quite open and plain, some had the space divided by fence-like walls covered with brown tapa cloth, which John Forster described as appearing like so many hurdles.[27] Low platform beds, apparently raised to keep off dampness, represented still another constructional option. Since farmers often kept their pigs in the house during the night, it was not uncommon to find a low pigsty which was covered over with planks to serve as a place of rest.[28] As for interior finishings, quite probably only the finer dwellings had their beams beautifully smoothed by the use of coral or the rough skin of a ray or shark. And it was strictly a chiefly prerogative to have the rafters of the home wrapped with fine matting or the braided fibers from the husk of the coconut.[29]

While the locations of chiefs' houses were reasonably permanent because of the size of these structures, this was not necessarily the case for smaller dwellings. These latter could be, and were, dismantled and moved to new locations as occasion, or a chiefly order, demanded. It was also not uncommon for small, rather crude, temporary structures to be built for limited use. Such were employed in the mountains during foodgathering trips, while others were constructed on the sacred grounds around a marae for the ceremonies surrounding the birth of a child. Unlike the regular dwellings, these were easily thatched—with coconut leaves for those on the coast, and *ti* leaves for those in the mountains.[30]

The theme of clean spaciousness in the Tahitian dwelling seems to have been carried through to include its furnishings. These were simple in the extreme and, since the interiors of houses were usually described as being quite open and uncluttered, it is probable that many of the items were placed around the edges of the dwellings, or even outdoors under the deep eaves. While floors were of well-compacted earth, they remained clean and neat by being amply covered with a layer of dried grass. So important was the cleanliness of this grass that etiquette did not permit persons to enter a house without first being sure that their feet were well cleaned. It was even reported that if one of the household desired to expectorate, he did so by first parting the straw, and then covering the offensive liquid by returning the grass to its original position.[31]

Certain to be found in many of the homes, though not all, were mats of various sizes upon which the Tahitians sat cross-legged in the daytime or slept during the night. These ranged in quality depending upon the material used. Some of the strongest were made of rushes, while others were made from pandanus leaves or the bark of young hibiscus.[32] In the dwellings of what the early explorers might have called the "better class" of people were often found at least one stool which appears to have been used by the head of the household. Stools were four-footed and carved out of a single piece of log. At least four different kinds of wood were suitable for their construction, including breadfruit and the lighter-weight hibiscus.[33] What looked like miniature, concave stools were, in fact, headrests or pillows for sleeping, and were probably found in all houses.[34] The Tahitians provided for storage by weaving a variety of baskets. Some were quickly plaited from coconut leaves, a method still used in the late twentieth century on some of the Polynesian islands, and were used to carry or store breadfruit, bananas, and probably fish. Others, of more permanent construction, were woven from prepared pandanus leaves or the rind from the trunk of the *fe'i* banana plant. There were even baskets made from matting, but the most likely to be found in a dwelling were pot-bellied, narrow-necked baskets woven from the vines of the *'ie'ie* plant. These latter were usually hung from the ceiling and were used to store casual gear as well as food.[35] Their lofty position was partly as a protection against the always-interested rat population. However, it was equally important to store one's prepared food where it could not be accidentally touched by any guests who had not gone through the ritual prescriptions which allowed them such a privilege. Should such a contact be made, even unintentionally, the owner of the food could not eat it.[36]

Since most foods were eaten raw, roasted, or more commonly covered with leaves and cooked in a pit oven, there was only a limited need for cooking utensils. One of these was a rather large, shallow bowl or tray of tamanu wood on which such foods as breadfruit, bananas, and taro were mashed up to make a wide variety of pastes, or *popoi*.[37] Intimately related to this was a gracefully designed pestle, or poi pounder, of highly polished, compact black volcanic rock.[38] While the normal practice seems to have been to serve meals on large freshly-picked green leaves, coconut shells and gourds were also used for both food and liquids. The coconut shells must have been quite handsome, for they were thinned down and rubbed smooth with coral, the shells of the young nuts ending up with a brownish-white tone, while more mature ones presented a polished black surface. According to the missionaries, these black bowls, when filled with water, also served as mirrors when occasion demanded. A few large sections cut from fully grown bamboo for use as bulk liquid containers, especially water,[39] and the sharpened edge of a shell or a sliver or two of bamboo for knives[40] completed the list of Tahitian utensils. As for raw or unprepared food, its proper storage was usually taken care of by constructing a hanging post outside the dwelling. Here baskets and gourds, the latter encased in plaited coconut fiber nets, could be slung well above the ground to protect their contents. However, the ever-hungry rats had to be considered, and so a rat guard disk of coconut shell or gourd was fastened around the middle of the post.[41]

Simple and efficient in terms of the lifestyle of the people, the Tahitian house was abundantly suited to its tropical environment. Shaded by broad-leaved trees and nestled in a surrounding of flowering shrubs and banana plants, it was both practical and comfortable day and night. Each must have reflected in some way its occupant's individual taste. Although the early European observers uniformly described impeccably neat little dwellings, surely there must have been a sliding scale of houses that included at its lower end at least a few somewhat disheveled affairs reflecting slovenly owners.

Be that as it may, a Tahitian's home included not only a house but also a parcel of land. The amount, and quite possibly the class, of land must have varied with the owner's rank in society. The chiefs, including the paramount chief, appear to have maintained the largest holdings. The boundaries of such lands were marked by crude images, some of them being carved in trees. If the property belonged to the chiefly class, little flags of material were added to these figures. These markers were, in effect, warning devices for any trespasser who might be of lower social rank and who was thus forced to show his respect for his social superiors by uncovering the upper part of his body while crossing this land. Should such an act of homage be openly neglected, the mother of the offended family would immediately complain symbolically by striking her head with a shark's tooth until it bled. If the offending party did not quickly make restitution by presenting the family with the standard symbol of peace, a young banana shoot, a brawl might well result. In fact, it was stated that there were times when whole extended families from both sides of the disagreement got into the fray with dire consequences. If such societal ranking became a stand-off and threatened the peace, it would appear that a district chief might be called in to sit in judgment.[42]

Rahui

There seems little doubt that ownership of individual property, whether a canoe, a tool, or the fruits of one's land, was a recognized fact among the population.[43] In this regard, one should not misconstrue Cook's statement that, on the occasion of his second voyage, all the pigs and fowl of Tahiti and the Taiarapu Peninsula were the property of the high chiefs of those two areas. The inference is that only the high chiefs, and not the rest of the population, owned these sources of flesh foods.[44] However, the very fact that Cook stated that there was an obvious scarcity of these creatures would indicate the probability that the high chiefs had placed a rahui, or taboo, on the eating or sale of chickens and pigs.

A rahui was a necessary protective mechanism used to insure the continued existence of the food resources of the island, and could be applied by chiefs or landowners to crops, animals, or even the products of the immediate lagoon. It could be applied not only because of increasing scarcity of a species but also to breed up additional food for an intended feast. The areas so tabooed were marked by white flags or banners. Upon removal of the rahui a hog or fish was offered up, and the individual who imposed the taboo was under the social obligation of furnishing a feast. Some of these, probably those given by chiefs, lasted several days and must have been memorable affairs. During this period the guests were entertained with food, wrestling, and dancing. Finally, to cap the event, large quantities of tapa cloth were tossed to the assembled crowd who then made sport of tearing off pieces of the material to take home as souvenirs of the great *'oro'a,* as the feast was called.[45]

It is clear that the laying on of a rahui by a chief did not divest a family of their property rights but merely placed a temporary control on the use of certain things that they owned. The rahui was enforced by the strength of religious restriction through fear of divine wrath. Another obligation, that of taxation, was carried out when chiefs called upon their districts to furnish them with food, clothing, mats, and other hard goods. If a district did not meet its desired quota, the chief, as governing authority, felt free to banish the delinquents from their land.[46]

Division of Labor

Once the ablutions of the morning had been completed, the daily work activities needed for comfortable existence took over. Often there was some gardening or harvesting to be done; if not, the men might apply themselves to such tasks as building a canoe, carving a much-needed paddle or canoe bailer, or perhaps fashioning a lance or war club. At another time they might occupy their morning in helping to build a house, for this too was men's work, as was the making of the thatching for the roof. If there were no major tasks to be performed, there was always the need to make new fishhooks, twist filaments into fishing lines, or soak a quantity of coconut husks in water so that they might later be beaten up and their fibers drawn into threads and plaited into cordage.[47]

While the men occupied themselves with their traditional roles of activity, the women busied themselves making and decorating yard upon yard of tapa, or bark cloth, weaving innumerable mats of varying texture and size, and fashioning clothing from both materials. On the Taiarapu Peninsula they also constructed ceremonial masks of plaited "grass."[48] This activity suggests that, although the women were not normally allowed within the precincts of a marae and did not usually participate in religious ceremonies, at least on the Peninsula they may have furnished certain of the religious accoutrements for such occasions. Whereas the construction of matting may have been a dominant woman's activity, it was not uniquely so, for there is at least one reference to a man constructing a mat.[49] Perhaps in this case the mat was to be used as a sail: since men built canoes, they may also have woven the mats that were used as sails.

Meals and Their Preparation

Like many people of the tropics, the Tahitians labored in the cooler hours of the day. By mid-morning it was time to rest and, if a warm meal was anticipated, to start the pit oven

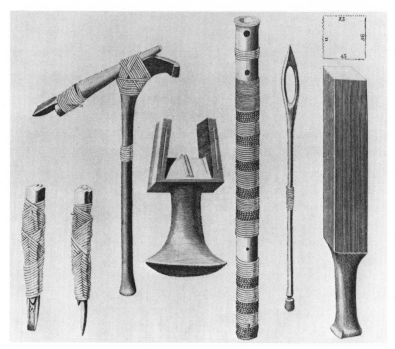

Tahitian implements. From left to right: *Two chisels, a small adz, a stone pestle or poi pounder, a nose flute, a roof thatching needle, and a tapa, or bark cloth, beater. The diagram above the tapa beater shows the number of ridges on each of the beater's four sides. Artist unidentified.*

fires burning. This was a brief period of quiet repose, a time to have a friend pick the lice from one's head and have him eat them in the bargain.[50] It was also a time to groom one's hair and, if necessary, to add a little more scented coconut oil, or *mono'i*, to it. Such oil, still used for grooming in Tahiti in the late twentieth century, was an important element in the daily routine and, according to John Forster's reasoning, had the additional advantage of tending to suffocate the lice population.[51] It was made by grating the fully ripened white meat of the coconut into a large wooden tray or trough, which was then covered and set in the shade for several days. Gradually the oil would begin to separate from the meat, and as it accumulated it was spooned out with a shell or carefully poured off into tree-gourd containers. Here a wide variety of parts of plants could be used alone or in various combinations to give fragrance to the oil. Omai, a Tahitian whom Cook took to England on his second voyage, claimed that no fewer than fourteen different plants could be used for such a purpose. One of these was the greatly prized fragrant sandalwood, which grew high in the mountains. Then, too, there were pungent leaves and flowers, and even the pollen from the blossoms of the pandanus tree. These were mixed into the clear oil and stirred frequently over a period of several weeks, after which the liquid was strained and put up for storage in large sections of bamboo. Although it seems to have been principally used in grooming the hair, it was also occasionally employed over the entire body.[52] How long such oil lasted without becoming rancid is not known. However, that it probably did become rancid was attested to by Cook, who found the Tahitians' olfactory delights too strong for his own nostrils.[53]

Once refreshed from the early morning activities, Tahitians turned their thoughts to food. Although none of the women were allowed to eat pig or dog, and women of less than chiefly status were prohibited from eating certain kinds of seafood,[54] the family was less concerned with what they ate than with who prepared the meal and who joined them in the eating of it. A man could not eat anything prepared by a woman, and the women could not touch the food of the men, unless they were near relatives who had undergone the special amo'a ceremony that allowed them to do so by removing certain taboos.[55] Neither could the sexes join in partaking of a repast, so they ate separately. In some cases this separation amounted to nothing more than the men eating at one end of the house and the women at the other. However, some appear to have followed a more rigid code that did not allow the women to eat within sight of the men.[56] To complicate a meal still further, there were additional restrictions within the sexes as to who might touch one's food and with whom one could, or could not, eat.

The total picture of eating restrictions is none too clear and far from complete. However, it appears that at least the choice of which relatives ate with one, or touched one's food, was traditionally determined by certain of the amo'a

ceremonies having to do with the life-cycle rites. The statements on this matter are, unfortunately, neither exhaustive
nor abundantly clear. It was said that before the newborn
child could be taken from the sacred grounds near the marae
an amo'a had to be performed by the father and the child's
uncles, and yet another by its mother and aunts before the
child could be returned to the house where the father and
uncles ate.[57] Not only are we left in doubt as to whether the
aunts and uncles were from one or another, or both, sides of
the family, but perhaps more important, there is no reference to the sex of the child. Considering the importance of
the separation of the sexes for cooking and eating purposes,
one cannot help but suspect that perhaps the ceremony involving father and uncles was conducted for a male child so
that he might eat with his male relatives, while the one involving mother and aunts was for a girl so that she might eat
with them. Later, upon the marriage of a daughter, her family gave two other amo'a ceremonies. The first of these allowed her father and uncles to eat with her husband and to
partake of any food that he may have touched. The second
ceremony allowed her mother and aunts to touch the food of
her husband without his having to throw it away, though
they still could not eat with him. Unfortunately, what was
not stated is whether these ceremonies allowed reciprocal
freedoms on the part of the groom's parents, uncles, and
aunts: that is to say, that upon completion of the two ceremonies the groom's mother and aunts could eat with his
bride and touch her food without tabooing it. Regardless,
there seems to have been a series of religiously based prescriptions surrounding the handling of one's food by relatives and the determination of which of them might be permitted to join one at mealtime. It was possibly the working
of these restrictive decrees that caused Cook to make the
observation that it was not common to find any two people
actually eating together.[58]

Since Máximo Rodríguez, in his year-long travels
around Tahiti, frequently referred to the meals served up to
himself and his Tahitian fellow travelers, it would seem to
follow that the eating restrictions within the sexes did not go

beyond a concern with one's relatives. This point is further reinforced by the missionary accounts of native hospitality practices toward friends and visitors from neighboring islands, which invariably included food.[59] Thus we may conclude that although the voracious appetites of many of the Tahitians left no doubt that food was for the eating, the gods had laid down certain ground rules for its preparation and consumption. Should such rules be broken, it followed that one might lose an eye or become crippled or deformed.[60] To Europeans, the extreme in Tahitian food restrictions was to be found among certain of the superior chiefs, including the paramount chief. As noted earlier, these unfortunate dignitaries were not allowed to touch a single morsel during certain periods of their lives, and thus had to be hand-fed by others. In so doing, they acted like so many small children in the eyes of at least some of the voyagers, who saw the custom as simply an affectation.[61]

Meals seem to have been ample but customarily did not consist of any wide variety of dishes. Out of a list of ten meals which various voyagers described, there were always at least some flesh foods. These appeared to be rather evenly divided between fish, chicken, and pork, one or another usually appearing at a meal. However, considering the vast number of people that frequented the reefs to fish in the evening, it may be that seafood was dominant when foreign guests were not present.[62] Such food was usually accompanied by either baked breadfruit or one of the many popoi, or vegetable paste, mixes. Coconuts and such fruit as the *vi* or perhaps ripe bananas might form an additional complement. Although we know that yams, sweet potatoes, taro, and fe'i bananas were grown in fair quantity on the island, they do not appear to have been served to the Europeans, and thus it is likely that they were either less desirable or largely limited to the lower classes. In a few cases, only meat and fruit sufficed. Such meals seemed to have been the norm for the common people and, to some extent, for the chiefs as well. However, these latter did enjoy a somewhat greater variety of dishes and certainly favored pork and dog, though they did not exclude chicken and fish from their diet. We know that dog was eaten as one of the flesh foods of the chiefs,[63] but William Broughton, writing in 1791, implied that dogs, as well as European-introduced cats, were regarded as proper food to be eaten by the lower classes, too.[64] Quite probably the sensitive Tahitians quickly learned that most of their foreign visitors looked with disgust at the enjoyment of canine flesh, and so they did not serve it in the presence of Europeans.

The average household menu was given a degree of variety by the assortment of recipes available for making popoi, as well as several kinds of dishes best described as puddings. The most common type of popoi consisted of freshly baked breadfruit which, with the addition of water and a little fermented breadfruit paste, or *mahi*, was thoroughly mashed and then eaten hot or cold. An improvement of this basic formula consisted of a mashed-up mixture of cooked breadfruit and bananas, to which might be added a little coconut milk. A stronger version of this latter recipe called for using only the soured, or well-fermented, breadfruit paste with the bananas and coconut milk. This, however, called for baking in the pit oven, as well it might. Then there was another baked paste which consisted of breadfruit, yams, plantains, and bananas.

I had about come to the conclusion that the Tahitians had never made a popoi without breadfruit, when I found three recipes which did not include this ubiquitous ingredient. One of these called for nothing more than the cooked and mashed fe'i banana, while another, said to be a breakfast and supper dish, consisted of the soft meat of young coconuts and bananas made into a paste. However, the third recipe, using taro, coconut cream, and if desired, bananas, sounded like a gourmet's delight. First there was the rich coconut cream to be extracted. This was done by grating the ripe coconut meat on a piece of coral and extracting the cream by placing the particles in a makeshift press of special grass and squeezing them by tightly twisting the bundle. After scraping away the outer skin of the raw taro corm, it too was grated and mixed in with the cream, along with some ripe bananas. Large banana leaves were then gathered and, after being held briefly over a fire to toughen them, were used to tie up individual portions of the concoction for overnight baking in a pit oven. This particular dish could be eaten hot or cold, and was said to last for several weeks. The starchy corm of the *pia* plant, or Polynesian arrowroot, which normally grew in the mountains, could be substituted in place of taro. However, if eaten in quantity, it was said to cause giddiness. This side effect may have been due to the residual bitter substance present in the raw plant. Since the recipe did not call for washing the gratings, the heat of the oven was probably counted on to remove this undesirable material.[65]

Another series of gastronomic delights were puddings. Starting out essentially as liquid batters, they jelled, or set, with the application of heated stones. William Bligh, looking ahead for additional uses for taro in the West Indies, carefully recorded the recipe for one of these. Taro corms, scraped clean of their outer skin, were first grated and made up into little loaves of about half a pound each. These were wrapped in leaves and baked in a pit oven for half an hour. A similar amount of coconut meat was then grated and the oil-rich cream extracted as described above. This was poured into a wooden vessel and heated by adding smooth-surfaced hot stones, probably waterworn cobbles. The baked taro gratings were then mixed into the cream and the contents stirred to keep it from burning. The resulting pudding was deemed ready to eat when the white cream turned to oil. Occasionally the tender green leaves of the taro plant were broken up and added to the batter. The same grating and stone-cooking technique was employed to make a breadfruit and coconut cream pudding.

The corm of the pia, as well as the mountain-growing *teve*, could also be made into puddings. In both cases, however, the bitter substance in the starchy flesh first required removal by a soaking technique. This was accomplished by using a piece of coral to grate the flesh into a wooden tray. Water was then added to cover the pulp and was decanted each morning for a period of five days. The tray was then emptied and the finely grated material allowed to dry in the sun. In this stage it had the appearance of flour and could be mixed with coconut cream. The batter thus formed was then warmed with hot stones until it set in a jelly-like mass which Sydney Parkinson likened to blancmange. The teve flour could be substituted for that of pia but seems not to have tasted as good as the pudding made from the latter.

Of the various recipes recorded by early voyagers, it remained for Cook to describe the pièce de résistance in the world of Tahitian puddings. This was one made up of no less than breadfruit, ripe bananas, taro, and the kernels of the pandanus fruit. Although he did not indicate which product got which treatment, he described them as having been grated, scraped, or beaten up. However, based upon the information above, it seems probable that the breadfruit was grated, once its tough outer rind had been scraped off with the sharp edge of a shell.[65] As for the taro, it almost certainly was treated in the same manner, while the bananas were probably mashed, and the soft but stringy inner ends of the pandanus segments may well have had their flesh removed by scraping. All of these items were then individually baked. In the meantime, a quantity of coconut cream was expressed into a large wooden tray and the baked materials were added. As with the other puddings, hot stones were then immersed in the liquid and the contents stirred until the coconut cream turned into oil. By this time the batter had, according to Cook, set to the consistency of an English hasty pudding and was now ready to be eaten.[67]

Flesh foods were eaten raw, broiled over an open fire, or baked in a pit oven. That is to say, fish and shellfish were eaten raw or cooked, while chicken, pig, and dog seem always to have been baked or broiled.[68] Thus, to prepare a hot meal a fire had first to be kindled. This was done by what anthropologists call the fire plow technique. The light wood of hibiscus was favored for this purpose. First a flat board had to be formed; then, using one's teeth or a sharp shell, another stick of hibiscus was sharpened at one end and firmly and quickly rubbed lengthwise along the grain of the base board. The friction of this rapid back-and-forth movement and the heavy pressure at the point of the stick quickly formed a groove and, in the process, created a certain amount of fine wood dust. As the intensive rubbing continued, often lasting up to two minutes, the heat of friction finally ignited the tinder dust. This was immediately dropped into a bundle of dried leaves or grass, and the whole swung in the air until it caught fire. Although dry wood, muscle, and rapid movement of the plow were sure to create fire, the Tahitian fire makers took no chances. As they moved the stick back and forth, they chanted a prayer to insure success. Since fire was for cooking, and cooking meant food, the male-female eating restrictions carried over into fire making, men and women each producing their own flames. On rainy days, when wood was apt to be damp, actual fire or glowing coals were carried wherever they might be needed.[69]

I have found no record of whether open fires for broiling were made directly on the flat surface of the ground or in prepared shallow depressions or fire pits. On Easter Island, for example, the archaeological record would seem to indicate shallow open pits,[70] but whether this held true for Tahiti must await the archaeologist's spade. At least Anders Sparrman was kind enough to leave us a hint of one of the techniques of cooking over an open fire: he wrote that he found breadfruit a very fine food when roasted over hot coals.[71]

While early voyagers neglected to describe the common cooking fire, they over-reacted in describing the Tahitian earth, or pit, oven, which was quite new to them. In its simplest form, this was nothing more than a hole dug in the ground in which a fire was kindled and stones tossed into the flame to be heated to a dull red glow. When this occurred the rocks were temporarily removed, the fire cleaned out of the pit, and the food, carefully wrapped in leaves, placed in the depression. The heated stones were then placed in and around the savory green packages and the whole covered with earth to seal in the heat emanating from the rocks. Cooking time varied from one or two hours to as much as half a day or more, depending upon the kind and quantity of food being prepared. Heat, and steam generated from the moisture in the leaves, did the cooking. Having partaken of meals cooked in this manner, I can readily agree with Captain Cook that food coming out of one of these ovens is juicier and more evenly cooked than food prepared by any other manner.[72] In fact, it is downright delicious.

The average family oven was a relatively small affair measuring a few feet across and ranging in depth from as little as six inches to as much as two feet. In some cases, the pit was first lined with stones before setting the fire, while in another reported case a basal lining was made only after the stones had been heated and the fire removed from the pit. The evidence is not altogether clear, but I suspect that such hot rock linings were employed only when flesh foods, such as pig and dog, were to be cooked, for there were several reports which indicated that no stone lining was employed. However, these latter instances all occurred on the Taiarapu Peninsula and thus might represent a slightly different cooking tradition than on the rest of the island.[73]

Although Tahitians might do battle with one another and draw blood, when it came to slaughtering their animals they depended upon strangulation or drowning to do away with life. In the case of dogs, the nose and mouth were held closed, while pigs were either drowned or strangled by wrapping a cord around their necks and twisting it tightly with the aid of a stick.[74] Then the animal's hair was singed off by holding the carcass over a fire. This was followed by scraping the skin with a coconut shell and rubbing the hide down with a rough stone. Only then was the body opened with a bamboo or shell knife and the entrails extracted. These could then be placed on hot stones and roasted for immediate eating. However, pig entrails were occasionally divided up among several coconut shell bowls and, after the addition of some coagulated blood and bits of the soft fat surrounding the intestines, were cooked by immersing a hot hot stone into each bowl. This resulted in a blackish pudding that was eaten as a pleasant appetizer while the pig was baking.

While the animal was being thus prepared, the pit oven fire slowly heated the fist-sized stones that were to do the cooking. While these were taking on more and more heat, the cleaned animal was being heavily wrapped in the large leaves of the breadfruit tree or the banana plant. When the proper rock temperature was reached, the stones were removed, except for those on the very bottom, and the remaining fire raked out. A layer of large leaves was then laid over the bottom lining of hot stones, and the leaf-encased animal placed on top of them. At this time the heart, lungs, and liver could be separately wrapped and placed in the pit as well. More hot stones were then dropped around and over the packages of meat and the whole topped by yet another layer of leaves. This, in turn, was then covered with earth and tamped down.[75] There was one thing to be said about this kind of cooking: timing had to be properly judged. After all, one could not conveniently keep opening the oven door to see how the roast was coming along! It was probably for this very reason of differing cooking times that dog and pig seem to have been cooked separately from fish, chicken, and vegetables. However, breadfruit, cooking bananas, and other plant food were often separately wrapped in leaf containers, then packed together in makeshift fresh coconut frond baskets and jointly cooked in a single pit oven.[76]

In addition to domesticated fowl and other animals, wild pigeons as well as some other birds were also caught and eaten. Others, however, were obtained purely for their feathers.[77] There appear to have been three techniques employed in this type of hunting. The simplest was accurate stoning. Finding a bird nesting or feeding on the ground, the hunter got an aim on the bird by pointing at it with his left forefinger and throwing his rock with the right hand. While success was usually achieved with a sitting target, once the bird took flight the Tahitian hunter had little luck.[78] Another device, used primarily to catch small birds, was birdlime spread on strips of bamboo. As might be expected, this sticky stuff was made from the black sap of the breadfruit tree.[79] However, considering that much of the ethnological literature of Tahiti is adamant in proclaiming the bow and arrow as having been uniquely used as a chiefly sport in distance shooting, it is interesting to note that José Amich found reed arrows with hard wood points being used on the Taiarapu Peninsula to hunt birds, while Wallis mentioned arrows tipped with round stones — useful, so he figured, for a similar purpose.[80]

Once a dinner was cooked, the large green leaves of *'ape*[81] or banana plants were plucked fresh and laid on the ground as a tablecloth, though occasionally a mat served the same purpose.[82] Since the Tahitians enjoyed using the direct approach of eating with their fingers, there were no eating implements. Nonetheless, there were a few essentials needed at each meal. One of these was a coconut shell of fresh water to keep one's hands clean while eating.[83] A second item was a coconut bowl which served to hold sea water to dip one's meat or fish into before eating it; if desired, the sea water could be dished up in one's hand and drunk.[84] This was the primary source of salt in the Tahitian diet for, unlike the ancient Hawaiians, the Tahitians did not know the art of extracting salt crystals from sea water. So important was sea water in the diet that those who lived inland brought it to their homes and stored it there in large sections of bamboo.[85]

The final piece of equipment needed for a proper meal was a fly flap. This consisted of a bunch of feathers fastened either to the end of a dried wing bone from a large fowl or to a plain or carved wooden handle about one foot in length. However, a small bough from the nearest tree could be made to serve the same purpose.[86] The annoyance factor certainly must have helped to create the fly flap, but more than that was the Tahitian's abhorrence of flies. If he found a dead fly in some food, he would promptly throw the particular offensive food item to the pigs. However, if he found a dead fly on his body, he would immediately go to a stream and take a bath.[87] Considering that these were people who thought nothing of eating head lice, this reaction to dead flies seems a little strange. That is to say, it seems strange until one reflects that all too often the exposed and rotting body of a relative was not far from one's dwelling, and it must have

been obvious to the Tahitians that the flies made little distinction in their choice of foods as they made their daily
rounds in search of a meal.

With the diners seated cross-legged on, or around, their
tablecloth, the steaming food from the pit oven was brought
forth on large green leaves or occasionally in bowls.[88] Before
eating, the Tahitians took small bits of their food and, after
first looking toward the sun and repeating some prayerful
phrase, placed them nearby as an offering to one of their
deities.[89] It was now time to eat, so in keeping with their
clean habits they first washed their hands and then commenced to gorge themselves. That Tahitians were real
trenchermen there can be little doubt, for the amount of food
that they could stuff in their mouths at one time, and the
quantity consumed at any one sitting, was a constant source
of amazement to the early Europeans. High chief Pomare
was said to have consumed two complete chickens and a
couple of pounds of pork, along with his various vegetable
dishes, in one sitting, while raw fish was wolfed down, gills,
guts, and all. With such consummate eating habits one
might picture a Tahitian meal as a rather quiet affair, the
silence being broken only by the contented munching
sounds emanating from countless overstuffed jowls. However, nothing could be further from the truth, for the Tahitians had perfected the art of shoving masses of food into
their mouths and conversing avidly at the same time.[90]

While vegetables and the various popoi mixes seem
never to have been eaten with sauces, the taste of meat,
poultry, and fish was often enhanced by dipping them in a
special sauce. This concoction was made by first taking the
soft white flesh of a young coconut and letting it ferment, or
sour, for a few days. To this was added a little fresh water
and a quantity of cleaned shrimp or, more likely, prawns, the
resulting thick mixture being then placed in a basket to
marinate for a day or two. It was important that the meat of a
young coconut be used, since, if the flesh were too mature, it
would contain vegetable oil which would soon become rancid and spoil the resulting curd-like paste. Although the
thickened curds could, it would appear, be eaten as such, it
was more usual to mix them with a little sea water to form a

sauce. It is said to have had a pleasingly tart taste, and it was so enjoyed that a basket of the paste frequently accompanied a gift of fish or pork.[91]

The Tahitians had several etiquette patterns related to food. One of these was a desire, or more probably a socially enforced custom, to share one's food with anyone who requested it, regardless of the smallness of the available amount.[92] This applied equally, if not more so, to the chiefs; James Wilson wrote of one poor chief who had to pass out so much of his meal that he later had to ask one of his men to bring him more food under the protective cover of darkness.[93] Another pattern, which I found still being observed on Easter Island as late as 1956, pertained to invited guests. In this case the host gave all of the remaining uneaten food to those who had been invited to dine, so that they might finish it up at their leisure.[94] On Easter Island the simple explanation of this custom was that the food had been cooked for the guests, and just because they could not eat it all at one sitting was no reason for them not to eat the remainder later on in the day. It had been prepared for them and, therefore, it was theirs to enjoy. Quite possibly the same reasoning prevailed in Tahiti.

While the number of people eating at one meal may normally never have been very large, there were occasional chiefly banquets attended by several hundred people. John Rickman briefly described one of these which was given for the two ship commanders, Cook and Charles Clerke, and Omai, the young Polynesian gallant who had gone with Cook to England on his second voyage, and who had now been brought back to the Societies on Cook's last voyage. On this occasion the high chief and his official guests each had two members of the chiefly rank attend them, while the serving of food was left to the capable hands of the servants, or teuteu. Not only did the wide variety of fish and fowl and the great quantity of barbecued pork and "stewed" yams impress Rickman, but the gracious ease with which it was all carried out quite overwhelmed him.[95]

A good many years before Rickman's experience, George Robertson, of Wallis's expedition, recorded a much fuller account given to him by two of the crew who accidentally stumbled onto an all-Tahitian formal banquet which was just commencing. The great quantities of food to be eaten on this occasion had been cooked in a series of little sheds located some distance from the eating grounds. When all was ready, the four to five hundred guests sat down in a large circle, in the middle of which was "Queen" Purea, a chiefess, who rested on a very fine mat. Around her clustered her two "feeding" ladies, and beyond them a number of others presumably of high rank. The teuteu now brought into the ring large quantities of food and set them down in front of the chiefess, who then ordered her "feeding" ladies to serve up individual helpings for each of the ranking members seated immediately around her. Wallis's gunner reported on another banquet in which the "queen" personally served up all the portions in separate coconut shell bowls which were then grouped on a large wooden tray and passed around to the guests. As for eating, there was no waiting for the "queen" to be served. As each person received his food, he removed a small portion of it and, looking toward the sun, muttered a short prayer, and then threw the portion away and immediately commenced stuffing down the meal. After this select group had been waited upon, the servants took on the difficult task of providing food for all of those who composed the large circle. While this was in process, a special meal was laid before the chiefess who, apparently being under religious prescriptions at that time, was hand-fed by the two "feeding" ladies on either side of her. As each one alternately reached for some food, she would first wash her feeding hand in a bowl of fresh water, and then grasp a morsel and stuff it into the chiefess's mouth.

As soon as the "queen" had completed her meal, the young "feeding" ladies were allowed to settle nearby and enjoy their own food, while being attended by a large group of other young women. Finally, and only after all others had been fed, the servants were allowed to congregate at a considerable distance from the banquet area and eat their own meals.[96] Here, then, in the instance of a full Tahitian formalized banquet, a ranked protocol of serving existed suggestive of the serving protocol employed in the twentieth-century ceremonial drinking of kava far to the west in Fiji, Tonga, and Samoa. Perhaps this latter, status-ranked serving protocol derived from a much earlier banquet pattern.

Once the meal was over, the left-over scraps of food were tossed hither and yon for the always-present rats to clean up.[97] The Tahitians again washed their hands and then followed the sensible tradition of enjoying a brief siesta.[98] This sometimes took the form of a short sleep, but more often seems to have been a time of quiet talk and some pleasant music.

Music

Tahitian music mainly consisted of singing to the accompaniment of a nose flute and one or more rhythmic devices. In fact, except for the human voice, the only musical instrument capable of a slight but continuous range of tone was the nose flute. This consisted of a bamboo tube with a hole at one end to breathe into, and two stop holes at the other end which were capable of producing three or four different notes. George Forster, who may have known more about music than the other Europeans and had a more delicate ear, claimed that the notes were, in fact, closer to half or quarter notes. While the great majority of these flutes were described as having only two stops, it is interesting to note that on the Taiarapu Peninsula at least one was observed which had three. In playing this softly musical instrument, the thumb of the left hand was used to close the left nostril, while the right breathed air into the instrument and presumably the right hand held the flute and played the stops. Some of these flutes were probably quite plain, but others were decorated with wrappings of coconut fiber cord.[99]

Drums came in a variety of sizes and were formed by hollowing out a log, setting it on end, and covering the upper opening with a stretched shark skin. According to Rodríguez, the drums used in the sacred marae were quite different from those employed in secular entertainment. The fact that at least three different kinds of wood could be used in their construction might be a reflection of their variations in size or, perhaps, the ceremonial or secular use for which the drum was to be employed. Such drums were always played by hand and, depending upon where the skin head was struck, could be made to produce up to six different tones.[100]

Another rhythmic device, which apparently occurred only on the Taiarapu Peninsula, consisted of a pair of what must have been small slit gong drums. These were described as consisting of two chunks of sonorous wood, each of different length and width. This sonorous quality almost certainly must have come from chiseling out a deep wide slot in one side of each instrument so as to create a soundboard effect when the wood was struck. These were played, usually in company with drums, by beating on them with two sticks.[101] Rhythm for dances was also obtained by the use of pearl shell clappers or castinets[102] and by clapping the hands.[102]

Records and the Calendar

The noonday rest being over and the heat of the day beginning to wane, some Tahitians returned to their unfinished tasks of the morning.[104] Others, who had no further chores for the day, sat idly by greeting friends or, one might guess, educating their young children or grandchildren in the requirements of their society. Not only were there taboos and proper social etiquette patterns to be learned but also such simple arts as counting, understanding the Tahitian calendar, or learning little tricks for improving one's memory. There were also the techniques of agriculture and the men's or women's crafts to master. However, these latter were probably learned by actually working side by side when the parent was involved in them.

For most Tahitians counting was a simple—and limited—matter. Numbers went only as far as ten and were counted on the fingers of both hands. However, those who were more educated could count as high as two hundred. This was accomplished by giving the proper name for each digit up through ten and then prefacing each digit with the name for ten, such as ten-one, ten-two, and so on, until they reached twenty. From that point onward, the word for twenty was employed and the count continued by the score, five "twenties" equalling one hundred, and ten equalling two hundred. Apparently there had never been a need to count beyond this ultimate figure.[105]

A few individuals who had trouble remembering where they were in their computations beyond their ten fingers employed leaves as a memory device. In fact, leaves and sticks, and even the marking of posts where a long-term record was needed, were used when one wished to determine the number in a group of things or the passage of time as counted by moons.[106] Distances were measured by how long it took to go from one place to another; fishing and other lines were measured either by the span from the tip of the thumb to the little finger of a spread-out hand, or by the fathom, that is, the distance between one's stretched-out arms.[107] When a variety of individual measurements had to be made, a cord was employed and a different kind of knot placed at the terminal of each measurement.[108]

As for the Tahitian calendar, its major aspects were probably known to most, if not all, of the population. Each day, as well as each night, was arbitrarily divided into six named segments representing two one-hour periods.[109] Each month was one lunation, including the two days when the moon was "dead," or could not be seen.[110] The finer intricacies of the calendar may well have been understood by only a few, and those probably of the priestly class. It was said that thirteen lunations, each with its individual name, composed one year. [111] Since one lunation is somewhat over twenty-nine and a half days, it is immediately obvious that the accumulated days of thirteen lunar months would well exceed the approximately 365-day solar year. This, then, would cause the beginning of each lunar year to advance in relation to each solar year. However, this does not seem to have been the case, for John Forster specifically noted that the new year commenced in March when the major bread-fruit crop of the year was fully ripe and ready to be plucked and reduced to mahi paste for storage.[112] Obviously, some factor other than purely lunar counts was introduced into the system to keep the new year consistent.

Although the early voyagers never worked out all of the factors in the Tahitian calendar, they did leave enough fragments of information that a calculated guess as to its operation can be made. Considering that the Tahitians were aware of the apparent northern and southern movement of the sun,[113] and that the new year began in March, I would suggest that the March 21 equinox was observed, and that its arrival heralded the beginning of the new year. Such observations of the movement of the sun were not unknown in ancient Polynesia, a sun "clock" having been excavated and visually confirmed for the solstices and equinox on Easter Island.[114] Furthermore, the solar year appears to have been tied in with an agricultural year which centered on the ripening time for different varieties of breadfruit. This agricultural year was divided into six parts, the last one being named after the breadfruit, plus one small interval called *tawa*, said to have occurred near the end of February.[115]

Although there are no early records of specific religious ceremonies being conducted on Tahiti at the end of the year, it is especially interesting to note that in the beginning of the 1800s Ellis reported a special ceremony called *maoa ra'a matahiti*, or the ripening or completing of the year, given annually on Huahine, one of the leeward islands of the Society group. This appears to have been an all-island affair for men, women, and children, though as usual, the women were excluded from the ceremonies at the marae. It was a period of great feasting, prayerful acknowledgment of their gods, and, on a family basis, a time of prayer at the family marae for those who had departed.[116] Although Ellis claimed the timing of this ceremony was determined by the flowering of certain reeds, the fact that it was termed the *ripening* of the year might be a reference to March, or the equinox, when the principal harvest of breadfruit normally commenced. Thus, the implication here is that the solar, or agricultural, year and the lunar year were forced into annual alignment at the time of the March equinox, and that tawa, the small agricultural year interval preceding the equinox, was a compressible or expandable period of days which was needed to make the calendrical adjustment. I would further suggest that it was during this flexible time interval that year-end feasting and perhaps ceremonialism were carried out, with the giant *'opio* breadfruit pit oven, described in a later chapter, serving as the center of regional and district festivities.

To the degree that the Tahitians had an annually disagreeing lunar and solar year calendrical system, a comparison can be made with the Aztec *tonalpohualli*, or dual calendrical system. However, in the latter case the two calendars came into conjunction once every fifty-two years,[117] while this does not seem to have been the case for the dual Tahitian system. In fact, if we can believe José de Andia y Varela, the Tahitians seldom kept track of more than thirty or forty lunar months,[118] and, according to John Forster, their individual years were neither numbered nor, apparently, named, great events in history being immortalized in verse rather than according to the calendrical year of their occurrence.[119]

As is readily apparent, the intricacies of the Tahitian calendar system probably represented more advanced knowledge than the normal family may have possessed. However, its superficial aspects were quite probably taught on a family level. Teaching, except for the chiefly class, must have been a rather casual affair, and if childhood learning was not the order of the afternoon, one probably sat back and enjoyed the cooling hours of the day by greeting friends and relations and exchanging the latest in gossip.

Greetings

So much has been made of the Maori of New Zealand greeting their friends by touching noses that it has become almost axiomatic that this was originally the characteristic greeting of all Polynesians. Nothing could be further from the truth. The first record of any kind of personal greeting on Tahiti was made by Wallis and Robertson on the occasion of their discovery of the island. This consisted of shaking hands,[120] and its temporary use by the islanders would certainly suggest that it was an introduction by the English. After all, Wallis and his men had just shown their military superiority over the natives on the occasion of the latter's attempt to take Wallis's ship. Having been rather thoroughly chastised, the natives would have immediately accepted and copied any symbol of friendship offered by Wallis's men in the interest of both peace and the promotion of what proved to be rather lucrative trade. That this was the case is well reflected in the historical record, since hand-shaking is not again noted until 1789, some twenty years later.[121] However, what appears to have been the indigenous form of greeting did occur as Wallis was about to leave the island, when the chiefess Purea embraced both him and his officers before leaving his ship.[122]

For those regarded as friends, a strong embrace was customary on meeting,[123] and if two people were very good friends this was accompanied by a kiss on the cheeks and temples.[124] A gift of one's own personal wrap or some fine tapa cloth might also accompany this stronger demonstration of friendliness, especially if one were of chiefly status.[125] However, where personal friendship was not involved, the pleasant term *taio*, or "friend," was spoken as one passed by.[126] These seemingly indigenous demonstrations of friendliness appear to have been in effect from the time of discovery of the island until as late as 1777. It was in this year that Cook, making his last fateful voyage into the Pacific, returned the Polynesian Omai to the Societies and left with him two young Maori boys as servants.[127] Whether or not these two boys alone were responsible for the introduction of the Maori technique of touching noses, and its complete replacement of the older form of Tahitian greeting, cannot be known for certain. Perhaps some of Cook's own men aided in the introduction of the Maori custom to Tahiti. However it happened, we do know that this custom did not obtain in 1777, but it was present to such an extent on the island in 1786 that Bligh referred to the touching of noses as the customary Tahitian manner of greeting.[128] The following year, and again in 1791, hand-shaking had come back as a form of greeting,[129] while nose-touching as well as the shaking of hands was still in evidence by 1797.[130] The former, in fact, had now so completely replaced the older embracing and kissing technique that the missionaries reported that Tahitians could not understand why Europeans showed affection by wetting people's faces with their lips![131]

Besides the more affectionate embracing, there was a formalized demonstration of friendliness which appears to have been practiced only in the earliest years of contact. This consisted of placing one's hands on one's own chest and uttering the term *taio,* or "friend."[132] Perhaps the earlier years of instability of relations between foreigners and Tahitians demanded the use of this more formalized greeting, since it was not reported after 1769 when more friendly and understanding relationships were established.

As previously mentioned, the greeting of two good friends was often accompanied by an exchange of gifts. This might consist of nothing more than foodstuffs, but a more appropriate gift was a manufactured item, usually tapa cloth. The reason for this was effectively explained to the missionaries by one Polynesian. As he put it, products of the land grew spontaneously, as they most certainly did in Tahiti, and therefore their use as a gift did not represent real generosity. However, anything that was manufactured represented labor and thus was more suitable as a gift of value.[133]

Since the making of fine tapa cloth required not only considerable time but also no small amount of labor, it served as the customary gift of value. So much so in fact that, considering the native recognition of differences in quality of the cloth, it might be said that Tahitians were on their way toward developing a cash economy based on tapa cloth. Be that as it may, in a few extreme cases in which a chief wished to emphasize his close friendship with an individual, he formalized the gift procedure to the extent of wrapping a young woman in roll after roll of tapa. Thus dressed in this oversized garment, she was presented before the intended receiver of the gift. Gradually divesting herself of one long strip of cloth after another, she deposited each length of material at the feet of the recipient, usually a chief, until all that she had left was a loincloth.[134] A more flamboyant technique was for a chief to order a special heiva dance, at the close of which both male and female dancers took off their tapa garments and, making pyramid of them, presented the lot to the honored guest.[135] However, it remained for Sir Joseph Banks to fondly describe the ceremony

Young woman bringing gift of tapa which has been wrapped around her. The two semicircular objects hanging on the tapa skirt are warrior's gorgets included in the gift. Painting by John Webber.

in which a gift of cloth was presented to him. In his case a large piece of tapa was spread out on the ground in front of him, after which a beautiful young woman stepped gracefully onto the cloth and stripped herself of all clothing. After turning slowly around in front of Banks, she retreated while another layer of cloth was placed on top of the first. With each presentation, she repeated her performance until the gift was complete, whereupon she stepped forward in all her nakedness and presented the whole to Banks, much to his surprise and enjoyment.[136]

The innumerable accounts of Tahitian hospitality and generosity, however, were not always the result of openness of heart. Just as often they represented an attempt to avoid social stigma. Hospitality to strangers was a way of life, and if such was not forthcoming, it was permissible for a stranger to freely pass the word along, to the complete social disgrace of the offending host.[137] Hospitality was a must in Tahiti, and it certainly served the useful purpose of allowing freedom of movement without the burdensome annoyance of having to travel with all of one's necessities. In turn, whatever a Tahitian received in hospitality, he was socially bound to repay when some stranger crossed his own home threshold.

As the lengthening shadows of a dying day stretched ever further across the plains of Tahiti, the workers in the fields and in the other areas of specialized labor turned homeward for the final activities of the day. For those who arrived weary from a hard day of work, there was always the treatment of *rumi*, or massage, to look forward to. This was a gentle squeezing of one's arms and legs, or if need be, the entire body. The result was complete relaxation and the loss of fatigue and muscle pain.[138] Thus relaxed, Tahitians enjoyed a small evening meal followed by a refreshing bath and perhaps a little dancing, spear throwing, or some other amusement with friends and relations.[139]

With the arrival of darkness it was time to get out the candles and light one's home for the evening. These devices were not of the wax and wick type, but consisted of a series of oily nuts from the candlenut tree stuck onto a sliver of wood or the midrib of a palm leaf. However, the nuts had first to be slightly scorched before making up the candlestick, since the charred surface seems to have served the same purpose as a wick.[140] For some it was now off to the reef for a few hours of torch fishing, while for others it was a quiet evening at home with family and friends.

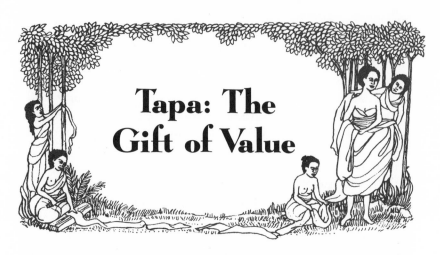

Tapa: The Gift of Value

A gift of value was one on which considerable labor had been expended, as noted in the previous chapter. Many different crafted items were available to allow one person to honor another. Canoes, nets, woven mats, and large feather-decorated crescent neckpieces were occasionally mentioned in this regard. However, it was tapa, the cloth derived from the beaten inner bark of a variety of trees, that become the characteristic, if not necessarily the most valuable, symbol with which to pay homage. Its fineness, decoration, and above all, its quantity and the manner in which it was presented all entered into the degree of value of the gift. Thus, as a dominant element of clothing and proper gift for innumerable occasions, tapa could be described as ancient Tahiti's principal item of mass manufacture.

Simple and effective as tapa was, it had certain drawbacks that caused an unending amount of work for the women who hammered out and decorated the material. The problem was in the fabric's inability to withstand the effects of moisture. Rain softened the fibers and probably dissolved the starchy paste that held the layers together, so that the tapa, or bark cloth, was easily torn or pulled apart. By the same token, neither could the material be washed, dried, and worn again as the same garment.[1] As a result, the Tahitians appear to have maintained a minimal back-up wardrobe of finely woven mat clothing to be worn when they worked in water or on rainy days.[2] Why they did not turn completely to matted clothing is hard to say. Perhaps it was not warm enough, and certainly it would not have been as soft to the skin as tapa. Also, fine mat weaving was a long and tedious task. Then again, perhaps bark cloth, despite its impracticality, was nothing more than a traditional way of dressing. Whatever the reason, tapa was the acceptable material for Tahitian gifts and clothing, and, since it could not be washed when dirty and immediately reused, the only answer was to build up a bark cloth industry that could continually supply new cloth as older items wore out or became too dirty for proper use. So effective was this female-dominated enterprise that, by the time Europeans began to visit the island, tapa production had gone beyond the simple needs of supply and demand. Chiefs assured themselves of surplus production for use as gifts and as symbols of material wealth by calling upon the women of their districts to make their tapa, large sheets being fabricated as a group effort.[3]

Materials and Manufacture

Tapa was made from the bark of at least three different trees: paper mulberry, breadfruit, and two species of figs, the *'aoa,* or *ora,* and *mati.*[4] Cloth from the bark of the mulberry appears to have been most preferred, Joseph Banks claiming that plantations of this tree covered the larger part of the cultivated land.[5] It was also the preferred cloth of the upper classes, as was the somewhat more water-resistant tapa, called *ora,* made from the bark of the fig trees. Clothing made from the latter was customarily worn in the morning,[6] perhaps because its special qualities lessened the normally damaging effect of tropical dew swept up on clothing as the Tahitians walked down narrow trails in the early hours of a dawning day. This, then, left the bark of the breadfruit as the material from which the common, or lower, classes of people made a cloth which was said to have been coarser than that made from the mulberry.[7] Since there were certainly more natives of the lower classes to support the upper ranks, one might be tempted to challenge Banks's observation with regard to the extent of mulberry plantations. However, on reflection, it seems possible that the poorer people of Tahiti were no different from their counterparts of today in making their clothing last as long as possible, hence the lack of need for innumerable fields of breadfruit plantings. Since many from this rank of society owned no land, or maintained only small holdings, it is possible that Louis Antoine de Bougainville's observation that the "bark tree" was cultivated by all Tahitians around their houses actually referred to household plantings of the working class who could not afford distinct plantations.[8]

Trees grown for the purpose of harvesting their bark could be easily recognized. In the first place, the young sprouts and saplings were pruned of their lower branches so that they stuck straight up like so many poles capped at their tops by crowns of leaves. Secondly, they were never allowed to grow for more than one or two years, by which time the trunks of the mulberry and fig trees had reached a height of from six to eight feet and had a diameter of about one inch. Only the breadfruit appears to have grown faster during this limited timespan, the diameter of its trunk being considerably larger than the other trees.[9] This greater size may help to account for the lower classes' preference for breadfruit, since a larger quantity of bark could be produced in the same timespan than from the other trees, though the resulting tapa was a bit coarser. In this regard, it is interesting to note that in the earlier years of European exploration the preferred mulberry tapa cloth came from stems only one inch or so in diameter, creating a very fine cloth. However, by the early 1790s European woven cloth was beginning to replace tapa for clothing, and the mulberry plantings were consequently beginning to show neglect.[10] It would seem, then, that the continued manufacture of bark cloth had become less a matter of clothing the population than preserving the traditional use of bark cloth as a gift, as well as a much sought-after item for Europeans. After all, in 1791 George Hamilton boasted that he had loaded his ship with several thousand yards of this material.[11] By 1797 mulberry bark plantings were allowed to grow to heights of up to twelve feet with trunks showing a diameter of three inches. This slight difference in size meant greater bark production for a given planting, but the texture of the finished product was slightly coarser than in earlier days. As is still the case, tourist goods have never been of the highest quality, and it would seem that perhaps the Tahitians were simply reacting as best they could to the European interest in collecting authentic Tahitian curios!

Although it is not clear whether breadfruit and fig trees planted for their bark were ever grown in protected gardens, or plantations, we do know that this was a practice with the paper mulberry. Such groves were located in areas of rich soil, and shells of all sorts were carefully mixed into the earth, reportedly as a form of manuring. The rootstock was then set out in formal rows, each plant being placed from eighteen to twenty-four inches away from its nearest neighbor. A deep trench surrounded each plantation which, according to John Forster and the missionaries, was designed to protect the field from the depredations of man and beast. Certainly such a precaution was necessary by 1797 when introduced goats were beginning to make nuisances of themselves. However, considering the admixture of shells to the soil, though admittedly this may have had a secondary effect of manuring, I would suggest that perhaps the overriding original purpose of both the shell mixture and the deep trenching that surrounded each plantation was that of needed soil drainage for this particular plant. Be that as it may, when the trunks of any one of the trees used in tapa production had reached their proper size they were immediately harvested. This was accomplished either by cutting them near the base and leaving the roots to sprout again, or by pulling each tree up bodily, cutting off the root and bushy top, and replanting any rootstock that was producing a young sprout. The resulting harvest was an unspectacular quantity of thin, rodlike tree trunks three to four feet in length.[12]

The sapling rods were now ready for peeling, unless one wished to produce a cloth with a darkened, cloudy effect. In that case the bark, still attached to the rods, was first cracked or broken by hitting it all over with a stone, after which the treated stems were wrapped in leaves for several days before removing the bark.[13] In either case, stripping was an easy affair. A longitudinal cut was made the full length of the rod and the bark peeled away as one entire piece. Such strips were then taken to a nearby stream where they were immersed in water to ret for several days, stones or weighted boards being used to anchor the material to the bottom of the channel.[14]

While men appear to have supplied the raw materials for making bark cloth, the task of manufacturing and decorating the tapa was women's work.[15] Because the women of the upper class oversaw the manufacturing process and participated in the final patching and decorating of the material, the missionaries gave them full credit for being the principal producers of the cloth.[16] However, Banks saw it differently and reported that it was the servant class of women who did the dirty, heavy work, while the women of higher rank did the lighter chores of final patching and decorating, much as upper-class women of eighteenth-century England spent their leisure time making items such as caps and ruffles.[17] Thus it was that with the retting of the bark completed, the servant women of a household stripped themselves and, sitting in the middle of a flowing stream with a large, smooth board of *toa* wood to work upon, proceeded to scrape the fragments of wet bark with the sharp edge of a bivalve shell.

Scraping and washing of the retted material continued through most of the day until all the tough outer bark and other substances had been removed, and only the finer fibers of the inner bark remained. By late afternoon the strips of prepared fiber, looking like so many lengths of ragged linen, were ready to be laid out for draining and partial drying. For this purpose a bed of banana leaves was laid out on the grass and the strips of fiber placed upon them to a thickness of two or three layers. Such strips were apparently placed in a lengthwise, overlapping pattern, much care being taken that each individual layer was the same thickness as the one adjacent to it. When the laying out of the strips was completed, the effect was that of an elongated fiber belt thirty or more feet in length and from one to three feet in width. The longer measurement represented the final length of the cloth, for the Tahitians knew that in the beating of the fibers to make the cloth there would be no appreciable lengthening of the filaments. However, it was quite a different matter when it came to determining the final width. This depended upon the thickness of the layers of fiber and the amount of lateral spreading that would take place as the material was pounded.[18] Widths of from six to twelve feet appear to have been normally anticipated, though tapa of much greater width was also reported.[19]

After the layered belt of fibers was constructed, it was left to drain during the night; by morning the individual elements had dried sufficiently so that the entire mass was stuck together and could be removed intact to those specialized areas where bark was beaten into tapa.[20] A slight variation in this procedure was recorded by the missionaries, who claimed that after the retting and scraping, the strips of fiber were encased in leaves for three days to "digest," after which the,' were ready for the beating process.[21] This may represent an alternate method of preparing the fibers, but it seems equally possible that what they observed was nothing more than a way of temporarily storing prepared bark fiber when the process of beating and spreading the material could not be carried out for several days because of other, more pressing activity.

Beating the layered belt of bark fibers was no easy task, indicating that at least the lower classes of Tahitian women who did this work kept themselves in fine physical condition. The anvil upon which the bark filaments were placed at right angles for widening consisted of a log beam of toa or *mara* wood. This was squared to six or eight inches in width and smoothly finished on its top, or working, surface. Some of these, perhaps representing family anvils of the lower classes, appear to have been rather short and designed for a single operator. Others, however, measured up to twelve feet in length.[22] Longer beams may also have been used to create still greater widths of cloth, for Anders Sparrman mentioned a tapa 18 feet wide, and the missionaries referred to yet another specimen having a length of some 240 feet and a width of about 24 feet.[23] However, the width of this latter, a showpiece, may well have been the result of careful pasting together of several smaller sections of cloth.

The bark beater used to forcibly spread the fibers was made of hard toa wood and ranged in length from one foot to as much as fifteen inches. Two-thirds of the length of the club was squared to form four flat beating surfaces which ranged in width from a mere two and one-half inches to as much as six inches. Each of these surfaces was ridged longitudinally by grooving, the starting surface being the coarsest with only about ten or eleven ridges separated by broad, deep grooves. Each succeeding face around the squared club exhibited an increase in the number of ridges and a corresponding decrease in the width and depth of the intervening grooves. The finest, or finishing, face had as many as sixty thin ridges extending the length of the rectangular surface. The remaining third of the bark beater was worked into a rounded stem to form a firm handle.[24]

To spread and thin the layered belt of prepared bark fibers it was necessary to place it at right angles to the anvil beam; laying one end upon the smoothed surface of the timber, the women proceeded to beat the fibers, first using the coarser surface of their tapa clubs. This part of the operation could have been managed by a single woman using the smaller anvils. However, it seems to have been customary, certainly when producing the larger pieces of cloth, for groups of women to sit on either side of the beam and beat the fibers out by striking the cloth in time to a tune sung by one of the nonlaboring members of the party. Since the fibers could not be struck in their dried state for fear of breakage, coconut shells filled with water were placed near at hand so that the material could be regularly sprinkled as the beating proceeded. In at least one instance, George Forster observed these containers filled with a "glutinous water" which he understood, apparently incorrectly, to have been concocted from *Hibiscus esculentus L.*, or okra. Whether or not his understanding of the formula was correct, a special liquid was apparently employed only for making exceptionally large pieces of tapa.[25] Captain

Women beating out tapa, or bark cloth, on a long wooden anvil. Unsigned pencil sketch by Sydney Parkinson.

Cook, on the other hand, claimed that the individual strips of prepared fibers were first pasted to each other to form the belt before the bark beaters were brought into play.

Once the beating commenced, the delicate fibers from the inner bark expanded rapidly. One of the tricks of the beating technique was to know just when to switch from one coarseness of ridges on the beater to the side with the next finer ridging. This appears to have been accomplished by simple observation. That is, whenever the ridges of the tapa beater created grooves in the cloth which made the tapa appear too thin, the club was given a quarter turn and the next finer surface of ridges was employed. This process continued until the finest ridges of the beater had been employed over the entire length and breadth of the cloth. By this time it was only natural to expect that here and there the bark fibers had stretched unevenly, leaving thin spots or even small gaps in the cloth. When this stage was reached, the beating was stopped and the holes and thin spots repaired by pasting patches of bark cloth over them to bring them up to the desired thickness. The paste employed was derived from the rhizome of the pia plant,[26] while the patches seem to have been made from bits and pieces of tapa trimmed from the ragged edges of the freshly beaten-out cloth. Such trimming was accomplished by the ladies of rank with nothing more than a knife made by using a fingernail to diagonally split off a long edge of bamboo so that a sharp, single-beveled blade was formed. This touching up and trimming seems to have been followed by the process of covering the entire cloth with a viscous white paste, probably also made from the pia plant, and again beating the cloth through the cycle of the four ridged surfaces of the club. The final result was a thin, single-ply piece of tapa, which was rubbed to break up its stiffness and then carefully washed and dried.[27]

There is some inferential evidence that these single sheets of tapa may have been used for clothing. However, the early literature seems to indicate that it was far more common to combine several sheets of tapa to make a warmer and softer product. This was accomplished by gluing together two or more layers of tapa, using the starchy paste of the pia and welding the layers still further by an additional cycle of beating the combined sheets with the tapa club. It was not always necessary to combine layers of tapa made from one type of bark. A sheet of breadfruit tapa could be welded to one of mulberry or, for that matter, tapa separately derived from mulberry, breadfruit, and fig could all be layered together to form a single, three-ply bolt of cloth.[28]

The finest of tapa was that called hobu, of which there were several varieties. It consisted of a number of layers of tapa pasted together, beaten, and then thoroughly rubbed and washed to produce a soft texture. According to Banks, a still softer hobu cloth could be produced by first wearing regular hobu material for a while, and then again subjecting it to washing and beating. All in all, there appear to have been a number of different kinds of tapa material, each with its special descriptive name. Besides the varieties of ora and hobu, there was a type that the missionaries referred to as *mara*. This was made from the bark of the paper mulberry and consisted of several layers of half-beaten tapa. It was used for upper garments and, as might be expected, presented the appearance of cloth of uneven thickness. Interestingly, the men of the 'arioi society of entertainers seem to have been especially adept at making this tapa, even though such work was normally left to women. Still another cloth, called *hopa*, was made from gray, unbleached cloth which had been worn for a while. This slightly used cloth was dyed brown and then lined with a layer of bleached white tapa by pasting the two sheets together.

Old and dirty tapa could be washed, but the results were unwearable. Cloth that was only slightly soiled could be cleaned by weighting it down with stones in a gently flowing fresh water stream. However, that which had become really filthy had to be soaked, squeezed, and wrung out. Actually, the washing of tapa was nothing more than an efficient recycling procedure, several sheets of laundered tapa being laid one on top of the other and the whole beaten together using the coarsest side of the bark beater. The result, according to Banks, had the finish and feel of a coarse broadcloth. Another technique, which gave more handsome results, was to take old, worn-out, brown tapa, mix it with the prepared bark from branches of a breadfruit tree, and beat them together into a new cloth which ended up having a mottled appearance. This was then dipped into a perfumed, light yellow dye, after which a lining of white tapa was glued to one face of the cloth. This use of a colored lining suggests the possibility that the Tahitians were attempting to duplicate, in their own material, the textile linings they had observed in some of the clothing worn by their European visitors. This view is further strengthened by the fact that such tapa linings were not reported as occurring until 1797.[29]

Except for the naturally russet-colored tapa produced from the bark of fig trees, finished bark cloth came off the anvil beam looking gray and rather unspectacular.[30] To improve this drab appearance the cloth was subjected to bleaching for several days. The accounts of this process suggest two different techniques. One was to wash, or more probably soak, the tapa in water and then expose it to the sunshine, while a later report stated that the cloth was stretched out on banana leaves to receive the early morning dew, and was removed only after the sun became too warm.[31] Whichever system was employed, the results seem to have rendered the cloth a pleasing white.[32] It was now ready for the wearer, unless it was to be dyed, stained, or otherwise decorated.

Techniques of Decoration

Only three colors—red, yellow, and brown, along with black—were used to decorate tapa. Since red and yellow appear to have been "royal" colors reserved for those of high chiefly status, it would seem that the commoner was left with brown and black if he chose to decorate his clothing.

Red was a tricky color to produce and could only be made of the juice from the basal stem of the mati fig, and then only when it was combined with the natural surface ingredients of certain leaves, those from the toa tree apparently being the most preferred. To obtain this juice the women bit off the footstalk quite close to where the fruit hung down. Upon doing this, a few drops of milky juice exuded. These were either shaken directly upon the leaves of the toa or, more commonly, dropped into a coconut shell container filled with fresh water or coconut liquid. In the former case the leaves with their droplets of juice were placed in a wooden tray, sprinkled with water, and gradually worked about until a red color appeared. The latter technique required about three or four quarts of these gooseberry-sized fruits to provide enough droplets of juice to properly infuse half a cup of coconut water. Once a proper mixture had been obtained, a quantity of the leaves of the toa tree was immersed in the liquid and then laid out on banana leaves. Here the women began to gently turn and shake them as the fluid soaked into the leaves and caused them to gradually become limp. As the fluid was taken up by the leaves, more liquid was added and the women began to gently squeeze each leaf, increasing the pressure as it became more limp. It was obviously important to the chemistry of this process that the leaves not be broken, a fact which Sydney Parkinson discovered when he attempted to crush some in his mortar and, adding their juice to that from the fig, obtained absolutely no results. After about five minutes of constant squeezing, the veins of the toa leaves began to turn red; after another five or six minutes the leaves had taken up all of the juice they could hold, and the women then squeezed them very hard in preparation for straining the resulting dye. When Banks observed this latter process, he noted that a kind of mesh was formed from the stripped fibers of a large grass; the toa leaves were enfolded in this and squeezed, and the resulting red dye was collected in banana leaves. John Forster, who later observed the making of this same red dye, reported that the strainer was constructed from the fibers of coconut husk. Regardless, not content with this initial extraction, the women collected the well-pressed leaves and, dipping them in the collected dye, again squeezed them forcibly to extract the last few drops of coloring matter.

Once the straining process had been completed, the leaves were thrown away, but the fibers of the grass strainer were carefully saved to be used as coarse paintbrushes to spread the dye over the surface of the tapa. First, however, a banana leaf was broken up so as to form a number of small cups or containers in which the red dye was poured and then passed around to each of the women who were involved in the work. The grass fibers were then dipped in the little leaf containers and brushed over the surface of the tapa. Although Banks referred only to this brushing technique, it would seem from George Forster's observations that the women's hands were employed in spreading the stain evenly over the entire surface of the cloth. This would account for Banks's statement that the women of rank who did this staining prided themselves on having their hands and fingernails covered with the red dye. No doubt, as Banks suggested, the color not only served as a mark of beauty but also clearly indicated their superiority of rank.

Overall red stain was applied only to one side of the heavier types of tapa. Banks noted, however, that thin sheets of tapa were stained red only around the edges, perhaps because the color tended to go completely through the finer fabric and did not create as pleasing an overall effect.

Yellow, usually used as a deep dye rather than a surface stain, was obtained from at least five different plants. The inner bark of the *nono* was made into a watery infusion and the cloth dipped into it.[33] The rhizomes of turmeric, probably the "ginger" of the Spaniards, were also used to create a yellow dye.[34] The fruit and leaves of the tamanu created a pale yellow tint.[35] This particular dye may have had special significance to those who wore it, for it gave off a peculiar aroma much appreciated by the Tahitians, though apparently not enticing to the nostrils of Banks. Furthermore, the tree from which the dye was derived had religious importance, for it was planted in the ceremonial centers, or marae, and regarded as sacred to the Tahitian god Tane. The fruit of the mati fig, when the juice was used alone, apparently also gave up a yellow dye. However, according to John Forster, the finest yellow dye was obtained from a concoction whose principal ingredient seems to have been the juice which dripped from the broken flower stalks of the *miro*.[36] Unfortunately, the details of creating color in each case were not noted in the literature.

The best brown dye appears to have been derived from the bark of the toa tree. Used in dyeing not only tapa but nets and fishing lines as well, its special advantage seems to have been that no amount of water could ever wash out the dye once it was set. Bark from the tree was steeped in water, and the cloth dipped into the resulting dye and then spread out in the sun. Apparently the tapa did not take up all of the dye with one wetting, thus allowing an individual to control the tint by repeated dipping and sun-drying until the desired depth of color had been obtained. The milky juice from the *piripiri* plant created a soft brown,[37] while two other plants, mentioned by Parkinson but neither described nor given botanical names, were also said to produce a brown dye.[38]

Black was obtained in two different ways. That probably used for staining patterns was obtained from the sap of the fe'i banana, though whether this was mixed with some other ingredient or used directly is not known. However, the missionaries described a rather interesting technique for overall dyeing of a piece of cloth that seems a bit out of keeping with normal Tahitian methods. First the tapa was buried beneath the roots of a coconut palm growing in swampy ground. After it was left to soak in this mucky situation for a day or two, it was exhumed and dried. Should the material not be dark enough, the process was repeated until a deep black had been obtained, after which the dye was fixed by washing it in salt water.[39]

Another treatment of tapa, waterproofing it by covering one side of it with a varnish-like coating, reflected considerable experimentation with plant substances on the part of the Tahitians. The islanders had discovered that soaking the bark of the *tutu'i,* or candlenut tree,[40] in fresh water produced a resinous substance which, when applied to the cloth, left a glossy waterproof coating. It was stated that this was applied only to brown tapa, possibly the ora cloth made from the bark of the fig tree, which in itself was partially water resistant.[41]

One might conclude that Tahitian clothing, though colorful within limitations, lacked any decorative appeal. Nothing could be farther from the truth. Using the stripped fibers of a type of grass called *mo'u,* the Tahitians created reasonably efficient paintbrushes with which to decorate their clothing with a variety of designs, including stripes, in the various colors of their dyes.[42] They had also learned the principle of the pattern stamp, though they had not carried the idea very far at the time of European discovery. In fact, all it consisted of was a bamboo reed whose circular end was dipped in dye and then stamped on the cloth to form patterns of rings.[43] However, the printed trade cloth they received from England as early as 1769 may have expanded their views of what could be done with this technique.[44] Thus, by 1791 Hamilton reported that the women were printing tapa with figures that were exactly the patterns which were in vogue in England when he departed for the Pacific. Such copy work was accomplished by picking out sprigs and leaves of different shapes, dipping them in dye, and pressing them onto the tapa cloth in a myriad of patterns.[45] Finally, there was an overlay technique of decoration which, it would appear, was especially well developed by the 'arioi society. This consisted of cutting out various designs from tapa of different colors and pasting them together to create decorative effects.[46] The fact that the 'arioi excelled in this work may indicate that these elaborate materials were used more as parts of costumes for entertainers than as everyday forms of normal dress.

In our world of automated looms and synthetic fibers the energy expended by the Tahitian women in producing their small array of tapa clothing seems curiously out of proportion to the limited range of their end products. However, one must recall that not too many years have passed since the hand labor employed in dressing our own population was equally energy-consuming, and almost certainly more time-consuming, than that of the Tahitian fabric makers. There is no doubt that tapa was far less efficient a material for garments than the European trade cloth brought to Polynesia, whose special qualities the Tahitians were quick to appreciate. Since prior to the arrival of European vessels the Tahitians had no tradition of spinning and loom weaving, even though wild cotton was present in the Society Islands,[47] bark cloth was adequate, though barely so. Dress and ornament in the humid tropics has always tended more to reflect cultural tradition and local concepts of beautification than to fulfill the physical requirements of bodily warmth and protection so important in the colder climes.

Recreation

Diversion is the piquant sauce that makes life worth living and breaks the bland routine of mere existence. Tahitians needed such sauce. Their tropical island regime and their workaday world combined to form a monotonously pleasant, but potentially dulling, lifestyle. However, there was nothing dull about Tahitian living, and part of what made it so stimulating was diversion—punctuating rounds of amusements for all to see, if not always to join in.

Most entertainments were of the spectator type, but the ocean was there for all to enjoy, and enjoy it they did. When the waves ran high it was surfing time, and while many contented themselves with body surfing, others used miniature surfboards. These consisted of nothing more than a small board, two and one-half feet long, which had been cut to a point at one end to resemble the bow of a canoe. On this the surfer rested his chest and, as he sped forward on the slope of a wave, he would drop one leg into the water to serve as a steering oar. While everybody seems to have enjoyed this sport, it would appear that the women of Tahiti were the true masters of the surfboard. As for swimming, the Europeans were continually amazed at the skill and endurance of the Tahitians. They spent hours contendedly swimming around the great vessels and diving for nails tossed into the water for the amusement of the crew.[1] In the eyes of George Forster, the fact that the girls wore no clothing while swimming added zest to the whole affair.[2]

Kite-flying was another sport well suited to Tahiti's location within the trade winds. Made of cane and covered with bark cloth, kites were flown by men and boys alike.[3] It was also the men who made a sport of practicing the martial arts. Spear-throwing was one of these, a banana stem target being placed some thirty or forty yards from the participants. Spears ranged from eight to fourteen feet in length and were tipped with a point made from pandanus wood. Grasping the shaft, the player aimed his spear, poising it on the forefinger of his left hand. While only a few usually participated in this sport, there were times when one district competed against another. Regardless of which side won, the hosting district provided entertainment at the close of the meet.[4]

The sling was another device of warfare which was also employed for amusement. It was plaited from a length of coconut fiber, the central part of the long sling band made wide enough to receive a stone. At one end of the sling a large loop was formed through which the right hand was slipped so that when the stone was released the sling did not leave the thrower's hand. To load the sling, the player held the two ends of the woven band in his right hand and placed a stone in the wide pocket at the bottom of the loop thus formed. The looped sling was then stretched across the back of the player's neck, the left hand holding the stone in its pouch. To hurl the stone, the player was said to first make a short jump, which was probably employed to plant his feet in a firm throwing stance. Releasing the pouch from behind his neck, he began twirling the sling over his head, using his now free left hand to reinforce his right arm by grasping the right wrist. On the third spin he let go of one end of the sling band, thus releasing the stone to shoot forward with remarkable speed. The force that could be developed through this centrifugal technique was such that it was common to find sling-stones buried in the bark of a tree at a distance of two hundred yards from the player.[5]

Wrestling and Boxing

Wrestling was essentially a spectator sport, though there were a few occasions when there were so many wrestlers in the ring at one time that one suspects these special overcrowded affairs might have been "amateur nights." Unlike the sports previously mentioned, wrestling was a rather formalized affair which might be put on as a special event, or be made to follow a heiva dance as part of a package of entertainment. Joseph Banks described a large courtyard, surrounded by a three-foot-high bamboo railing, which was used as a wrestling arena. The regent, who had called this particular match, sat at one end with members of his entourage forming a half circle around him. At another point along the perimeter of the court was an open house in which some old men stood and watched the competition. When one wrestler succeeded in throwing his opponent on his back, thus ending the fight, the old men loudly repeated three times a set of words which, apparently, formed a short chant of sorts. Then some other men danced briefly before the next wrestling challenge was made. However, not all wrestling matches appear to have had these special features, suggesting that some may have had ceremonial or religious overtones, while others were purely secular.

Once a large ring of spectators had been formed, one or more prominent wrestlers appeared in the arena walking slowly in a slightly bent-over posture. As each one did so, he signaled his desire to challenge another by bending his left arm close to his body and, taking the open palm of his right hand, forcibly slapping the inner angle of the left elbow, or at times the upper arm, in such a way that the noise could be heard for a considerable distance. This slapping signal was frequently repeated so many times, and with so much gusto, that the skin was bruised and, occasionally, left broken and bleeding. When a challenger appeared from the crowd he stretched his arms forward in front of him, the first wrestler doing the same. In this position they approached one another until their fingertips were actually touching. At this point, the challenger bent his elbows slightly and wiggled them up and down as a signal that he wished to compete. If the first wrestler accepted the challenge, he then wiggled his own elbows, not a word being spoken, and the two would immediately separate into a grappling posture.

The idea of Tahitian wrestling was to drop one's opponent on his back, which immediately ended the battle. However, to do so was not an easy matter, for it seems that no specialized holds were employed. The principal goal appears to have been to grab the opponent's thighs and thus upend him. This was no mean accomplishment, the wrestler frequently closing by catching his opponent's hair, arms, or loincloth, after which the final fall was largely determined by strength alone. Often no fall was made, and the wrestlers parted of their own free will or were separated after a certain length of time by their friends or relatives. In such an event, no victory was declared. During all of this time, the wrestlers contorted their faces in angry grimaces, but when one was defeated neither the victor nor the vanquished exhibited any further signs of exhilaration or anger. As quickly as one wrestler won his match, he resumed his stroll around the arena, smacking his arm to signal that he was again available to take on yet another challenger.

Wrestling was not limited to men alone, women having their own particular matches which were conducted in the same manner as those of their male counterparts. However, while male wrestlers seldom showed any emotion after a match, the women athletes were said to be more prone to exhibitions of anger at having been defeated.

Interdistrict wrestling matches were occasionally promoted in which the women first exhibited their prowess in this sport, after which the male contenders entered the ring. When different districts were on a friendly basis, such matches were orderly affairs. However, it occasionally happened that emotions ran high, and a general melee ensued as spectators and wrestlers armed themselves to defend their honor.[6]

Whether boxing as such was an indigenous sport in Tahiti is open to question. Although John Ledyard, writing of his trip with Captain James Cook in 1777, seemed to list boxing as a separate, individual sport,[7] I have found no description of such an event during the early period with which we are concerned. By the 1790s, however, it appeared that the art of grappling had come to include direct blows with the bare fists, and even with the top of the head.[8] Such a mixture of combative techniques well describes British boxing matches of the 1770s and 1780s, when every technique of barroom brawling was used to gain an advantage. In the first quarter of the nineteenth century William Ellis reported that wrestling and boxing were now quite separate sports, the latter, however, being less favored by Tahitians than their more traditional wrestling. In fact, Ellis found that boxing was rather limited to the lower classes and servants (though not completely so, since he admitted that several chiefs and priests were also renowned for their ability in this sport).[9] It would thus appear possible, if not probable, that the techniques of early British boxing were diffused into the Tahitian sporting world, probably through the example of sailor competitions, via the traditional wrestling matches. Only later in Tahiti's history did boxing become an individual sport in its own right.

Archery

Surfing, kite-flying, spear-throwing, stone-slinging, and wrestling were sports that could be enjoyed by many, though not everyone participated. However, there was one sport whose membership was strictly limited to the upper chiefly class, and, although the public does not seem to have been excluded from watching the affair, only limited interest seems to have been shown. This was the archery match, which, to this writer, is one of the more interesting anomalies in Tahitian culture.

Archery as a chiefly sport was somehow linked to religion, inasmuch as the participants first retired to a marae where they bared their shoulders in pious humility while a priest conducted prayers, part of which included a request to the divinity that the bowmen should do well. To further assure sanctified success, the priest also invoked a taboo against any fires within, presumably, a prescribed area surrounding the site of the match. That such a decree was serious business is indicated by the fact that anyone who lit a fire during such a contest, which might last several days, was said to expose himself to the wrath of his god. Since a god might conceivably overlook the desecration of such a taboo, an added incentive for compliance took the form of an immediate punishment and fine by the chiefs themselves.

With the completion of prayers the archers left the marae and, dressing themselves in clothing especially designed for such an occasion, proceeded to a special shooting platform. Although this structure was never described in the early literature, Ellis reported one on Huahine which was said to have been used for this purpose. It was basically triangular in floor plan with one side slightly convex, and it stood between three and four feet in height.[10] However, Kenneth Emory, who conducted an archaeological survey in Tahiti in 1925–26, was taken to several stone structures which his informants identified as archery platforms. In floor plan these looked a little like greatly enlarged bootjacks, the normal V cut at one end of the bootjack being replaced by a deeply concave end wall.[11] Thus, it was probably on some such specialized platform that each archer took his turn. Raising his bow at a high angle, he drew back the arrow and, at the sound of drums, released his missile. As the arrow shot upwards, young men stationed high in trees along its intended route shouted its progress and helped to spot its precise landing.

While in the martial sports of spear-throwing and stone-slinging both distance and accuracy of aim were important, as well they should have been, the only goal of the archery match was distance. The chief whose arrow covered the greatest distance was proclaimed the winner of the match, while the loser was he whose arrow covered the least distance from the platform. In this particular sport it was the loser who, at the close of the meet, had to supply his fellow archers with a feast and dancing.[12]

While the archery bow was made of soft *purau* wood and the bowstring of roava bark, the arrow was nothing more than an unfeathered bamboo shaft with a toa wood point fixed to the forepart of the shaft with breadfruit gum.[13] Although bows and arrows were occasionally used on the Taiarapu Peninsula to hunt birds, there is no early record of their having been used in warfare, and they certainly were not employed as fighting tools during the historic period.

Indeed, it was José de Andia y Varela who quickly recognized the fact that the chiefly archers were unfamiliar with the requirements of the bow and arrow in warfare since they wore no wrist, or bow, guard to protect themselves. Thus, when an archer released his arrow, he simultaneously dropped the bow to avoid the sharp backlash of the bowstring on his inner wrist.[14] Such a technique would hardly have done while in the throes of a heated battle. Besides, had they used archery as a martial sport to keep themselves in training, as suggested by E. S. C. Handy,[15] distance would have been of less importance than accuracy of aim, yet no target was employed.

While the bow and arrow was used in battle by the Tongans, it has been assumed, and rightly so, that the impetus to use this weapon came from the neighboring Melanesian islands of Fiji.[16] However, Peter Buck found evidence that such a weapon had once been employed in warfare on the island of Mangareva, well to the east of Tahiti, though by the early nineteenth century it was apparently no longer used for such a purpose.[17] It would thus appear that there was the anomalous situation in Polynesia of the existence of a prime fighting weapon in parts of this island world which, by historic times, had been reduced in function to a minor hunting tool and, in Tahiti, to a poorly adapted sport for the upper chiefly class. Yet, far to the west, in Melanesia, the bow and arrow remained a weapon of warfare among many of those people. Thus, rather than a Polynesian primal introduction of the bow and arrow, which was later tabooed for their own protection, as suggested by Handy,[18] a still earlier introduction may have taken place. That is to say, the Polynesians, advancing into their eventually chosen part of the Pacific, may have found certain islands already inhabited by proto-Polynesians armed with bows and arrows; once they were subdued, a taboo was placed upon the use of their weapon, except for minor hunting and, in the case of Tahiti, chiefly sport.

The Performing Arts

While Tahitian sports gave vent to the exhibition of physical prowess and added a degree of amusement and exhilaration to the less athletically inclined spectators, the island also maintained a theatrical art form for all to enjoy. This was the heiva, which one early European likened to an opera-ballet.[19] Actually, the term *heiva* seems to have been employed to describe any formalized theatrical production. It could be a play, a dance, or a combination of the two. There was even a record of a dance-and-play routine with an intermission for the participants during which time the crowds were entertained by a special display of interpersonal techniques of attack and defense used in warfare. Yet another heiva, usually consisting of a dance routine, was given in honor of a chief or other important person and was closed by presenting the honored guest with a series of gifts. There were other less formal dances and entertainments which were not always referred to as heiva in the literature. The principal differences between these and heiva appear to have been that the latter were sponsored by a chief, a paramount chief, or the latter's regent, and usually involved actors and dancers from the chiefly ranks, while the former were put on by commoners or the 'arioi, or entertainers', society.[20]

The site for a heiva was a very large building capable of holding one hundred or more people. It was open at both ends and along one side, the opposite long side being walled by a plaiting of coconut leaves which must have served as a simple backdrop. Extending out from both ends of the building was a one-foot-high fence, or railing, which came forward to enclose an open-air performing arena. Thus designed, the theater was prepared to cope with evening performances, held inside the building by torchlight because of the cool night air, or matinees, held out of doors in the adjoining arena. Here the audience arranged itself outside the enclosing fence, though seats of honor for chiefs and their guests were allowed within the confines of the railing. When a heiva was about to take place, heavy mats of pandanus leaves were unrolled to serve as a smooth dancing surface. Some of these were as large as seventy by twelve feet, and when matched together they added a pleasing artistic effect by being decorated in black stripes or checks.[21]

Heiva dancers performing on woven mats in an open dance arena. The headdresses of the women are of plaited human hair. Drawing by John Webber.

While the Tahitian dancing girl of the late twentieth century wears a sexy, shredded hula skirt resting low on her hips, and demurely covers her breasts with a more or less adequate brassiere when dancing in public, her costume bears no resemblance whatsoever to that of her eighteenth-century counterpart. The heiva dancer of the late 1700s was about as heavily clothed as a Victorian grand dame. A long white tapa cloth skirt fell from her hips to the ground and effectively covered her feet, while tassels of black feathers were wound around her waist and their ends made to drop down over the skirt to her knees. Her body from waist to armpits was also thoroughly masked by a bolt of white or colored cloth. However, this latter element of dress was decorated by a bunch of black feathers fastened onto the tapa cloth at the point of each breast. Across her back, and extending from her shoulders to her hips, were two large pieces of tapa which were deeply pleated into crescent shapes so that they extended out on either side of her body like fluffy wings. Sometimes her hair was gaily decorated with beads, colorful shells, and garlands of flowers, while at other times a coronet of black feathers enhanced her features. On other occasions a remarkably long braided cord of human hair was wrapped around her head in an expanding, tubular fashion, giving the impression of an upward-flaring hat. This, too, might be decorated with anything from flowers and beads to gleaming white sharks' teeth.

Although the above seems to have represented the basic costume of the Tahitian dancing girl, there must have been variations, for there were occasional mentions of heiva in which the girls came forth with completely new and different costumes. Red trim and stripes were also said to decorate the skirt or pleated wing elements and, because this was a chiefly color, probably helped to symbolize the social position of the particular dancer, as did red or black feathers placed on the forefinger of each hand.[22]

With a dance costume of such Victorian primness, it should come as no surprise that the Europeans were startled by what a Tahitian woman could do inside that bundle of clothing! They were said to place their bodies in innumerable "extravagant" postures, to "waggle" themselves, and to swing their hips in a rotary motion at "high velocity," even

Dancing girls dressed in tapa costumes in various positions of a dance. Unsigned pencil sketch by Sydney Parkinson.

when resting prostrate on their knees and elbows. While John Forster saw this hip-wiggling as "strange and indelicate," he found the movement of the dancers' hands to be more in keeping with his own artistic traditions and described them as "elegant."[23] In some routines, paired dancers joined hands and moved them to the beat of the rhythm, while other dances called for the hands and fingers to be bent far back to form a gracefully curved arc.

If there was anything that really spoiled the Tahitian dance routines for Europeans it was the "wry mouth," or occasional distortion of the dancer's mouth. Based upon the native applause this contortion usually received, it must have been a dancer's cherished, though not particularly beautifying, ability. It often consisted of suddenly raising one corner of the mouth while lowering the other, thus converting it from its normal horizontal position to one at a steep angle. Its meaning, or purpose, has never really been made clear. Perhaps it was the ultimate in muscle control in a dance technique in which suppleness of body and limbs was of the essence.[24]

Such elegant dancing needed rhythm to match, and this was supplied by songs, pearl-shell clappers, and finger-beaten drums whose tones could be changed slightly to correspond with different movements of the dance.[25] The full routines of a heiva were never left to the performers themselves. A dancing master directed the affair by signaling each new movement by song, shouts, or a special clapping of the hands. These masters were also the dance instructors kept by many of the more important chiefs, young girls being sent to them for special instruction and improvement in their heiva performances.[26] All in all, it would appear that although men usually served as instructors, and occasionally performed with their students, the dance in Tahiti was dominated by the women.[27]

While the wiggling and waggling of the well-clothed dancers in the more formalized heiva performances startled Europeans, they were delightfully ill-prepared to cope with the culture shock engendered by what they termed the "lascivious" dances. These were especially disconcerting because many of the female performers, when away from the dance arena, seemingly conducted themselves in a manner

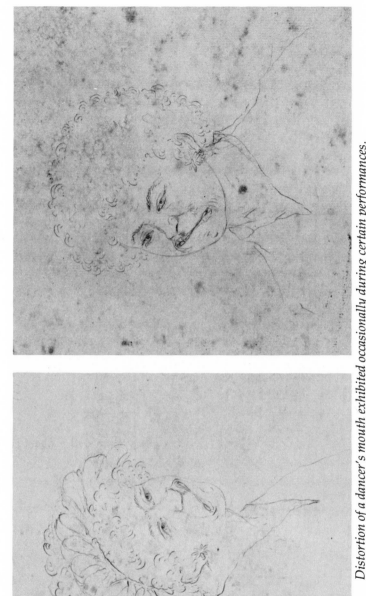

Distortion of a dancer's mouth exhibited occasionally during certain performances.
Unsigned pencil sketch by Sydney Parkinson.

fully conformable with European views of how a proper lady was supposed to act, at least in public.[28] Blas de Barreda, for example, reported a heiva dance in which the girls were totally nude and danced in licentious abandon,[29] while George Hamilton wrote of another in which the girls appeared in all their costume finery, only to finish the dance by undressing completely and walking the full length of the dance court to present themselves before the honored guests. True to English aplomb, Hamilton and his men arose and complimented the ladies by bowing deeply "with all the honours of war."[30]

Not all dances were formalized heiva, nor were all intrinsically designed to heighten sexual instincts. However, there were certainly some that would have set an old-line burlesque house in an uproar.[31] William Anderson described one of these in which the dancers alternately dressed and undressed, while the female dance master earned the loud approbation of the native male audience by continually lifting her skirt to satisfy their curiosity as to what lay beneath her robes.[32]

Traditional Tahitian dancing seems to have maintained its supple art form for quite some time—partly, perhaps, because foreign visitors were more enthralled than appalled by much of its overt physical symbolism. However, even by 1773, change was already in the making, for Cook reported that young Tahitian women were then attempting to imitate the hornpipe and country dances of his own English sailors.[33] By 1777 John Rickman commented that Tahitian dancing had greatly improved as a result of copying the European technique. As for the hornpipe, the women were then said to exceed the ability of their original instructors.[34] Thus it is that unenforced culture change often moves in little increments over a broad spectrum of daily living.

Although dancing seems to have been a more common feature of heiva, and its employment was aimed primarily at creating sensual pleasure for the audience, the heiva play was another matter. Often these were brief comedies with an exceedingly light story line made funny by the actors' looks and gestures during delivery.[35] John Forster outlined one such play in which a man, presumably a chief, entrusts the care of some goods to his servants. They, in time, become sleepy and decide that the best way to protect the merchandise is to fall asleep on top of the material. From this point onward, the comedy builds up as thieves cleverly steal one item after another from beneath the sleeping guards. Variations of this theme either allowed the thieves to get away with their act, or had them surprised and caught.[36]

Love stories with an earthy touch also had their place in comedy. One involved the worldwide story of a girl's love for a young man and her father's dislike for the same gentleman. Although the father tries to protect his daughter from her lover, the young man succeeds in spiriting her away. In a short time the young daughter reappears, ready to give birth to a child. It is here that the comedy rises to earthy heights as the girl goes into labor and soon produces a full-grown boy who immediately runs about the theater waving his umbilical cord and afterbirth. During these moments of slapstick routine, the young boy is chased by a midwife who desperately tries to catch him. At this point, the girl's father catches sight of the cleverness of his newly-arrived grandson in evading the midwife and is thus reconciled to the elopement. While the Europeans might have viewed the waving of a placenta on a public stage as a bit too crude for comedy relief, John Forster understandingly pointed out that since Tahitian children, even those as young as four or five years of age, were fully familiar with the occurrences at birth, such a presentation simply exaggerated realistic events which were not regarded as unseemly.[37]

Serious dramatic performances were not well reported but may have been more common than the early literature would indicate. After all, their value as entertainment for Europeans may well have been limited, because, in order to understand them, the audience needed a more complete knowledge of the local language than most visitors commanded. However, that such did exist seems indicated from Rickman's account of a play in which the audience reacted in a more grave and composed manner than he had ever seen before.[38]

There was one form of the Tahitian dramatic art that had a very real social function, and that was satire. John Forster recounted a satirical act played on the island of Huahine when Cook's vessel brought back a young girl who had run away to Tahiti with her lover. Apparently, her list of misdeeds and their consequence to family and friends were brought forth in such sharp satirical wit that the numerous barbs and the laughter of the crowd finally brought her to tears of contrition. Having served as a mark of satirical ridicule for her wrongdoing, and thus as a warning to young peers who might have had similar notions of eloping, she was then comforted and welcomed back to the fold.[39] Such satirical derision was not limited to the young alone, for if a chief stepped out of line in his conduct toward others, he too was fair game for public condemnation via the medium of the satirical play.[40] Here it is interesting to note that Europeans were not exempt from being the targets of this form of theatrical art, usually through the use of extravagant mimicry. Perhaps unfortunately, the Europeans saw themselves as simply being mimicked for any ludicrous or absurd happening the natives might have seen on shipboard, when, in fact, they were probably being publicly humiliated for indiscretions they had committed against Tahitian mores.[41]

The 'Arioi Society

Intimately connected with the world of sports and the performing arts was a society of people known as the 'arioi. On the surface of things, their sole function seems to have been to serve as entertainers in the fields of sports, the hieva, and very indecent dancing.[42] Rickman and James Wilson likened them to the strolling players of England.[43] Whenever they performed, they were paid in gifts ranging from provisions to yards of tapa cloth or anything else that an audience, or the people of a district, might be able to afford.[44] No doubt there were times when they overemphasized their demands, since Anders Sparrman claimed that the common people were heavily taxed by the members of this society.[45] On top of this, the members of the 'arioi lived under the rule that all children born to them must be killed at birth.[46] Unfortunately, this combination of infanticide, lack of a clearly defined Christian work ethic, and their unseemly, if not immoral, dancing brought forth the full wrath of missionary zeal and moral verbosity. This put an early end to the society before its true history and function within the culture could be determined from the members themselves. What followed after its historic dissolution was a series of confused memory accounts given to the nineteenth-century missionaries and others by converted Tahitians. These informants seem to have been strongly imbued with ideas of Christian morality, and they appear to have wished nothing more than to illustrate how far up the ladder of cultured civilzation they had climbed as compared to their heathen ancestors. Here it must be kept in mind that the democratic principles of Christianity offered a heretofore unavailable route—the only other being genealogical—toward public elitism if one subscribed to the new ethic and, in so doing, critically overemphasized the immorality of one's non-Christian ancestors.

Although it was not clearly described in the eighteenth-century accounts, the 'arioi society appears not to have been limited to Tahiti alone but had branches, as it were, in all of the major islands of the Society group.[47] While Cook, Sparrman, and Wilson inferred that only the upper levels of the chiefly class were admitted to its ranks,[48] such astute observers as Rickman and William Bligh suggested that the lower ranks of chiefs were also included. Rickman, for example, stated that the 'arioi included members from a middle social rank between the manahune, or landowning commoners, and the ruling chiefs,[49] while Bligh claimed that many of the members were distinguished by their valor, and almost all the males were fighting men.[50] Both of these descriptions suggest that the 'arioi society included individuals from the lower chiefly class, or to'ofa, as well as from the higher chiefly ranks. Since Bligh seemed to be adamant in insisting that the lower classes were never admitted as members of the 'arioi, it would seem reasonable to conclude from these pre-missionary accounts that the society drew its membership from the full range of the chiefly class, but not beyond it, an arrangement conformable with Tahiti's class-structured society. Since there were seven ranks within the 'arioi to which a member could aspire, each rank being symbolized by special tatoo designs,[51] upward mobility within the chiefly ranks was possible, but only through and within the 'arioi society. Since infanticide was a condition of membership, such upward mobility was limited to the individual during his lifetime, or the length of his membership within the 'arioi. Thus the entertainment society was not, as Irving Goldman concluded, a device for upward mobility for all classes within Tahitian society as a whole,[52] but only offered advancement within one major class, and that one the highest of the orders.

What, then, was the 'arioi function in the society of early Tahiti? It is a question that no longer can be clearly, or definitely, answered. The licentious dances and tricks of the 'arioi men and women have, with some reason, been interpreted as indications of an agricultural fertility cult or organization.[53] This may well have been one of its important functions in helping to insure continued agricultural production. However, there may have been another, more covert, function, since not all of their public performances and attributes can be interpreted in the above light. Perhaps Bligh has given us a clue by pointing out the apparent incongruity of the 'arioi claim that their use of infanticide was because they had "too many children, and too many men."[54] While Bligh took this comment to refer to the total population of Tahiti, it is more probable that it referred only to the population of the chiefly class from which the 'arioi derived.

As previously pointed out, infanticide was used by more Tahitians than the 'arioi members to keep genealogical and inheritance lines clean. However, there was another problem within the chiefly class. Since only the oldest son inherited his father's property and position, and thus had a job and a source of income, what could the chiefly class do with additional siblings who inherited nothing, and had no formalized positions in life to step into? There were, of course, a few positions, such as that of to'ofa or metua, which might be filled by some of these lower-ranking children, and there was always the need for well-conditioned young warriors as occasion demanded. Nonetheless, a surplus of children among the chiefly class was a very real problem. Should arable land have been taken from the land-owning commoners to be given to the children of chiefly rank, the whole economic system would, in time, have collapsed, since the traditional commoner support of the chiefly class would gradually have been eroded away. Thus, in this light the statement to Bligh that the chiefly class had too many children makes abundant sense.

The answer to the problem of overpopulation in the chiefly classes of Tahiti and the other Society Islands was the 'arioi society. This organization effectively absorbed these otherwise useless members of the chiefly class, gave them goals of achievement via upward mobility within the society and, by the rules of infanticide, assured the nonproliferation of additional children of chiefly rank who might have added to the population problem of that particular social order. At the same time, such a society needed an overt function within Tahitian culture as a whole, and so they became entertainers, perhaps with overtones of religious fertility, while the men additionally served as a standby warrior class when needed. The chiefs and commoners would have to support this overpopulation of chiefly siblings whether there was an 'arioi society or not, but at least the performances and other functions of these entertainers gave the rest of society something in return.

Thus it was that the common routine of daily living was broken from time to time by diversions that could be enjoyed equally by participants and spectators. Practice in the martial arts served to maintain a trained militia, while satirical plays provided amusement for many and a stern public rebuke for those who crossed the lines of traditional ethical behavior. And finally, there was the entertaining 'arioi, whose very presence assured the continued existence of the traditional sequence of inheritance within the ruling chiefly class. Recreational activities, at least for Tahitians, functioned both in the realm of pleasurable experience and in the integration of the society as a whole.

From Birth to Death

The life cycle is present in all living things. In man it is the biological curve that begins with the first cry of a newborn babe, moves upward to the excitement of puberty, levels off with the years of mating and procreation, and—with the continuance of the species assured—slips gently into the quiet decline from old age to death. Man has dressed his life cycle with a cloth of customs and beliefs which appear like varied costume at the critical periods of his natural span; these differ from culture to culture. This chapter attempts to re-create, through the observations of the European voyagers, the Tahitians' views, ceremonies, and beliefs concerning the critical moments in their own cycle of biological existence.

Infanticide

The beginning of new human life and the birth of that life are often recognized by societies as two distinct phases, each of which may be dealt with in a different but culturally acceptable manner. Thus, the intentional aborting of a fetus is legally and socially acceptable in some areas of the world, while in others it is not only frowned upon but is illegal and, among certain faiths, is regarded as murder. In other words, even among sophisticated societies of the twentieth century the question of when the taking of an immature human life is culturally acceptable, and when it is regarded as murder, is still unclear. Only after the actual emergence, or birth, of a child is the answer to the question crystallized in our own society: the taking of life from a newborn child is murder.

The arguments for and against human abortion are long and bitter. However, if they do nothing else, they serve to point up the fact that many societies have at one time or another found the need to culturally justify the taking of young, developing life at one of its very early stages. Where the technique of abortion is known, the life-and-death decision tends to center on the pre-birth phase. However, what happens in simpler societies in which cultural patterns prescribe death to certain unwanted children, but the technique of abortion is unknown? The Tahitians, who were in this very dilemma, solved their problem to the everlasting horror of European seamen and missionaries alike: they practiced infanticide. As in some other societies, they chose a point at which new life might be taken, but after which it became murder in their own eyes. Since contraception and fetal abortion were unknown to them, custom allowed the parents to smother or strangle an unwanted child immediately upon birth. However, if the death sentence was not carried out at the prescribed moment, it could not be carried out at all without, presumably, its being condemned as murder.[1]

Except for the fertility-oriented 'arioi society, which allowed promiscuous cohabiting among its members but forbade any of them from maintaining the resulting offspring,[2] infanticide seems to have been limited to situations which the Tahitians may well have regarded as realistically practical. Thus, since chiefly status was inherited through chiefly lines, it would not do for a woman of this rank to give birth to a child fathered by a man of lower status, and so infanticide resolved the situation. By the same token, a lower-class woman giving birth to a child fathered by a member of the chiefly rank was forced to destroy the infant at the moment of birth.[3] Obviously, this custom did away with any possibility of status challenge by a child who had lower-class blood in his veins.

Although female adultery, except in the chiefly ranks, does not seem to have been common, when it did occur and resulted in the birth of a child, the husband could demand its death.[4] This, again, may have been the Tahitians' realistic way of being sure that one's legitimate children inherited all of one's land and property. Finally, James Wilson claimed that in a few cases in which a wife refused to bring up a child, it was put to death. However, this was not always mandatory if the reverse was true and the husband was not eager to have a baby.[5] In this case a little persuasion on the part of the wife, who was occasionally assisted by neighborly friends, often saved the baby's life.

Infanticide in the 'arioi society, a mandatory practice, was explained to William Bligh as an attempt to control the population.[6] However, with promiscuity a feature of society membership, it is clear that numerous problems of genealogy, inheritance, and social rank would have resulted had the children been allowed to live. Besides, the 'arioi moved continuously from island to island within the Society Island group, and a large population of children would thus have been a heavy incumbrance to this troupe of traveling entertainers and ritual specialists.

While infanticide in ancient Tahiti took the place of abortion in various modern societies, it did not reflect in any way a Tahitian abhorrence for children and their proper rearing. On the contrary, the severest critics of Tahitian infanticide were forced to admit that children were well cared for and abundantly loved.[7]

Birth and Removal of Taboos

While the physical birth of a child was a relatively simple matter for Tahitian women, who found no need for postpartum rest and care,[8] it was nonetheless a time of critical taboos to be followed with great care. Immediately upon the birth of a child a small sweat lodge of matting and tapa cloth was raised within the dwelling and the mother placed within it. Hot stones were then brought, and these in turn were covered with grass and sweet herbs, and the whole doused with water to create steam. In this Tahitian version of a Swedish sauna the mother rested until she could endure the heat no longer, whereupon she dashed to the nearest stream and plunged into the cooling water. After washing herself thoroughly, she dressed, bathed the baby, and immediately took him to the family marae. Here the father made an offer-

ing of a banana plant and a pig or fowl, after which a priest
cut off all but ten inches of the baby's navel cord, which was
then buried in the grounds of the marae. The priest was
given either a hog or a piece of tapa cloth for his services.

From the moment of birth a child was looked upon as a
highly sacred being, the restrictions surrounding him bearing a remarkable resemblance to those surrounding a youthful high chief before he was invested with the authority of
his position. Thus, the mother, having handled the sacred
child, could no longer touch her own food but had to be fed
by another person. Should that person, or any other for that
matter, touch the child, he or she immediately came under
the same taboo. Should the baby reach out and touch anything, it too became sacred and was immediately approp-
riated to the child's use. Likewise, if something touched the
baby as he was being moved or carried about, that object
became sacred and had to be deposited in a small, consec-
rated enclosure near the house. The passing on of this sacredness of the baby to any contacting object went so far as
to even include trees which then had to be cut down. Since
the tree had become sacred by the child's having come into
contact with it, any adjacent tree or bush whose bark might
have been broken as the sacred tree fell also became sacred
and had to be treated in a similar manner. As is readily
apparent, these restrictive taboos could not last for any
length of time without causing considerable disruption in
the family circle. Somehow the sacred character of the child
had to be dispersed, or profaned, and this was done through
a series of rites known as amo'a.

Once the priest had cut the lower portion of the umbilical cord of the baby, a temporary house was constructed on
the sacred grounds adjacent to the marae, and there the
mother and child lived until the remainder of the navel cord
dropped off and was buried in the marae, or sacred grounds.
Although the dropping of the cord may have been one of the
ritual specifications for this period of isolation, the sex of the
child also seems to have entered into the length of the stay,
for this isolation was said to last for two weeks in the case of
a boy, and three weeks for a girl. During all of this time the
child was critically sacred, and the mother therefore had to

be fed by another person. At the end of this initial period of seculsion the first ritual step was taken in the gradual profaning of the child. This amo'a rite involved the offering of a pig or chicken and resulted in the release of the mother, and any other person who might have touched the child, from having to be fed. It seems to have extended to the father as well, for after the ceremony the child was moved to yet another temporary dwelling built on sacred ground, but closer to the family's dwelling, and there the father, too, might touch the child. However, the parents were still restricted to the extent that they could not touch the child if they were wearing the clothes that they had worn while eating their own food. Obviously, a few more amo'a were in order. One of these, the second in the series, not only allowed the father to touch the child regardless of what clothes he might be wearing, but it extended to the baby's uncles as well. The third rite removed the same restrictions for the mother and also applied to the child's aunts. It seems probable that it was at this stage that a small window-like opening was cut into the wall of the temporary house through which the baby's food was passed, since the food of the mother and that of the child could not come in by the same opening. And should the two have need to travel during this period, the infant's food had to be taken along in a separate canoe.

There was now a need for only two more amo'a rites to profane the child to the point at which he could mix with his own extended family and friends within the everyday pattern of normal, restrictive taboos. Thus, the fourth amo'a was performed by the father and uncles, and the fifth by the mother and aunts, after which the child left the temporary dwelling and entered his real home as a full member of the family. There might be other amo'a to follow, but they would be later in life. In the meantime, as each rite of deconsecration was fulfilled, it was celebrated by happy festivities. However, care had to be maintained at all times for the child's head, since, until the fifth ceremony was performed, the head was regarded as vitally sacred. In fact, throughout a Tahitian's life his head was regarded as very much his own business and was not to be touched by others. Neither did he ever carry anything on his head, and any hair clippings were cautiously buried at his marae. With the completion of the five amo'a, there remained but one final act to be performed. A tattooing specialist was called upon to tattoo a special mark on the inside of the child's arms, just above the elbow, to indicate forever more that the five rituals had been completed and that the child now had the right to touch his father's and mother's food without making it sacred, and thus inedible for them.[9] The sacred child had at last, and for better or worse, now become a human.

While the child was still very young and his bones still supple, the mother worked on her baby's legs to be sure they were straight and well formed. At the same time the nose was depressed slightly, since a somewhat flattened, broad nose was regarded as a mark of beauty. The development of a well-formed, unblemished body was the full responsibility of the mother, to such an extent that if the child grew up bowlegged or knock-kneed, she was condemned for her lack of knowledge of proper child care.[10]

Growing Up in Tahiti

Early youth was a carefree existence. By the time the baby had begun to crawl, he was introduced to the sea, and he was swimming by the time he could walk. Before too long he was indulging in that delightful sport of body surfing on the smaller waves along the beach. No wonder the Tahitians were as much at home in the ocean as they were on the land! Like so many other children in the warmer tropics, they went about naked until they were six or seven years of age. And, like children the world over, they enjoyed sweet between-meal snacks: they chewed on the sweetish stalks of a local plant,[11] or talked their parents into breaking open the ripe orange fruit of the pandanus and, taking a number of the hard "keys" of the fruit, sucked the sweet juice from their soft inner tips.[12]

As the child grew older, there were games to be played and knowledge to be acquired. There were cat's-cradle string figures to be drawn tight between one's opposing fingers, kites to fly, and stilts to make one tall. Then, too, there was rope to swing on or jump through and the art of Tahitian wrestling to be developed by both boys and girls, who, in later life, might give public exhibitions of their talent. For the boys, from even a tender age, there were various aspects of the martial arts to be learned by defending and attacking with nothing more than a simple quarterstaff. There were probably several varieties of group amusements, but, unfortunately, most of the early European explorers and sailors were more interested in the adults' sports and activities. However, Sydney Parkinson mentioned a kind of ball game played by two opposing teams of young girls, the ball in this case being a fruit. Unfortunately, he was so impressed by the crudity and lewdness of certain defiant actions taken at various moments of the game by one team or the other that he failed to record the main points of the sport.[13] There were also heiva, or secular group dances and the like, for young people, which may have helped to train the children in the art of group participation. However, not all was fun and games. At least some children, probably of the chiefly class, were given a degree of formal education through teachers of the chiefly class called ta'ata 'orero, while the young high chief, during his minority years, was instructed by the high priest. This is not to say that the rest of the children remained ignorant. They appear to have been informally instructed, probably by their own parents and members of their extended family, in the practical aspects of making a living. This may well have taken the form of actual participation with their elders in building a house, forming a canoe, gardening, and at least the simpler aspects of sailing and navigation.[14]

This casual, joyous life of the young continued until suddenly one day the boys discovered girls and the girls discovered boys. Puberty was reached by the girls around the age of eleven or twelve, and by the boys at thirteen or fourteen.[15] Although there appear to have been no formal ceremonies marking this biological transition, certain customary events did take place to clearly indicate to all that the boy or girl had reached the age of procreation. Primarily, this was achieved by the painful ordeal of having one's buttocks completely blackened by tattooing, above which were added a series of arched, tattooed bands extending as far up as the lower ribs. Other designs on the arms and legs might also be

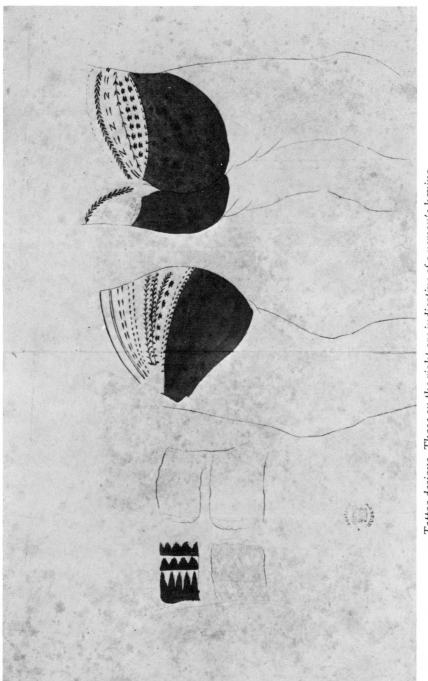

Tattoo designs. Those on the right are indicative of a person's having reached puberty. Ink drawing, artist not recorded.

added at this time, but these appear to have been optional to some degree.[16] In addition, the boys went through the operation of circumcision, the prepuce being slit by nothing more delicate than a sharpened shell, or a shark's tooth, after which ashes were rubbed into the open wound.[17] For these rites of pain the tattooing specialist, who also performed the circumcision, was given either a pig or a piece of tapa cloth. If the tattooing was done on a chief or the head of a family—that is, a firstborn son—the tattooing instruments were taken to a marae and destroyed at the completion of the operation.[18]

If the unceremonious rite of passage was painful to the participant, the postoperative years were ones of pleasant exploration of the opposite sex, unencumbered by the inhibiting frustrations of Christian moral ethics.[19] There were prohibitions, of course, for incest, at least within the immediate family, was forbidden. Also, if a man had gone through the ceremony of becoming a taio, or formal friend, of a married man, he might cohabit with his friend's wife but not with his sisters or daughters, as they were then considered equivalent to his own blood sisters and daughters. Similarly, taio of opposite sex were equivalent to blood brothers and sisters, and thus no intercourse between them could be permitted on the basis of the incest taboo.[20] This was the age for mate-searching, and, since intercourse was not only condoned, but anything short of it would have been looked upon as peculiarly unsocial, occasional pregnancies were bound to occur from time to time. However, since under other birth-taboo conditions infanticide would have normally solved the problem of a socially undesirable baby, the taboo on incestuous cohabitation, which extended to the taio as a member of the family, must have had deep significance. Quite possibly it represented a religious, rather than social, stricture. Beyond this restriction, however, the game of "dating" was carried on by the young unmarried with as much gusto as it is in the late twentieth century among the adolescents of the United States. The big difference was that it was carried on with little, if any, parental interference. In fact, this was probably the time when young Tahitians moved out of the family dwelling and set up housekeeping on their own.[21]

One need hardly imagine the effect of this premarital sexual license on European crews, their officers, naturalists, and, in the course of time, the first permanent missionaries. And in all fairness to the Tahitians, they most certainly understood the needs of sailors after a long and rugged cruise. In the case of Louis Antoine de Bougainville, for example, they sent canoe-loads of young naked girls to cruise around his ship that all might better appreciate the best qualities of their island.[22] Here it must be remembered that the Tahitians had quickly learned from Samuel Wallis's visit the year before that European sailors lavished gifts for such loving female understanding. As a matter of fact, had Wallis not left when he did, his ship might conceivably have fallen apart for lack of nails, which his sailors had quickly found to be marketable items.[23]

Since the common sailor, and perhaps some of the officers as well, paid in goods for their lovemaking, they tended to look upon their youthful partners as not much better than the girls back home who accepted money for an evening of pleasure. This view may easily have been heightened by the fact that, at least in Wallis's time, girls who were interested in a little lovemaking with a particular individual merrily employed a special hand signal. This consisted of holding up the right hand with the first finger firmly straight and then grasping the wrist with the left hand and rapidly wiggling the fingers of the right. Unaccountably, George Robertson, who was the only man to actually describe this signal, had to have its meaning explained to him by the gunner of his vessel![24] Such goings-on were hardly conducive to thinking of Tahitian girls as anything better than ladies of the night, and their fathers and other male relatives who generously proffered them as somewhat lower than commercial pimps. However, in terms of Tahitian custom and tradition, there was nothing particularly immoral about the situation. Needless to say, though, there is certainly no doubt that the

Tahitians capitalized on what, to them, was no more of an indecency than a British pub owner's hiring exceptionally pretty barmaids to entice the customers into staying a bit longer and thus leaving a few bob more on the counter. Here it should be noted that, for the sailors at least, it would appear that most of their evening playmates may well have come from the lowest classes,[25] though this did not seem to hold for the officers of a vessel, for whom a more sophisticated exchange of gifts might often take place.[26]

Marriage, Divorce, and Concubinage

With society's approval of sexual license for the unmarried, there was no great biological urge to drive one into early matrimony. However, should a girl become pregnant, and the father be of suitable station so that infanticide was not in order, the two were regarded as husband and wife and were treated as such.[27] This satisfactory arrangement may, or may not, have held for the chiefly class, since we have at least one record of early betrothal within this group.[28] Be that as it may, without the force of pregnancy, a young couple desiring to be married had first to obtain the permission of their parents.[29] There seems to have been some kind of a formal wedding ceremony for at last those of the chiefly class. Unfortunately, however, the young midshipman on Cook's second voyage who was lucky enough to have seen such a wedding was incapable of describing any of its features to George Forster, who wished to record it for posterity.[30] Years later, Captain Bligh endeavored to determine if a common marriage ceremony ever took place and arrived at the conclusion that such was not general within the society. Perhaps Bligh expected too much, though, for he did admit that when the parents of a young couple approved their marriage, a ceremony of prayer was conducted at a marae.[31] On the other hand, the missionaries categorically stated that no wedding ceremony existed.[32] This wide variation in observations, though perhaps a bit confusing, suggests the simplistic view that perhaps there was a wide variation, depending upon one's station in life and, very possibly, one's ability to pay the priests who may have officiated.

Since in Tahitian society heterosexuality appeared, at least overtly, to be the norm, it comes as a bit of a surprise to read that near the end of the eighteenth century male homosexual transvestites were discovered living as socially acceptable members of the community. The first hint of this comes from the pen of George Mortimer who, visiting Tahiti in 1789, recounted how one of his friends became quite enamored of a dancing girl only to discover to his embarrassment and great disappointment that "she" was a "he" dressed in female dancing attire.[33] A few years later, in 1791, George Hamilton observed that certain young men were kept for "abominable" reasons.[34]

It remained for Wilson, of the missionary ship *Duff*, to provide a clear description of this seemingly anomalous situation. These men, of whom there were no more than eight scattered in various districts of the island, were called *mahu* and were kept by the principal chiefs. They were said to have started at an early age to dress like women, and even imitated female voices and other details of expression. Since they affected the life and dress of women, the Tahitians logically applied all female taboos to them to the extent that they lived with women, did women's work, and could not eat with men or partake of any male food. They are also said to have cohabited with male partners and to have shunned any love life with women.[35] The fact that these male transvestites appear to have been acceptably integrated into Tahitian society suggests that transvestism within the male population may have been of long standing. However, in spite of the successful disguise that caused Mortimer's friend such embarrassment, it is likely that, had such homosexual female impersonators existed within the chiefly entourage much before 1789, they would have been recognized and reported upon in earlier journals. After all, the young man Mortimer referred to was dressed in an elaborate dancing costume, while under everyday conditions the more casual and open female attire would presumably have been worn, and thus a transvestite would have been more easily recognizable. Although a degree of homosexuality can be expected in all societies and is reported for several Polynesian islands, its social approbation, as in Tahiti, was not always assured. As for transvestism, its only other reported occurrence in Polynesia was in 1797 in the Marquesas where, perhaps significantly, the name for a transvestite was similar to that used in Tahiti.[36]

Although we shall probably never know the real origin of socially acceptable male homosexual transvestism in Tahiti, there is one possibility that seems not to have been considered before. That is that male homosexuality as an accepted way of life might have been introduced by one or more of the all-male crews of European ships. Since most European contacts were with the chiefly class, its acceptance into this privileged rank is at least a distinct possibility. Once homosexuality was accepted as a way of life for some Tahitian men, transvestism followed as a logical sequel.

Early accounts concerning marriage were anything but consistent with regard to whether polygamy was practiced on Tahiti.[37] However, on an island where a family's economic needs and food requirements hardly needed additional hands, and where divorce for the commoner was a simple matter of mutual separation,[38] multiple wives would appear to have been superfluous. Where at least part of the confusion seems to have arisen is in the early misinterpretation of concubinage among the chiefly class. Whereas divorce and remarriage within the chiefly ranks appear to have taken place,[39] availability of marriageable mates within one's chiefly status must normally have been quite limited. Hence, it would appear that when chiefly marriage partners failed to satisfy one another for any of several reasons, they might choose to remain nominally husband and wife but turn to concubinage with people of the lower ranks for sexual satisfaction.[40] As previously noted, any children resulting from such arrangements were killed immediately upon birth in order to keep the genealogical blood line pure. This was obviously the case with Pomare's wife, Ideah, who killed her child by a lower-class man but explained that had it been fathered by Pomare it would have lived.[41]

While concubinage, at least under the circumstance of a spouse's dissatisfaction, seems to have been socially acceptable within the chiefly class, under more normal marital conditions it was looked upon as adultery. Thus, Máximo

Rodríguez mentioned how a high priest complained to the high chief Tu that one of Tu's own uncles had been caught in adultery with the high priest's wife. Tu immediately ordered banishment for his uncle.[42] However, not all such cases were dealt with so severely, especially among the common people. If a husband caught his wife having an affair with another man he might beat her, and if he could catch the man he might well inflict punishment on him as well.[43] As for the woman's side of the story, if a wife caught a young girl in the arms of her husband, she applied some well-placed fisticuffs to the young intruder's ears, and let her husband know her views on the matter in the strongest language she was capable of using.[44]

While adulterous intercourse was obviously not enjoyed by the nonparticipating spouse, it did not necessarily lead to divorce. Perhaps that was because sex was not considered the exclusive right of only the husband and wife. In Tahiti when a woman married, both she and her husband could expect that from time to time he and his brothers might have intercourse with each other's wives. This seems to have been especially true with regard to older brothers and the wives of younger brothers.[45] Also, should the husband have a male taio, or formal friend, one of the taio's prerogatives was ready access to his wife.[46] This privilege caused Hamilton, surgeon of the *Pandora,* a bit of a problem when his chiefly taio offered him his wife for the evening. When Hamilton at first refused the offer, the chief immediately began to take umbrage. Seeing that he had committed a diplomatic faux pas, Hamilton manfully rose to the occasion even though, as he put it, he was no longer young and had already been enjoying a week of recreational activity on the island. Having gallantly saved the situation, he then found his taio in a distressed state of mind. It seems that his wife was already six months along in pregnancy, and the chief was now worried that as a result of his taio's lovemaking she might produce a piebald, or brown-and-white spotted baby![47]

With the advent of marriage, Tahitians settled down into the routine business of making a living and raising a family. These were the working years which, with the advancement of time, gradually tapered off into old age. This latter stage of life was a period of serene contemplation coupled with the pleasantries of having others respect one for the advanced age that had been reached.[48]

Illnesses and the Healing Arts

Although the Tahitians were a remarkably healthy lot, some did suffer from illnesses which must have been brought to the island by Polynesian immigrants before European contact. One of these was elephantiasis, which, however, does not seem to have been too common.[49] Another may well have been yaws. Since this latter affliction presents many of the visible symptoms of veneral infection, and because venereal disease was introduced to Tahiti by the earliest European ships, its presence can only be inferred and is, therefore, in some doubt. However, John Forster remarked that a young Borabora man told him that his mother had died of "venereal" disease before European ships ever reached the Society Islands.[50] Also, Bligh observed large numbers of people who suffered from swollen glands and sores which they insisted were not the result of venereal disease, and to which statements Bligh's surgeon agreed.[51] Yet another disease, which James Cook and John Forster regarded as a kind of leprosy, resulted in the formation of large, white, scabby blotches over the skin and, in advanced cases, weakened the individual so much that he could no longer walk.[52]

Besides these diseases, which appear to have been communicable, there were less virulent physical ailments that appeared occasionally in the population. A case of jaundice was mentioned by Rodríguez,[53] while one chief was described as suffering from a painful swelling of his legs and feet much as in gout.[54] A skin infection in the mastoid area directly behind the ear was also reported,[55] but beyond these, the most common problems appear to have been occasional inflammation of the eyes, sores, and what was usually described as "the itch."[56] Although not necessarily physical ailments, cases of hallucinations were reported,[57] and the missionaries claimed that periods of temporary insanity occurred among some people during the periods of high sun.[58]

Sores, inflamed eyes, and "the itch" seem to have been treated by the afflicted individual himself. The juice of certain plants was used to cure sores and "the itch," the crushed fibers of the plants being applied to the affected area as a poultice.[59] Sore eyes were treated by making a concoction from the paper mulberry and taking it internally.[60] Broken bones and open wounds were more serious problems which often called for the abilities of a special class of priest known as the *tahu'a-ma'i,* or wound dresser. Not all were masters of their profession, and crude scars were to be found on some individuals. However, there were others of considerable ability, Bligh being especially impressed with the neatness with which an arm had been removed below the elbow and the stump smoothly covered over. Such wounds, once closed, were then subjected to poultices of crushed plants or the ground nut of the tamanu tree.[61]

Broken arm bones were set in splints but, according to the missionaries, a terrific urge for mobility caused the Tahitians to refuse to have such restrictive devices placed upon their legs.[62] If this was the case, one can only conclude either that all such sufferers died of infection or that legs were not often broken. An unimmobilized broken leg would almost certainly have resulted in some form of permanent lameness, but I have found no reference to such in the literature, though the presence of a few hunchbacks was noted.[63] Only the open sores that occasionally occurred behind the ears were not treated with poultices but were simply kept clean by washing. The reason for this was religious: since one could not pass the numerous sacred grounds of marae without uncovering one's head and shoulders, a poultice was deemed a bothersome nonessential.[64] Oddly enough, hernias resulting from wrestling and overexertion seem not to have been treated.[65]

The search for new cures and poultices must have been a continuous one, and at times gave rise to some interesting accounts. For example, naturalist Joseph Banks related that he had been bothered with flies in his tent and, in an effort to catch them, had concocted a mixture of tar and molasses which, unfortunately, failed to entice his worrisome guests. Placing the sticky dish outside his tent, he soon noted a

Tahitian quietly slipping up to the plate. It seems he had a large sore on his backside and, viewing the dark viscous mess, he grabbed a handful of it and applied it to his sore. For all of Banks's scientific curiosity, he regrettably failed to follow through to determine the success or failure of his flytrap-turned-poultice.[66] Where a poultice came from also seems to have been important. Rodríguez recounted how a native who had been badly cut up by his father-in-law had used a local herb poultice with little success. He therefore approached Rodríguez for aid, explaining that had the cuts been made by something of local manufacture, the poultice would have worked. However, his father-in-law had carved him up with a knife which the Spaniards had brought from Lima, and, therefore, a poultice made from material from that locality would surely be more effective.[67]

While broken bones and open sores were obvious complaints that could be treated, the less obvious sources of discomfort were quite a different matter. These were looked upon as having been caused by the patient's having somehow angered his god. While relatives assembled to make the patient comfortable, a priest was called — or if the family was wealthy, several priests — to intercede with the sufferer's deity. Bringing a young plantain shoot, the priest commenced his round of prayers.[68] To render the patient cured, it was apparently necessary for the god to descend to earth. To aid him in his landing, sprigs of the "ginger" plant, in all probability turmeric, were waved over the sick person to cause a breeze, for it was believed that the god always came down in a whirl of wind.[69] If prayers and breezes failed to help, the next step was that of making offerings at the patient's marae. In the case of a chief, especially a high chief, this reached a crescendo with the offering of one or more human sacrifices.[70] However, such activities were only performed for those deemed still too young to die. Thus, when premature death seemed imminent, as in the case of the young high chief of Taiarapu, Vehiatua, a near-maniacal appeal to deity was offered by priests and subjects alike. In the final hours of his demise, a wailing mob surrounded his house, and people ran hither and yon grabbing anything that might constitute an offering to appease the angered god who must surely be causing this youth to die.[71] However, natural death through aging seems to have been recognized as inevitable, and was not considered the result of the wrath of the gods. Thus, old Mahow, the reigning chief of Moorea Island, was given every attention to the desires of his final days. Too weak to walk, he was carried in a litter to spend evenings in George Vancouver's camp, and on other occasions was placed in a canoe and paddled around the great British ships so that he might view them in all of their glory. Vancouver saw all of this activity as a callous way to treat an aged man and complained that such constant moving about was only assuring the chief's early demise. However, the Tahitians saw it differently, and explained that all they had done was to try to fulfill Mahow's wishes during his final days of life.[72] Death was inevitable for the aged, but if their desire to see more of life was greater than their desire for creature comforts, the thoughtful behavior of the Tahitians was to acquiesce.

Death and Mourning

In Tahiti as in many societies, even before the bereaved had time to control the initial trauma of a loved one's death, the formalized rituals of mourning procedure and religious prescriptions moved in to set the pattern for proper behavior and ceremonial needs. For the poor, or lower classes, little was recorded of the formalized behavioral patterns. Bligh, who heard of such a death and immediately went to the scene to record the event, arrived too late. By the time he reached the locale, the body had been taken from the home and placed upon a bier, or rectangular raised platform. Here the corpse rested on its back and was quite naked, except for a piece of tapa cloth across its loins and another around the neck. One hand had been placed upon the chest, while the other rested on the stomach. On a finger of each hand was a band of plaited coconut fiber to which was attached a small bunch of red feathers. Beneath the bier, a grave had already been dug to receive the body.[73] On this particular occasion, Bligh was informed that the deceased would lie in state for a month before burial. However, this may have been in error, for during his second visit to the island he reported that corpses belonging to the "lower order" of people were buried immediately after a short period of mourning.[74] From all indications, this period appears to have lasted from two to three days.[75] However, on the Taiarapu Peninsula the period of lying in state, at least for certain members of the society, may have been a bit longer, since the corpse was said not to be interred until the body tissue had begun to decompose.[76]

This form of primary burial, that is to say, interment of the entire body, was the most common Tahitian method of disposing of the dead. Not only were the bodies of commoners treated in this manner, but also those of lesser chiefs, sacrificial victims, and warriors who fell in battle.[77] However, among the upper levels of the chiefly class a different method of body disposal obtained. This consisted of exposing the body on a raised bier until the flesh rotted away.[78] Among the highest chiefly class the length of exposure was enormously increased, up to perhaps a year, by removing the viscera of the corpse and then subjecting the remaining flesh to an extended treatment with scented coconut oil. To conduct this lengthy operation an especially long, raised bier was constructed, one half of which was roofed and thatched over. At least some, if not all, had rat guards on the upright posts to keep these voracious creatures from making a meal off the cadaver. On clear days the body was moved out onto the open section of the bier for oiling and so that the sun might do its job of gradual desiccation. However, the moment any rain began to fall, the body was immediately brought back under the roofed area for protection. Unfortunately, the early accounts did not reveal just how long this operation lasted. Quite probably it was not a matter of a predetermined length of time, but rather depended upon weather conditions and the amount of fatty tissue on the corpse which had to be dehydrated. Fascinatingly, the oil treatment was so efficient that its deep penetration into the drying tissues made them sufficiently pliable to often allow the joints of the body to remain quite flexible, so that when occasion demanded, the corpse could be made to sit up.

The individuals who had the unenviable task of taking care of dehydrating a chiefly body represented a specialized class known as *miri*. Whether they performed the initial visceration is not clear, for there is some indication that this

Desiccation of the well-oiled remains of a chief, propped up into a sitting position. Engraving from a drawing by John Webber.

may have been undertaken by certain priests, or tahu'a. However, the oiling and sunning of the body was certainly in their hands. There were both male and female miri and, considering the separation of the sexes in such matters as the preparation and eating of food, it seems likely that this division extended to the treatment of the dead, men taking care of male corpses and women handling female bodies. The probable existence of this arrangement is supported by the fact that in the single case that I have found in which a female corpse was dehydrated, the miri was a woman, while all the descriptions of treatment of male corpses specifically mentioned male miri in attendance.

As one can readily imagine, the initial days—if not weeks—of treating the body required the miri to have a strong stomach or a none-too-sensitive nose. To lessen the stench of decaying flesh the body was initially stuffed with tapa cloth into which a quantity of sandalwood gratings had been sprinkled. In addition, the coconut oil used in wiping down the body was heavily scented, and the bier was decorated with strong-smelling flowers and plants as well as mats, colored tapa cloth and, at times, tassels of feathers.[79] Since a body under treatment had to be attended both day and night, the miri customarily lived in a temporary house nearby. It would appear that during this period of working with the dead, and perhaps for a month afterwards, the miri took on a sacred character and could not touch any visitor; furthermore, they could not touch any food but had to be fed by others.[80]

Desiccation of the body in order to preserve it and the occasional practice of carefully conserving parts of bodies, such as the head, bits of hair, and even fingernails, appeared to the missionaries to represent a testimonial of the affection the living had for the departed.[81] It was a kindly surmise on their part, but the record would seem to indicate a more practical reason for maintaining such relics. These remains were somehow linked to land and, in some cases, represented title inheritance from the deceased party. Thus, Banks explained that the removal of a female corpse from Matavai to another district was a necessary adjunct to the property inherited by a native from the deceased woman.[82]

Wilson, in turn, mentioned a female skull, carefully wrapped and hanging from the roof of a dwelling. The woman had died on Moorea, and, after the body had been desiccated, the head had been cut off and brought to this home where she had owned land and which, quite obviously, she had willed to another.[83]

The importance of saving the complete and preserved chiefly bodies as a testament to one's rightful inheritance of land and title was clearly stated in at least two different sources. Should a son allow the corpse of his father to be destroyed or stolen, he would lose his inherited title and land, both being passed on to the next heir.[84] Also, in times of war the capture of such a complete relic was more important than slaying an enemy, for the captor of such a desiccated body had the right to assume the dead chief's name and might also lay claim to the land formerly owned by the deceased. It was for this reason that such bodies were taken to the mountains and hidden during times of impending warfare.[85] Since a high chief might have owned property in several different regions, the Tahitians solved the problem of where to permanently place his remains by allowing the corpse to remain in each of these areas for a length of time, and then placing it on its final bier in the locality where he had customarily resided.[86]

One thing seems clear: the need to retain such grisly relics must have been limited to keeping those of the deceased person from whom one had directly inherited land or title. Had this not been the case, and had the relics been kept in perpetuity, Tahiti would have appeared as one giant charnel house. And this was certainly not the case when Europeans arrived. In fact, it was stated that in due course of time, after the flesh of even the dehydrated bodies had disintegrated, the bones of these dead were buried.[87] However, an intriguing twist to the final destination of these bones was presented in a bit of information obtained by José de Andia y Varela. Working on the Taiarapu Peninsula, he reported that it was claimed that if the preserved dead had living relatives, the bones were cremated, while the bones of those who lacked such relatives were buried.[88] Since it is almost inconceivable on an island that one would not have relatives nearby, Andia y Varela's informant may have referred to immediate blood relatives rather than any and all relations. Be that as it may, the important factor is that cremation of the bones of at least certain individuals on Tahiti appears to have occurred at the time of European contact.

On the surface of things the trait of cremation in Tahiti may not seem important. However, its sporadic occurrence in Melanesia and at the two opposite extremes of Polynesia—New Zealand in the southwest and Easter Island on the eastern perimeter of this insular culture area[89]— suggests that its distribution in time and space may have potential significance in helping to unravel the sources of cultural and migratory influences in Polynesia.

Although we lack information on the ritual and behavioral prescriptions for death among the Tahitian commoners, just the fact that their description was neglected by the early European voyagers suggests that they were anything but elaborate. Since commoners were not normally allowed in the larger marae, or sacred precincts, it seems doubtful that any ceremonies for their dead were carried on in these specialized areas. However, among the chiefly class there was a basic pattern, to which were appended certain variations depending, it would seem, on the status of the deceased. Fundamentally, the procedure consisted of exposing the body on a bier so that a formalized pattern of mourning could be carried out by chiefly relatives of the deceased. Rodríguez participated in one of these entourages and was thus able to leave us one of the more accurate descriptions of the formalized behavioral pattern expected on such an occasion.[90]

As soon as the chief mourning party had been assembled and the location of the bier had been determined, two women of the group were appointed to undertake the formalized emotional aspect of the ritual. This consisted of bloodletting by striking their heads and shoulders with a shark's tooth embedded in a stick of wood, smearing the blood over their bodies, and wailing on cue. Since this was a rather messy business, the women sensibly slipped out of their normal tapa cloth vestments and donned ones of fine matting. After all, these latter could be readily washed and

reused, while the former could not. Once they were prepared for their masochistic demonstration, the other women
of the party were each issued a roll of fine tapa cloth to be
used as offerings to the dead. The men, in turn, each pulled
up a small banana sprout for their ritualistic presentation to
the bereaved. This accomplished, the party moved on to
within a short distance of where the body lay. Since it would
have been inappropriate to catch the bereaved unprepared
to receive the mourning party, one of the commoners was
assigned the task of setting up a mournful howling as a
signal that the group was about to make its entrance. A line
was now formed with the men in the lead. This arrangement, however, may have varied with different groups, for
Andia y Varela described a double line of mourners preceded
by the bloodletting women.[91] Nonetheless, in this case the
men went first and, after forming a circle in front of the
house of the bereaved, placed their banana shoot offerings
on the ground, quite probably as a symbolic prayer offering
for the relatives of the deceased. The women then came
forward in slow and solemn step, the bloodletting individuals seating themselves near the head of the corpse, where
they proceeded to weep. The others, on passing the bier, left
their offerings of tapa cloth for the dead. After a short period
of time, the weeping of the women came to an abrupt halt,
and from then on everyone indulged in quiet talk until evening, when they retired to prepare for their return home the
following day.

With the termination of the initial mourning ceremonies, the body of the deceased was carried to its marae,
and there the priests conducted prayers. It was after these
ceremonies that the final disposition of the corpse took
place. In the case of the district chief whose mourning ceremonies were described above, the body was returned and
immediately buried near his home.[92] For those whose rank
determined that their remains were to be exposed to rot,
they too were returned to a point not far distant from their
dwellings where they were placed on a prepared bier. However, the bodies of those of the highest ranks were preserved
by dehydration. In such cases the corpses appear to have
been first taken to the marae for prayers, and then were

moved to a special, and strongly tabooed, sacred area where they were eviscerated before being placed on a drying bier located in the vicinity of a marae.[93]

Since mourning rites were now again in order, the bier was surrounded by a protective fence of bamboo within which no one could enter except the mortuary specialist, or miri. It was his, or her, job to see to the proper oiling and drying of the body and, as occasion demanded, to dress the corpse in the tapa cloth offerings which had been left for the departed.[94] Outside the bamboo fence, which outlined the area tabooed to the visitor, was an altar-like structure for receiving offerings of food. Such gifts, however, were not designed for the use of the dead, but rather were for the gods who, if not properly fed, might eat the departed, soul and all.[95] At a central location on the outside perimeter of the fence was a specialized area, occasionally consisting of a temporary house, where relatives came to weep and bleed themselves with the shark's-tooth instrument. The blood was allowed to drip onto swatches of tapa cloth which were then placed on the bier alongside the corpse.[96] Since it was only women who underwent this formalized weeping and bleeding ceremony,[97] one may presume that this particular spot was largely reserved for the female relatives of the dead. Off to one side was a temporary house for the chief mourner, who was said to represent the person most closely related to the deceased.[98] However, there may have been a bit more to it than that, for George Forster contended that a man would represent the chief mourner in the event of a female death, while a woman would be chosen in the case of a deceased male.[99]

It was the duty of the chief mourner, during a period of two or three days, to don a shell-masked costume called a *parae*.[100] Thus attired, and with a long stick or a shaft edged with shark's teeth, he or she first prayed near the body, then again near the temporary house, and finally sallied forth in the early evening accompanied by several club-wielding, charcoal-besmudged individuals who chased people into hiding in the immediately surrounding area.[101] However, it was doubtful if anyone got hurt during this ceremony, since the chief mourner carried two large pearl shells in one hand. These were kept clacking together as a warning that the mourner and accompanying henchmen were abroad. The clacking of two large shells was quite a loud alarm on quiet Tahiti, according to John Forster. [102]

The mourner's costume consisted of several elements of dress designed to cover him as completely as possible, except for the feet. First, the body was encased in three tiputa, or poncho-like garments. The inner one, of matting or tapa cloth, was of the everyday wide variety, and might be decorated in white or red. Over this was yet another tiputa, brown in color and somewhat narrower than the inner garment. Finally, a third, and still narrower, poncho of strongly made material was added. This latter had the distinction of being longer in the front than in the back and was decorated in front with horizontal rows of coconut shell disks, or buttons. These were one inch to one and a half inches in diameter and firmly sewn to the underlying material. This rather bulky assemblage was then tied around the waist by a two-ply twisted rope of brown and white tapa cloth. Over the back of the individual was fastened a large netted mantle, or cloak, whose outer surface was covered with glossy, bluish pigeon feathers.

The headgear was another composite of various materials. The foundation, or basic element, was a piece of matting tied together to form a cone. On the back and sides of this were pasted alternating horizontal strips of red, brown, and white tapa cloth, the entire gear being wide enough to cover the ears, and long enough so that the neck and shoulders of the individual could not be seen. On top of the conical cap was placed a thick garland of glossy, dark green pigeon feathers, to which were occasionally added small bunches of red and yellow feathers. A turban-like affair was then created by winding a two-ply rope of twisted brown and white tapa cloth around the cone. This was further enhanced by wrapping the rope with black and red dyed strands of vines.

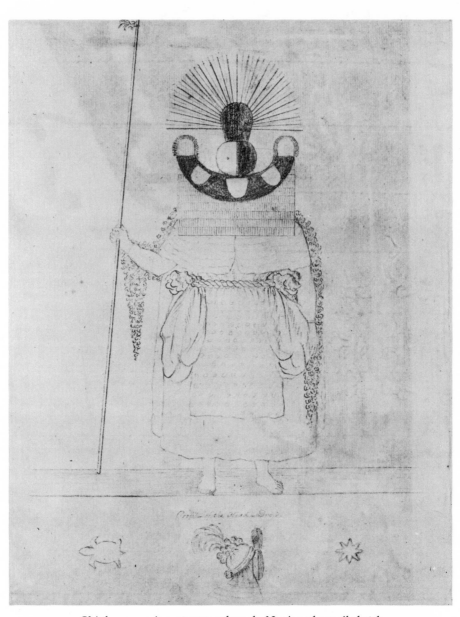

Chief mourner's costume and mask. Unsigned pencil sketch.

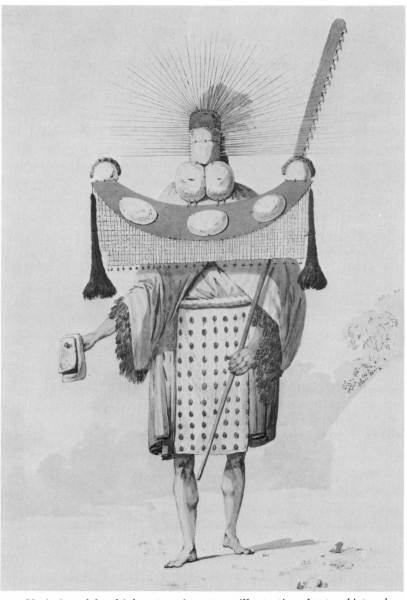

Variation of the chief mourner's costume illustrating shorter skirt and wider mask. The mourner carries a shaft edged with shark's teeth and a pearl-shell clapper. Watercolor by unidentified artist.

Up to this point there was nothing particularly special or outstanding about the chief mourner's costume. Between the body clothing and the headgear he was now quite well hidden, except for his face. However, it was the face covering, a flat vertical mask, that represented the patience of Job in its construction and the wealth of the upper classes in obtaining the necessary materials.

Made of nothing more than wood, feathers, mother-of-pearl shell, and coconut fiber string to hold it all together, the mask's intrinsic value would not seem overly great to us. However, pearl shells appear to have become scarce in the lagoons, or perhaps were always rare in the waters of Tahiti. According to Rodríquez, who once went searching for pearl shell for such a mask, a single shell of the desired type could bring the price of one entire hog.[103] Whereas the decorative pigeon feathers could have been obtained with no great effort, this could hardly be said for the long, white tail feathers of the tropic bird which formed a half sunburst effect on the top of the mask. These birds made their nests in small pockets in the vertical faces of high sea cliffs. To obtain their tail feathers, a man would be lowered by rope over the face of the cliff, with nothing but the smashing sea and jagged talus rock below him. Seated on a small cross stick fastened to the end of the rope, he would swing from one nest to another, plucking the tail feathers of any unfortunate bird found nesting.[104] Certainly the risk, and the prolonged effort, must have brought no small reward to these Tahitian feather merchants.

The basic unit of this face mask consisted of a thin, flat piece of dark wood shaped into a segment of a circle, or in some cases, a tapered, round-ended crescent. This was placed horizontally, convex side downwards, so that it appeared a little like a grinning mouth. The smaller crescent boards had a four-inch vertical width at the center, and a horizontal breadth of about two feet, while larger ones were as much as seven inches in vertical width, and up to three feet from one rounded end to the other. On the outer surface of this board were fastened four or five polished shell disks, whose rims had been drilled to correspond to similar holes in the wood so that they could be sewn into place. The two disks, or occasionally half-disks, that covered the two rounded ends of the crescent were drilled around their outer edges so that a fringe of blue-green pigeon feathers could be attached.

Fastened to the central, concave upper edge of this basic unit were two half-moon-shaped pearl shells whose two straight edges were fitted together vertically so that the composite effect was that of a large disk, or occasionally an oval. Since this discoidal assemblage covered the face of the mourner, a single small hole was cut in one of the shells so that the individual could see to move about.

On top of the composite disk was lashed still another shell that looked like half of an upright, large flattened oval, the straight-cut edge being fastened to the discoidal shells below. The outer surface of this shell faced forward, the technical reason for this being that its original rough surface had been ground off just sufficiently to reveal the immediately underlying colored portion, which was then polished and left intact. This resulted in the shell's presenting a·pleasing purple, or in some cases brown, surface nine to ten inches high. Some had the edges fringed with shiny, dark green pigeon feathers, while others appear to have been quite plain. Sewn around the back edge of the upper half of the shell was a narrow band of woven coconut fiber which served to hold the lower ends of countless, long, tropic bird tail feathers radiating out from the round edge of the shell to create a large, half-circle fan effect.

While the radiating tail feathers created a delicately beautiful fan at the very top of the mask, the stranded apron of shell work which hung from the lower edge of the wooden crescent was more a representation of the Tahitian shell workers' abundant patience than a fanciful work of art. This was formed from ten, to as many as twenty, strands of elongated rectangular shell fragments ground down to a width of about one-eighth of an inch and a length of from one to two inches. A hole drilled at each end of these individual elements allowed them to be tied end-to-end to form single strands. Each element had to be of a precise length, for, in assembling the strands into an apron, the shell worker's aim was to have adjacent elements match each other so that they appeared as horizontal bands running across the apron. The real trick in maintaining this illusion of banding came in shortening the topmost shell element of each strand where it fastened into the convex lower edge of the crescent board, so that the horizontal band effect could be maintained despite the curved edge of the board. Finally, the plainness of this wide shimmering mass of some two thousand white bits of worked shell was relieved somewhat by two long, hanging tassels of green and yellow feathers, one on either side of the apron, attached to each end of the wooden crescent. [105]

The chief mourner's mask was obviously an impressive affair which must have required a great deal of time in shaping and drilling the numerous fragments of shell required in its construction. However, from a technical point of view, I fail to agree with some of the early voyagers who looked upon it as the epitome of Tahitian craftsmanship: that accolade I would reserve for the construction of canoes. Nonetheless, it was a masterful demonstration of simple shell shaping, and the drilling of thousands of holes with nothing more than a pointed shell, a shark's tooth, or perhaps a bone tool must have required countless hours of work. Little wonder that the total costume was regarded as the greatest gift that one could give to another. [106]

Interestingly enough, the wearing of this mourning costume was not always limited to the scare tactics described above. On the occasion of the death of Vehiatua, the chief of the district of Atehuru came dressed in such a costume, while his entourage went through the customary mourning rituals of bloodletting. [107] Later, when Blas de Barreda paid his respects to the dead chief's mother, he was allowed to view an especially sober dance in which all of the participants were dressed in this shell-masked attire. [108]

Ceremonialism connected with death among the chiefly class may have changed, or become more complex, the higher the social rank of the deceased. Unfortunately, the record is insufficient in this regard. What is clear, however, is that in the event of the death of a high chief, such as Mahow of Moorea and Vehiatua of the Taiarapu Peninsula, a three-day mourning period accompanied by taboos was declared for the district in which the individual had died. Such a restriction did not go into effect immediately upon death, since apparently there was a delay of at least twelve hours or so. Here I am inclined to agree with Vancouver's suspicion that the delay was purposeful and necessary. After all, during these next few days of mourning, silence was to be observed and no one in the district was to maintain a fire, nor could anyone go fishing.[109] Neither could one plead lack of knowledge of the taboo since flags, or streamers, announcing the restrictions were placed along all of the principal pathways.[110] Thus twelve hours of lead time allowed the populace to obtain and prepare food in advance of the laying down of the mourning taboos. However, the old adage that rules are made to be broken applied as much to Tahiti as anywhere else, for Rodriguez noted that a few desperate natives sneaked in a little fishing during one of these periods.[111]

If there was an increase in funeral ceremonialism associated with rank, it would appear to have been in the number of people who came to mourn the deceased and in the quantity of tapa cloth they brought as offerings for the dead.[112] Although not necessarily common or traditional, the extreme in funeral rites for a high chief would appear to have been the offering of a human sacrifice, as occurred on the occasion of Vehiatua's death rituals.[113]

Once the funeral formalities were over, it remained for a near female relative, usually a wife or a mother, to occasionally burst forth in the ritual mourning pattern of weeping.[114] At times this was accompanied by bloodletting, the blood being collected on pieces of tapa cloth and later thrown into the sea.[115] So seemingly genuine was this outburst of ritual emoting, and so suddenly could it be turned off and cheerful conversation resumed, that some of the Tahtitians' European guests were left in a quandary.[116] Only Parkinson seems to have recognized it for what it was: a ceremonial rite to be conducted under certain circumstances.[117] Just what the circumstances had to be to promote this occurrence cannot be determined from the literature.

Another, less violent, way to show that a death had occurred in a family was for the relatives of the deceased to cut their hair in patterns. This was accomplished by using a shark's tooth, which was occasionally set in a piece of rough shell.[118] The range of designs suggests that there was no prescribed style, but rather that this was a bizarre outburst of freedom of expression. Some shaved all of their hair off, others cut out a circular patch on the crown of the head, while still others reversed this pattern. There were styles consisting of cutting the hair short on only one side of the head, or of trimming off the hair on the front, crown, and back, thus leaving long hanks suspended from either side of the skull. Some even cut their hair in circular designs, while yet another method was to shave off all but a small, square forelock. In the eyes of the Europeans it was bad enough that such outlandish hairstyles had to be created, but worse yet was the fact that they had to be maintained for two or three years![119]

Thus it was that the Tahitians passed through the days of their lives, respecting the secular traditions of their culture, fearing the god-given taboos of their religious heritage, and generally enjoying a quietly productive existence, until their final demise. Was it all to end when death closed tired eyes or cut down the strong while the excitement of life still glowed? As with us, their notions of life after death, of a spiritual existence beyond the corporeal body, seem to have varied with the individual, or perhaps the group.

Captain Bligh could find no evidence of a belief in an afterlife, only in a state of nothingness.[120] However, other Tahitians believed differently. There were two elements to life: the material body, which withered away and was finally destroyed, and the spirit, which carried on indefinitely.[121] John Forster's queries in this regard brought forth the information that the soul left the body upon death but hovered about the corpse for some little time before taking up its permanent abode in one of the carved wooden statues erected in the places of burial. From here it must have sallied forth occasionally, since the afterlife was pictured as a happy one with sunny days where one feasted on breadfruit and even the meat required no cooking.[122] Since upward social mobility was inconceivable for the living, why should it exist in the hereafter? The servant remained a servant, the chief a chief.[123]

Another view pictured the spirit as a lively individual who, during life, shared the excitement of its occasional evening wanderings by relaying accounts of them to its corporeal body via the medium of dreams. Upon death, it slipped away and, passing through the "god bird" that frequented marae and was thought to be a messenger of the gods, was purified and became one of the lesser deities. As such, it had to be propitiated by the living with prayers and offerings since, as an employee of the higher deity, it was known to watch over the living by curing their illnesses or inflicting punishment on those who deserved it.[124] However, of all of the explanations of what happened in death, perhaps the most effectively simple one was that given to Wilson when he asked where the departed had gone. His Tahitian informant smiled politely and answered, *"Harre po,"* or, "Gone to the night."[125]

Food From the Land

Food scarcity was never much of a problem in eighteenth-century Tahiti. There were, of course, brief periods between harvests of breadfruit when less desirable foods had to be eaten. However, that could be expected, for there are not many places in the world, even in the tropics, where nature provides a year-round harvest of all its foods. Undoubtedly, though, there had been more than one drought on the island, for there were forest foods, notably special fern roots, which were said to have been eaten in times of necessity.[1] However, as far as the European explorers could observe, most periods of near famine on any part of the island were man-made and not the result of nature's caprice.

Warfare, accompanied by the destruction of the enemy's tree and root crops by the victorious, was a firmly fixed tradition in Tahiti. Mass murder and land accumulation seemed not the ultimate goal, but rather the destruction of material goods and the food base of the enemy. After all, how else could one keep his enemy down and yet not depopulate the island? However, these localized, man-made famines were not total disaster. There were always the fish of the sea and the wild foods of the mountain to sustain life while new gardens were planted and new trees and banana plants set out. Nature, it would seem, was not the Tahitian's enemy. On the contrary, the soils and gentle climate had gratefully accepted the domesticated food crops that had been hand-delivered by the migrants to the island. A still wider variety of crops from European vessels were to be successfully transplanted. That many of these later innovations did not immediately "take" was not always the fault of the island's environment but rather of local disinclination.

Just when each domesticated animal or food crop was established on Tahiti may never be known, though archaeological investigations and pollen studies may eventually provide some clues. One might visualize the original immigrants as intentional colonizers in search of a new home. Whether such imaginary colonizers landed on Tahiti and raised some other high island in the Societies would make little difference. Once established, they could easily expand to each of the other nearby islands in the group. One viewpoint, steeped in European and American traditions, might picture these immigrants as being like the Jamestown colonizers or perhaps the more successful Puritans. These doughty souls brought with them all of the basic necessities to build a colony, including all the seeds necessary to plant and raise their most familiar and useful food crops. Only common sense dictates such a strategy, and since Polynesians had an abundance of such sense certainly they must have colonized in the same manner.

Many Polynesians, though certainly not all, were keen sailors, but the early voyaging colonizers of America had two things in their favor that would-be Polynesian colonizers lacked. They knew that a whole continent lay to the west, and, even if they missed their intended landfall by many a mile, there were bound to be a few thousand miles of coastland that could be raised and followed to their intended destination. In contrast, the early Polynesians had only a hoped-for island, or island group, to find. Furthermore, such an island, or the natural indicators of one, would have to lie within sight of their sailing track. Without previous exploration they could not know where they were going, and, if they got to an island, they would not know where they were.

The European colonizers had the tradition of seed cultivation and were thus able to store a wide variety of seed stock in small, dry containers where the seeds could easily remain viable during long voyages. The Polynesians, on the other hand, had the disadvantage of depending upon plant cuttings, since most of their basic food plants no longer bore seed. Such cuttings not only required more storage space aboard the double canoes, but on a long voyage they ran the risk of salt spray damage and dehydration. About the only advantage the Polynesians had over the European colonizers was that they were not tied to a metal technology. They did not have to carry the tools of their trade nor the material to make them, for they were quite capable of shaping them from stone, shell, coral, and wood once a landfall had been made.

The voyaging canoes of the Tahitians were large for their class of vessel, up to fifty or sixty feet in length.[2] However, it seems virtually impossible, if not downright comical, to envision such a colonizing canoe. It would have been loaded to its gunwales with pigs, chickens, dogs, quantities of root stock, voyaging food supplies, and people, not to mention the ubiquitous Polynesian rat. For short, interisland trips such a Polynesian ark might survive, but on indefinitely long voyages on the high seas in search of some unknown island, the probable result would be chaos and eventual disaster.

It seems far more likely that the first immigrants to Tahiti or the Society Island group were colonizers by mistake. Where they might have come from is not really known. However, since the earliest radiocarbon dates from prehistoric Polynesian sites are far to the west in Samoa, Tonga, and Fiji, it is probable that they originated to the west of Tahiti. Quite possibly, the group was rather small and may have been sailing from one known island to another in their original insular homeland when a storm threw them off their track and they ended up in the Societies. There are ample records of such accidental voyages, so the notion is not beyond the realm of possibility. At the same time, it is equally possible that the first canoe-load of people represented purposeful explorers who found these new and fertile lands and decided to stay. In either case, they would not have carried the food and plant stock of a colonizing expedition. Coconuts might well have been aboard as a source of liquid refreshment as well as food and could have been planted. Yams, too, might have been aboard, for they were said to be good sea stock on a long voyage.[3] Actually, when one comes right down to it, the earliest immigrant group could have landed on Tahiti without a single plant and still made a successful first colony. After all, there was ample fresh water to drink, the indigenous forest could furnish a degree of nourishing vegetable food, and the quiet lagoons offered all of the fish protein that could possibly be desired.

It seems doubtful that all of the domesticated plants and animals that reached Tahiti arrived on one great colonizing voyage. Far more plausible is the view that the inventory of introduced animals and plants grew by small increments. Tahiti is not isolated, like lonely Easter Island, and thus if the island group could be discovered once, it could be discovered again and again by voyagers from disparate surrounding islands. Each such landfall would carry the potential of introducing a new food plant until, by the eighteenth century, all of the basic Polynesian domesticated plants and animals had arrived and been fitted into the island population's needs and desires.

Domesticated Crops

Agriculture took two forms in ancient Tahiti, one in the uplands and high mountain valleys, and the other on the rich flatlands of the coastal plain and the attenuated floors of the youthful, steep-walled valleys whose streams drained the interior of the island. The former area seems to have been limited to a few hardy crops which could use more rainfall and endure the poorer mountain soils and cooler weather of the uplands. Once planted, they could, and did, fend for themselves as essentially feral plants.[4] In contrast, the agricultural methods used on the flatlands took on all of the basic aspects of subsistence farming.

Farming as the European explorers knew it was not a Tahitian way of life. Perhaps their method could best be described as a form of mixed horticultural farming characterized by gardening techniques more than any other. In fact, to the water-weary European voyagers the flat and narrow coastal plain looked for all the world like one elongated garden plot, behind which rose barren, ochre-red hills. Above the deep red of these leached lower slopes lay a backdrop of high rugged mountains, dark green with forest and wildly gashed by steep-walled valleys and sheer cliffs of barren rock. Extending inland from the gardened plains were lush green belts of crops on either side of twisting, clear-water streams.[5]

This idyllic picture described the lee side of the island. However, on the windward side, wherever the barrier reef was nonexistent or too deep to break the force of the waves, there was quite a different scene. Here hills and high ridges often extended right to the water's edge where waves cut them off into high, faceted cliffs. River valleys could scarcely build up their rich alluvial fans, for, as fast as the streams could deposit their silty load, the waves picked up the tiny particles and carried them seaward. The natives of the Tautira region of the Taiarapu Peninsula had controlled this problem to some extent by building masonry sea walls. In fact, their need for rich, bottomland soil was such that they had even confined their streams into narrow, stone-walled channels.[6] However, such expertise was exceptional and appears to have been limited to that immediate area.

To eighteenth-century Europeans the garden culture of Tahiti must have been an enigma. Nowhere was there the formal layout of the English countryside. Groves of breadfruit trees and lofty coconut palms rose above banana plants and fruit trees, and in the spaces in between were plantings of taro, yam, and sugar cane.[7] Beneath it all, the land was picked clean of stones and weeds, leaving only a grassy sward crisscrossed with numerous trails which led to the dispersed houses of the natives.[8] As if this mixed-up, scattered garden were not enough, each house had its own immediate garden of flowers and readily available little patches of food plants.[9] Formality was not the Tahitians' way of gardening. Not until 1797 was there recorded a description of a formalized planting of kava in fenced beds forming "regular parallelograms" which, according to Wilson's view, looked precisely like European gardens.[10] Perhaps those mutineers of the *Bounty* who stayed behind in Tahiti introduced this European style of planting by the example of their own gardens.

View of Tahitian coastal plain. Note the open house and breadfruit tree with baskets at its base on the right, the taro plants in the left foreground, and the canoe shed in the background. Pen-and-wash drawing by Sydney Parkinson.

Breadfruit was, above all else, the preferred staple of the island.[11] John Forster listed three varieties, while William Bligh, who certainly became familiar with Tahitian breadfruit, claimed that the natives recognized up to eight.[12] One of these, superior to any at Matavai where Bligh collected them, was raised exclusively on the Taiarapu Peninsula.[13] So great was the Tahitians' love of breadfruit that the periods between harvests were regarded as dreary times when other foods, probably of equal nutritional value but less palatable, had to be eaten. However, taro and bananas rated high and were carefully cultivated. Although breadfruit, once planted and growing strong, needed little attention, Tahitian taro was planted in watery beds.[14] Where naturally marshy areas of the coast occurred, the tops of the plants were stuck in the muddy soil and stone weirs were built across the adjacent streams to raise the water sufficiently to allow it to flow down hand-dug channels into the taro beds.[15] Besides the starchy corm, the green tops of this plant could be cooked in a pit oven and, according to the English missionaries, tasted as good as spinach.[16]

Of all the crops of Tahiti the banana presented the greatest number of varieties. John Forster and John Ledyard set the number at thirteen, while Sydney Parkinson and the Spaniard José de Andia y Varela claimed the natives recognized over twenty, and Daniel Solander listed twenty-three.[17] Lowland bananas were carefully tended and certainly formed part of the chiefly diet.[18] They were planted in the richer soils and the new shoots carefully guarded against hogs, dogs, and children by surrounding them with pegs and sticks until they were strong enough to withstand such onslaught.[19] While the lowland varieties may have been the more desirable food, it is obvious from the record that fe'i banana,[20] planted in the mountains and virtually unattended, was regarded as an important staple for the common people. Joseph Banks, and later John Forster, referred to the large plantings of the fe'i in the mountains, and Jame Wilson described how the people of the interior valleys brought the fe'i to the coast to barter for fish and other seafood.[21] The fe'i was certainly distinctive and differed from other forms of

banana. The stalk, around the top of which the fruit clustered tightly, was thick, upright, and of a deep purple color.
The leaves, too, were larger than other banana plants and of
a deeper green. When ripe, the fruit's skin was a reddish
brown and the flesh a strong yellow. Andia was the first to
note that this fruit, which had to be cooked before eating,
had the peculiarity of coloring the urine of anyone partaking
of it. [22]

Several varieties of yams and the two varieties of sweet
potatoes, one yellow and the other red, also were included
in the list of staples. Of the former, the upland yam was
deemed best by Europeans, while the red type of sweet
potato was "exceedingly well tasted." According to the early
missionaries, this particular variety had the strange trait of
growing its potatoes on the stalk, much like tomatoes. [23] Reports would seem to indicate that neither one of these crops
was on the most-favored list of vegetable foods, apparently
being eaten in quantity only when breadfruit was not available. However, since many of the early voyagers tended to
reflect the thinking and tastes of their chiefly hosts, it seems
likely that, on the basis of the quantity grown, both crops
represented basic foods of the commoners and teuteu. The
multipurpose coconut completed the list of staples.

There were other domesticates available to the Tahitians, but they seem to have served as supplements to the
normal diet. Across the plains and up the valleys grew the
vi, or Polynesian plum, whose bright golden fruit was said to
taste somewhat like a peach. [24] There, also, grew the *'ahia,*
rose-colored and consistently likened by Europeans to an
apple. [25] The rather astringent fruit of the fara, or pandanus,
was also to be had, though voyagers paid little attention to
it. [26] The Tahitian chestnut, called *'ihi* or *rata,* and the south
sea almond were equally scattered across the lowlands. [27]
Pia, or Polynesian arrowroot, and teve represented additional food whose tubers, however, needed special preparation before consumption. [28] Finally, there were the sweet,
tuberous roots of the *ti* plant, as well as the scattered stands
of sugar cane, unattended and growing in large clumps.
Some of this older cane reached a thickness of six inches;

sections of it were simply chewed for the refreshing juice. When clumps of cane became too large, or a new field was needed for another crop, they were burned over and the land cleared.[29]

One other consumable crop, though hardly a food, was the kava plant, whose roots, when properly prepared by chewing and mixing with water, served as a mild toxicant. It was a commodity principally, though not exclusively, indulged in by the chiefly class and cultivated by their teuteu.[30] What is fascinating about kava is that it may represent the last plant introduction into the Society Islands before European contact, and certainly the last into Tahiti. It was first mentioned by Parkinson in 1769, who also listed a nontoxic variety which was offered to the gods at the ceremonial marae.[31] Apparently, chiefs could enjoy the stronger variety, but gods had more sober work to do! By 1773 kava was still not common on Tahiti, being "scarce and little used," although at that time there were large plantations of it growing on Huahine and the other Society Islands to the west.[32] The active diffusion of this shrub eastward from the leeward islands to Tahiti was still going on as late as 1774–75. Tomás Gayangos, for example, told of how the two paramount chiefs, Tu of Tahiti nui and Vehiatua of Tahiti iti, commissioned two of the Tahitians going with him to Raiatea to bring back more kava root stock.[33] In fact, it was still sufficiently rare at this time that Máximo Rodríguez mentioned how he begged some kava root for the chief of one of the districts which had not a single one of the plants.[34] However, two years later kava had become so common that its use had developed a number of problem drinkers among the Tahitian chiefs.[35] By 1797 there were large, neatly laid out kava fields protected by fences and ditches.[36]

The ceremonialism so intimately connected with kava drinking in Tonga and Samoa seems not to have arrived with the plant. This suggests that the original island from which it was dispersed did not have such ceremonies, or that its original introduction into the western Societies was the result of an accidental voyage by Polynesians who did not know the prescribed formalities. However, once established in the western islands of the group, kava gradually diffused eastward, arriving in Tahiti not too long before Samuel Wallis discovered that island for Europeans. That such a reconstruction may be correct is reinforced to some extent by the fact that, although kava had been introduced in pre-European times to the north of Tahiti in Hawaii and the Marquesas,[37] even as late as 1804 it had still not caught on as a popular beverage in the latter island group.[38] Also, it is not believed to have been a contact-period crop on Mangareva to the east,[39] while it was nonexistent further eastward on Easter Island.[40]

Gardening apparently was never heavy work for the Tahitians except, perhaps, after the ravaging of a victorious enemy. At such times crops, as well as houses, were destroyed, taro patches drained, and even the precious breadfruit trees barked. However, the manahune, who cultivated their own fields as a family unit, and the teuteu, who worked the large landholdings of the chiefs,[41] were fully capable of bringing new life to a decimated district. The arts of transplanting and pruning both the young and the well-developed plants were thoroughly understood.[42] They had even developed a technique designed to save the life of a barked tree. According to Bligh, this consisted of covering the barked area with a clayish soil which was held in place by a "bandage" of leaves. Bligh was especially impressed by this technique since, apparently, one closely similar to it had only recently been experimented with in England.[43]

Considering that the entire coastal plain was virtually one immense garden, the tools of the farmer were indeed few and simple. Quite possibly a crudely pointed digging stick may have been used at times, though such was not reported in any of the accounts that I have read. However, in William Ellis's time, the early 1800s, the preferred tool was a long stick, on the end of which was a sharp piece of iron shaped like a broad chisel.[44] That such a tool, though employing a shell chisel, was in use when Wallis discovered the island was suggested by George Robertson, who mentioned that pearl shell was used for many things, including fishhooks and "shovels to dig the earth with."[45] Similar shell-bladed tools were reported for Micronesia and the Tuamotus.[46] According to Ellis, this improved digging stick was employed somewhat in the manner of a foot plow, though it lacked the necessary footrest. Instead of using his foot, the farmer assumed a crouching position, and, after forcing the narrow blade into the ground by the strength of his arms and back, pulled the stick downward, allowing the blade to break out the soil.[47] No doubt this modified digging stick met most, if not all, of the soil-excavating needs of the Tahitians. It was fully capable of loosening the ground to prepare a taro pit or to dig the narrow irrigation channel that led to it. Even the deep trenches that surrounded kava fields and plantings of young paper mulberry trees could be handled by this tool, although the loosened soil was probably lifted out by hand, or perhaps in a simple coconut leaf basket, as in Micronesia.[48] Weeding in the damp, loose, coastal soil required no special tool and appears to have been done by hand.[49]

As with so many unsophisticated horticultural farmers, the tools of the Tahitian gardener were few and largely unspecialized. The only instrument that appears to have had but one use, though it could have also been employed in gathering the fruit of the vi and 'ahia, was the breadfruit picker. This consisted of a long pole, occasionally made of bamboo, with a fork on one end designed to pluck the fruit from its stem.[50] Although they were not mentioned in the literature, bamboo or ground-shell knives, such as those used in other occupations, were probably employed in cutting new shoots for transplanting, as well as in harvesting stems of bananas. As for taro, it could be pulled from its muddy bed by hand, as could most of the other root crops when they were ready for harvesting.[51] What could not be accomplished by hand could easily be undertaken with the shell-shod digging stick.

Harvesting the lofty coconut palm would have been no problem had Tahitians been satisfied to use only the ripened nuts that fell from the tree. Some of these were used for seedlings and for oil, but the greener nuts, with their shells still rather thin and the inner meat not yet fully firm, were much preferred for food and for their large quantity of water.[52] To obtain these more desirable nuts, it was necessary to climb the tree. To do so, the Tahitian stretched his feet just wide enough apart to encompass the trunk of the tree and then tied a length of the tough rind of a banana stalk from one foot to the other.[53] Lashed in this manner, and using his feet and the banana binding as a brace against the trunk, he could easily climb the tree in a series of vaulting motions. Once up among the cluster of coconuts, he could break a green one free by twisting it. If only a few coconuts were needed, he dropped each one safely to the ground by first giving it a spinning motion so that the force of the fall on the still thin-shelled nut would be diffused and the nut would not break on contact. If a larger quantity was desired, it was easier to cut an entire bunch and lower it by rope. Parkinson noted that the Tahitians tore off the tough wiry husk with their teeth and then cracked the nut open with any handy rock. However, when a large supply of coconuts was needed, a stake was forced into the ground and the nuts driven down on its upper, pointed end; then the husks were easily ripped off.[54] This technique is still employed by many islanders in the late twentieth century, though now a steel spike is preferred.

A cursory reading of early accounts leaves one with the impression that for three or four months of each year the seasonal nature of Tahitian staples conspired to reduce the population to a marginal existence. However, a careful plotting of all such statements, with dates and crops involved, clarifies the situation considerably. It was the overriding palatal love for breadfruit that accounted for this apparent period of distress. In the meantime, coconuts, taro, yams, sweet potatoes, and even bananas were nonseasonal, so that while certain of these crops were being harvested, others were approaching full ripeness in a continuous chain of food production.

Of all the Tahitian staples, only breadfruit had a defined season when most of the trees dropped their fruit. After eight months of bearing and then a brief rest, they began to bear anew.[55] Because of climatic variation, breadfruit began to get ripe on the north coast around the latter part of October, and on the south coast in early January.[56] Its peak production, at least in the area of Matavai where most European ships anchored, appears to have been from March

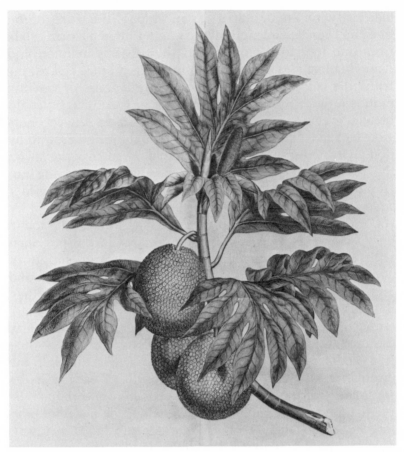

Breadfruit, one of the staples of the Tahitians. Engraving from a sepia drawing by John Frederick Miller.

through May.[57] By early June the Tahitians, knowing that the final annual crop was about to drop, furiously picked the last of the fruits to preserve them in mahi pits.[58] By the middle or latter part of June the trees were bare, and not until September could the small beginnings of a new crop be seen.

The breadfruit season was prolonged slightly by plantings of trees on the slopes of valleys where, perhaps because of cooler temperatures or different soil conditions, the harvest season began later than on the coast and, therefore, continued somewhat beyond the season on the flatlands. It

was also said that there were a few trees which, because of
their peculiar geographic position, bore fruit during the
normal off-season.[59] However, these small and scattered
off-season harvests were reserved for the chiefly class that
they might not suffer, for a Tahitian without breadfruit,
especially a chiefly Tahitian, was never satisfied at meal
time. During these distressful four-month periods, the taro
plants kept right on producing and yams and sweet potatoes
were available for the digging; the stately coconut knew no
season. It is possible that the banana had one short period in
August when it produced but little fruit, for several of the
voyagers noted a scarcity at this time of what were probably
the coastal varieties.[60] The fact that this was one of the drier
months of the year may have accounted for this brief period
of plant inactivity. However, one cannot help but suspect
that the reported scarcity at this time was due to the population's turning to the more favored lowland varieties of
banana in place of the missing breadfruit, and thus causing
the shortage. After all, by August even the breadfruit stored
in the mahi pits would have been greatly reduced.

There is certainly no doubt that Tahitians enjoyed their
breadfruit. However, there is equally little doubt that during
the few months when this fruit was unavailable they were
not necessarily living a marginal existence. Had this been
so, there would have been no reason why the yam and
sweet potato plantations and the wet taro fields could not
have been expanded, even terraced up the valley slopes, as
happened on Rapa.[61] Here again, it is likely that the voyagers' accounts reflected the attitudes of the chiefly class
with whom they consorted—and the chiefs were not happy
without their breadfruit. Bananas would do, and the fruits of
the vi and 'ahia, whose short nonproductive season did not
correspond with that of the breadfruit, could be tolerated,
along with *mape* or the Tahitian chestnut. In the meantime, it
seems altogether probable that the commoners and servants
continued to eat reasonably well on the root foods and the
mountain fe'i banana, which appears to have always borne
in large quantity. Thus, the annual period of distress would
appear to have been one of the palate, and not one of real
scarcity.

As might have been expected under such circumstances, excess breadfruit was picked and preserved for the four-month period of scarcity. By March the trees had reached their height of production, and fruit that would not normally be eaten was picked and prepared for storage. As the season progressed, the picking of excess fruit increased, reaching a crescendo of activity in June, when the last of the fruit was about to fall. Since not everyone owned his own breadfruit tree, and most certainly not the laborers, there were methods of distributing the crop among the inhabitants. Primarily this took the form of what was essentially a tax levied by the chief of a district on the people living in his domain to provide food for redistribution. Should those of any area not produce the desired amount, they were banned from the district, sometimes forcibly.[62] Although the chief undoubtedly saved a large quantity of the food to maintain himself and his entourage, the remainder appears to have been divided among the populace. Parkinson described such a redistribution of breadfruit as resembling a market, with some bringing in large baskets of the fruit, others dividing it, and still others carrying away their share in equally large containers.[63] Such redistribution of wealth also extended to handcrafted objects such as tapa cloth and even canoes, and was accompanied by a gala affair which under certain circumstances included the intentional destruction of objects.[64]

Preservation of Breadfruit

The process of storing and preserving breadfruit was one of fermentation. The descriptions of the preparation of the fruit vary somewhat and may reflect distinctions in the final taste of the sour paste, or mahi, as the end product was called. Since one method required more work than the others, its final taste and lasting qualities may have been more desirable and thus quite possibly may have represented the mahi of the chiefs.

In its simplest form of preparation, the rind of the near-ripened fruit was scraped off and the cleaned breadfruit stacked on the ground and covered with leaves. Piling it in this manner for several days must have completed the ripening process, for James Cook found that the resulting product was soft and sweet.[65] In the meantime, a large pit had been dug, and when all was ready it was lined with grass or ti leaves and the thoroughly ripened fruit tossed into it. When filled, the pit was closely covered over with leaves and weighted down with stones. Packed in this manner, the breadfruit fermented into a sour paste which remained usable for a period of ten to twelve months. Under these conditions, the mahi could be tapped at will and the pit again sealed over. Upon removing a quantity of the sour fruit, the core of each was extracted and the remainder made into small balls or "loaves." These were wrapped in leaves and either stored in shallow pits, some of which were located within the houses,[66] or immediately baked in a pit oven. Once baked they could be eaten hot or cold.[67]

A minor variation on the above technique consisted of removing the cores before depositing the fruit in the pit. This appears to have resulted in a much lighter colored mahi but seems to have reduced the length of time the paste could be successfully stored.[68] Another process, requiring considerably more effort, was recorded by Parkinson. In this, the breadfruit was first baked, the core removed, and the remainder placed in a a wooden trough or tray and mashed into a paste with a stone pestle or poi pounder. Thus prepared, the mass was deposited in the leaf-lined pit and covered over to ferment. When fermentation was completed, the paste could be removed as needed, wrapped in leaves, and again baked. At least one of the advantages of this more complex technique was that, once baked the second time, the breadfruit would last in the fresh air for several months and could even be taken on voyages as sea rations.[69]

There was still another, even simpler technique for preserving breadfruit, though for a limited time only. This was the annual construction of a giant pit oven called *'opio*, sometimes dug to a depth of nine feet, in which it was said that up to 1500 to 2000 pounds of prepared fruit was cooked at one time. Considering the number of people likely to be involved in such a large project, this appears to have virtually represented a breadfruit harvest festival. It was a cooperative venture which, apparently, could be called by a chief or any of his landholding subjects, whether or not they individually owned even one breadfruit tree. The primary prerequisite was that the person undertaking the project call upon enough willing hands to manage all of the jobs required for a successful operation. Perhaps one might best describe it as the Tahitian equivalent of an old-fashioned American barn-raising. There were hundreds of breadfruit to be scraped, enormous quantities of wood to be brought down from the forests to fire up the oven and, of course, the giant maw itself to be dug out and properly lined and filled with the special kind of stones that could survive the intense heat of the oven. As for obtaining the necessary breadfruit, tradition made the gathering a formal procedure. However, custom or not, no doubt the total project was preceded by an assessment of the potential degree of participation of friends and relatives. Be that as it may, a quantity of a shrub called *perepeere*,[70] which grew in such a way as to form a hollow in the center of its branches, was gathered and sent to members of one's own rank to be filled with breadfruit and brought to the site of the oven. Although a chief who wished to undertake such a project could have ordered his subjects to send in the required fruit, it seems that on these particular occasions he, too, sent the traditional shrubs or, lacking them, sent coconut leaves to be formed into breadfruit baskets.

Obviously, this was a period of festivity as dozens of people gathered to work, eat, laugh, and tell stories. Once the roaring fire had done its job, the red-hot stones were separated and spread out in the pit with long poles, and then covered with a layer of green leaves and crushed banana stalks as a protection, as well as to create steam. The pit was now ready to receive the vast quantity of breadfruit which, once deposited, was covered with more leaves and banana stalks, over which the remaining embers of the fire were scattered. Finally, the entire mass was given a heavy thatch of grass and leaves, and the whole was covered over with the dirt that had been excavated from the pit. Cooking time depended upon the size of the pit and the amount of breadfruit to be baked. Usually two, or sometimes three, days were needed. However, from the moment the breadfruit was ready to eat, all who had participated in the operation began to gorge themselves.[71] How long the feasting went on is not altogether clear, but it seems to have lasted several weeks. Since mahi pits were the dominant form of preserving breadfruit, and did so for longer periods of time than any other method, it is at least a possibility that this harvest festival with its giant oven represented, among other things, a means of consuming large quantities of breadfruit that could not be stuffed into the prepared mahi pits. However, as suggested in an earlier chapter, it seems more likely to have represented festivities marking the end of one Tahitian calendar year and the beginning of another. Ellis claimed that in the early days the period of the giant 'opio breadfruit oven had been marked by general debauchery and excesses, with all normal work coming to a standstill. However, he admitted that at the time of his writing, in the first quarter of the nineteenth century, these ovens had become rather small, and the harvest festival was disappearing as an annual event.[72] This could have resulted from the direct intervention of the missionaries to save Tahitians from the effects of their debauchery. However, it seems more probable that with the advent of European settlers, the end of the calendar year had been changed to that of the Europeans, and thus no longer terminated with the March equinox and the period of maximum breadfruit harvest. In other words, in Ellis's time the 'opio oven with its festivities was no longer a meaningful event and thus was rapidly becoming a traditional relic within the culture.

Thus it was that a shortage of vegetal food for the Tahitians seems never to have been a critical problem, except from the ravages of war, or rarely from storms or drought. Since there was no extreme dry season, as in a tropical savannah, and no period when temperatures became too cool to induce growth, as in the temperate regions of Europe and America, farming could be—and was—maintained in the rich coastal soils throughout the year. In fact, had it not been for the Tahitians' all-consuming love of breadfruit, there would have been no real need to develop techniques for the extended storage of food. Instead, it would seem that the mountain plantings of unattended food crops, such as the fe'i banana, yams, and ti, served as an ever-present source of survival both in time of need and in time of plenty. These were all obviously hardy crops capable of surviving under a variety of climatic and soil conditions and would appear to have competed successfully with the indigenous mountain growth. Should a drought occur, its effects would be most strongly felt on the low coastal farmlands, leaving the robust mountain crops to survive in their naturally more moist upland environment. If all else failed, there were always wild fern roots and other undomesticated plants in the undeveloped mountains that one could survive upon. No wonder that in times of war the defeated took to the mountains until a peace could be arranged. Up there was a degree of security and adequate food for the taking.

Animal Husbandry

Tahiti was one of several fortunate islands that eventually received all of the Polynesian domesticated animals and, more importantly, maintained them. There were not many to be sure—only the pig, dog, rat, and chicken. However, in light of the fact that some of the Pacific islands received only one or another of these animals, while others may have received more but lost their breeding stock through natural disaster or overkill, Tahiti stands out as indeed fortunate. That these animals arrived at all is a minor miracle, for they either had to arrive in pairs or, if singly, within the breeding life of each mate.

The prime meat producer was the Tahitian pig, whose flesh was said to have the tender taste of veal and whose fat was not as rich and heavy as that of its larger European counterpart. It was a small breed, weighing between eighty and one hundred pounds, and had a long back and pendant belly and erect, rather than floppy, ears. It was early recognized by the Europeans to be a Chinese breed,[73] and, on the basis of more recent studies, would seem to have been the south China one, or one of the closely allied breeds of Vietnam, Laos, and Thailand.[74] There was also an aboriginal breed in Taiwan that compared equally well with the description of the Tahitian pig.[75] The fact that all of these were sty, rather than herding, pigs further supports the view that the original ancestors of the Tahitian pig were located somewhere in southeast Asia.[76]

Tahitian pigs were a clean lot who did not enjoy that characteristically hoggish delight of wallowing in the mud.[77] During the day they were allowed to graze around the house, but at night they were brought inside and placed in a simple sty which was covered over with boards to form a raised platform bed for the owners of the house.[78] Other, apparently open-air, sties could be found adjacent to certain of the marae, or ceremonial centers, where pigs were sacrificed.[79] Although women were not allowed to eat the flesh of hog or dog, the care and feeding of these animals, as well as the chicken, was left in their hands.[80] The primary food of the pig appears to have been plantains, although taro and probably other vegetal foods were also used for this purpose.[81]

On the basis of meat production, the dog was rated second to the pig. However, in terms of chiefly palatal delight, its cooked flesh was regarded as superior to that of the pig. Quite probably there had been several different introductions of dogs into the Society Islands, for there appear to have been a number of different breeds ranging from small varieties to others which were quite large and hairy.[82] These latter, which had bushy tails, were especially appreciated, for they furnished not only food but also hair to decorate chiefly breastplates.[83] George Forster described the Tahitian dog as ranging from the size of a lap dog to that of a large spaniel. Their heads were broad, snouts pointed, and ears upright. Although hair color differed, he described it as most commonly white or brown. He further contended that these animals did not bark, an observation corroborated by Andia y Varela, but merely howled occasionally.[84] Although such a description lacks the detail needed for direct comparison, I feel that Margaret Titcomb's arguments for the Polynesian dog's having descended from the early Southeast Asian pariah dog are well within reason.[85] In this regard, there is the intriguing, but perhaps only coincidental, fact that the Tahitian pig compares well with the south China breed and that in this same general area the pariah dog was, as in Tahiti, used for food, though not exclusively.[86]

Regardless of the original source of the Tahitian dog, its primary purpose in life was to be raised for slaughter. Cook, who tried some of the flesh, likened it to English lamb,[87] a similarity which surely would not have been shared by the chiefs, who found lamb most distasteful. Although dogs were certainly a chiefly food, the early accounts do not indicate whether it was eaten by the common man as well. However, it may have been reserved by them for special occasions, since dogs were sufficiently common that John Forster observed that by every house some of them lay stretched out at their ease.[88] One might expect that the normally carnivorous dogs would have sooner or later gone after the chickens or piglets, but such does not seem to have been the case. Instead, they were basically vegetarians, eating such things as coconut meat, breadfruit, and yams.[89]

Of the three mammals brought by Polynesians to Tahiti, only the rat seems not to have been used for food, at least at the time of European contact. They were, however, quite edible, as some of Cook's "gentlemen" found out when, to the revulsion of the natives, they fried a few and found them to be good eating.[90] These rodents were not of the large European variety, *Rattus norvegicus*, but rather were *Rattus exulans*, and were sufficiently small that Raimundo Bonacorsi mistakenly referred to them as mice.[91] Their spread throughout most, if not all, of Polynesia has generally been accounted for by the explanation that they came as stowaways on voyaging canoes. Such a view seems biased by the knowledge that in the deep, broad holds of European sailing vessels there was ample room for rats to live and hide successfully. That they did so is well recorded in historical logs and journals. However, the relatively narrow, shallow-draft voyaging canoes of the Polynesians were hardly suited to such clandestine rodent activity. Had they slipped aboard unnoticed, their early discovery, probably among the sea stores, would have been assured. Had they been regarded as undesirable, they would have most probably been thrown overboard, for, in Tahiti at least, drowning was one of the acceptable methods of killing both animals and men. Obviously, this did not happen, and the more logical conclusion would appear to be that they were intentional guests of the Polynesian voyagers.

If the Polynesian rat was an acceptable import to Tahiti, and yet not deemed worthy of eating, then it must have served some other useful purpose. The record on this seems abundantly clear: it was the Tahitians' highly mobile garbage collector and sewage disposal unit. Anders Sparrman and the Forsters considered them public benefactors who consumed the fruit and vegetable refuse left on the ground after a healthy Tahitian dinner, and who quickly ate up the human excrement that was left scattered along the Tahitian pathways.[92] Unlike the Europeans, who generally displayed an attitude of disgust toward the rats, the Tahitians obviously enjoyed them, even feeding them scraps of food during meal time.[93] Given such an amiable attitude on the part of the Tahitians, and the propensity toward breeding on the part of the rat, it is little wonder that from 1768 to the arrival of the English missionaries in 1797, accounts were uniform in stating that the rat population on the island was numerous.[94]

The Tahitian chicken almost certainly had its origins in that same Southeast Asian center of early domestication as the Polynesian dog and pig.[95] Unfortunately for us, the finer points of chicken description seem to have been neglected by the otherwise observant European voyagers. To the Englishman Robertson they looked like the same ones that his countrymen raised back home, while the best that the Spaniards could do was to comment on the smallness of the hens.[96] As with the other animals, they were fed on vegetal foods and were allowed to run free. However, when evening came, they cautiously perched in nearby fruit trees.[97] Although their number never appears to have been great, every house seems to have had a few cocks and hens,[98] and there were numerous references to Europeans having been served pit-oven-cooked chicken, whether they were visiting in the house of a chief or that of a commoner.

While domesticated fowl were primarily raised for food, the missionary Ellis, writing in the early nineteenth century, characterized cockfighting as virtually a national pastime of Tahiti.[99] Years later, in 1930, E. S. C. Handy perpetuated this view by describing cockfighting as one of the indigenous sports of his ari'i culture of Tahiti.[100] The early records, however, do not support this contention. Certainly had cockfighting been as common on the island in the eighteenth century as it seems to have been during the following one hundred years, Cook, the Forsters, or perhaps Bligh or George Vancouver—and most certainly the first load of English missionaries in 1797—would have mentioned it.

On the contrary, the earliest mention of cockfighting in the literature occurred in 1773 and had to do with Cook's own sailors, which, of course, is not surprising since the sport was common in eighteenth-century England. What makes this reference particularly interesting is that it came from the pen of George Forster, who, with considerable disgust, described how the sailors purchased fowls at Huahine and spent the voyage from there to Tongatapu bedeviling the birds and otherwise incensing them to fight one another.[101] His obvious dislike of the sport surely would have excited some comment in his journal had cockfighting been a recreational activity of Tahitians. From his account it appears that the Society Island fowl were easily trained to fight, and it is thus possible that Cook's own men introduced the sport during their stay on Tahiti. That they did not introduce it to Tongatapu was at least partly due to the fact that they were unsuccessful in their training techniques with the much larger Tongan fowls and, to assuage their frustrations, ended up killing and eating the birds. That 1773 may well have been the date of the introduction of this sport to Tahiti was supported to a considerable extent by the Spaniard Rodríguez, who was the first to mention the sport as existing, at least on the Taiarapu Peninsula, during his stay on the island in 1774–75.[102] However, it would seem that it was not until the nineteenth century that cockfighting became such a common sport that Ellis found it already enshrined in legendary traditions of origin and surrounded with a degree of ceremony.

The ancient Tahitians were fortunate to have settled on an island where their introduced plants and domesticated animals thrived; natural shortages were rare, but even in the event of the destruction of trees and gardens by a victorious army, the land still provided the untended mountain crops and ample wild foods.

Food From the Sea

There is little wonder that the accounts of Tahiti brought back by the eighteenth-century sailors and naturalists were interpreted by their countrymen as descriptions of paradise itself. Certainly for the ground-grubbing north European and English farmers of the time the casual but amply productive agricultural practices of the Tahitians would have appeared as either heaven on earth or, as in the eyes of the missionaries, as downright un-Christian in their lack of constant toil. As for the hardened North Sea fishermen, the descriptions of the warm, quiet waters of Tahiti's lagoons, with their manifold varieties of seafood for the taking, may well have been incomprehensible and sloughed off as over-expansive storytelling. However, if nature had been kind to the Tahitians by allowing their land crops to grow and mature with minimal agricultural effort and little technology, she had certainly challenged their ingenuity before allowing them to wrest her products from the sea. It was here, in farming the sea, that the Tahitians shone most brilliantly— not only in their knowledge and use of ocean life but also in their development of simple but effective devices to reap that harvest.

The best word to describe the male Tahitian seafood eating habits is "omniverous." The women would probably have matched the men in this respect except that custom forbade any woman of less than chiefly status from eating albacore, dolphin, shark, porpoise, whale, and turtle.[1] The turtle, which did not occur in quantity around Tahiti, was regarded as sacred and eaten only by chiefs.[2] In addition, a few fish and a miniature red crab were said to be poisonous.[3] However, this still left plenty of sea life to be devoured, and devoured it was. The range extended from jellyfish, octopus, and squid, to such shelled delights as oysters, mussels, periwinkles, and sea urchins, to lobsters and crabs of immense size. There was also a large assortment of fish ranging from small fry and eels to dolphin, albacore, and bonito; among the larger sea animals eaten were porpoise and, when accidentally stranded, whale. John Forster was able to list forty-eight different fish that were regarded as edible, and he further noted that Captain Cook had informed him that on the occasion of his first voyage he had collected a record-breaking list of one hundred and fifty names of edible sea life in Tahiti.[4] Be that as it may, a list of specifically mentioned fish which I gleaned from voyage accounts made between 1767 and 1797 ran to twenty-six in number and may represent the more abundant, or at least the more sought-after, fish in Tahitian waters. On the other hand, it might represent nothing more than the fish enjoyed or recognized by the European observers. Some, however, were intentionally sought out by Tahitian fishermen and thus must have been preferred food.

Saltwater fishing, and the making of all the appurtenances that went with it, was men's work.[5] Interestingly enough, this distinction apparently did not extend to fresh water, for there was at least one account of women fishing with bag nets in one of the streams.[6] Unfortunately, there is no hint as to any division of labor in the collection of such shell food as periwinkles, oysters, clams, and conches. All we do know is that whenever the tide was low the reefs were covered with Tahitians collecting these delicacies.[7] Such collecting represented no mean source of food, for the periwinkles were said to be of remarkable size,[8] and José de Andia y Varela reported mussels measuring seventeen inches in length and from nine to ten inches in width.[9] This was sea harvesting at its simplest level and has probably been employed by shore-dwelling cultures throughout the greater part of human existence.

The Tahitians, like most—but not all—Polynesians, were expert swimmers and expanded their nontechnical gathering of seafood to include diving for fish. Rock fish, though often caught in pots, were frequently caught by hand, while such diving seems to have been the only method employed in catching the hedgehog fish. To obtain this latter, whose defense was to dart from one dark hole in the reef to another, not only did the surface of the lagoon have to be smooth for optimum underwater lighting, but the diver had to be prepared to stay under water a fair time while chasing the proposed catch from one protective hole to another. Since it was a spiny fish, the method for bringing it up to the surface was to push one's fingers into its eyes and haul it up in this manner. Some divers were expert enough in this sport to bring up two such fish during a single dive.[10]

There were at least two forms of sea life which were not intentionally hunted but were dispatched and eaten whenever opportunity presented itself. One of these was the whale, usually a young one. These mammoths of the deep occasionally got stranded on the reef, or were even washed into the lagoons. On such occasions the men armed themselves with war spears and, surrounding the partly beached mammal with their canoes, attempted to dispatch him as best they could. There is little doubt that this was dangerous sport, and more than one canoe was said to have been dashed to pieces.[11] Although the danger in this kind of an operation is obvious, what is more intriguing is how the Tahitians were able to cut up that much meat with nothing more than ground shell or sharpened bamboo knives. Quite probably the whale tooth ornaments occasionally found in archaeological excavations in Polynesia derived from such strandings.

Another, and delicious, resident of the briny deep which was not intentionally fished but whose aggressive habits were known and appreciated by the Tahitians, was the swordfish. When the men fished late at night for dolphin, it sometimes happened that one of their canoes was attacked by a swordfish. Rather than attempting to avoid such an assault, the fishermen would allow the attacker to continue ramming their vessel until the fish drove its sword sufficiently through the canoe to become stuck. As soon as this happened, one of the men quickly grabbed a rope and, forming a running noose in it, dropped over the side and secured the fish. Here it might be added that the next point of business was to bail like mad and return to shore as quickly as possible before the canoe sank.[12] Although there was special gear to catch shark, the running noose was occasionally employed by Tahitians when one of these grim-toothed monsters approached their canoe for the purpose of feeding on the smaller fish swimming about beneath the hull of the vessel.[13]

Local poisoning of freshwater streams and the quiet salt waters of the lagoons was yet another method of collecting fish, although it seems not to have been used to any great extent at the time of European contact.[14] The vegetatively derived poisons used by the Tahitians had the property of stupefying fish so that they floated helplessly to the surface, where they could be gathered by hand. There was no need for special processing of fish caught in this manner, for the poisons employed did not affect the eating quality of the meat.[15] Sydney Parkinson and John Forster agreed on three such plants employed for this purpose, while the latter noted yet another.[16] In the case of three of these, the plant was macerated and mixed with a little chopped meat of shell- or crayfish and thrown into the water. The fourth plant was a tree which produced a long, oval nut whose meat was apparently ground or otherwise reduced and, after being mixed with the chopped flesh of shell- or crayfish, was thrown into the water. This latter appears to have been the more popular.[17] The regular inclusion of a little shell- or crayfish to the poison probably served as a form of bait to attract more fish into the locally affected area.

Such a simplified technique as fish poisoning may well be ancient and could conceivably predate the development of seine and bag nets for obtaining a large quantity of fish in one operation. Its use required no real technical knowledge, and its local discovery, whether originally on Tahiti or brought in from elsewhere, was undoubtedly through accident followed by observation of results. The fact that it was no longer employed to any great extent in Tahiti when the Europeans arrived suggests that with the advent of the elongated nets, which could be quickly carried around a school of fish, and the use of weirs and bag nets in freshwater streams, this archaic and time-consuming technique was being superseded by more sophisticated methods.

Spear-, net-, and line-fishing appear to have been the principal techniques employed by the majority of Tahitians for obtaining fish in quantity. Pots and stone-walled fish traps may have been of equal importance, but, because they were not always readily observable, they were largely overlooked by the eighteenth-century European visitors. The former were basket-woven and made from a running shrub or vine called 'ie 'ie. They were used to catch "quantities of fine rock fish" as well as shellfish.[18] Captain Bligh, on the occasion of his second voyage to Tahiti, mentioned a stone weir which had recently been constructed for the chief Tinah off Point Venus. Although he failed to describe the trap, he did give us a fleeting glimpse of the religious customs observed at the completion of such a structure. At least in part, these consisted of making a special miniature altar, or marae, of stones, the entire construction being only a few feet square. On top of this altar Bligh found pieces of plaited coconut leaves and some taro. Nearby was an offertory consisting of a palm stump topped by a platform on which had been placed a coral coconut grater, some coconuts, and an empty basket. Here he was told priests had performed a ceremony of prayer to insure that the newly constructed weir would be successful in catching fish.[19]

William Ellis, writing in the early nineteenth century, described one of these stone weirs and pointed out that at that time such traps were so numerous in the shallow parts of the lagoon, or "lake" as he put it, that it seemed impossible for any fish to escape. The seaward, or deep-water, end of the trap consisted of a circular stone wall nine to twelve feet in diameter and built up from the bottom of the lagoon to the very surface of the water. On the landward edge of this masonry ring a small rectangular notch, two feet wide and six to eight inches deep, had been left in the top of the wall. Flaring out from either side of this were stone walls extending landward a distance of from fifty to one hundred yards and forming, in effect, a funnel to guide the fish into the trap. The landward-facing funnel and the rather shallow notch in the top of the circular stone wall suggest that the trap was designed to take advantage of the fish when high tide changed and the fish began seeking deeper water as the tide receded. Once caught in the funnel-like stone corridor, their instinct to seek deeper water would lead them eventually through the notch and into the circular enclosure. Here they were easily caught by nothing more than a spear or a scoop net.[20]

Such traps appear not to have been overly effective in terms of quantity caught. However, they did have the advantage of serving as holding ponds where fish could be obtained as needed. Such a holding operation should not be construed to mean that these traps served as true fishponds for the breeding and raising of fish, as occurred in the Hawaiian Islands.

In Ellis's time fish traps were the property of individuals who had sole rights to the entrapped fish.[21] Bligh's reference to a chief's having built a stone weir at least suggests the possibility that in pre-missionary times such traps were the property of the chiefly class, each chief having the right to the fish caught in his own personal weir.

Fishing With Spear and Net

Spear-fishing, especially on the reefs in the early evening, seems to have been an occupation of the multitude, rather than restricted to the more specialized fishermen. Since it required no more technical equipment than a spear and, for night fishing, a bundle of grass for a torch,[22] it seems reasonable to suggest that rich and poor, chief or servant, could participate. Certain it is that innumerable people took part in torch fishing on the reef, for George Robertson, who kept a record of lure lights on the reefs during Samuel Wallis's stay on the island, recorded one occasion when several thousand people were fishing on the southwest reef alone.[23] Since fish represented the dominant form of protein for the middle and lower classes, it seems reasonable to conclude that their fish diet was not completely under the control of the relatively few experienced fishermen who seem to have represented a class of tradesmen.

Fish spears had wooden shafts of toa or hibiscus, though some were of reed, while their single or multiple points were of hard wood.[24] The single-pointed spear, or harpoon, was barbed like an arrow,[25] but whether the multi-pronged spears were plain or notched was not reported. As could be expected, spear-fishing was not always a nighttime sport, nor was it always practiced on the reefs. Two- and three-pronged spears were occasionally thrown at fish from the beach.[26] Since none of these had a return line fastened to it, the fisherman simply dove into the water to recover it and hoped that a fish would be squirming on the end of the prongs. There was another type of spear that had numerous prongs and was thrown from a canoe into a school of fish. If the school was dense enough, one such spear could transfix two or even three fish in one toss.[27] However, it seems clear that for the common Tahitian who had mouths to feed and work to do, fishing was less a casual sport than a necessity, and therefore he often chose the most efficient way to spear as many fish as possible in the least amount of time. Nighttime spear-fishing on the reef with grass torches to lure the fish within range of his spear was both simple and effective. Thus, for the common working man, it was off to the reef when the sun went down to help feed the family.

Nets for fishing appear to have been numerous; they ranged from crude, essentially temporary, devices to ones of finely twisted and knotted cordage, the quality of construction depending upon the type of fish intended to be caught. The most common permanent net referred to was the seine, which ranged from small ones that could be handled by two men to others having a length of from forty to fifty fathoms—that is, from 240 to 300 feet.[28] Their depth varied as well, some being but 6 feet, while the larger examples were reported to be as deep as 70 feet.[29] Two other types were bag nets, used to catch fish in the rivers, and lading, or

scoop, nets. There also appear to have been casting nets, for
Máximo Rodríguez mentioned that"... in three casts of the
net, which is a very large one, they got more than sixteen
arrobas [about 400 pounds] of scad ...."[30] Since Bengt Anell
has made a case for the introduction of the circular casting
net to Tahiti in historic times, it is probable that this earlier
net referred to by Rodríguez was square.[31]

The crudest seines were of temporary construction and,
presumably, made up in a hurry when flooding rivers
brought down numerous small fry, or an especially large
school of fish showed up in the lagoon, particularly during
spawning seasons.[32] One of these, observed by Cook, was
made of a plant he thought to be a type of flag which was
twisted and tied together into a thick, heavy net ranging
from sixty to eighty fathoms in length. It was employed only
in shallow water. J. C. Beaglehole has suggested that the
flag-type of material was probably pandanus,[33] but it seems
more probable that it was the strand plant *Ipomoea pes-caprae*
(L.) R. My reasoning here is that the naturalist Parkinson,
who accompanied Cook on this particular expedition, referred to men dragging for fish with a "sort of net" made of
Convolvulus leaves.[34] Somewhat later in his text he explained
that *Convolvulus brasiliensis*, which has been identified by
Elmer D. Merrill as *Ipomoea pes-caprae*, was used to "... make
a sort of seine which they use in such ground where they
cannot use another."[35]

One other temporary seine was made of tightly inter-
woven coconut palm leaves and firmly fastened to a long
head rope. The one reported by Andia y Varela was between
eighty and one hundred fathoms in length. According to his
understanding, it was stretched across the mouths of
streams to catch small fry which became entangled in the
close mesh.[36] John Henry Martin, who was on Cook's third
expedition, saw what must have been a similarly constructed
net of coconut leaves being used in a lagoon. This same type
of temporary net was still being employed in lagoon-fishing
as late as 1797.[37]

Obviously, the size alone of such a lengthy temporary
net implies a fairly large labor force, and, judging from Martin's description, that labor force, and perhaps a bit more,

was readily available for launching the net—and for making the catch. On such occasions, the first order of business was for several manned canoes to quietly stretch the net around a large school of fish. With that concluded, the fun began. As the seine was gradually drawn in toward shallow water, the canoe men, acting like a bunch of waterborne cowboys, drove the fish landward by beating the water with long sticks. Finally, when the net had been drawn into water shallow enough to stand in, the waiting male populace moved around the inside of the net to form a closed circle. This was the moment for great expectations. The chiefs, who undoubtedly organized and directed the entire operation, were given first choice. Small seines and scoop nets were handed out to the teuteu, or servants of the chiefs, who then proceeded to catch the amount and kind of fish their particular chiefs desired. This accomplished, the entire crowd broke loose in the wildest confusion as the numerous men in the circle attempted to catch as many fish as they could. The chiefs, attempting to keep some semblance of order, desperately flayed out with their clubs, and, although they occasionally made contact, no serious harm seems to have been done. This was one of the very few times that even the women got into the act, diving into the watery melee and grasping for their own fish. Their participation in this final act of seining does not, I believe, represent an exception to the general taboo noted earlier against women's participation in saltwater fishing. After all, it was the men who surrounded the catch with a net and it was they who drove the fish into shallow water. It was only when the fish had been effectively entrapped that the women were allowed to join the action.

These temporary nets, because of their unprepared "green" construction, could not have been used for any length of time. With their eventual drying their suppleness would have been lost, and the desiccated leaves and stems would have cracked and broken under strain. Permanent nets, however, were a different matter and seem to have been owned by individuals, including chiefs.[38] They were all made of prepared cordage, the fibers of the plant employed and the size of the mesh being dependent upon its intended use. The stalks of the plant *Phaseolus truxillensis* MBK., or *pipi,* and the bark of the mati tree, *Ficus tinctoria* Forst., appear to have been generally employed.[39] The bark of another tree, variously referred to as *majagua* or *maho,* and since identified as the Tahitian purau, or *Hibiscus tiliaceus* L., was also employed for this purpose,[40] while its lightweight wood served to make floats. This identification is probably correct, since the bark of hibiscus was said to have been made into various sorts of cordage and fishing lines,[41] and thus its employment in the manufacture of nets seems probable. However, the finest seines, as well as the finest fishing lines, were made from cordage derived from the beaten stalk of the nettle, *roa,* or *Pipturus argenteus* (Forst. f.) Wedd., which was not only strong but did not rot in salt water.[42]

To make the necessary cordage for fishing lines and nets, the prepared filaments were twisted by rolling them between the hand and the thigh. Both two- and three-ply cordage was said to have been made in this manner, the former being preferred for fishing lines since it had less of a tendency to kink and thus was less apt to snap when playing a large fish.[43] Quite possibly the three-ply cordage was employed in the larger nets, the two-ply being used in the smaller ones.

There was not a great deal said in the early literature about any special deployment of the more permanent types of seines. Rodríguez mentioned obtaining large amounts of scad by seine-fishing, and Cook, on his third voyage, referred to great quantities of mackerel having been caught inside the reef by similar nets.[44] Seines measuring some ninety feet in length and nine feet in depth were taken in small canoes out into deep water and used to surround flying fish. Once the net was in place, the technique was then to frighten the fish by splashing the water with paddles and hitting the sides of the net to force them to dart into the meshes, where they became entrapped. Occasionally, when the weather was calm and several fishing canoes encountered a school of fish, they would join their nets together and surround the entire school. Any fish that were not caught in the composite net were captured by the expedient of diving into the encircled area and catching them by hand.[45]

Scoop, or lading, nets were, for the most part, auxiliary equipment used to pick up fish that had been caught in stone weirs or surrounded by a seine. However, they were used as primary fishing devices on those occasions when fishermen went out in the dark of night to lure fish around their canoes by torchlight, scooping up the unwary game in lading nets.[46]

Bag nets appear to have been limited in their use to freshwater streams and rivers. One type, whose size was not mentioned, was used in connection with a dam-and-sluice arrangement. Wherever a river was shallow, a dam with one or more sluices might be constructed. A bag net was then fixed so that its mouth covered the sluice opening where it could catch the fish driven downstream by beaters. Another, of rather small size, was designed to be operated by one person. The single mention I have found of this smaller net referred only to its use by women. Thus, on occasions when rain brought freshets down a river, the women took their individual bag nets and, a number of them forming a line across the stream, anchored the nets with their feet and pulled the mouths of the bags open with their hands. As quickly as a fish was caught, it was thrown into a waiting basket, the operation continuing until the baskets were full. It was said that even the "queen" and her mother often participated in this form of freshwater fishing.

The largest bag nets were employed at the mouths of streams to catch innumerable small fry during periods of stream freshets. Made of coconut husks sewn together, they appear to have been of a permanent construction, thus implying a certain amount of pre-treatment of the fibrous husks. Such nets must have been rather deep, for they had very wide mouths designed to receive most of the stream water. Such a bag was anchored on the bottom with stones and, apparently, was held open by hand. In this case it was not enough to wait for the fish to swim down into the bag. Instead, coconut sweeps were employed upstream to force the fry down into the net. It was claimed that bushels of these small fish were caught during a single sweep.[47]

As previously mentioned, nets were held as private property. However, the owner of a net could entrust it to another to do his fishing for him. It such cases it would seem that, whether the owner was a commoner or a chief, he must pay his entrusted net fisherman by giving him pigs, cloth, and fruit.[48] Apparently the social level of the net owner, and that of the user, could also make a difference. For example, when the Taiarapu high chief Vehiatua gave Rodríguez a net, the native to whom he entrusted it to do his fishing refused to store it in his home. He explained to Rodríguez that since the net had come from a chief, and he and his home belonged to the common class, he did not dare store it for fear of personal banishment. While searching for alternate storage quarters, Rodríguez came up against still another restriction forbidding storage of the net in a house where women had been living.[49] This latter taboo would seem to go along with the general taboo regarding women and saltwater fishing. Interestingly, however, this net-storage restriction did not seem to extend to a man's daughters, since this same fisherman later returned Rodríguez's net to him, explaining that his daughters now had a net he would use.[50] How many other precepts there were surrounding the use of nets or particular types of nets was not recorded for the period with which we are concerned. How interesting it would be to know how the fisherman's daughters came to own a net and, once acquiring it, whether they—or only their father—could use it in saltwater fishing! Obviously, the small bag nets were employed by women, but did this restrict men from using them? And if men made their own fishing gear, did the women make their own bag nets? So many questions and so few answers.

A special little contrivance was employed among the reef rock to capture octopus. Its entire construction and use was based upon a keen knowledge of the octopus's inquisitiveness and food-searching habits and was so effective that neither hook nor live bait was needed. The device consisted of a straight, polished stick of hard wood about one foot long and perhaps one half inch thick. Near one end of this a number of pieces of tiger shell cowrie were fastened, probably over a rounded stone, like the scales of a fish, until the whole was about the size of a turkey egg; a fishing line was then attached at a balancing point to allow the lure to hang horizontally. The fisherman then lowered the contraption almost to the bottom of the lagoon and began to gently jerk the line, causing the shell fragments to move as if a small fish might be wiggling around inside. The brightness of the shells, and the apparent indication that live food was readily available, caused the octopus to investigate. First one arm shot out to enclose the object, but this resulting in nothing, another and yet another arm reached out to deal with the situation until the octopus was thoroughly attached to the stick. By this time it had become so involved, and was perhaps so stubborn, that the fisherman had no trouble bringing it up and dropping it in the canoe.[51]

I have found no indication in the early literature that any of the above fishing methods were limited to any particular class or group. Since most of these techniques were employed on or inside the reef or in the numerous fresh water streams, it would seem that these were the areas of fishing open to all. However, this was not the case for the bulk of deep-water fishing. Thus, it was reported that between fifty and sixty canoes were employed out of Matavai alone during the dolphin season. Such seemingly professional fishermen also formed at least a part of the Tahitian trading fleet during the off-season between the end of the dolphin season, about March, and the beginning of that for albacore and bonito.[52] To a degree, the Tahitian fishing complex may be likened to that in modern Europe and the Americas, where sport-fishing in rivers and lakes and along the immediate shore line is potentially for everyone, while deep-water fishing is only for the well-equipped few and the experienced professional.

Line-Fishing

Line-fishing in Tahiti reflected a solid knowledge of what was required to catch any of the desired fish, as well as a clear understanding of the limits of the equipment employed. Lines, as mentioned above, were made of two-ply twisted fiber to reduce the possibility of kinking and consequent snapping. The strongest ones, made from the nettle roa, were normally reserved for taking the larger and stronger fish, such as dolphin, bonito, and albacore. Other, less demanding fish were caught on lines made from pipi

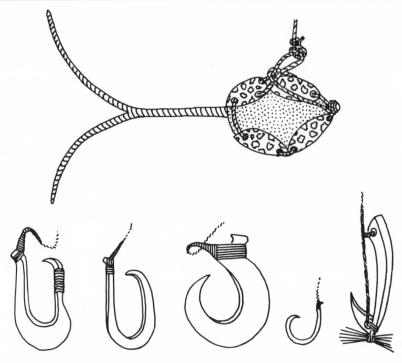

Tahitian fishing implements. Top: *octopus lure;* bottom, from left to right: *wooden fishhook with shell point, three varieties of simple shell fishhooks, composite shell fishhook of the aviti type. Redrawn from illustration in Sydney Parkinson,* A Journal of a Voyage to the South Seas . . . ,1784.

and the bark of such trees as the *mohu,* purau or hibiscus, and mati.[53] Fr. José Amich mentioned the use of coconut husk fiber as well as plaited human hair for fishing lines on the Taiarapu Peninsula.[54] However, since long strands of finely plaited hair wound around a woman's head was a special decoration for certain occasions, it is possible that in this case Amich drew an unjustified conclusion from having merely seen a ball of such prepared material.

While other fishing devices were relatively limited in range and variety, this certainly was not the case with Tahitian fishhooks. Of all the fishing paraphernalia that caught the eye of Europeans, nothing drew more admiration and respect than the wide range of fishhooks. Their construction, sometimes elaborate, involved no more complicated tools than a drill, which was probably a shark's tooth, and a file of coral or hard rock.[55] The simplest of the fishhooks, designed from one piece of shell, could be shaped and finished in a mere quarter of an hour. First a square fishhook blank was cut from its parent shell by sawing it with the sharpened edge of another bivalve, after which a file was used to shape the outside of the intended hook. This completed, a hole was drilled through the face of the blank by means of a pointed bit of stone lashed to a stick and twisted back and forth between the palms of one's hands. Once through, the hole was enlarged and the inner shape of the hook completed by again employing a coral file.[56]

Most fishhooks were made of shell, especially pearl shell, but there were others of turtle, bone, or wood. There was even one said to have been made from the thorn of a tree and used for catching very small fish.[57] Shape and type varied depending upon the kind of fish the hook was designed to catch, and whether or not it was to carry bait. Generally, according to John Forster,[58] small fish were caught on simple, one-piece shell hooks, while those of a middle size, whatever that might be, were caught on composite hooks. These latter were made of two pieces, the shank being formed from the bright, glossy part of the pearl shell, and the hook being fastened to it by lashing the two pieces together by means of small holes drilled into each segment. This type of baitless spinner, known as *aviti,* was often, if not always, decorated for decoying by the addition of hair, feathers, or a bit of thread. Parkinson described a still more elaborately decoyed hook in which the backs of two shells had been drilled and tied together to give the appearance of a fish, a small cowrie forming the head, and plaited grass the tail. Beneath this hung the hook.[59]

Wooden hooks were usually described as being very large and used for shark and, perhaps, other large fish.[60] However, there was at least one early mention of smaller hooks of wood pointed with bone.[61] Over thirty years later, these small wooden hooks were again mentioned, this time by Ellis.[62] Those seen by him were no more than two to four inches in length and remarkably strong for their size. The best were made from the small roots of the casuarina, or ironwood. The living root was first twisted into the desired shape and then allowed to grow until it had reached a size sufficiently large that the soft outer layer could be removed and the inner heart wood still would remain thick enough to serve as a hook. Some of these, so he claimed, were no thicker than a quill. The earlier use of root stock for wooden fish-hooks was attested to by Amich, who observed them in 1772.[63] Most of the large wooden fishhooks appear to have been relatively plain. However, John Forster described others as having shanks of wood or bone covered with brown mother-of-pearl and a point of turtle shell, occasionally lashed in two pieces.[64]

Bamboo poles were normally used in fishing—except for catching albacore and bonito, which required a special rig.[65] Surf fishing for sea chubb, white mullet, and the like required a long pole, the fisherman frequently standing in the sea up to his shoulders.[66] However, most fishing was done from canoes, those going outside the reef often being composed of makeshift double hulls.

One of the sure ways to locate a school of fish was to sight a large number of birds hovering over a particular spot. On such occasions the fishing canoes, with sails set, immediately embarked for the area. Approaching the school, the fishermen extended long fishing poles on either side of the canoe from which dropped lines with aviti, or unbaited spinner hooks. Making numerous passes through the school, they were assured of a good catch.[67]

Dolphin were fished with lines baited with flying fish, while red mullet was used for albacore and bonito.[68] Some of the former bait was probably caught in seine nets, as described above, but float lines were also employed. These consisted of thin white sticks six to eight feet long, weighted on one end with a stone so that they stood upright in the water. Attached to the bottom of each pole was a short line to which was fastened a bone hook baited with coconut meat. These were dropped at regular intervals as the sailing canoes moved out to the dolphin grounds some four to five miles off shore. On their return the bobbing white sticks were picked up, usually with a flying fish well caught on the bone hook, though occasionally other fish as well. As for the actual fish-

*Fishing crane used in catching albacore
and bonito. Unidentified artist.*

ing for dolphin, though the record is not clear, it would appear to have been done by trolling. However, the lines were never put out until the fisherman was sure that he had discovered a dolphin. When one was seen, the hook was immediately baited with a prepared flying fish and the line let out. Once hooked, the dolphin was played until worn out and then gradually brought alongside. However, it was never heaved over the side of the canoe by line. Instead, it was grabbed by the tail and lifted inboard.[69]

One of the most ingenious fishing devices was that employed for catching albacore and bonito. It consisted of a fixed fore-and-aft rigged crane arrangement hanging well forward of the central forepart of a double canoe. Its base was hinged by a transverse log lashed to a longer and thicker thwart which held the fore part of the two canoes at a given distance apart. This latter was firmly lashed to the gunwales of each canoe and extended about two feet beyond the starboard and port sides of the paired hulls. These latter extensions appear to have been for the purpose of running control lines from their extremities to the crane arm to assure that when that element was hoisted inboard its movement was confined to a fore-and-aft plane. The crane shaft itself formed a graceful double curve, the lower and thicker pole curving concavely upwards, and the thinner and shorter upper element, which was firmly lashed to the lower pole, arching forward and slightly downward. At the extreme point of this latter was a forked stick lashed horizontally. The fishing line appears to have passed upward through the fork and was then fastened to the upper end of the crane. The fork seems to have served as a lateral control for the fishing line, especially when the crane was lifted and the line swung inboard. In front of the crane hinge, and resting crosswise on the flat, horizontal prows of the canoes, was a movable log on which the crane arm rested when leaning forward. Its mobility appears to have been designed to raise or lower the forward angle of the crane arm by either moving the log closer to the hinge point to increase the angle of repose, or moving it forward to lessen it. A short length of rope lashed to one of the canoe prows looped upwards and was fastened at its other end to the lower portion of the crane arm. Its use appears to have been that of a stopping mechanism so that the crane could not be raised to a fully upright position, which might have resulted in its falling backwards on the fishermen. As for the hoisting gear, it was nothing more than a long, heavy rope fastened near the top of the crane and extending aft to the rear transverse thwart that held the sterns of the two canoes at a given distance apart. Although Admiral F. E. Paris's detailed drawing illustrated a single-pronged crane,[70] Bligh clearly indicated that at least some had the upper crane element divided into two pronged elements,[71] thus doubling the possibility of a strike. Such double-pronged cranes were still in use in Ellis's time, as he described and illustrated one.[72]

Fishing with this crane was the work of several men. It required at least two aft to paddle and to pull on the long rope to raise the crane when a fish was caught. Up forward only one man was needed. As the floating crane, for such it was, moved into a school of fish, it was the forward fisherman's job to bait the hook, which Ellis described as having been of pearl shell, and to swing the line forward so that the hook and bait just skimmed the water. As the canoe moved along, he would scoop up water and throw it forward, along with an occasional small fish, in an effort to attract the larger fish.[73] The minute an albacore or bonito took the hook, he signaled the men aft and they immediately raised the crane, thus pulling the fish out of water before it could fight. Swinging it inboard, the forward fisherman unhooked it and dropped it into a large oval basket which had been carried across the stern of the double canoe on the way out to the fishing grounds. However, once fishing had commenced, the basket was moved forward and fastened lengthwise between the two canoe hulls so that its lower portion was actually below water level. This served as a holding basket in which the fish could be kept alive until the canoe returned to the island.[74] Since light canoes, because of their greater speed, were frequently lashed together for this type of operation,[75] it was not uncommon for an albacore to be hooked that weighed so much that, unless great care was taken, it carried the fore part of the canoe under the water. This usually resulted in the loss of fish, hook, and line.[76]

There was no mention in the eighteenth-century published records of the type of fishhook used in albacore and bonito fishing. However, Ellis, living in Tahiti in the early 1800s, specifically mentioned that pearl shell hooks were employed. This would seem to counter John Forster's earlier observation that small and middle-sized fish were caught on pearl shell hooks, the latter being fished with composite types, and, presumably, that large fish were caught with hooks of wood. Here, unfortunately, there is the problem of what Forster regarded as a middle-sized fish. If Forster and Ellis were both correct in their observations, then albacore and bonito were regarded by Forster as of middle size. This leaves the problem of what large fish were caught with the big wooden hooks. Their use in shark-fishing was specifically mentioned as early as Captain Cook's first voyage, and was referred to much later by Ellis.[77] Since none of the existing large, early wooden hooks appear to belong to the ruvettus type,[78] it is unlikely that ruvettus was fished in Tahitian waters at the time of contact. As it presently stands, available information would seem to limit use of the large wooden hook to fishing the shark and perhaps a few other fish of comparable size, though the question should remain open.

Based upon the above record, there is no doubt that the Tahitians obtained ample protein from the sea. It is therefore of little wonder that the pig, dog, and even the chicken were not raised in any large number on the land. While the sea fed the fish at no expense to the plant economy of the islanders, the pig and the dog, at least, shared in the domestic food crops. For that reason, if none other, they could have been regarded as a somewhat wasteful commodity which could be tolerated as a delicacy but would always be limited to the excess available food that Tahitians were willing to expend on them. Although commoners did raise and eat a few of these domestic animals, their main consumption was as banquet, ceremonial, and chiefly food; as in other cultures, dearly gotten food was a symbol of importance and wealth.

Trade and Transportation

There is at least a possibility that there was a time in man's earliest beginnings when a family could fend for itself with no need to balance out necessities or material desires by trading its surpluses with its neighbors. However, it is unlikely that this isolation could have lasted for long, since man is a social animal and, while the ostensible purpose of trading is economic necessity, it can also be a viable excuse for socializing.

Agricultural and man-made products can, and do, move in simple one-to-one exchanges. However, more often than not, the movement of such goods is enmeshed in a complex skein of social, religious, and political requirements rendering these objects accessible to the members of a society. Such intricately threaded skeins are often difficult to follow within a living society, while those of a long-dead social order are nigh impossible to track. Unfortunately, the illiterate dead do not rise again, except as they have left the unintentional record of their past through archaeological debris. As it stands, the Europeans' observations tend to record the end points, as it were, of a trading mechanism whose intricate social and religious threads were lost before the explorers had time to recognize and understand them. What remains gives us a suggestion of how things moved from one person to another within the island, and what items were traded beyond Tahiti. While this part of the record is miserably incomplete, the European seafarers made up for this lack by satisfying their inborn curiosity as to the vessels employed in moving goods, the techniques of sailing, and the Tahitians' knowledge of the island world that lay broadly scattered around them.

As with all environments, Tahiti's potential for human subsistence must be gauged by its response to the material and technical resources of the people occupying the island. Using this as a measure, Tahiti's potential in the eighteenth century was more than adequate. Although only a few of its indigenous plants were used for food, the domesticated crops brought piecemeal by migrants to the island responded magnificently to Tahiti's soils and gentle weather. Meanwhile, in the surrounding ocean and quiet lagoons the varied life that swam, crawled, or fixed itself in sandy beaches or on well-washed rocks easily succumbed to the varied fishing techniques that the islanders had brought with them or had developed on the spot. All in all, the picture was one of abundance, so much so that early European vessels normally reported little trouble in refurbishing their supplies from what was not, perhaps, a genuine island surplus but certainly represented a generously adequate production of staples.

With crops so plentiful, one might question the need for trade or redistribution of native-grown food. However, not all island areas were capable of growing the full range of basic staples, either because of limited land space, or because the immediate environment did not favor the production of certain plants. The more extreme examples of this were the fe'i banana, the pia, or arrowroot, and certain of the yams which did best in the higher hills and lower mountain slopes. As for the general lack of trading for pigs and dogs, whose production seems never to have been adequate to meet the needs of the entire population, cultural restrictions—rather than blatant ecological controls—seem to have been the determining factor. Surely these animals could have been bred up to a point of being a staple in every Tahitian household, but this never seems to have happened. The Tahitians may have realized that, since these animals were fed domesticated food crops, it was more efficient for natives to eat the plant food themselves than to have it converted into meat, hence the use of animals as religious offerings, feast foods, and as gift exchanges limited to the chiefly class. It would appear that the trade and redistribution of basic staples was never too strongly formalized, most of it occurring on a level not readily observable by European travelers. However, this informal arrangement was certainly not the case with the more specialized, handcrafted goods. These, which were always regarded as more valuable than food, were prominent elements in exchanges of a more formalized nature, and their movement was thus more readily visible to the foreign explorers.

Methods of Acquiring Goods

The movement of material goods and foodstuffs throughout the population took on a variety of forms in Tahiti. At its simplest level it consisted of a request to a person, or family, for food or some item which, quite probably, was of no great value. This was interpreted by Europeans as representing an innate sense of hospitality on the part of Tahitians but, in fact, was a form of deferred exchange in which the person who received the request was forced from fear of social stigma to honor the request if it was in his power to so.[1] However, by the same token, the donor knew that he, too, was free to acquire minor needs from another under the same rules of social pressure, just as the recipient knew that at some time in the future he would have to give of what was available upon request. Thus, although the passage of goods was in one direction only in any given transaction, its reciprocity was simply deferred until a request was made by the donor, or some other individual, at some future date. The same type of deferred exchange system, though primarily involving food, was still in operation on Easter Island as late as 1945.[2] While such a system took care of what were probably minor necessities, a direct form of barter also appears to have been in operation on Tahiti. How far this extended, and what goods it included, is not known. However, Anders Sparrman reported that mountain, or fe'i, bananas were brought to the seashore by people from the interior and bartered for fish and other products of the sea.[3]

The movement of materials was also noticeable to European voyagers in the Tahitian system of forced gift exchange, a practice which still survives on such islands as Tikopia and Easter Island in the late twentieth century.[4] While gifts were often proffered freely, and Tahitians of chiefly rank customarily gave and received bundles of tapa as welcoming or departing gifts,[5] other such offerings carried a price tag. These latter were employed as a means of forcing the recipient to give in return something of value which the donor needed or desired. Since European goods were desired by all Tahitians, they quickly invoked this technique as a means of acquiring such goods in fair quantity. As John Marra pointed out, such gifts were always offered as if they came out of the generosity of some chiefly heart, but if a return was not immediately forthcoming and was not of equal or greater value, the giver was quick to show his dismay.[6] However, it was the ever-observant James Cook who soon learned that whenever a gift was proffered, the Tahitian donor let it be known in one way or another exactly what he would like in return.[7] Cook fully recognized the forced gift exchange system for what it was: an adept and gracious form of trading in which one could assure himself of obtaining something he needed or desired. Operating within the Tahitian culture, that assurance was probably strengthened by social pressures of conformity. Such exchanges were not always limited to one person's accumulation of his personal property, for there were occasions when relatives also contributed to the stock. This was observed by both Cook and William Bligh, the latter explaining that his return offering had been immediately divided among those who had, apparently, contributed their due share to the original gift.[8]

While the above techniques took care of individual and family needs and certainly accounted for considerable redistribution of materials within the island, the most conspicuous movement of goods through the populace was by periodic and formalized mass distribution. This should not be confused with the numerous feasts conducted throughout the year for a variety of ceremonial occasions. Many of these were nothing more than banquets and, in terms of the flow of goods through the community, amounted to not much more than the left-over cooked food that the guests had a right to take home after first stuffing themselves. In other words, the economic effect of such eating and entertainment, was, if anything, decidedly negative in that large quantities of food had to be gathered but were then consumed in a relatively short time. However, there were certain occasions when food or manufactured goods were brought together and redistributed. One of these, which seems to have lacked any special festivities, was briefly witnessed by Sydney Parkinson. On this occasion masses of ripe breadfruit were brought to a large open space and were divided up and handed out to members of the assemblage. To Parkinson it gave the appearance of a large breadfruit market.[9] However, there were other more formalized distributive affairs which appear to have centered on the removal of a rahui, or period during which a specified area and crop, or crops, had been under taboo so that no one could harvest them.

As described in an earlier chapter, the fundamental purpose of a rahui was to allow time for crops to increase, or for domesticated animals or seafood to breed. It could be used to taboo an individual farm, a subdistrict, or a district, or a paramount chief could declare a rahui over his entire domain. Whether or not a feast was given at the termination of an individual's personal farm rahui was not indicated in the literature. However, it would appear that a taboo over any area which included the lands of several individuals invariably terminated with a feast and a limited distribution of goods by whomever had originally prescribed the rahui. In some cases the goods so distributed amounted to nothing more than pigs and tapa cloth. However, when a chief terminated a rahui over his entire district, he gave away large quantities of items ranging from live hogs and fowl to bamboo sections filled with coconut oil, rolls of tapa, and even fully rigged canoes. Such an affair was not limited to inhabitants of the district, for it was attended by chiefs and innumerable 'arioi.[10] The fact that no plant foods were mentioned as items of redistribution tends to strengthen the notion that such basic staples moved through the population, when needed, via other systems.

The rahui termination feast may not have been the only formalized affair in which conspicuous redistribution of products was undertaken. There were occasional references to district chiefs making their rounds to collect "taxes in kind" from those living under their jurisdiction. Such collections may may have ended in some form of redistributive feast. At least we do know that at one point in 1797 "King" Pomare apologized for his lack of attention to a European, explaining that he needed to collect hogs, tapa, canoes and other items for a great feast at Papara. During these festivities his accumulation of wealth would be given out to various chiefs and *'arioi,* which would result, as he put it, in the entire island looking up to him.[11]

Perhaps because of its very conspicuousness in assembling large quantities of materials for public distribution, this technique has been accepted by some as the primary system of redistribution of goods within the island. Since such gatherings were usually conducted by chiefs, it was obviously one of the more overt chiefly means of gaining prestige, and thus a certain amount of power, over the people and chiefs subordinate to them. Correct as this view may be, one must question whether these massive redistributional affairs, which occurred only periodically, really accounted for much in comparison to the almost daily movement of goods via barter and the other less spectacular techniques already mentioned. To a degree, this method of conspicuous distribution of goods may have been a political technique aimed at gratifying the people by its apparent, and immediate, effect, but which was more cosmetic than real.

Although the record of exchange systems operating in Tahiti is fragmental at best, the techniques so briefly noted by early Europeans seem ample to have taken care of the simple distributional needs of the majority of the people. All of the basic necessities of life were grown, bred, or handcrafted on the island, and modes of distributing them wherever and whenever needed had been worked out. Thus it would appear that there was no need for external trade. However, trade there was, some of it on a regular basis. While canoes made regular passages between Tahiti and the clearly visible island of Moorea,[12] others sailed northward to the atoll of Tetiaroa, owned and operated by the Tu family from which the paramount chief was chosen. Since the atoll produced little in the way of crops, these vessels moved northward loaded with provisions and returned with quantities of coconut oil, fish, and a special fish sauce dear to the chiefly palates.[13] Farther to the west, annual voyages were made, when the winds were right, to the islands of Borabora, Taha, and Raiatea. While no trade items were specifically mentioned as being exchanged at the latter island, something special was certainly going on, since Raiateans reciprocated these Tahitian visits, also on an annual basis.[14] As for Taha and Borabora, the Tahitians were said to have brought great quantities of tapa cloth there to exchange for coconut oil, which was produced in larger quantities on those islands than on Tahiti. Though the island of Fenua ura (now Motu one), still further west and a ten-day sail from Tahiti, was said to be unpopulated, the Tahitians made occasional visits to this little atoll to collect the much-prized red parakeet feathers so important in their religious life.[15]

To the east of Tahiti, but at no great distance, lay the little high island of Mehetia, which was subject to the paramount chief of Taiarapu. Here again, annual trading trips were made, the voyages eastward being conducted during the season of the northwest winds, the return being made during the longer period of the easterly trade winds.[16] Tahitians made occasional trips to the Tuamotu atolls, taking with them tapa cloth, provisions to trade for pearls, and a special white dog hair used in decorating their breast plates,[17] but Mehetia may have served as the more customary trade center through which Tahitian goods flowed to the low islands and, in turn, products of the atolls reached Tahiti. A hint of this possible trade situation is found in a report on Tahiti's trade relations with Mehetia. Here it was stated that wooden bowls, stools, and other manufactures were shipped to the island in exchange for pearls and pearl shells, both dominant products of the atolls. By historic times fabricated iron in different forms was being sent to Mehetia, from which point it was passed on to the atolls in exchange for their local products.[18] Thus, while Tahitians were aware of the more distant islands and may even have voyaged to some of them, regular trade relations were largely limited to the Society Islands, with occasional expeditions into the western Tuamotus.

While trading canoes peacefully plied the waters beteen the islands of the Society group, this was apparently not the case for vessels whose occupants were strangers to these lands. The canoes of such foreigners were immediately raided and stripped of their cargo, as were the passengers of their personal belongings. The idea, it would seem, was not necessarily to kill the unfortunate intruders, but rather to deprive them of all that they carried. Once cleaned of their belongings, they were allowed to go free. However, any resistance precipitated a fight and, in the case of one vessel that landed on Mehetia, resulted in all but a young boy and a woman being killed. This raiding seems also to have applied to any vessels whose passengers were obviously in distress or, for that matter, even a known trading vessel which may have crashed on a reef.[19]

So firmly implanted was the above custom that it was a common sport for the supply vessel of a chief who might be visiting his counterpart in another district of Tahiti to be treated to a rough-and-tumble, though friendly, raiding party made up of the subjects of the hosting chief. However, in such cases the chief saw to it that his own food was removed from the canoe before the commencement of the raid.[20] Robbing a foreign vessel, then, was a special traditional device which allowed new, though fortuitously encountered, goods to enter the public domain. What makes it appear incongruous is that stealing among Tahitians was said to have been punished by death,[21] and this was a clear case of forced robbery! Obviously, then, the raiding of a foreign or stranded vessel was not regarded as theft but rather was viewed as a permissible means of gaining new goods.

This custom could explain the Tahitian trait that caused Europeans no end of trouble—constant theft. When the first European vessel arrived in Tahitian waters, the natives dutifully attempted a massive raid on it, only to be beaten off by superior weaponry of powder and shot.[22] It took only this first defeat for the Tahitians to learn that they were ill-prepared to strip the well-armed European vessels and crews. However, this initial failure in no way denied them their traditional right to rob foreigners of anything that they could get their hands on. Little wonder that the early voyagers voiced consternation over the fact that chiefs and commoners alike showed no compunction about stealing what they could of European goods.[23] Nor did it help relieve this consternation to have the chiefs intercede on behalf of thieves in an effort to have their punishment reduced from that prescribed by some ship's captain.[24] After all, in the eyes of the chiefs the poor prisoners may have upset the Europeans a little, but they certainly had committed no Tahitian crime. Since, according to some voyagers, much of this stolen property ended up in the chiefs' hands,[25] it is possible that another aspect of the custom dictated that valuable items so obtained should be turned over to the subject's chief.

Although these actions were a constant annoyance to Europeans, they fairly admitted that if an object had been taken which proved of no value to the light-fingered heister, it was returned or left where it would surely be found.[26] In fact, the Tahitians thoroughly enjoyed the joke on themselves when they lifted handkerchiefs from George Forster and Sparrman only to find that the gentlemen were using sheets of tapa cloth from the island which were of no value to the pilferers.[27] Thus, although the Europeans viewed the Tahitians as unmitigated thieves, it would seem that in terms of native custom, the Tahitians were living well within their customary code of proper ethical behavior. To them the Europeans and their ships were no different from a foreign canoe with its occupants, and it was thus quite proper to treat them in the same manner and divest them of what they had. The only difference lay in the superior weaponry which forced the Tahitians to take a more indirect approach to the matter.

Transportation

Just as necessary as exchange techniques for the economic well-being of a culture are the physical means of moving goods and people from one place to another. On a continental land mass nothing more technical than foot trails

trodden by human beasts of burden are required for the
extensive movement of goods, ideas, and people over vast
areas. Probably the finest example of this type of network
was the prehistoric trade development in Mesoamerica,
where Toltecs, Zapotecs, and Mayas appear to have been in
continuous contact for hundreds of years. However, on a
small island in the middle of the Pacific, foot trails become
secondary, while the development of water navigational
skills and the vessels to match them becomes vitally important. They determine how far one can, or wishes to, move
about and, in the process, what things are available for trade
in other parts of the oceanic world. Obviously, Tahitians had
already developed a degree of seamanship when they discovered and settled their island over a period of years. What
we do not yet know, however, is whether the sailing and
navigational prowess of the early Tahitians was sufficient to
undertake extended two-way voyages. Certainly at the time
of European discovery there were crafts capable of such
long-range voyaging.

Canoes and other types of watercraft were the Tahitians'
primary means of transportation. As a result, foot trails received only casual, if not perfunctory, attention. Coastal
tracks and those running up into the foothills were reasonably maintained and well compacted from constant use.
However, those which extended up into the remoter parts of
valleys and across the mountains appear to have been little
more than unattended pathways. These often followed the
narrow crests of steeply sloping hills, while others, especially on the windward side, crossed the bare faces of sea
cliffs. These later amounted to nothing more than narrow
ledges whose outer edges dropped vertically to where the
sea pounded the rocks hundreds of feet below.[28] Although
there were a number of these trails which followed up valleys and crossed the mountains, they became so impassable
during periods of heavy rain that the Tahitians turned to
their canoes to make the circuitous trip rather than face the
muddy spectacle of the rugged interior.[29] Nor could they
possibly have made it through the upper valleys, for some of
the trails amounted to nothing more than the beds of

streams, which would have been flooded during heavy rains.[30]

Since Tahitians lacked the wheel and had no pack animals, loads were carried on the human back or hung from each end of a four-foot-long pole whose balance point rested on one shoulder of the packer.[31] Humans, too, were carried astride men's shoulders, though the sick and the elderly were given the comfort of a crude litter which was likened by Cook to a handbarrow.[32]

From the description above, there seems little doubt that Tahitians were not land-oriented in terms of transportation. Paths could get them from one place to another without having to go through dew-wet grass or snagging burrs, but beyond that there was no need to perfect them. As for bridges, or even a slippery log, why should one bother? The Tahitians had grown up both in and on water, so that wading a stream or borrowing a canoe to cross a stretch of deep water came naturally.

It was on the water that the Tahitians showed off their resourcefulness to best advantage. It was here, where no man-made furrows forced movement along already determined lines, that they excelled. The ocean and lagoons offered myriads of routes over which one could move and leave no record of the passage. The sea could be kind, nigh generous to a fault, when the fish were running and the wind was right. But it could also be demanding of travelers and the crafts they chose to sail in. While most Tahitians enjoyed the unruffled waters of the protected lagoons or fished at no great distance beyond their abrupt-walled barrier reefs, a few others committed themselves to deep-water sailing to other islands of the Society group as well as a few that lay beyond it.

The simplest craft to be found in Tahitian waters was the raft. So simple, and perhaps so temporary, was its construction that the only record of its existence in the eighteenth century is in wash drawings by Parkinson. One of these illustrates a small, flat platform of poles squared off at both ends and being paddled through the water by its lone occupant.[33] Still more intriguing is what appears to be a rough sketch of a fair-sized, high-decked raft which carries a typical Tahitian sprit sail.[34] If this interpretation of the craft is correct, one would tend to question the early use of kites as standard towing devices for Tahitian rafts as mentioned by James Hornell.[35]

Rafts may well have been used by the poor, while larger ones may have been employed for exceptionally awkward or heavy loads or, for that matter, may have simply constituted an efficient technique for shipping lumber from one place to another around the island. Certainly they were never the dominant craft, that position being easily held by the canoe.

Types of Canoes

Canoes were divided into two basic hull designs known as the *va'a* and the *pahi*. Of the two, the former was used for more varied purposes than the latter, whose primary employment was in deep-water voyaging.[36]

The va'a ranged in length from a mere ten feet to as much as seventy-two feet, the smallest ones being nothing more than hollowed-out logs, or dugouts. In fact, the bottoms of all larger va'a-type canoes were formed by two or more hollowed-out logs whose ends were made to abut one another; they were then drilled and lashed together with cords to bind them firmly end to end. According to Joseph Banks, the bottom, or base, of the log hull was flat, though Cook claimed it was rounded and the hollow log dressed down to a thickness of about three inches. Early illustrations suggest that both men may have been correct, vessels seeming to have either one or the other basal configuration. Regardless, the sides were essentially vertical and, on the larger vessels, raised by the addition of one, or occasionally two, planks or strakes set on edge, the height from bottom to gunwale never exceeding three to three-and-one-half feet.

The sides of the central portions of these vessels were straight but not parallel; the stern, apparently where it rose out of the water, was from eighteen to twenty inches in width, and the fore part was about one third smaller. Up front the cutwater of the va'a beveled smoothly into a vertical knife-like edge which was overlaid by a horizontally projecting flat board extending, on the larger canoes, from four

Double sailing canoe of the va'a type off the island of Taha, Society Islands. Note the small raft in the lower right foreground. Unsigned wash drawing.

to as much as eight feet forward of the hull. This plank, according to Louis Antoine de Bougainville, served to keep the vessel from plunging during heavy seas.[37] As for the stern of the vessel, the entire hollow hull rose out of the water in a curve and, often narrowing with height, was squared off at its terminus. On very small va'a this rise amounted to only a slight upward trend of the hull,[38] while on sailing and fishing vessels of this type the upward curve might, according to Banks, reach a height of from four to five feet. However, this estimate may be slightly off, for early illustrations indicate a somewhat greater stern height was employed on some vessels of this class.[39] There was probably an upward limit to the curving stern pieces when it came to sailing, since there were other va'a, designed for paddling within lagoon waters, whose sterns rose as high as fourteen feet into the air. A good part of this height, however, was not made up of the hull, but consisted of an upright, carved pillar which might be several feet in circumference and was hollowed out, presumably to reduce its weight. Smaller and thinner carved pillars might also be found on sailing va'a.[40] According to the missionaries, the stern height, including the pillar, reflected the degree of chiefly status of the vessel's owner.[41]

The other type of canoe, the pahi, had a far more sophisticated hull design than did the va'a. It had what was essentially a keel, wedge-shaped on its outside, or bottom, which was hollowed the length of the desired hull by abutting the ends of shaped logs and lashing them together with cords pulled through holes drilled at the ends of each keel segment. On either side of this basal member, diverging board panels were lashed, forming, at this point in construction, a V-shaped cross-section. On top of this latter row of boards was lashed a second range consisting of vertically convex boards designed to curve in sharply near their upper edge. On top of this was sewn a vertical strake, the top edge of which had been carved into a gunwale. The resulting construction gave the hull of a pahi a cross-section resembling the shape of an inverted spade in a deck of cards. What was especially unique in the construction of this hull was the use of interior timbers, or ribs, which strengthened the entire

Double sailing canoe of the pahi type at Raiatea, Society Islands. Unsigned wash drawing.

vessel. The pahi again differed from the va'a in that both prow and stern rose out of the water in an upward curve — the prow, however, always being lower than the stern. Where the hull rose out of the water, it narrowed with height and was capped at its highest point with a single figure of a man carved out of a block of wood. While the main body of the canoe hull remained open between the gunwales, the rising prow and stern sections were decked over — a wise precaution in a voyaging canoe.

These vessels, because of their more limited use for voyaging, were never small, their range in length being from thirty to as much as seventy-six feet. Banks described the hulls as widening slightly in the middle, one being eighteen inches at the midpoint of the hatch and thirty-six inches directly below at the bilge. The difference, however, between this and the extreme points where the two ends of the hull curved out of the water was no more than three or four inches. This is obviously the configuration for two of the pahi illustrated by Parkinson and John Webber.[42] However, Cook, on his first voyage, must have seen a somewhat different pahi, for he described it as being broad in the middle.[43] It thus seems possible that this vessel was the same kind of broad-beamed pahi later illustrated by Webber on the occasion of Cook's third voyage to Tahiti and considered by some as rather un-Tahitian.[44] Just as there were both round- and flat-bottomed va'a, there seems little reason why there could not have been a range in style among vessels of the pahi type.

While there was no question that va'a were constructed locally on Tahiti, as they seem to have been on the other Society Islands to the west, this is not true of the pahi. When Cook first arrived in Tahiti, he claimed to have seen only six pahi, and those, he was told, were not made there.[45] Banks, after leaving Tahiti and having moved through the leeward islands to the west, seemed to support Cook's view when he stated that the va'a was the only craft used by Tahitians, but that Raiatea, Huahine, and other islands employed both the pahi and the va'a, the former being used for long voyages.[46] However, prior to Banks's visit to the leeward islands, he and Cook had visited the domain of

Tahiti iti on the Taiarapu Peninsula. There he was not only amazed at the vast number of large canoes that he saw, but he reported that they were of a different build than those of Tahiti nui and had higher heads and sterns.[47] As we have already noted, the Tahitian va'a was never raised at the head, that portion being formed by a horizontally projecting board. However, the pahi did curve upward at the prow. Here one might reason that these canoes at Tahiti iti were neither va'a nor pahi, but were of some other construction which failed to be detailed in the early literature. This argument, however, does not hold up, for only three years after Banks's observations Domingo Boenechea also commented about the vast number of large canoes on the peninsula, 1,500 to 2,000 by his guess,[48] while his companion, Juan de Herve, added that each chief had his own pahi.[49] It thus seems probable that the canoes seen by Banks were, in fact, pahi; perhaps since he and Cook spent so little time on the peninsula of Tahiti iti, he failed to recall the pahi's existence when summarizing his data on canoes after leaving the Societies. In fact, he even failed to mention the six pahi seen by Cook at Tahiti when he stated that the va'a was the only craft employed on that island.

Should the above reasoning be correct, it would appear that by 1769 pahi in some numbers were to be found not only on the leeward islands of the Societies, but on the Taiarapu Peninsula as well. Since their seemingly large number at this latter location virtually eliminates the possibility that they were all traded in from Raiatea or another of the leeward islands,[50] one must conclude that pahi were, even then, being constructed in Tahiti iti. Since Tahiti iti was, at this time, a quite separate governmental unit from Tahiti nui, the fact that Cook, who was almost certainly referring to the area around Matavai where his ship was anchored, saw only six of these craft is not necessarily surprising. Also, the statement made to him that these vessels had not been made there may have meant that they had been made in Tahiti iti. Thus, the six pahi could have represented gifts or articles of trade from the leeward islands, possibly Raiatea, or from physically adjacent Tahiti iti on the Taiarapu Peninsula. On the face of things, all of this may not be too important except

that it suggests not only a close cultural tie at this time between Tahiti iti and the leeward islands, but further that the
pahi-type vessel was, in 1769, only beginning to diffuse into
Tahiti nui. By 1774, when Cook returned on his second voyage, pahi-type hulls were being constructed on Tahiti nui.
This he proved conclusively in his detailed drawing of the
double war canoe which was being constructed at that time
by Tu, who wished to give it the grand name of *Britannia*.[51]

The broad distribution and use of the va'a in the Society
Islands can be readily understood: its simplified constructional requirements allowed almost anyone to build his own
craft. In its smallest form it was nothing more than a
carved-out log, and its growth in size amounted to little
more than a horizontal and vertical extension of the basic
dugout unit. The fact that even in its finest form it reflected
its humble beginnings suggests that the original vessels
which brought the first settlers to Tahiti were simplified va'a
which only later evolved into larger and finer craft. After all,
even the record left us from Cook's time indicated that simple dugouts and lofty-sterned vessels—representing a complete evolutionary range of these craft—existed side by side.
However, this was not the case for the pahi. There were no
obvious progenitors, unless the broad-beamed pahi mentioned by Cook and illustrated by Webber represented such a
craft. Instead, the pahi seems to have suddenly appeared in
Tahitian waters full blown, or nearly so. The inference would
thus seem to be that its original development took place
outside this area, and its arrival represented contact influence from elsewhere. E. S. C. Handy, with little comparative
proof, suggested that it arrived late, along with his so-called
Arii Culture of Polynesians who came to dominate the government of the islands.[52] However, lacking more recent research, I tend to agree with James Hornell's argument of
1936 for the pahi's having had its origin in the nearby
Tuamotu atolls, where voyaging canoes were a virtual necessity and trade contacts with the Society Islands had become
established.[53]

Like numerous other Polynesian canoes, Tahitian crafts
of the same type could be lashed together to form highly

stable double canoes, or they could remain single. In this latter case, however, a float attachment on one side was needed to keep the slender hull from capsizing. This device was nothing more than a narrow log of light wood equal to or sometimes two-thirds the length of the vessel. Occasionally this might be trimmed like the hull of a canoe or given a triangular cross-section. It lay parallel to the canoe on the port, or left, side at a distance ranging from six to ten feet, depending upon the size of the vessel to be balanced. Its primary connection to the vessel's hull was by a main spar lashed athwart the gunwales at or just forward of the midpoint of the vessel and indirectly connected downwards to the float in the water by a series of small sticks inserted at angles. The after spar, similarly lashed across the gunwales near the stern of the canoe, was much lighter and arched downwards to make a direct attachment to the float.[54] While such an outrigger did much to balance a narrow canoe, it was not, and is not, totally foolproof, as this writer and also the journal of Sir Joseph Banks can attest![55]

Single outrigger canoes could be paddled or sailed, though the ones under about twenty-five feet in length were usually, if not solely, moved by paddle.[56] For a single-hulled craft to carry sail it needed no only a mast, which was stepped just forward of the midpoint of the canoe, but also a combined shroud and balance board. This extended out over the water on the starboard, or right, side of the narrow vessel directly opposite the main spar of the outrigger, which might also carry an extension of these boards. To this, as well as to the outrigger spar, were fastened paired shroud lines which supported the mast laterally, while two stays, fastened fore and aft, kept the mast from moving in that plane.[57] To trim the vessel when under sail a man crawled out on the balance board, or heavy stones were employed for the same purpose.[58]

The sail of this type of vessel was made of especially strong mats sewn together. Set fore and aft, it was narrow and tall, its curved upper portion extending about one-third higher than the mast, and the leech rounding blade-like back to a point directly above the masthead. While two-thirds of the luff was lashed to the mast, the foot and leech of the sail were fastened to a boom at the base which, judging from early illustrations, curved or formed a rounded angle upwards and then, thinning with height, became a form of sprit which held the sail spread out. This allowed the vessel to sail remarkably close to the wind. However, there was no easy means by which the sail could be reefed or furled in bad weather, except to unlash it at the foot and roll it up to some extent. Supplementary features consisted of either a bunch of young branches of a tree or from one to three outward-facing funnel arrangements of wickerwork, placed at the very top of the mast. Also, from the highest point of the sail hung one or two long streamers, or pendants, of feathers and bark.[59] While the purpose of the branches or wickerwork funnels at the masthead is unknown, José de Andia y Varela claimed—with some reason—that the feather streamers were used to quickly ascertain change in wind so that the sail could be trimmed accordingly.[60]

Another contrivance, consisting of a light rectangular framework lashed vertically to a mast, appeared on some, but not all, sailing canoes. In Parkinson's drawings, this was fastened to the front of a mast crosswise to the length of the vessel and had a single crosspiece at the midpoint of the two longer sides of the frame.[61] A drawing made some eight years later by Webber of a similar device, but having a greater number of crosspieces, suggested to Edward Dodd that this was a ladder for mounting the mast.[62] However, its lack of consistent use, and the considerable distance between the rungs in those illustrated by Parkinson, would seem to make this an unlikely supposition. Its spotty occurrence perhaps indicates that it was an attempt to strengthen a weak mast.

While some of the larger Tahitian canoes were designed to go double, especially those va'a with extremely high sterns, many of the others were adaptable to the exigencies of the moment.[63] Matching single canoes could be made double by removing their outriggers and lashing the two hulls nearly together, or one could reverse the order and reinstate the hulls to singleness. Canoes going double were usually spaced from three to four feet apart and kept at this

distance by a series of spars lashed athwart the two hulls.[64]
Held in this manner, a portion of the area over and between
the two hulls could be decked over as a flooring for one or
two cabins, or open-sided shelters. On va'a-type double
canoes these were occasionally set well forward, even over
the horizontal bow boards.[65] Since this would have been a
rather cumbersome, if not wet, location for deep-water
sailing, I suggest that these bow cabins were used within the
lagoons and probably represented the little structures, mentioned in an earlier chapter, which chiefs were wont to un-
load for temporary housing on land. Other cabins, better
fitted for travel beyond the reefs, were located aft or amidships; Parkinson even illustrated a two-masted pahi double
canoe with one cabin well forward and another amidships.[66]

Sailing double canoes carried one or two masts to which
were attached the same kind of sails as those described
above. In the case of a single mast it was placed forward and
stepped between the hulls on a wide, heavy planking set
across the two hulls and extending several feet beyond them
on both sides. These extensions served to fasten the shroud
lines and may have aided in trimming the vessel during
heavy weather.[67] When two masts were employed, these
were either stepped on planking between the two hulls,[68] as
with the single-masted vessel, or one was placed in each hull
of the double canoe.[69] These two-masted vessels also carried
transverse planking extensions abreast of the masts to carry
the shroud lines.[70] The single-masted double canoe of the
va'a type in Webber's fine illustration of 1777 does not, oddly
enough, carry the seemingly characteristic overhanging
shroud planks, as do those illustrated some years earlier.
Instead, its shrouds are fitted more in the fashion of the
Tuamotu sailing double canoe.[71] This configuration may be
additional evidence of the influence of Tuamotu construction
techniques on Tahitian canoe-building.

It should be noted in passing that Tahiti's master canoe
builders were also employed in making double canoes for
strictly ceremonial purposes, as well as the giant double-
hulled craft employed in naval battles, described in the following chapter. Even without including these more
specialized vessels, however, I believe one can fairly state

that the construction of canoes, especially the pahi, represented Tahitian craftsmanship at its best. This is not to say that al! canoes represented the epitome of the woodworker's art, for undoubtedly the smaller, single-hulled vessels were less perfectly finished. As Boenechea pointed out, the canoes of commoners were all of the "flimsiest construction."[72]

Canoe Construction

Although it was reported that every fisherman built his own canoe, and the great chief Tu, at least, maintained a regular dockyard for the construction of his vessels,[73] not all commoners may have been adept in this specialty. This possibility is suggested by the rather concentrated production of medium-sized canoes on the east, or windward, coast of Tahiti nui, an observation reported by Wilson during his trip around the island.[74] It seems possible that the limited agricultural potential of this zone, due to extensive sea cliffing and the absence of broad valleys, may have aided in the development of what appears to have been a regional specialization. Since none of these vessels was of the larger variety customarily used by chiefs, it is likely that they were designed to be traded to other areas of the island in exchange for needed foodstuffs.

Canoes required wood, and, since the coastal plain had largely been taken over for agriculture, the source of most lumber had to be the hills, upper valleys, and mountains of the interior. Fortunately, these areas were capable of furnishing a wide assortment of trees which were found suitable for one or more of the elements that made up a canoe. Parkinson listed twelve such trees, and in 1797 the missionaries added the names of three more to this rather substantial list.[75] Interestingly enough, two of the trees so noted represented food-producing domesticates, the vi and the breadfruit, which had been brought to the island by Polynesians.

While the building of a ceremonial canoe, and most likely a war canoe, was marked by a variety of religious ceremonies at critical stages of its construction,[76] such activity was probably conducted on a generally reduced scale for the more common canoe. Quite probably a vessel's intended use and ownership predetermined the degree of ceremonialism to be employed during its construction.

The most difficult job in preparing to build a canoe was the initial felling of the necessary trees. According to Banks, to fell a large one required the labor of a number of people during several days.[77] Samuel Wallis, who seems to have actually seen a large tree cut down and split, reported that an adz of a tough, greenish stone was employed in this operation.[78] Should a felled tree be marked for use as the hollowed-out log forming the bottom of a va'a, it was shaped and hollowed by the use of adzes. Banks claimed a log could be hollowed with Tahitian stone tools as quickly as a European carpenter could do it with iron implements.[79] However, he later amended this statement by explaining that such speed was accomplished only where there was ample room for a heavy adz to break out long splinters of wood.[80] Since the early missionaries reported that hollowing was accomplished by burning,[81] it is probable that the size and character of the particular wood being dealt with dictated the technique to be employed.

Planking, so vital in the construction of both types of Tahitian canoes, was obtained in a rather ingenious manner. Once a tree had been felled, the trunk was cut into logs whose lengths matched that of the planks which were to be split from it. This accomplished, one end of the log was heated, though it is not known by what means, until it began to crack lengthwise. Hardwood wedges were then driven into these cracks to split them down the length of the log. In this manner, rough boards were obtained measuring as much as two feet in width and up to twenty feet in length. The faces of these planks were then adzed down until the board had a thickness of about one inch. While a number of men might have worked on a single plank, this kind of dubbing must have gone slowly, for the stone tools required constant sharpening, each carpenter carrying with him a coconut shell full of water and a whetstone for this purpose.[82] In the hands of a good carpenter these stone adzes, which were smaller than those used for felling,[83] could be made to cut off a skin of wood no greater than one-sixteenth of an inch in thickness.[84]

Since no canoe planks were ever bent to shape, each board had to be individually carved to fit its particular location in the vessel, be it the bilge of a pahi or the upturned stern of a va'a.[85] Such carving was accomplished not only with stone adzes, but also with gouges and chisels made from human leg or upper arm bones, the same material even being used for drills.[86] The final touch was to smooth each wooden element. This followed several methods, probably depending upon the fineness to which the surface was to be smoothed. One of these, probably for coarse work, employed nothing more than a certain type of coral, while another involved the use of coral with sand.[87] Banks mentioned not only the use of a coconut husk to rub coral sand over wood, but also the employment of the rough skin of a ray for smoothing.[88]

With the completion of the various elements of a canoe, preparations were begun for tying the entire thing together, dowels and other such devices never having been employed to fix one board to another. At this time all adjacent elements had to be matched with one another so that the holes to be drilled along the margins of each board were sure to be opposite those of adjoining members. For va'a these holes appear to have been set in pairs on each board, with several inches separating each set of paired holes. However, this does not seem to have been the case for pahi, for which opposing holes were evenly spaced along the edges of planks.[89] The drilling of these holes was, according to Banks, the most difficult operation of building a canoe. The tool used was nothing more than a sharpened human bone set into the center of a stick which was, apparently, set crosswise to the axis of the drill, giving it the form of a gimlet.[90] When the drilling was completed, the entire hull of the canoe was mocked up to be sure that all segments fitted properly. In the case of a va'a the hollowed-out log forming the keel was set on blocks and the other boards wedged together and held in place with stanchions.[91] However, the narrow keel of a pahi apparently made the use of blocks difficult, and so the keel was literally hung by ropes extending from the roof of the canoe shed in which the work was carried on. The remaining sections of the vessel were then forced together and held in place by the usual stanchions.[92]

With all parts trimmed and fitted, it was time to caulk and sew the vessel together. The edges of each contacting segment of the canoe were first smeared with prepared resin and the finely beaten, dried husk of coconut.[93] Both the Tahitian apple, or vi, and the breadfruit tree produced a sap capable of being used for caulking.[94] That from the breadfruit tree was prepared by wrapping the gummy material around a series of oily candlenuts which had been skewered, one on top of another, onto the midrib of a coconut leaf. The nuts were then lit, and the sap, being heated, was allowed to drip into a container of water, after which the water was squeezed out of it and it was then ready to be used as a caulking compound.[95] Unfortunately, the Europeans did not describe the preparational procedures for the resin of the vi.

Once the edges were covered with caulking, each element of the canoe was immediately forced into its proper location, and braided coconut fiber rope was passed through the prepared holes and brought up tightly.[96] To obtain maximum leverage in this operation a forked stick was employed, the butt end of one branch of the fork serving as a sort of fulcrum. The rope which had been passed through the adjoining sewing holes was twisted around the other branch of the fork, which was then used to lever the rope tight. When full strength had been exerted to stretch the rope as far as possible, a peg was driven into the hole to wedge the rope firmly in place.[97]

With the completion of the difficult job of sewing the hull together, there was left only the simpler operation of completing the superstructure of the vessel. However, a canoe once completed had to be maintained if it were to remain useful. Since coconut fiber tended to rot when in long contact with salt water, it was necessary from time to time to cut loose all of the old sewing cords and apply new ones. At such times all boards and fittings were examined for wear.[98] No wonder canoes were hauled up on land when not in use and placed under special canoe sheds.[99] These were open-ended affairs and were, apparently, as wide and as long as was necessary to cover the single or double canoe to be housed. They had no walls and, at least in the larger sheds, the roofs curved upwards from the ground like a Gothic arch, the whole being heavily thatched down to, or within a few feet of, the ground.[100] Such care of canoes was indeed warranted, for, although the description of their construction sounds simple enough, even a medium-sized canoe made with stone and bone tools was said to require nearly ten months of work. Later, with the advent of iron, this time period was reduced to about thirty days.[101]

Such seaworthy vessels are never born—they evolve bit by bit, reflecting, as it were, the increasing knowledge of wave, wind, and navigational aids of their builders. It is the attempt to live with, but not conquer, the natural elements of the ocean that presents man with the creative challenge to build upon his cultural heritage and, using the environmental potential surrounding him, create the watercraft best suited to his needs and desires. Not all cultures have cared to accept the challenge, nor have all been in a geographic position to do so. Those that did, however, have presented the world with a fine array of vessel types, making it clear that the oceans require no single design for living on their ever-changing surfaces. The voyaging va'a and pahi represented the Tahitian culture's answer to this challenge. Even though the creation of the latter vessel may have had its roots in the Tuamotus, or elsewhere for that matter, knowledge of its design and construction technique had been absorbed into Tahitian culture and surfaced with that culture's own peculiar stamp upon it.

Tahitian sailing canoes, as we know them, had at least two characteristics which we would have regarded as bothersome. Since their washstrakes were purposely kept low for paddling, and their hatch was open throughout the greater length of the hull, they shipped water easily and had to be bailed by hand almost continuously.[102] Their sails, although efficient in catching the wind, could not be lowered or furled in bad weather except by unlashing the foot and rolling it up a little.[103] This inadequacy occasionally resulted in upset or dismasting, though the common trick in the event of a squall was to luff up and hold her there, even if it meant diving overboard and manually holding her head into the wind.[104] Troublesome as this may seem, to a Tahitian who had virtually been born and brought up in water, it was probably only a minor inconvenience. After all, even when an outrigger was upset and her sail was resting in the water, no other vessel came to assist in righting her.[105]

Navigational Limits of the Tahitians

Sailors the Tahitians had, as well as the vessels to put them in. Navigators, however, represented a more limited class of people with highly specialized knowledge. Since they lacked a magnetic compass, their cardinal points were two—the rising and the setting of the sun which, of course, changed with the seasons of the year. Their compass card was the horizon of the sea around them and was visually divided into sixteen named segments. These served to designate the direction in which any island lay from one's starting point, and they also served as a means of control by which one could determine the angle at which swell, wave, and wind struck the vessel upon leaving port. These factors helped to set the initial heading of the vessel, and their change in direction, as determined by the horizon compass card, had to be observed to maintain one's proper heading.

Although Tahitians were good at predicting the weather for about twenty-four hours in advance, longer predictions were, like our own, only occasionally correct.[106] Since some voyages between islands took several days of open-sea navigation, unpredicted bad weather and low cloud cover were occasionally encountered. At such times their horizon compass card was not operational. Thus, while any change in the angle of attack by swell or wave could not be easily established, the long feather pendants that hung from the peak of the sail reacted quickly to a change in wind direction and were, therefore, of some navigational help.[107] As for clear evenings, the navigators knew the celestial heavens of their own latitude and had long ago determined which stars would lead them to which islands within their range of navigational knowledge.[108]

The two factors which Tahitian sailors could not determine when once out of sight of land were the direction and strength of ocean currents. On short runs between islands the locations of currents could surely be determined through constant travel. Thus, if a consistent deviance was noted in raising a given island, a correction would eventually be built into the sailing directions for that particular piece of land. This, however, was an essentially unusable technique for long voyages of exploration during which a vessel would be out of sight of land for days on end. While latitude within the limits of one's original reference point might be determined by the change in location of known heavenly bodies, there was no observational technique, or primitive instrumentation, that allowed the Tahitians to determine their own longitude on the high seas, let alone that of any island that they might discover. Unfortunately, even the voyage of a Hawaiian-style double canoe from Hawaii to Tahiti in 1976, conducted to prove the accuracy of ancient Polynesian navigational techniques over great distances, established little or nothing in this regard. After all, in 1976 the geographic position of the islands was already known, and the force and direction of the various currents to be encountered had long been charted, thus allowing course corrections for their set. Based upon the plotted track of this experimental vessel, such corrections appear to have been taken into consideration during the voyage southward, something no ancient Polynesian mariner would have been capable of doing.[109] While populating the Pacific islands in prehistoric times obviously required intentional, or accidental, distant voyaging, such journeys were probably one-way affairs, legendary accounts to the contrary notwithstanding. Here one must remember that such unwritten stories take on new elements in the telling; over the years European and Polynesian ships' crews provided much geographic material for such aggrandizing additions to the legends that had come down from the unwritten past.

Tahitian claims to voyaging fame rest mainly on their knowing the names of numerous islands which early Europeans were eager to locate in order to advance their own explorations. As for their actual sailing activities, George Forster concluded that they were limited to short runs between islands.[110] However, Banks claimed that the Polynesian navigator Tupaia set about twenty days as the maximum duration a crew could last on an intentional voyage without refurbishing supplies,[111] a figure somewhat supported by information supplied to Bougainville.[112] It was this same Tupaia whose great list of island names not only impressed Cook in 1769, but so caught the imagination of Banks, an otherwise stable naturalist, that he came to write that Tupaia had personally visited most of these seventy-odd islands.[113] This same statement was to be repeated later by an equally staid naturalist, John Forster.[114] However, after checking Cook's own record of Tupaia's list, it becomes clear that the number of islands which Tupaia claimed to have visited is merely twelve, all but two being within the cluster that forms the Society Islands group![115] This reduction in no way should be thought of as a disparagement of Tupaia's navigational skills nor, even more importantly, of his knowledge of other islands. Whether all of the names noted by Tupaia, as well as those listed by the Spaniards, represent individual islands and complete atolls, or whether individual islets within a single atoll have helped to expand the list unduly, will never be known. Since the earlier names of innumerable islands have been lost for all time, many that appear on these lists may never be geographically identified. However, perhaps all is not lost.

While Tupaia may have been, and probably was, a very exceptional geographer in that he had acquired a considerable knowledge of other islands, the directions he gave for some of them were quite wrong, occasionally even the reverse of their true locations. This would certainly suggest that their existence was not learned via direct exploratory journeys, since Tupaia was also a navigator whose very life on the high seas depended upon accuracy of direction. On the contrary, a more logical assumption would be that over the years at least one vessel from each of these wrongly located islands had become lost and had landed on one of the Society Islands from a direction that did not accord with the true location of the land from which it had come. The crews of such vessels could be expected to report the name of their home island, and perhaps others nearby, just as Bligh and Wilson had been queried about the islands that they had seen during their voyages.[116] Since such waifs were possibly no longer sure of the true location of their island home, they, or their host listeners, may have taken the location to be in the direction from which the craft had descended upon the particular island raised within the Societies. Since some, if not many, would have been single occurrences, the knowledge of these islands and the presumed locations would not necessarily have become common information—hence their inclusion on some lists and not on others. Such accidental voyages were common in the South Pacific, a list of over one hundred and fifty having been recorded.[117] The Europeans apparently never thought to ask Tupaia and the other native navigators who helped in compiling these early historical lists how they had come by their knowledge of each particular island.

That the name of more than one island had been picked up through waif voyagers would certainly seem to be indicated in Tomás Gayangos's annotated list, which includes brief statements about each island. Here, out of forty-three islands noted, six were known only as being inhabited, four others as simply existing, while three have no explanatory data at all.[118] While Tupaia's list, as recorded by Cook, lacks descriptive annotations, it does give the generalized direction in which each island was said to lie relative to Tahiti. J. C. Beaglehole, as editor extraordinaire of Cook's journals, was able to identify, either as older names of islands or as obvious equivalents of contemporary names, slightly fewer than half of these island names.[119] Twelve of these recognizable islands are within the Society group, and their broad directions from Tahiti are correct—as they should be, since Tupaia claimed to have visited them. However, of the remaining nineteen, nine are given a wrong direction in relation to Tahiti, four of them—Mururoa, Mangareva, Timoe, and Pitcairn—being in the opposite direction of that recorded by Tupaia. Two islands outside the Society group had been visited by Tupaia. One of these, Manua, has not been identified, but the other, Rurutu, under its earlier name of Heteroa, was given its proper direction, thus verifying Tupaia's claim of having visited the place. One curious point of interest is the wrong direction indicated for Raivavae, given as between north-by-west and west, rather than its proper south and south-by-east location. It was from this island that, according to John Forster, Tupaia claimed fine "hatchets" (probably adzes) had been brought to Raiatea in the Society Islands. With such trade going on, the direction of Raivavae should have been known. Perhaps in this instance Tupaia had mistakenly given the proper broad direction in which Raiatea lay from Raivavae, rather than the reverse.

While the above information tends to support my contention that the listing of an unknown number of islands in these early European accounts was the result of information supplied to the Tahitians by waif voyagers, this is not to say that they were the only source for such geographic knowledge. There seems very little doubt from Gayangos's annotated island list that the people of Tahiti iti at least, from whom he obtained his information, had made frequent visits to the Tuamotus. Bolton Corney was able to identify thirteen atolls of this group to which Gayangos had appended such pertinent information as sailing time between certain atolls. He also noted the basic crops to be found, as well as such trade goods as mats, pearls, and dogs, which supplied hair for ornamentation. Tupaia, whose original home was Raiatea, may not have been as familiar with this area as his counterparts in Tahiti iti, for only six recognizable atoll names in the western Tuamotus have been identified in his list, all of which appear in Gayangos's enumeration.

As for the islands to the southwest and south, that is, the Southern Cooks and the Australs, the recognizable island data suggests that, while these islands may have been

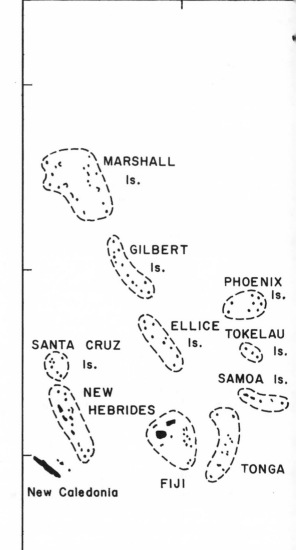

The eastern Pacific. Heavy black line outlines the probable geographic extent of eighteenth-century, two-way voyaging by Tahitians; dashed lines enclose island groups.

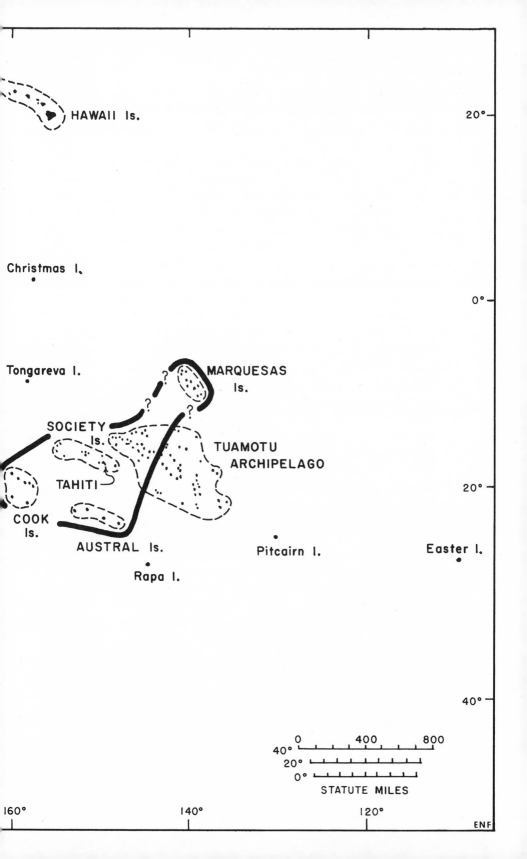

HAWAII Is.

Christmas I.

Tongareva I.

MARQUESAS
Is.

SOCIETY
Is.

TUAMOTU
ARCHIPELAGO

TAHITI

COOK
Is.

AUSTRAL Is.

Pitcairn I.

Easter I.

Rapa I.

20°

0°

20°

40°

0   400   800

40°
20°
0°
STATUTE MILES

160°   140°   120°

ENF

visited on occasion, the traffic was considerably less than to the western Tuamotus. Thus, Mangaia, noted by its older name of Ahuahu, is found on the lists of Tupaia, Boenechea, Andia y Varela, and Gayangos.[120] While Tupaia had its location wrong, Boenechea noted it correctly as being to the southwest, and Gayangos added that it had coconuts, plantains, and pigs. Atiu was almost certainly known, its name occurring on all three Spanish lists; Boenechea not only gave its proper southwest location but added that it was a ten-day sail from the island of Tahiti.[121] Manuae, by its old name of Uritete, was reported by Gayangos as being west of Tahiti and being both large and productive.[122] Although his direction would appear to be wrong, it is obvious from his list that he was locating islands as being either east or west of a north-south meridian passing through Tahiti. While Rarotonga appears on Tupaia's list, its direction is wrong; Gayangos's informant vouched for a limited knowledge of this island by admitting that all that he knew of the place was that it was inhabited.[123] Although the other islands of the Southern Cooks do not appear, at least not in readily identifiable forms, it seems reasonable to suspect that they were known to the Tahitians, who would have learned of them while visiting Mangaia or Atiu. As for the Australs, Rurutu (under its earlier name of Heteroa) had specifically been visited by Tupaia, and, as mentioned earlier, he was sufficiently aware of Raivavae to know that fine "hatchets" were produced there for trade with Raiatea.[124] Rimatara occurs on John Forster's, Andia y Varela's and Gayangos's lists, the latter reporting that the island produced coconuts, plantains, and pigs, though Tubuai, to the east, was known only to be inhabited.[125]

Such, it would seem, was the known and visited world of Tahiti in the late eighteenth century. It extended from the western Tuamotus, approximately from the longitude of Makemo atoll, west and southward to include the Southern Cook Islands and those of the Australs as far east as Raivavae. Perhaps, but only perhaps, we can include the Marquesas Islands to the northeast, since Fatu Hiva and

Hivaoa are identifiable in Tupaia's list, and their direction from Tahiti is approximately correct.[126] On the other hand, the extreme curiosity about these islands expressed by Tahitians in their intense questioning of Wilson and the missionaries about the Marquesans and their culture suggests that the Marquesas had not been visited.[127] Had they been known through direct contact in Tupaia's time, it is difficult to believe that such directly obtained information about these islands would have been lost to Tahitians in a period of fewer than thirty years.

Much farther afield, Beaglehole was able to identify names of such far western islands as Tutuila and Upolu in Tupaia's list, and even Rotuma much farther to the west.[128] Perhaps these hark back to distant, bygone voyagers who made landfalls in the Society Islands. Certainly the occurrence of the two Samoan islands in Tupaia's list was not the result of recent voyages for, while the direction of Upolu is basically correct, its within-sight neighbor, Tutuila, has been given a completely wrong directional location! Thus, while romantics enjoy using legends of doubtful value to strengthen a case for long-distance, two-way voyages between, for example, Hawaii and Tahiti, and set aside the above eighteenth-century evidence as reflecting a late decline in the sailing abilities of Tahitians, perhaps anthropologists will eventually clarify the situation. As it stands, when Captain Cook weighed his anchors at Tahiti in 1777 to explore the north Pacific Ocean, he could only write in his journal that his Tahitian friends knew of no islands to the north and northwest of their homeland.[129] Had the memory of distant northern islands been lost through time, or was there no knowledge of them to be lost? Travelers on ancient one-way sailings sent no messages back to the homeland.

Warfare

Except for the Spaniards, who observed a highly localized revolt in Tahiti iti, no eighteenth-century writer of Tahitian history ever saw the actual clash of two major opposing parties. Regrettably, Captain Cook failed in his bid to observe an impending naval battle between Tahiti and the island of Moorea in 1774,[1] while William Bligh, admitting a war was actually going on at the time of his 1792 visit, cautiously restrained his normal ethnographic curiosity and kept to his breadfruit business.[2] Nonetheless, there are some firsthand descriptions of battle preparations and demonstrations of fighting techniques, as well as some secondhand accounts of battles and the ravages of war that were left behind.

Had population decimation been the goal of warfare on Tahiti, that island might well have returned to its original, virgin state. During the twenty-five years between Samuel Wallis's discovery of the island in 1767 and Bligh's second voyage after breadfruit in 1792, there were no fewer than eight wars, not counting a minor revolt or two. Whereas a few conflicts appear to have resulted in considerable bloodshed, there were others in which the tide of victory was determined by the slaying of no more than one or two individuals. Although great warrior chiefs were expected to lead their troops and, if necessary, fall while facing their enemies,[3] the less-than-mighty had quite a different attitude toward battle. As the missionaries described it, the Tahitian commoner did not feel an obligation to fight any longer than he wanted to, and he thought it much less disgraceful to run away from a fight with his body intact than to stand his ground and end up wounded. To do the latter was just plain foolish.[4] Bligh, too, felt compelled to admit that, although a massed group of warriors armed with spears was an awesome sight, they seldom hurt each other with such weapons. They much preferred to stand at distance and use their slings, which, with some luck, occasionally killed sombody.[5]

Overt excuses for war were often as nonsensical as those of our modern day. Bligh, for example, reported a potential war brewing between a chief and his brother due, it would seem, to a trivial disagreement between their wives[6] while the ill-fated attack of the regent Tuteha against Vehiatua of Tahiti iti was said to be owing to some insult that had once been shown his family.[7] However, one begins to get a glimmer of the truth of things when it is discovered that the rights to chiefly succession were also stated reasons for war, not only on Tahiti, but also between that island and the nearby one of Moorea.[8] Thus, although it was never so explicitly stated, political power through prestige, rather than revenge or sheer accumulation of landed wealth, seems to have been the fundamental cause of the major, formalized conflicts. The desire for landed wealth and direct political power over new territory was a somewhat later development. As it originally stood, however, a chief, once beaten in battle, might actually look forward to continuing to rule his district, though with the primary stipulation that he accept his chiefly victor as his superior.[9] At worst, a potentially too-powerful chief might lose his position to a relative.[10] However, in none of these earlier cases is there evidence that, except for the immediate spoils of battle, the victor gained appreciable wealth via any such Old World system as demanding tribute from the conquered. True opulence was not part of the chiefly way of life, but success in war brought prestige, and this was remunerative in the attention paid one's physical and emotional needs. Little wonder that the average Tahitian was not averse to running away in the heat of battle: for him there was very little to be gained in staying.

Although our data is necessarily limited, the above attitude toward warfare and the results to be gained from it in chiefly prestige seem to hold reasonably constant until around 1790 or 1791 when a change occurred. At this time the purpose of successful warfare, as exemplified by Pomare, shifted toward a European pattern of extending landed wealth and placing direct family political power into the governmental control of conquered territories. In almost no time at all Pomare extended his direct political authority over all of the districts of Tahiti nui, as well as Tahiti iti,[11] and shortly after these victories he defeated his own sister, widowed by the death of her Moorean high-chief husband. In this latter case, he placed another member of his family in direct political control of what had come to be his sister's island.[12] This proved to be only the beginning of a new trend toward conquest and control.

How had this new concept of war gains come about? Since traditional attitudes and ways of life in simple societies are not normally subject to sudden change from within, perhaps the European presence was a dominant factor. As noted earlier, personal acquisition of vast amounts of material wealth had not been a chiefly tradition, at least it had not been until Europeans began bringing exotic goods to the island. These they used to purchase the favor of chiefs and, through them, the food necessary to keep their crews alive and well. By 1777 the chiefly desire for personal trade goods had so overcome the regent, Tu, that he requested Cook to make him a storage chest large enough that he could sleep on it to secure its contents.[13] Food was the initial goal of such European transactions, and, as more and more ships arrived on the island, a greedy chief such as Pomare was forced to look farther afield for the foodstuffs required to gain the enticing new products which each ship brought in its holds. The need for more resources would eventually require the acquisition of more land under one's direct control, and thus the seeds of conquest and control could have been born in Tahiti. There is also, however, a good possibility that this concept was promoted by some of those mutineers of the

Bounty whom Fletcher Christian had left on Tahiti in the fall of 1789 and who, with their muskets, aided Pomare in carrying out his newly developed concept of the purpose of war.

Pomare's wars of conquest were departures from traditional Tahitian practices and therefore do not concern us here, except as a possible example of European-induced culture change. As for the old ways of war, if they had any advantage for Tahitians it was in the democratic approach employed, which kept even the paramount chief from becoming a governmental despot. True, the democratic process pertained only to the chiefly class—more precisely, the district chiefs—but at least its presence served as a deterrent to ambitions of dictatorship.

Tahitian Naval Battles

Wars, beyond local uprisings, were formal affairs and were fought on open water or on land, canoes occasionally being used to land troops in a beachhead invasion. Cook, in 1774 and again in 1777, witnessed the Tahitian preparations for a naval battle with the nearby island of Moorea. He was rather unprepared for the sudden appearance of innumerable giant war canoes in 1774 and thus missed the initial ceremonial proceedings, as well as the battle and any following peace or other ceremonial gathering that might have occurred. Although he went so far as to offer to accompany the fleet to observe the battle and record it for posterity, he failed in his efforts, since the chiefs, with malice aforethought, conveniently set the date for battle as being on the fifth day after Cook left Tahiti, whenever that might be.[14] He and the Forsters thus contented themselves with observations on the great vessels of war and their deployment. However, in 1777 the opportunity again presented itself to Cook, and he made the most of it, although he did not witness the brief battle that ended in a truce. The observations he and others recorded of these two events give us the best composite of the conduct of Tahitian warfare.

The 1777 war began essentially with the arrival of a messenger from Moorea announcing that some of Tu's people had been set upon by the Mooreans and had taken to the hills in self-defense. A council of chiefs was immediately assembled in Tu's larger house and the messenger brought before them. After some kind of a formalized introduction on his part, the messenger explained the happenings at Moorea, and the chiefs immediately went into a debate as to what should be done. One chief at a time was allowed to present his views and, although he was apparently inter-rupted or challenged at times and words became a bit heated, coolness was always quickly re-established and the conference continued. During all of this discussion Tu, as paramount chief, remained silent except for an occasional word or two with a few of the speakers.

On this particular occasion not all of the chiefs appear to have concurred on going to war, for Cook explained how those who wished to prosecute the war approached him for aid. While no district chief could be forced to participate in a war that he did not approve of, it seems clear that those who wished to go forward in battle could not be detained. Such war council meetings were not limited to the question of whether or not to go to war, but also included the problem of time and place of battle, as well as the method of attack to be employed. However, during all of these deliberations the common Tahitians went about their daily chores as though nothing of import were even in the making.

It was good to know one's strength in arms before going to battle, but it was even better, if not imperative, to have the deity approve the undertaking. Thus, the day following the council meeting the great warrior chief Towha, of the district of Atehuru, advised Tu that he had obtained a human sacri-ficial victim for the proper marae ceremony designed to en-sure divine assistance in battle. The body had been taken to the great sacrificial marae, then located in the district of Ate-huru. Here Tu, as paramount chief, participated in the rituals conducted by four priests. Two of these came from Tu's district of Pare, while the other two priests were from Atehuru, the district which had furnished the human victim. After first praying over the body of the victim while holding sacred red feathers in one hand and a bit of kava root in the other, a priest then extracted some hair from the victim, as well as one eyeball, and offered this up to the deity. This was followed by extracting the other eye of the dead man and symbolically offering it to Tu.

It was now time to bring out the ceremonial bundles, the one enclosing the sacred maro, or loincloth, and the other representing the god Oro. However, in this first day of ceremony neither package was opened, both simply being displayed in the arms of one of the attending priests. Their presentation before the great crowd of male spectators who surrounded the marae, no women being present, apparently was a signal for the commencement of the prime prayer of the ceremony. It also so happened that just as the packages were revealed to the audience, one of the sacred birds of the marae, in this case a kingfisher, conveniently made a noise, and Tu happily informed Cook that the sound was that of their god. The prayer now began in earnest, the god being asked to deliver not only Moorea into the hands of the Tahitian warriors, but their chiefs, hogs, and women as well. With this accomplished, a shallow grave was dug near the foot of the ahu and the victim unceremoniously dropped into it and covered with dirt, though not before a young boy had sent up a high, squeaky note which was purported to be the god speaking. While the priests now prayed over the covered body, others killed a sacrificial dog and prepared it as if for cooking. With that completed, another youth let go with two shrill squeaks which were designed to request the god to eat, and the uncooked remains were then placed on the marae rack for sacrificial foods. Thus ended the first day of pre-battle ritual.

The second day of ceremonies was known as the "chief's prayer," and, though prayers were conducted and a pig sacrificed, its most important element seems to have been reading an augury of the dead pig's liver. During this particular occasion the sacred maro was not only unwrapped but spread out full length on the ground and prayed over. After this, the package representing the god Oro was opened and the spasmodic jerkings of the pig's liver carefully analyzed. With the augury appearing to favor the upcoming battle, the loincloth, already folded and resting on the ahu, was wrapped up; the red feathers that had been used in the ceremony were placed in the Oro god package, and that also was wrapped; and the two bundles were taken away to their little storage shed.

While this second day of ritual was getting under way, four double canoes were drawn up on the nearby beach. These were known as the "marae" canoes, and on the fore part of each was a kind of platform of palm fronds on which various morsels of breadfruit, coconuts, bananas, and even fish and some piglets were placed. These were vessels for the deity and would go with the fleet against Moorea. Obviously, a god with a full stomach would be more sympathetic to the success of his subjects than one who was hungry. Canoes by this same name, and with basically similar decoration, had been previously reported by Cook during the preparations for the 1774 war with Moorea. At that time, however, Cook understood them to act in the capacity of floating hearses to return the dead from battle. As in the present instance, there were remarkably few of them, so few that Cook was forced to conclude that either they carried only the chiefly dead, or there were very few who ever died in battle.[15] Since enemy victims of warfare were offered to deity at the sacrificial marae,[16] it is very possible that these specialized small canoes served both sacred purposes.

Agreement having been reached, at least by some, to enter into battle, and the proper ritual observances having been completed, it now remained for the paramount chief to call in review the intended naval force and, in the process, give its sailors, officers, and warriors a bit of pre-battle training. In the meantime, messengers must have been moving back and forth between Tahiti and Moorea, for once war had been agreed upon by one party or another, the gentlemanly, traditional thing to do was to come to an agreement with the enemy as to the place and time of battle. This accomplished, the preceding day and night before the agreed-upon day of action was devoted to feasting. Curiously enough, and for unstated reasons, the 1777 battle became fouled up through some misunderstanding. Twelve days after the marae ceremonies, Towha and the chiefs of two other districts in Tahiti sallied forth with thirty war canoes to meet the enemy before the back-up forces were ready, and before the customary review had taken place. The result was predictable. Towha began sending urgent messages back describing his stalemated position within a circle of enemy vessels and pleading for succor. In the meantime, those left behind continued discussions on the pros and cons of fighting Moorea and were just getting ready to review the remaining fleet when, after eight days of indecisive skirmishing, a very angry Towha returned with the news of a truce he had been forced to conclude with the enemy.[17]

While the full might of a Tahitian navy was never reviewed in 1777, the 1774 exhibition was one that would not be easily forgotten by any of Cook's men. The assembled fleet was made up of war canoes and ancillary vessels from only two districts, and consisted of between 300 and 350 craft, depending upon whether one selects John Forster's or Cook's count, the larger figure belonging to the latter.[18] Of this number, between 200 and 210 were specialized war canoes, while the great majority of the others seem to have been supply vessels which, with their little shelters aft, also served as sleeping quarters for the chiefs.[19] Besides these, there were a very few of those sacred "marae" canoes mentioned previously.[20] As if this were not enough, Tahiti iti was said to be sending its own fleet which, unfortunately, had not yet arrived when Cook left the island.[21]

I doubt if any author, and certainly not this one, could do verbal justice to the spectacle of this massive, all-canoe naval assemblage with its complement of warriors and crew, estimated by George Forster to have been about 5,500 men and by Cook at around 7,760 personnel in all.[22] Here one would do well to look at the four illustrations of this event prepared by William Hodges, artist on Cook's second voyage, and published together by Edward Dodd in his fine volume, *Polynesian Seafaring.*[23]

While the ancillary vessels appear to have been common canoes, the double-hulled war canoes were impressive affairs ranging from fifty to ninety feet in length.[24] Although built along the standard lines of either a pahi or va'a, their sterns rose much higher out of the water. Those of the va'a type of construction had their high sterns surmounted with an exceptionally tall, carved post, some reaching a height of twenty feet above the water and decorated with black feathers.[25] Each hull lay parallel, but somewhat separated, from its neighbor, the two being firmly held in place by from fifteen to eighteen transverse beams. In some vessels these beams were made exceptionally long so that they extended beyond the outer edge of each hull. Thus, by adding lengthwise timbers, two or three out over the water on either side of the double canoe and one between the two hulls, a kind of open-work platform was created which stretched the length of the horizontal portion of the vessel. Since none of these canoes bore sail, their gunwales were only two or three feet above the water line to allow for paddling.[26]

On the fore part of each war canoe was a fighting stage, or platform, standing from four to six feet above the gunwales and resting on six or eight carved posts. These stages seem to have ranged from ten or twelve feet in length and from six or eight feet in width to as large as twenty or twenty-four feet by eight or ten feet.[27] Besides these structural features, some war canoes carried a large sheet of white tapa cloth fastened between the raised sterns of the two hulls, while others bore variously decorated pieces of cloth which, according to George Forster, represented naval division emblems.[28]

These pre-battle fleet reviews were full-scale dress rehearsals. The complete range of Tahitian armament was placed in its proper position for battle. On the stage were sling stones, neatly piled up in the manner of cannon balls, while in at least some canoes special sockets held spears and thrusting lances in an upright, ready position.[29] These, made from the wood of either the tough *ararua* or the toa,[30] seem to have ranged in length from eight to as much as twenty feet, although Cook mentioned an extreme example of thirty feet. Undoubtedly, the longer of these served as lances which, according to Sydney Parkinson, were often rubbed with the flower of the *'aute* to give them a reddish hue,[31] and tapered gently from the grasping end to the thrusting point. These latter, like the spears, were armed with the barbed sting of a stingray fish.[32] Fighting clubs, made from the same woods, seem to have come in two size ranges. Some were relatively small, being from four to six

Tahitian war canoes assembled at Pare. Wash drawing by William Hodges.

feet in length, while others were long affairs ranging up to eight or nine feet. These latter were probably the so-called battle axes referred to by John Rickman and George Forster. Cook described these longer clubs as having their upper half flattish, thus forming two edges, and, if we can trust Hodges' illustrations, these blades broadened toward the top of the club.[33] This, then, was the Tahitian armament: spear, lance, club, and sling, which, from the record, appear to have been standard for both land and sea fighting. According to Cook, naval engagements began with a blast of stones, after which the opposing canoes closed, and the lances, spears, and clubs came into play.[34]

The part of the fleet rehearsal which most appalled Cook was the matter of warrior dress. The functional part of their clothing consisted of at least three tapa cloth, poncho-like garments, the inner one being white, the middle one red, and a smaller outside one brown.[35] However, some may have worn considerably more clothing to blunt any spear attack, for Cook took the time to watch them undress after the review and ended up wondering how they could fight with the great weight of the clothing that surrounded them.[36] In an impulsive effort to improve their fighting ability, he gave his Tahitian friends a visual presentation of how an Englishman prepared for battle by stripping the clothes off his back. However, it all went for naught, since no one seemed to care how the English undressed for battle.[37] In addition to the heavy clothing that surrounded each warrior, a second practical accoutrement was a heavier-than-usual turban of tapa cloth, obviously designed to soften the blow of an enemy's club. A few of these were decorated, perhaps symbolically, with the dried branches of some shrub on which white feathers had been fastened.[38]

One element which may have had the secondary use of warding off the thrust of a spear was a semicircular gorget notched in the center of its one straight edge so that it could fit around the front half of the warrior's neck and hang down over his upper chest. The basic frame was of wickerwork overlaid with a series of expanding semicircles of coconut fiber. These, in turn, were covered with glossy pigeon feathers and were set off in curving bands by two or three cres-

Tahitian wearing helmet, or headdress, and gorget:
Engraving from a drawing by Sydney Parkinson.

cent rows of white shark teeth. Around the curved edge of
the gorget was a fringe of fine, white dog hair.[39] Most, if not
all, of the warriors wore these decorative devices which, like
their spears, and probably the rest of their war paraphernalia, had been made by men, rather than women.[40] However, the finest, but physically nonfunctional, piece of military decoration was a tall helmet. Its basic element was a
wickerwork cylinder some four feet tall on the front of which
was fastened an upright semicylindrical device of a finer
basketweave which expanded upwards and, breaking away
from the basic helmet, curved gracefully forward at the top.

The front of this was completely covered with the glossy, blue-green feathers of a particular variety of pigeon. The finest of these were further decorated by an edging of white feathers from which radiated innumerable long, thin tail feathers of a tropic bird, giving the effect of a delicately diverging halo surrounding the helmet. There were only a few of these beautiful headpieces in the reviewing fleet, and thus it is likely, especially since the chief warrior, Towha, wore none, that they were the headgear of high priests. This Tahitian version of a shako had no chin strap to hold it in place but was merely jammed down on top of a large cloth turban. Not surprisingly, the wearers displayed this precariously balanced piece of finery for only a short time during the review and then placed it on the fighting stage, where it was not apt to be blown away by the ocean breeze.[41]

José de Andia y Varela, writing about the chiefly warriors of the Taiarapu Peninsula, briefly described somewhat similar helmets, except that those he saw had some kind of small skirt which dropped down over the face of the warrior. Another piece of headgear, which he inadequately described as a sort of crown made from braided coconut husk fibers, appears to have been limited to the use of one person. Andia y Varela reasoned, and perhaps rightly, that that one person was probably the paramount chief, or at least his representative in any battle.[42]

Thus did the bold prepare to storm their enemy on what was probably not the high seas but instead the quieter waters of reef-protected lagoons. Cook tried hard, with a little information and a lot of reasoning, to determine how a Tahitian naval engagement was undertaken. He envisioned that the fight progressed by fleet divisions, the aggressors' and defenders' canoes lining up facing one another at some little distance. They then advanced on one another under fire of sling stones, and finally closed to a point where the fighting stage of each canoe was abreast of its opposing counterpart. It was then that the clubs and spears went into action. Although the fighting platforms were capable of holding up to eight or ten men, Cook's old friend, the chief Tupaia of his first voyage, had previously explained to him that no more than one or two men actually fought on the stage at any one time. When one was killed or wounded, another warrior took his place.[43] One thing Cook seemed certain of was that the battle never lasted very long, and its outcome settled the dispute, at least for the time being.[44] This conclusion is amply supported by accounts of other Tahitian wars.

It was not until 1777 that Cook, still not able to view an actual sea battle, was treated to a mock fight between two war canoes. During this make-believe battle Omai, having just been brought back from England by Cook, took command of one canoe, while paramount chief Tu, with Cook and James King aboard, commanded the opposing vessel. After coming about and facing each other at a distance, the canoes proceeded to make a number of closing drives, only to suddenly retreat just as precipitously. The movement and control of the paddlers was under the direction of Tu in Cook's canoe, and Omai in the opposite vessel. Cook saw these preliminary maneuvers as attempts to obtain the best advantage in closing and admiringly confessed that it took fine judgment and a quick eye. During all of this time the warriors flourished their weapons and, one gathers, attempted to frighten the opposing forces by various fiendish antics. Finally, the vessels closed with their fighting stages side by side and, after a moment of mock battle, Omai's warriors pretended to have won the affair and promptly boarded Tu's canoe. Here, Cook witnessed the normal procedure for the defeated, as, in one great series of splashes, the entire crew of his vessel, including the great Tu, took to the water and swam for safety.[45]

While Tu and Omai were playing their war game, poor Towha was arranging a temporary truce with his very real foe in Moorea. The actual terms of the truce were brought to Tu by a messenger who first placed the usual plantain shoot, indicative of peace, at Tu's feet before delivering the information. Within the same day, yet another messenger arrived with a plantain shoot. This one came from Towha with the information that Tu must come to the great marae at Atehuru to take his part in what appears to have been a ceremony confirming the truce. The following day Tu arrived at the marae and, although Towha and his fellow chiefs who had participated in the war had not yet arrived, the brother of the paramount chief of Moorea was there. After Tu was presented with the plantain shoot of peace plus a small pig, both men settled down to a long discussion of the war. Apparently the reasons for the late conflict were brought up from time to time, since the Moorean was heard on several occasions to cry out, "False! False!" These conversations had little to do with the formalized ceremony which was to follow the next day, and thus they were carried on outside the marae. However, in preparation for the upcoming ritual, the "marae" canoes, which earlier had taken the god to war, now returned to their original location and bore pigs as offerings.

The following morning eight large canoes arrived, one of them bearing Towha, who was too lame (probably as a result of the conflict) to get out and participate. The assembled group of chiefs now entered the marae where Tu's chief priest and two others began a long ritual of prayer and song, to which no one seems to have paid the least attention. This was followed by bringing out the symbol of Oro and the package containing the sacred loincloth. On this occasion, the maro was properly wrapped around Tu's loins as paramount chief and, while a priest began praying, a man ran out from the surrounding crowd and yelled, "Heiva!" and the crowd answered with, "Ari'i!" or "chief." This having happened three times, those within the marae then moved to the opposite side of the masonry platform, or ahu, where a series of prayers, answered from time to time by other priests and onlookers, was presented. Again the call of "Heiva" and its answer, "Ari'i," was repeated three times. With this the sacred maro was returned to its package and, with the god symbol, taken to its storage shed.

The deific part of the truce had now been completed. However, there remained a secular ceremony which was conducted in Tu's large assembly house nearby. Here, those in attendance sat in a circle, Tu being at one end of the house with the usual plantain stem at his feet and his talking chief alongside him. A series of speeches now commenced, the Tahitian chiefs speaking first. This aspect was terminated with a speech by Tu's talking chief, after which the brother of Moorea's paramount chief presented a statement and was immediately followed by an elderly gentleman also from Moorea. It was during these latter talks that a symbolic gesture took place: a man from Towha's district of Atehuru walked about inside the circle of chiefs, carrying a large stone on one shoulder and having a sling fastened to his waist. He seems to have kept repeating some statement in a rather musical tone and, upon the completion of the two Moorean speeches, allowed his stone to drop within the circle of the chiefs. After this gesture, two more brief speeches were made and the stone, along with the plantain peace symbol, was removed to the marae. Here, attended by Tu, the priests prayed over the two items and thus ended the ceremony confirming the truce. And truce it was, for it was to last no more than six months, after which either side could again find reason to perpetrate yet another battle. As it ended up, Towha brought back one Moorean war canoe, apparently the sole trophy of at least one successful engagement during the brief war.[46]

Effects of Defeat

Not all battles were conducted at sea, although canoes, undoubtedly war canoes, must have occasionally carried troops to beachheads, for when Vehiatua invaded Papara he was said to have landed his forces there.[47] Such landings must have been spectacular affairs. In the maneuvers of 1774, Cook and George Forster described how a complement of forty war canoes slipped, one by one, through an opening in the reef. Once inside the lagoon they all turned their heads toward the beach and, with groups of canoes lashed abreast of each other, formed one long line which moved hastily toward shore with such precision that all of the vessels touched the beach at virtually the same time. The commander of this remarkable naval maneuver was a lone man who stood in a canoe in the middle of the long line of vessels and signaled the paddlers with nothing more than a green branch held in one hand.[48]

While most battles, whether decisive or not, seem to have terminated the immediate disagreement between two warring parties, the war between Tahiti nui and Tahiti iti in 1773 was an exception. In this case it would appear that the

war council of Tahiti nui had agreed to a naval battle against
Vehiatua of Tahiti iti. However, this naval engagement, under
the command of Tuteha, the governing regent of Tahiti nui,
was indecisive. This seems to have annoyed Tuteha to such
an extent that he soon after rallied a few other chiefs and,
against the wishes of his own family, moved his troops over-
land to meet Vehiatua's warriors at the Isthmus of Taravao.
The result was a smashing defeat for his forces in which he
and several other chiefs were killed. While Tuteha's troops,
as well as the young paramount chief whom he had taken
along, ran for the mountains, Vehiatua marched his forces
on Pare and Matavai districts, where he burned houses and
canoes and took away all of the hogs that he could find.[49]
So thorough was this raid that when Cook landed there
the same year he was barely able to purchase a pig or
two. However, when he returned eight months later, in
1774, hogs were in plentiful supply again, many new houses
had been constructed, and others were in the process of
being built.[50]

Not all such battles were as easy to recover from as that
of 1773. In 1788 Bligh found both Matavai and Pare still in
pitiful condition after a war successfully prosecuted against
them by Moorea in about 1782.[51] The fine houses that Bligh
had seen when he was with Cook in 1777 were gone, and the
inhabitants were now living in little portable sheds.[52] No
doubt this war had resulted in near total destruction of crop-
lands and breadfruit trees, which would have required the
defeated to first tend to replanting their food base before
bothering with new housing. After all, according to George
Hamilton, the Tahitian war technique of barking breadfruit
trees resulted in a loss of that basic food source for a period
of four or five years, the same amount of time it took for new
trees to be planted and begin bearing fruit.[53]

One of the standard by-products of war, the prisoner,
was searched for in vain by John Forster. He concluded that
either the Tahitians took no prisoners or, if prisoners did
exist, they were not socially stigmatized by being treated as
slaves or forced into subservient labor.[54] It was understandable that he could find no trace of such people, for, as Bligh
finally discovered, prisoners were served up as human sac-

rifices. Like any other sacrificial victim, the prisoner was killed and one of his eyes was offered to deity while the other was symbolically proffered to the paramount chief.[55] No wonder Tahitians were quick to run from the scene of battle at the first sign that the fight might be going against them! It just did not pay to be too curious at a time like that.

Bodies of enemies killed in battle were given rather special treatment. The lower jaw of each of these individuals was carefully excised, cleaned of flesh, and hung up in the victorious warrior's house. Cook and Joseph Banks saw fifteen such clean, white jaws hanging from a semicircular board, while some years later Máximo Rodríguez witnessed three hung up in a dwelling.[56] The remainder of the bodies of these unfortunate souls appear to have been collected from the field of battle and taken to the sacrificial marae, where they were buried in a common grave at the foot of the ahu.[57] Although sacrificial victims were initially buried in the marae, their bodies were left there only long enough for the flesh to rot and, most likely, be eaten by beetles. Once the bones had been thus naturally cleaned, they appear to have been exhumed, the skulls placed on a platform extension of the ahu, and, presumably, the remainder thrown out.[58] This, quite likely, was the fate of those enemy bodies buried at the sacrificial marae. Thus, the mass of human vertebrae and rib bones found by Banks along the seaside trail not far from the marae was probably the thrown-out sacrificial bones of enemy slain in 1768 when Vehiatua made war on Papara, rather than the remains of rotting bodies left in the field of battle.[59]

Enemy chiefs killed in battle appear to have been given a somewhat more permanent type of burial at the same marae. Tuteha and the other chiefs killed in the land battle against Vehiatua were said by Cook to have been taken to the sacrificial marae and, after evisceration, buried in separate places within the ahu.[60]

While larger wars involving several districts required the action of a war council, as well as the deific benefits to be derived from ceremonies at the marae, this does not seem to have been true for lesser brawls. When the people of Vaitepiha Canyon decided to rebel against Vehiatua for having banished them to the hills for not supplying him with their proper quota of goods, the young chief quickly taught them a lesson. As soon as the revolutionaries were ready to march they dutifully sent word to Vehiatua, who immediately summoned his forces and met them at the mouth of the canyon. The initial battle lasted but a short time, for, when two of the rebels were killed, the revolutionaries broke and ran for the hills, with Vehiatua and his men in hot pursuit. In less than two hours' time, Vehiatua's warriors had routed the enemy, burned their homes, destroyed their gardens and fruit trees, and made off with anything they could find that was movable. With the completion of the rout, each subchief of Vehiatua's forces submitted his plantain shoot to his high chief in a symbolic gesture indicating that peace had been restored, and by high noon Vehiatua was comfortably enjoying a lunch served aboard the Spaniards' ship.[61] In this particular brief battle two items of special interest are to be noted. Some of Vehiatua's warriors appeared on the scene wearing grotesque masks,[62] a feature not mentioned in other early accounts of warfare, and the signal for the battle to begin was given on a drum.[63] This latter observation is particularly interesting, for although Wallis, describing the Tahitians' attack on his vessel which occurred soon after he discovered the island, twice referred to the sound of conch trumpets,[64] George Robertson, on the same vessel, did not mention them at all. Furthermore, I have found no other mention of such trumpets in the published eighteenth-century literature on Tahiti. It therefore seems possible that Wallis, who admitted to having been sick and confined to bed during most of his stay at Tahiti and even questioned his own accuracy of reporting,[65] may well have been confused. On the other hand, he may have been simply adding what he thought he should have heard because conch shell trumpets were known for other Polynesian islands. I suggest this partly on the basis that he claimed to have heard both shell trumpet blasts and flutes, which could only have been nose flutes, at the same time. Anyone who has heard the delicate, light tones of such a flute realizes that the two could hardly have been heard simultaneously on shipboard, and surely a nose flute was hardly an instrument to incite anyone to battle!

The fascinating thing about the shell trumpet is that except for Wallis, in 1767, none of the explorers mentioned such an instrument until William Ellis, writing in the first quarter of the nineteenth century, reported it in constant use in Tahiti for warfare and for ceremonies at marae.[66] This evidence suggests that either there were remarkably few conch shell trumpets used during the previous century or, more likely, they did not exist on the island at that time and were brought in from other islands, perhaps on some turn-of-the-century European vessel. A number of such additions to Tahitian culture seem to have arrived in this manner, as witness Ellis's description of a three- or four-bladed "short sword" edged with shark's teeth and used in warfare.[67] This item was certainly not in the eighteenth-century armament of a Tahitian warrior. However, even by 1792, warfare was changing. No longer was there a gentlemanly agreement as to the time and place of battle; nighttime attacks were preferred, and the use of specialized war canoes was rapidly becoming a thing of the past.[68]

All in all, old Tahitian warfare was dangerous to life and limb for only a relatively few. However, for the defeated, the destruction of homes, gardens, and tree crops was temporarily devastating. The most pleasing account of warfare I have discovered concerns the battle that did not come off between the districts of Taiarapu and Ahui. The two armed forces had decided to face each other in battle not far from the little house of the Spanish priests who had been left on the island for a year. When informed by the Spaniards that if a battle ensued, a Spanish ship would come and destroy them by cannon, the two warring parties immediately approached each other, agreed on a peace, and sat down to roast pig. After a pleasant and satisfying meal they all returned home.[69] Would that all wars could be so pleasingly defused.

To Accept or Reject

Whatever contact Tahitians might have had with other islands in prehistoric days, or with strange craft from even
more distant lands, their combined impact could not com-
pare with that of the itinerant European voyagers who in-
termittently visited the island during the period from 1767 to
1797. In ships loaded with exotics, they brought innumerable
trade goods as gifts or for barter. They planted strange seeds
which developed into still stranger plants, and they landed a
small variety of two- and four-footed animals, of which only
the pig, dog, and chicken were recognizable food to the islanders. As if this were not enough, they came wearing tailored clothing, a new concept to Tahitians, prepared strange
food in something other than a pit oven, and ate from a
raised, flat board while sitting on a wooden frame. As if
unappreciative of the full usefulness of one's hands, they ate
with the help of a small, pronged, metal bar placed in one
hand, and a knife of iron in the other. But above all, their
seemingly giant vessels brought with them those instruments of death, the cannon, musket, and pistol, which
needed but one good demonstration by Samuel Wallis in
1767 to prove to the Tahitians that détente with these pale-
skinned foreigners was a wise course.

All of this and more the first Europeans presented in
what, to the Tahitians, must have been an awe-inspiring
panoply of the new and different. This suite of European

culture was at first presented to the islanders with no overt attempt to forcibly change their style of living. They were free to accept or reject that which was offered to them, or to copy at will those customs which appeared as normal behavior for European sailors and officers. Thus it was that during the first thirty years of European contact, Tahitians, inspired by new goods and new lifestyles, commenced to noticeably modify their culture as they came to perceive new needs and idiosyncratic desires. The changes that occurred were not overly great, but they were the Tahitians' own selections, and as such they are worth noting as a record of culture change through freedom of choice. Unfortunately, such freedom was soon lost. From 1797 onwards, forced culture change—acculturation, as it is called—reared its questionable head as English missionaries, and somewhat later the French, began their efforts to Europeanize what was once a self-sufficient and, up through the first thirty years after discovery, a self-satisfying culture.

Effects of European Trade Goods

The initial reaction of the Tahitians to the goods, trinkets, and more solid hardware that the European voyagers brought with them was somewhat like that of a small boy with a fistful of money encountering his first variety store. Money for the Tahitians, of course, consisted of fruits and vegetables, or pigs and chickens, all of which their foreign visitors eagerly sought after months of living on restricted sea rations. There were other items of hand manufacture —curiosities, the Europeans called them—which could occasionally be traded off, while tapa cloth in quantity was offered up as the customary gift of value. However, gift though it might be, it was expected to be matched eventually by some exotic object of equal quality. Then, too, there were the young women who, though not really selling themselves, responded to a sailor's desires with greater alacrity if an appropriate foreign gift was occasionally forthcoming.

Thus it was that after the initial skirmishing during Wallis's first contact with the islanders, it was not long before Tahitian and European were presenting one another with whatever each had to offer in exchange for that which seemed useful or intriguing. While most of the Tahitian offerings quickly disappeared down the hungry gullets of grateful sailors, the European trade goods were of a longer lasting nature. The full range of these highly portable artifacts will probably never be known. Although each vessel carried a store of goods specifically designated for trade, and records of them may still exist, there was yet another source of goods. This latter was the ship's own company, each of whom had his personal collection of bits and pieces of things stowed in his locker. These unrecorded objects seem to have been passed out for trade when personal desire overcame the knowlege that such pieces of gear might well be comforting a little later on during the long voyage home.[1]

While the record of European trade goods is far from complete, the voyagers occasionally documented some of the things that they gave away or traded. A very few, like the ever-thoughtful Captain Cook, took the trouble to summarize those items for which there seemed a real demand, so that later seafarers might profit from previous experiences. On the basis of this kind of information we can obtain a reasonably good picture of what European trade goods were accepted fully into Tahitian culture. At the same time, we can determine which items were only initially found acceptable and, finally, which were accepted a few times, perhaps out of curiosity or politeness, but appear never to have effectively entered the Tahitian lifestyle.

With but few explorers before him, Wallis had little opportunity to choose his trade goods for his voyage into Polynesia on the basis of the previous experiences of others. However, in spite of this handicap, he did not do badly, although such items as ribbons, earrings, buttons, and "toys," the latter probably reflecting the European preconceived notion of the Polynesian personality, did not do well.[2] In fact, "toys" and ribbons disappeared from the trade lists of later voyagers, though buttons continued to be passed out by Bougainville in 1768, and again by Cook in 1769.[3] However, until tailored clothing began to arrive in some quantity toward the end of the century, such buttons were doomed in terms of their intended function, since the purposely loose garments of the Tahitians hardly called for their use as fasteners. Quite probably, they were initially employed as decorative features which could be easily tied onto mourning and dance costumes, just as were drilled shell and coconut disks. As for earrings, they never appear to have competed favorably with the pearls, worked shell, and, above all, fragrant flowers that the Tahitians loved to insert in their punctured earlobes. In fact, by 1774 John Marra could report that the natives had little regard for European earrings of any sort.[4]

Wallis's bead collection was a different story. These little items were immediately appreciated, as well they might have been.[5] After all, the art of drilling and hand-grinding such miniature specimens from shell or other hard material was tedious and time-consuming, especially in view of the fact that their sole purpose was decorative. So, to be suddenly confronted by hundreds of these decorative elements already formed and in a variety of shapes and colors must have been a pleasurable encounter for the Tahitians, although they never traded anything of much value for them. Nonetheless, by 1768, and again in 1774, Cook was able to recommend them as a valuable trade item for future voyagers to Tahiti.[6] However, the islanders had now narrowed their preference to white cut-glass beads, which in their color and luster must have reflected the Tahitian taste for pearl shell, which had become rare in the surrounding lagoons. Whether European beads became a glut on the market or, as purely decorative objects, were eventually overshadowed by the desire for more practical goods, is not at all clear. Perhaps both factors were in operation. All we do know is that, although such beads continued to be passed out occasionally by Europeans right into 1797, their value as a trade item had essentially disappeared by 1777.[7]

With so many indigenous natural elements, such as flowers, with which to decorate their bodies, it is understandable how the Tahitians might have been willing to reject beads as an item of trade. However, this was far from true of one piece of toiletry introduced by Wallis which remained a valuable article of trade over the years, for George Vancouver called attention to its usefulness as late as 1792.

This item was nothing more than the simple mirror,[8] which may also have aided the eventual full acceptance of scissors, which Wallis first introduced, but whose usefulness in trimming Tahitian beards and hair was not fully appreciated until Cook's second voyage to the island in 1773.[9] From that time onwards, however, the scissors ranked well as an article of value in the Tahitian world of trade — especially, according to Vancouver, among the women.[10] Compared to the sharpened edge of a shell or a split fragment of bamboo, which had formerly been used to cut hair, the scissors must have seemed a miracle of painless efficiency.

Completing this ensemble of toiletry, the comb, first introduced by Wallis but brought to the island in quantity by the Spaniards in 1772, was listed by Marra the following year as a chief item of trade during Cook's second voyage.[11] While these combs served the normal purpose of adjusting one's hair, John Forster claimed they had an additional salutary use in helping to rid Tahitian heads of "vermin," a task which traditionally had been accomplished through the indelicate art of hand-picking one another's hair.[12]

While none of the above really struck at the essentials of Tahitian living, the Europeans right from the beginning brought two commodities which were destined to become integral components of Tahitian culture. In the process of doing so, they were to replace older and less efficient materials and condemn the Tahitians to an essential dependence upon European trade. These items were textiles and iron.

The one great drawback of traditional Tahitian bark cloth, or tapa, was its tendency to fall apart with moisture as the starchy paste that held much of it together began to dissolve. Not only did one have to run for cover in the event of a sudden shower, or risk an embarrassing revelation, but this unfortunate aspect of the cloth kept it from being laundered, clean clothes invariably meaning new clothes. In this respect, it was a capitalist's dream of built-in, rapid obsolescence. However, the Tahitians were no capitalists, and when they discovered that European textiles stood up to rain and washing, they were understandably quick to appreciate these superior and longer-lasting qualities. In fact, since it was the women who spent long hours beating out innumerable yards of tapa cloth, it may well have been they who first encouraged the ready acceptance of these foreign-made textiles.

Accustomed to using large sheets of tapa to drape their bodies, the Tahitians readily received these new-found textiles in the form of yard goods. Cook found cloth to be a dominant trade article, in both plain and printed form, as early as 1769.[13] Although yard goods continued to maintain a superior position in trade inventories right into 1792[14] and beyond, Cook tried an interesting innovation on the occasion of his second voyage. At that time he brought along a quantity of bed sheets—but they were not for beds.[15] He reasoned correctly that they were about the same size as the normal tapa robe that customarily draped the Tahitian body, and they had the advantage over yard goods of being already cut to size and hemmed. The Spaniards, too, found sheets a worthy trade item in 1774–75,[16] but there was no further mention of them in later literature. Since the Spaniards of 1772 brought to Tahiti some two thousand sewing needles[17] (first introduced to Tahiti by Wallis[18]), perhaps the Tahitians eventually learned their use in hemming yard goods, and thus manufactured sheets became less enticing than they had been in the trade of 1775.

In the warm, moist climate of the tropics Tahitians must have often wondered inwardly at the hot and essentially constricting, tailored clothing of their foreign visitors. While a few breeches and a jacket or two found their way into the population, probably as a curiosity more than anything else, elements of European clothing were indeed slow to catch on, except for the light and loosely designed shirt of the day. This garment, first introduced by Wallis's men, gradually gained in popularity, until in 1772, much to the dismay of the Spaniards, the Tahitians began demanding shirts and more finely woven textiles for the very goods that they had originally been quite willing to part with for more inferior articles.[19] By the time Cook arrived on his second voyage, shirts were all the rage, especially when it came to trading with the women.[20] This seeming burst of popularity appears to have been a bit faddish for, although there were reports of an occasional shirt being given away in later years, there was no indication that it was a greatly desired article of trade.

When it came to clothing, Tahitians as a whole exhibited remarkably good sense in maintaining their well-adapted, loose tropical dress. Even as late as 1777, David Samwell could report that the islanders generally preferred their own clothing to that of Europeans.[21] Unfortunately, however, that year of 1777 may have been a fateful one for Tahitian dress. Omai, the native Society Islander whom Cook had taken with him to England in 1774, and who had been wined and dined in the best of British company, returned with Cook on his final voyage. Resplendent in European dress, he was magnificently loquacious in describing British finery to any Tahitian who cared to listen to him. The Admiralty fueled this new interest by sending the native Odiddy, who had sailed with Cook into Antarctic waters in 1773–74, a complete suit of clothes. And even the young paramount chief, Tu, was given a linen suit and a gold lace hat by Cook.[22] Obviously, a few fancy clothes had arrived before this date, for when Samwell met the young chief, he was wearing a pair of overly-large, lace-trimmed, Spanish breeches that draped from his hips all the way down to his ankles.[23] However, up until Cook's third voyage, there were no reports to indicate a previous surge toward accepting European clothing.

From 1777 onward a new element seems to have been gradually substituted for the former Tahitian concept of practicality in clothing. Vanity was perhaps involved, but there also seems to have been a strong desire, especially on the part of chiefs, to begin copying the more fancy attire of those Englishmen of consequence whom they saw, that is, the ships' officers, or whom they heard about, such as the king of "Pretaine." Thus, among the Tahitians as among ourselves, it would appear that the upper class set the trend for the less fortunate to follow as best they could. It took some fifteen years, but by 1792 a thoroughly disgusted Captain Bligh complained of the quantity of old clothes that had been dropped off at Tahiti by various ships. General dress was now a dirty shirt and an old coat and waistcoat, while it was rare indeed to see anyone wearing the ample but simple robes of the earlier days. To Bligh the Tahitians now looked like a bunch of ragamuffins.[24] However, the picture of Tahitian change in clothing may not have been quite as complete as Bligh described it. In 1797 some islanders must still have been wearing traditional dress, for Wilson mentioned that he lent clothes to several natives who were eager to dress in the English manner.[25] Nonetheless, the trend toward Europeanization of clothing had become well established, and traditional Tahitian dress was no longer *de rigueur;* even foreign dresses for the women had been introduced.[26]

For people of a traditional, self-sufficient society to appreciate the practical aspects of any new commodity they must have time to use it, to experiment with it to see if it is truly advantageous in terms of their own cultural requirements. The initial acceptance may be due to curiosity or the fact that the new object clearly serves a purpose similar to something already existing within the society. This latter must have been the case with woven yard goods, which simulated in form and function the bark cloth of Tahiti. In this instance, there was a short time lapse of about two years before the islanders came to recognize the practical advantages of this newly introduced cloth over the beaten-out tapa they had been accustomed to wearing. However, this expectable time lapse between initial acceptance and either final rejection or full appreciation and integration did not occur when it came to iron. Iron in any form was immediately accepted and appreciated by the Tahitians when they cautiously began to trade with Wallis's men. Although George Robertson put it that nails were preferred over anything else they had,[27] his comment may reflect the limited number of other iron tools, notably hatchets, which Wallis carried for trade. Thus the immediate and astonishingly favorable response to iron as a trade item may have caught Wallis by surprise, forcing him into exchanging the ubiquitous nail, with which the carpenters had probably been well supplied before leaving England, though for quite a different purpose.

It was not just nails which became highly acceptable, but actually any sort of iron that was made available. Here, then, one can only conclude that the Tahitians were already familiar with the cutting qualities and malleability of metal. Since no metal occurs naturally on the volcanic islands and coral atolls of Polynesia, the source of this knowledge had to come from beyond this insular world. A very good possibility, if not probability, is that this knowledge derived from the wreck of one of Jacob Roggeveen's ships, the *Africaansche Galey*, on the Tuamotu atoll of Takapoto in 1722.[28] The natives of that atoll may have first learned the value of nails and metal fittings from that derelict, whose crew and, presumably, supplies had been transferred to Roggeveen's other ships, thus leaving only the vessel to be scavenged. Quite possibly in their desultory trade with other atolls, they passed on some of the metal, as well as the knowledge they had derived about the qualities of this new material, and some of it eventually reached Tahiti. Since there is no evidence to the contrary, this seems as good an explanation as any for the source of Tahitian knowledge of iron during Wallis's time. However, until considerably more archaeological work has been conducted in the Society Islands it should be kept in mind that the source could have been earlier and non-European, that is, Asiatic. After all, the eroded iron knife in the hand of a Kauai native who boarded Cook's vessel at the time of the "discovery" of the Hawaiian Islands has not yet been satisfactorily explained away as the result of an alleged but unrecorded Spanish landing.[29] Many of the Asiatics, especially the Japanese and Chinese, were as much at home on the high seas in the sixteenth and seventeenth centuries as were Europeans, and their deep-water craft were equally as seaworthy.

Whatever the original source of Tahitian knowledge of iron, they not only wanted the metal, but they put it to work almost immediately. Nails, however, were not for driving, some being mounted as drills and small ones being bent into serviceable fishhooks, while modified spike nails quickly came to replace the less efficient chisels and gouges which had traditionally been made from bone.[30] Apparently, a sufficient number of small nails had been introduced by Wallis so that Cook, arriving two years later, found that only large nails and spikes were counted as truly worthwhile trade items.[31] However, with the Spanish introduction of no fewer than six thousand small fishhooks and three hundred large ones in 1772,[32] and Cook's introduction of a quantity of English woodworking tools the following year,[33] the need for nails to be modified into useful artifacts began to diminish. By 1777 Cook found need to grumble that the Tahitians would no longer even look at a nail when it came to trading.[34] For the Tahitians, nails had never been for building, and now the numerous manufactured tools and fishhooks which had been brought to the islands by Europeans eliminated the necessity for modifying spikes and the like to fit these purposes.

While nails as trade items were an immediate, but temporary, success, the same cannot be said of the ax. This tool, in all sizes, became the most sought-after instrument available to the Tahitians, and it remained so through 1797. What makes its full acceptance so interesting is that traditionally Tahitians employed the adz as their only chopping tool. Since the techniques and motor habits used with the ax and the adz are markedly different, it would seem that the Tahitians made a remarkably fast adjustment to a totally new technique of woodworking. The fact that metal adzes were introduced on at least two different occasions but never seem to have gained a popularity similar to the ax would appear to further this view.[35] This was not the case, however, for in 1797 James Wilson revealed the true state of affairs with regard to the ax. He discovered that the Tahitians had simply been taking the ax head off the handle and, by fixing it at right angles to the end of a helve, had been effectively converting it from an ax to an adz.[36] Thus, traditional woodworking habits in Tahiti had actually been maintained.

Why, if the Tahitians were determined to maintain their adz tradition, had they not more readily accepted the few metal adzes that had been offered them? Had they done so, it was almost assured that following ships would have brought them in abundance. However, as late as 1792, Vancouver still found the ax a favorite object of trade.[37] The answer to this question may well rest in the hafting mechanism of these two English tools. By long custom this always consisted of a hole in the metal cutting head for the helve, or handle, to pass through and be fixed. Such a socketed attachment, however, may have clashed with the Tahitian traditional method of attachment which called for binding the head of the stone adz to a knee joint formed at the working end of a wooden handle. With this in mind, one can immediately see that a European ax mounted crosswise, like an adz, on the end of a Tahitian adz handle had certain advantages. As with its stone adz counterpart, it would present a relatively flat surface which could be easily made to fit firmly against the smooth knee joint of the handle. Furthermore, with the built-in helve attachment hole now running crosswise to the handle, the tunnel-like opening would serve as an ideal passage through which the traditional lashings could be drawn in order to fasten the head to the handle. The European adz, on the contrary, would not present such a smooth attachment surface and, with its helve hole, or socket, in line with the handle and its deeper construction at the attachment head, would be far more difficult than an ax to fasten to the knee joint by the traditional method of patterned lashings. In other words, the Tahitians were most willing to substitute what was obviously a superior chopping material for their former stone adzes, but they saw no reason to exchange their time-tried method of hafting for that of the Europeans, even though the new tool was specifically designed for it. Since the ax lent itself more readily to their method of hafting than did the metal adz, the former became the preferred instrument. Whether these assumptions are correct cannot be ascertained at this time. However, they supply what seems the only logical explanation available as to why the Tahitians tended to neglect metal adz heads while readily accepting European ax blades for remounting as adzes.

There must have been innumerable other objects of iron that passed into Tahitian hands for which no written document preserved the record. A few tools, such as the mattocks, picks, and spades brought over by the Spaniards from

Lima, seem never to have caught on.[38] The Tahitians no doubt found their own digging stick quite adequate for the relatively small amount of cultivating that their gardens required. Interestingly, Marra reported razors being much in demand during Cook's second voyage,[39] though there is no mention of them before or after this record until 1797.[40] Perhaps they were originally accepted simply as another form of knife, but whether the Tahitians attempted to use them for the purpose for which they were intended is not known. The keen cutting edge may have initially attracted the islanders to this instrument, but it would not have taken long for them to find that its often brittle edge made it unsuitable for the normal uses of a knife. Thus, one suspects that the renewed request for the razor in 1797 may have been the result of finally understanding its intended purpose.

One iron object, the cast-iron pot, presented the Tahitians with a whole new concept in cooking. Although the islanders occasionally roasted some food over a fire or dropped hot stones into liquids contained in a wooden bowl, the bulk of their cooking was done in a pit oven. Such techniques were a necessity since they had no fire-proof container for boiling or frying. However, with the arrival of Wallis the Tahitians were offered the unusual spectacle of one of the ship's company boiling meat in an iron pot. The cooking potential of this exotic vessel immediately caught the fancy of a few Tahitians, so Wallis generously gave away several of the metal vessels to chiefs, including the chiefess, Purea. From that moment on, they began boiling meat in their little black pots while dozens of their fellow countrymen flocked around to watch the bubbling contents. They looked, according to Wallis, like rural folk in England watching a puppet show at some country fair.[41] However, the boiled meat of British delight was obviously no gourmet dish to the Tahitians, for after this initial experiment it took another thirty years before a Tahitian chief again asked for a similar cooking pot.[42]

Although we have but scratched the surface of the quantity of foreign trade materials that must have entered Tahiti between 1767 and 1797, it is obvious that the two major commodities, iron implements and textiles, became so integrated into Tahitian culture that the islanders would have suffered severe withdrawal pains had foreign vessels suddenly ceased their Pacific wanderings. While Bligh viewed the culture change, especially in clothing, as an unfortunately ugly choice of the Tahitians, Vancouver saw it all in a far more humanistic vein. He clearly recognized that the obviously superior European implements, as well as other objects which were less essential to Tahitian living, had, in 1792, become so integrated into the society that the people would have found it difficult to live without them. The old and traditional implements of stone and bone had been so completely replaced by ones of metal that Vancouver could acquire only poor copies of the working originals, and these were made, so he said, only for the tourist trade. In fact, so essential had cloth and iron become that the trade price of food to obtain them had dropped some two hundred percent since Cook's last visit in 1777. Under such circumstances, Vancouver felt forced to recommend that Europeans, for humanitarian reasons if nothing more, continue regularly to furnish Tahitians with at least the most important articles, gaining, in return, their customary supplies of food.[43]

While one can only admire Vancouver's concern over the future welfare of the Tahitians, the very cultural adaptability shown by the islanders in accepting European commodities would have again come into play had foreign ships ceased to arrive in Tahitian waters. In such an event, one can only speculate as to how much of the former European presence would have remained on the island, or within the culture, had such material objects ceased to arrive and the old ones disappeared through disintegration, wear, and loss. Perhaps some copies in local materials may have persisted, but far more promising would be those other European introductions whose staying power was less dependent on continuous foreign imports. One of these was foreign agricultural imports, including livestock, which held the potential of continued reproduction either as a food source or as escaped and unattended wild plants or animals.

Introduction of Foreign Crops

While the early explorers brought solid goods to trade with the islanders, they were also concerned with what they regarded as an attempt to upgrade the nutritive potential of the islands they visited. Understandably, this took the form of introducing crops and livestock that they were familiar with and whose advantages, they presumed, would be just as obvious to Polynesians as they were to Europeans. However, they were faced with the problem of introducing many new and unfamiliar-tasting foods to tradition-bound islanders who, like so many people of the world, were quite content with what they already had. Their food, after all, had for the most part obviously kept them in a fine state of health over countless years. Also, to further discourage their own good intentions, the early Europeans seldom stayed long enough on an island to show the people when a particular crop was ripe and, in certain cases, how to prepare it for eating once it was harvested.

Fruits, especially tree fruits, were among some of the first exotics to be brought to Tahiti, Wallis alone planting the first limes, lemons, oranges, peaches, cherries, and plums.[44] Of these, the last three, more acclimated to northern environments, probably would never have succeeded naturally. At least cherries and plums were never heard of or introduced again, and, although Máximo Rodríguez also planted peach stones in 1774–75,[45] he never reported on their growth, nor did anyone else. However, the more tropically adaptable citrus fruits also failed to succeed, apparently for lack of interest on the part of Tahitians. Joseph Banks, in 1769, not only did not mention these fruits left by Wallis, but made a very sincere effort to again plant lime, lemon, and orange seeds in the different soils to be found around Matavai.[46] These also must have failed in the end, for Bligh, in 1788, did not mention them but, in his turn, planted two orange trees which he happily reported were flourishing before he left the island.[47] Unfortunately for Bligh, his two little trees could not have flourished for long, since in 1791 yet another attempt was made to plant the originally introduced triumverate of citrus fruit. This time, however, Edward Edwards came to realize that the acidity of the fruits caused the Tahitians, who were used to a bland diet, not to bother taking care of the young trees. He thus concocted a scheme to make them more enticing by coating his limes, lemons, and oranges with sugar and feeding them to various chiefs.[48] The trick did not work, though, for after Bligh again planted oranges, and Vancouver lemons and oranges in 1792, the missionaries of 1797 mentioned only lemons and limes still growing on the island, though neither one was regarded as of much value by the Tahitians.[49]

Other Old World fruits fared as badly as the earlier citrus trees. The citrons, pomegranates, and quince introduced by Bligh in 1792[50] appear to have gone for naught, as did the American endemics, the cherimoyas introduced by the Spaniards in 1774–75,[51] and the guava planted in 1792.[52] Shaddocks, or pummelos *(Citrus grandis)*, found growing in the Tongan Islands and brought to Tahiti by Cook in 1777[53] were, like other citrus fruit, unappreciated by the Tahitians. However, these trees adapted well, and Bligh planted slips, probably from the original introductions, in other parts of the island in 1789. These latter were found to be producing in abundance when he returned in 1792.[54]

Grapes, possibly of Old World origin, were apparently first brought to Tahiti by the Spanish.[55] However, in 1777 they were found much the worse for trampling. It seems that the Tahitians, not knowing when the fruit was ready for plucking, ate some of the grapes well before they were ready for harvesting. Finding them sour in the extreme, they immediately concluded that they were poisonous and attempted to destroy them.[56] Later efforts by Bligh in 1788, and again by Vancouver in 1792, to reintroduce the vine appear to have failed.[57] For the Tahitians that first impression of the grape was quite sufficient.

In 1788 Bligh introduced the Old World fig and reported that one planted upcountry at a chief's house was doing well.[58] He brought more with him in 1792.[59] Whether these survived unrecognized by the missionaries in 1797 is open to question, for they could have been mistakenly taken for the endemic figs used in making a red dye. In fact, it is possible that the fruit of this imported fig may never have been eaten, though the sap may have been employed, as with the local species, in making the red dye for tapa. Unfortunately, we shall probably never know.

Because of the historic commercial production of pineapples in Hawaii, that fruit has often erroneously been regarded as an indigenous Polynesian crop. Actually, its origin was in tropical America, and, although the commercial varieties bear no seeds, there are others that do. It was the seeds of the latter which were introduced to Tahiti by way of England, and through the courtesy of Cook in 1769. Two more plants were started by him in 1777, and another two by Bligh in 1788. Still more were brought to the island in 1791, and Bligh planted another dozen the following year.[60] These plants appear to have reacted well to their favored tropical environment and, at long last, the Tahitians seem to have taken a liking to them and continued to plant them in their normal unsystematic manner. At least we do know that they were still growing in 1797, since Wilson reported that two of the missionaries who visited the district of Pare returned with no fewer than twenty pineapple plants.[61] Thus, out of fifteen exotic fruit-bearing plants brought to the island by 1797, only the pineapple, perhaps because some are remarkably sweet when fully ripened, seems to have ended up as a viable food plant for the Tahitians.

Considering the fleshy foods that formed the bulk of the traditional Tahitian diet, the islanders must have indeed looked with bewilderment at the grain crops springing up where European voyagers had sowed them broadcast in prepared plots. Louis Antoine de Bougainville was the first to plant wheat, barley, oats, rice, and maize, or Indian corn, in 1768.[62] Since all of these were grasses, only the maize with its heavy stalk and ears of corn would have stood out as something special to the Tahitians, the remainder looking like just another grass, a plant which, of course, the islanders had never attempted to eat. Cook, too, introduced more "grains" the following year,[63] and the Spaniards between 1772 and 1775 again planted wheat and rice, in addition to the Andean Indian grain, quinoa, or *Chenopodium quinoa* Willd.[64] It may have been a generous thought to bring in these European staples, but even had the Tahitians recognized that the hardened seeds of the smaller grains were the edible portion of the plant, it would have done little good. After all, they were totally unfamiliar with the grain preparation complex of thrashing, winnowing, grinding where needed, and finally cooking the resultant product. Some of these grains quite probably died out because of the adverse tropical environment in which they were planted. However, at least wheat, which was never touched by the Tahitians, was able to successfully compete with the local grasses, since some was found, apparently growing wild, as late as 1791.[65]

Maize, or Indian corn, had quite a different history in Tahiti than the smaller grains. Besides its original introduction in 1768, the Spanish brought in still more in 1772 and again in 1774–75.[66] By then Tahitians were actively growing the crop, for Rodríguez mentioned looking over the maize planted locally by the natives.[67] Bligh, who introduced still more maize in 1788, had some of his own crop stolen by the islanders who, he happily reported, immediately planted the grain in their own garden plots.[68] From that point onwards to 1797 at least some maize was found growing on the island.[69] The acceptance of maize by the Tahitians presupposes that they had discovered a way of consuming it. Although there is no explanation in the literature of how the Tahitians prepared their maize for eating, our knowledge of their cooking habits suggests one possible method. Since the islanders were unfamiliar with grinding hardened grain, there is a distinct possibility that they picked the ears while they were still somewhat green and the kernels were soft, like those of sweet corn. Since they were accustomed to wrapping many of their foods in green leaves before placing them in a pit oven for cooking, it is even possible that with the ears of maize already naturally wrapped by their own husks, the Tahitians placed them, husk and all, in their earth ovens. The result would have been delicious, steam-baked corn on the cob. In other words, here was a grain which could be cooked and eaten in its green state by using the available culinary arts. It was, therefore, accepted by them, though only as a decidedly secondary source of food.

The botanist Elmer D. Merrill gave Wallis credit for introducing the first American squash into Tahiti, but since Wallis failed to specifically mention this crop as being planted, and Merrill failed to reference his statement, the time and source of the introduction remain in question.[70] In terms of plant dispersals, the question is important, for while Merrill claimed that Cook, in 1769, found that the Tahitians had accepted the squash "first planted by Wallis," Cook's own statement actually read that he found pumpkins had gotten a footing in Tahitian soil and, rather than giving credit to Wallis for their introduction, he presumed that the Spanish had brought them in.[71]

While Cook was wrong in presuming a Spanish introduction, since the latter had not yet touched at Tahiti, Daniel Carl Solander's botanical manuscript of that first voyage listed a squash as having been found there. Unfortunately, he failed to describe the specimen, probably regarding it as a European introduction of an American Indian crop. Solander either had knowledge unavailable to Cook, or, in his turn, did a bit of presuming when he recorded that the plant was a volunteer which had first been introduced by Wallis.[72] He may have presumed correctly. While Wallis identified some of the crops he planted on the island, not including squash, he added that he planted "several sorts of garden seed" among which may have been squash.[73] The importance of all of this is simply that if neither Wallis nor Bougainville, who followed him, planted squashes (and neither one mentions having done so), the plant could represent a prehistoric introduction from America where *Cucurbita* are known to antedate European contact.[74] It is, of course, barely possible that Solander erroneously identified a gourd, or *Lagenaria*, as a squash, a similar error having once been made by a botanist in Hawaii.[75] However, this seems unlikely, since he and Banks collected such a specimen in Tahiti, describing it at that time as *Cucurbita lagenaria* L. This Merrill has since identified as *Lagenaria siceraria*.[76] The point here is that *Lagenaria* do not present the dispersal problem that *Cucurbita*, or squashes, do in that they are pantropical in distribution, being found in Africa, Asia, the Americas, and

Polynesia,[77] and almost certainly represented the gourds used by Tahitians to bring water out to Wallis's ship.[78]

Although the likelihood that either Wallis or Bougainville brought the first squashes to Tahiti is good, the only clear-cut record of Europeans introducing squashes to the island is to be found in the Spanish records of their voyage to Tahiti in 1772.[79] One thing is sure: the Spanish introduction seems to have been taken up by the natives. In 1774–75 Rodríguez was made a present of some Tahitian-grown "zapallos," or squashes, known under the botanical name of *Cucurbita maxima,*[80] and as late as 1788 Bligh reported that he not only saw many pumpkins growing, but was offered some for sale.[81] They must have continued to do well, for in the early nineteenth century William Ellis reported that pumpkins were growing nicely in the island environment.[82]

Because there is no longer a question as to the prehistoric introduction and assimilation of the American sweet potato into Tahitian culture, since, as noted earlier, it was there when the first European vessels arrived, there is little doubt that the seeds and slips of this same plant, brought from Peru by the Spaniards in 1772, had little trouble being immediately accepted by the local inhabitants, who would have recognized their value.[83] With the sweet potato well established as a Tahitian secondary food source, it would seem likely that the "Irish" potatoes brought out by these same Spaniards, and again by Cook in 1777,[84] would be picked up by the islanders as an additional form of root crop. However, this did not happen, and the reason finally became clear some years later when the missionary Ellis attempted to grow them in his own garden. He quickly found that the local tropical environment was totally unsuited to this crop. With the first planting the fleshy rhizomes developed only to the size of a spring potato, while a second planting produced still smaller specimens which were found to be considerably less tasty than the local sweet potato.[85]

The number of foreign plants deposited in Tahitian soil over the first thirty years of European contact must have been rather remarkable, although many may have been duplicates of previous historic introductions. Unfortunately, we can never know the full range, for, although the voyagers often took the trouble to note what they may have regarded as the more important crops planted, they all too often concluded with the teasingly simple comment that they also planted "all sorts of garden seed,"[86] "seeds of different kinds from the Cape of Good Hope,"[87] or, as the Spanish put it, "all the most useful seeds and plants of the Realm of Peru."[88] With statements like that, the cosmopolitan nature of the plant introductions to Tahiti can hardly be questioned! Beyond those imports already mentioned above, we can add onions, garlic, turnips, tomatoes, cucumbers, okra, mustard, parsley, lettuce, broccoli, endives, cabbages, and chili peppers.[89] Of all of these, the cabbage must have at least been tried by the Tahitians, since they stole some from Rodríguez's garden.[90] However, the attempt to use the plant must have ended in disappointment, for although some were found to be still growing in 1777, the natives now proclaimed a real dislike for the leafy vegetable.[91] As for the chili peppers, or capsicums, the bland diet of the Tahitians virtually assured their rejection of this Spanish-introduced crop, although they offered some for sale to Bligh in 1788.[92] Nonetheless, even though the Tahitians may not have liked the plant, the chili peppers found the Tahitian soils and climate very much to their own liking, and by 1797 they had dispersed themselves completely around the island.[93]

Not all of the botanical imports to Tahiti were meant to be eaten. Although tobacco seems not to have been introduced to the island until 1774–75, when the Spaniard Rodríguez reported planting some,[94] at least one islander had already lived through a disastrous experience with the product as early as 1769. Seeing Cook's sailors chewing the dried leaves, he successfully begged a sample to try for himself. Not realizing that the resultant brown saliva was to be spit out, he manfully swallowed the juice and quickly learned what many a young farm boy has learned, with equally discouraging effects.[95] Tobacco never needed cultivating by the Tahitians for, like chili peppers, it spread over the island under its own initiative.[96] While the missionaries reported that its red blossom was particularly enjoyed by the natives,[97] the islanders were now, apparently, familiar with its intended use. Thus, when Wilson attempted to deride their use of kava, they explained to him that its use only made them want to dance, just as tobacco did.[98] Obviously, they were no longer swallowing the juice!

Considering all of the derision that has been heaped upon the character of Captain Bligh who, in fact, was a rather fine ethnographic observer, it seems proper to conclude this listing of plant imports to Tahiti with two sentimentally inspired introductions by Bligh. In 1788 he brought in rose seeds because, as he explained, the Tahitians loved the sweet smell of flowers, and the women enjoyed decorating themselves with the blossoms.[99] His sentimentality overtook him again in 1792, when he introduced aloe plants because of their flower. On this latter occasion, however, he also exhibited some very sound thinking by introducing some fir trees and another type of tree which he referred to as "metrocederas" and which, when grown, would furnish the islanders with long, straight logs from which they could cut planks for boats.[100]

While European intentions in introducing new crops to Tahiti were of the noblest, some of their choices, and their lack of illustration of how to prepare various of them for eating, left much to be desired. As time went on, they gradually began to see their efforts going for naught. Unthinkingly, they at first saw this failure as completely the fault of the Tahitians. By as early as 1777, Cook complained that, although he had planted a number of items in a prepared garden, he seriously doubted that the islanders would ever look after them.[101] Bligh, who on his first voyage always seemed so optimistically pleased when a new crop appeared to be doing well, was a bit chagrined one day when he discovered that not only had his garden plot been thoroughly trampled, but the chiefs did not seem to be particularly upset by the damage.[102]

Tahitians had never had to do much cultivating in their own casually laid out gardens, because these were usually planted by slips or sprouts. Thus they did not need the careful soil preparation and early weed-hoeing required of seed cultivation. For them, extensive weeding and isolating of crop plants from potential competitors had never been too important. The use of the shod digging stick was their basic agricultural technique, although they seem to have been somewhat more thoughtful when it came to their kava fields. The Europeans were slow to understand Tahitian gardening techniques, for even as late as 1789 the complaint was being made that many of the plants formerly left by voyagers had been found growing luxuriantly but completely choked up with weeds.[103] Even Bligh ruefully came to the conclusion in 1792 that it was useless to bring the Tahitians any kind of plants that required care.[104] However, it took the reflective Vancouver to realize that, since the Tahitians had so many varieties of their own vegetables, they understandably had little desire for new ones. In addition, he reasoned, the unmanaged condition of those introduced crops which still survived indicated that if such were ever to be of any use to the Tahitians, it would have to be through the example of Old World agricultural techniques eventually supplied by resident European gardeners. The concept was basically sound, but his additional thought that Tahitians might come to imitate the Europeans' example of hard physical labor in cultivating the soil may have been unrealistic.[105]

Introduction of Foreign Livestock

As for that other aspect of agriculture, livestock and fowl, the Europeans were equally persistent in their attempts to create a wider variety of flesh foods for their Tahitian friends. Had it not been for a devastating war and a culinary error on the part of the islanders, this aspect of the welfare program might have had greater success than that involving plants. Since Tahitians had long been accustomed to chickens as a source of food, they had little trouble accepting European domesticated fowl brought in by the foreigners. A pair of turkeys and geese, as well as three guinea hens, were the first to be left on the island in 1767, followed the next year by another pair of turkeys and the further addition of drakes and ducks.[106] Although nobody reported ever having seen the guinea hens again, Banks encountered one of the turkeys and a pleasantly plump goose left by Wallis, both of which were quite tame and were thoroughly enjoyed by the islanders.[107] However, Bougainville's contribution of two turkeys and some ducks may have lasted only long enough to serve as tasty morsels, since Rodríguez, in 1774–75, reported having been shown only one goose that had been left on the island.[108] This particular creature must have led a charmed life or, like some geese, had a frightening disposition, for he was probably the same gander that Cook saw in 1777, identified by the islanders as one left by Wallis.[109]

The European chicken, introduced by the Spanish in 1772 or 1774,[110] must have soon interbred with the Tahitians' local Asian variety. Since the results would be essentially unidentifiable by other than specialists, they were not noted by later explorers. On his third voyage Cook brought the Tahitians another series of turkeys, geese, and ducks and, in addition, introduced a peacock and hen.[111] However, this generous restocking of the exotic fowl population eventually went for naught. Although in 1788 Bligh was able to report that the geese and ducks had been allowed to increase their progeny to a considerable extent, though the turkeys and peacocks had shown no proclivities in this direction, these favorable results were terminated abruptly in 1782. This was the year that the island of Moorea teamed up with the warriors of the district of Atehuru to wage a successful war against the paramount chief, Tu of Pare. The result was that all of these exotics were joyfully eaten as part of the destructive aftermath that usually accompanied such a military success.[112] Geese were again introduced in 1791, and yet again the following year,[113] so that by 1795 they were found to be well established.[114] Ducks, however, were not brought in again until 1797.[115]

Considering the number of common flesh food animals of the Old World, it was almost inevitable that sooner or later the European voyagers would attempt to introduce some to the Tahitians. The first of these, the goat, was imported to Tahiti by the Spaniards in 1772, and again in 1774,[116] while in between these two dates the English left a male and a female, the latter producing kids before the expedition left the island.[117] By 1777 the goats had bred to such an extent

that Cook reported that there was hardly a chief on the island who did not have some.[118] In fact, they were by then so
plentiful that Cook felt no compunction in begging four
goats from the paramount chief so that he might take one
pair to Raiatea, where they had none, and keep the other
pair for introduction to any island that he might find on his
journey into the northern Pacific.[119] So well did the goats do
that for a short time Tahiti became an exporter of the animals. In 1788 Bligh bought a goat and kid as part of his ship's
stores, and the *Bounty* mutineers, after unceremoniously
dumping Bligh and his loyal companions, returned to Tahiti
and, among other things, picked up thirty-eight goats and
eventually deposited them on the island of Tabuai.[120] Again,
in 1792, Vancouver collected a number of the same animals with the idea of introducing them to the Hawaiian
Islands.[121]

Obviously, there was no question but that the goats did
well in Tahiti. They should have, for the Tahitians developed
a distinct dislike for the meat as well as the smell of the
animals, and thus left them alone to breed.[122] By the 1790s
they had offered them up to ships in such quantity that they
were said to have been greatly reduced in number.[123] However, this report may have been unfounded, for the missionaries claimed that the goats had caused so much trouble
in the plantations of paper mulberry trees, quite probably
barking them, that many of them had been driven into the
mountains.[124] So disliked were these mischievous creatures
that in the destructive war of 1782 they were the only animals imported specifically as a potential source of food that
were not even touched by the victorious Mooreans!

The next animals to be introduced were three sheep in
1773. These had been castrated and were thus incapable of
breeding but the chiefs wanted them, so Cook let them go.
The following year the Spanish left a pair, but the ewe soon
died without issue. However, in 1777 Cook successfully introduced one ram and four ewes which produced ten young
before all were destroyed by the victorious Mooreans and
Atehurun warriors.[125] It must have been after this momen-
tous victory and feasting that the word went out that the

meat of sheep was highly offensive. There can certainly be little doubt about this appraisal, for the sheep had been prepared and cooked in the same fashion as a dog or a pig. That is, rather than skinning the animals, the Tahitians had carefully singed the wool off the hide and cooked the whole, as customary, in an earth oven.[126] As anyone who has smelled the stench of burning wool knows, the final taste of the smoke-infested hide and meat would be gastronomically offensive in the extreme. Although the missionaries dutifully reintroduced sheep to the island,[127] it is probable that they, and they alone, enjoyed the resulting roasts and chops for some years to come.

Although Tomás Gayangos claimed that several varieties of cattle were left on Tahiti by the Spanish from Lima,[128] either he was in error, or all but one young bull perished, for Rodríguez mentioned only the latter.[129] Cook, who saw the animal in 1777, described him as a remarkably fine beast.[130] Charles Clerke, however, observed the bull in a more pitiful light, explaining that it was the only being on the entire island that was incapable of finding any solace for itself through a little "amorous dalliance."[131] The bull must have been in agreement, for no sooner had Cook landed the three cows he had on board than he shortly noted that all three cows had accepted the love-starved animal.[132] The cows eventually produced eight calves and, although the Moorean warriors attempted to eat some of the cattle, they ended up taking some of them, a bull included, back to their island.[133] However, when Bligh arrived in 1788, he found both a bull and a cow still on Tahiti, but their separate location in two different districts was not helping in the least to breed up a stock. Through purchase of the bull, Bligh finally rectified this dismal situation and brought the two animals together.[134] Unfortunately, his efforts were wasted, for the mutineers of his ship, the *Bounty,* picked up the animals with a view to breeding them in Tubuai. Regrettably, the bull died on shipboard, and the cow was slaughtered on Tubuai.[135] By 1792 Vancouver discovered that the Moorean cattle had increased to four cows and a bull. The latter, however, had become crippled and could no longer breed.[136] Five years later it was found that the bull had been destroyed, while the cows had become so wild that the Mooreans did not dare to approach them.[137]

The culmination of this rather frustrating story is that, even had the cattle succeeded, it is somewhat doubtful if the islanders would have accepted this ample source of meat. Just as the Tahitians had done with the sheep, the Moorean warriors had cooked some of the beef, hide and all, and quickly discovered that even their strong teeth could not penetrate thoroughly cooked cow hide.[138] Here again, demonstration of preparation techniques by the Europeans might have saved the day or, on second thought, might have resulted in over-eager slaughtering before the stock could have bred up in sufficient quantity to maintain itself.

Fortunately, not all of the four-footed animals introduced to Tahiti failed so completely. An outstanding success was the variety of large European hogs introduced by the Spanish in 1774.[139] The Tahitian pig of Asiatic origin was a small breed and so, with the introduction of the much larger European variety, the Tahitians seem to have quickly accepted the animals and, no doubt, encouraged crossbreeding with their own stock. By 1777 William Anderson reported seeing a quantity of hogs which were noticeably larger than those originally found on the island.[140] In terms of the difficulty of human dispersal of the Asiatic pig into Polynesia, an interesting point was brought to light by Samwell and repeated later by Cook when off Kauai. It seems that on his previous voyages Cook had discovered that the original Tahitian pig did not stay alive on shipboard for any length of time. Thus, in preparing his ship's stores for his voyage northward he made the effort to purchase the Spanish hogs not just because they were larger, but also because they were known to be good sailors.[141] By 1788 Bligh reported that the European hog had supplanted the early Tahitian variety, though the animals he saw were probably the result of cross-breeding.[142] Certainly by 1797 the size of Tahitian pigs had increased enormously, Wilson mentioning an exceptionally fine example that dressed out at 340 pounds.[143]

While the European pig had been brought in specifically as a flesh food animal, two other creatures were introduced for quite different reasons. However, they ended up, as far as the Tahitians were concerned, as excellent sources of food. These were the cat and the dog. Actually, a cat, pregnant with kittens, was probably the first European animal introduced to Tahiti: Wallis gave it to the chiefess Purea as a gift in 1767. Cook dropped off twenty more in 1774, and by the end of the following year the Spanish had added still more to the island.[144]

With the numerous small Polynesian rats on the island for food there was little doubt that the cats would survive and multiply. Others may also have been introduced from time to time without a record of the event. Be that as it may, by 1777 some had already gone wild and were living off what they could find in the mountains.[145] By 1789 Bligh found it worthy of note that the cats had done such a fine job of ridding the island of its rats that he had scarcely seen any of them.[146] However, perhaps they had become temporarily satiated with their diet, since in 1797 Wilson complained to the paramount chief about the damage being done by rats and was immediately issued four cats to take care of the matter.[147]

As noted much earlier, Tahitians were never perturbed by their rat population, regardless of its effect upon their foreign guests. In fact, they enjoyed feeding them scraps of food at mealtime and kept them from doing damage by placing rat guards on their food posts and at other locations where they were not desirable companions. However, at the same time they never seem to have been annoyed by the cats' ability to keep the rat population low. This apparent inconsistency may well have been due to the fact that a well-fed cat meant a future good meal, Tahitians having discovered that feline flesh was quite edible.

Since dogs had always been an acceptable form of food for Tahitians, the new and different breeds brought by the Europeans were readily received by the local population. Although Rodríguez suggested that the first foreign dog import may have come from the Spanish in 1772,[149] the first reliable record is of the shaggy, tar-covered dog of John Forster, which, for diplomatic reasons, he was rather forced to give to the paramount chief, Tu, who had begged for the animal.[150] This may not have been the only dog left on the island during Cook's second voyage, since the following year Rodríguez specifically mentioned seeing spaniels which, the Tahitians explained, had been left by the English.[151] However, the Spanish were not to be outdone, so they introduced some dogs from Lima.[152] These appear to have represented two or three different types whose viciousness made no friends of the British in 1777 when the dogs attacked the English sheep which Cook had painstakingly brought to the island.[153] Cook succinctly summarized his views of the Spanish dogs when he wrote that the Spaniards would have done the island a lot more good if they had hung the beasts instead of landing them.[154] Over the years more dogs must have been landed—Bligh, for example, left a pointer[155]—so that little by the little the original character of the Tahitian dog disappeared through miscegenation with a wide selection of imported canines.

Finally, it should be mentioned that that rapid multiplier of its kind, the rabbit, was given the opportunity to exhibit its proclivities in a Tahitian setting. As Wilson so blithely put it, "If they prosper, the hills will soon breed them in abundance."[156] Unlike Australia, Tahiti was fortunate in that the rabbit did not thrive in this tropical environment, even though Ellis stated that several attempts were made to introduce them.[157]

Thus goes the story of the first thirty years of intentional European introduction of their domesticated plants and animals. The acceptance rate of these agricultural products was frustratingly low. Some plants, as well as the rabbit, did not thrive because of adverse natural environmental conditions, while other plants might well have survived under proper European-style cultivation, but failed under the traditional, but casual, gardening techniques of the Tahitians. Unaccustomed taste also played a role, as did the lack of knowledge of what to look for when a particular crop was ripe for plucking. And above all, there was the need to know the process by which some of the foreign crops, as well as the animals, were made ready for human consumption.

Although the great bulk of domesticates were unacceptable to Tahitians, the European presence on Tahitian soil was marked, if not for all time, certainly for many years to come. Here it is interesting to note, however, that of the few exotic crops seemingly accepted by the Tahitians — namely pineapples, maize, and probably squash, not to mention the chili peppers and tobacco that ran wild throughout the island — all were of American Indian origin, yet none had been brought to the island by the natives of that continent. However, there were still some European fruit trees, unused but growing strong, as well as various Old World exotics which undoubtedly ended up growing wild, owing to their ability to effectively compete with the local indigenous flora. As for the introduced fauna, some of the fowl and other animals might have disappeared without continued European intervention, but I rather suspect that the wily goat and the cat would have survived unattended in the inner mountain sanctuaries of the island.

Further Effects of European Contact

Those things that the early voyagers intentionally set before the Tahitians for them to accept or reject as they saw fit were not the only outside influences, for the very presence of these foreigners afforded the islanders further opportunities to observe new lifeways and, through constant questioning born of curiosity, to learn something of the thoughts and attitudes of these foreign visitors. These, too, represented potential sources for culture change through imitation or thoughtful reflection on the part of the Tahitians. They were not, for the most part, intentional offerings by the Europeans, but they were there nonetheless to be accepted or rejected at the will of the islanders.

When Tahitian chiefs were invited aboard European ships for a meal, they attempted to copy the table manners of their hosts as a diplomatic gesture. Although used to sitting on the ground with their food spread out before them, they accommodated themselves to the dining table. At first they found the chairs awkward to get into but finally came to appreciate their convenience[158] — so much so in fact, that by

1788 Bligh was asked to arrange for King George of England to send not just any chairs, but specifically high-backed, "elbow" chairs.[159] By 1797 the missionaries reported that although the islanders still were accustomed to sitting on the ground, the average home always had a seat or two for the comfort of guests.[160] The table, however, seems not to have been fully appreciated, at least during the first thirty years of contact. However, in 1777 and again in 1797 there were mentions of chiefs who served their foreign guests on such a piece of furniture.[161] Nonetheless, there are no records of direct requests for such an item, nor did the missionaries note them as part of the furnishing of a common house.

Shipboard dining was more than just sitting at a table, for, unlike the Tahitians, each European was armed with a knife and fork and occasionally a spoon. The use of these instruments posed a problem, as witness Wallis's description of one native whose valiant attempt with a fork was at first doomed to failure by his own well-implanted motor habits. Accustomed to eating with his hands, he raised his well-filled fork from the plate, but his hand insisted on moving to his mouth, thus leaving the fork and its contents waving precariously near one ear.[162] It all took time, for there were such oddities as putting "oil," actually butter, on one's breadfruit, and learning to drink the hot water that the English called tea. New to them also was salt which one put on food, rather than dipping a morsel into sea water to gain the same effect.[163]

At first the copying of European table manners took the form of Tahitian politeness in attempting to conform to the customs of their foreign friends whenever they were invited aboard their ships. However, a few of the chiefs occasionally attempted to extend this gesture by duplicating, as best they could, the Europeans' eating paraphernalia and techniques when they invited foreign guests to their homes. In one such instance, a large kitchen knife and individual bamboo sticks served in the place of individual knives and forks.[164] However, by 1777 Samwell reported going to a chief's home for dinner and, to his complete surprise, finding a table covered with a "tablecloth" of green leaves and the whole surrounded with benches forming, in a effect, a rough copy of what the host had seen in the midshipmen's quarters aboard ship.[165]

What originally started out as a gesture of politeness when eating with Europeans gradually became a sincere habit on the part of Tahitians to copy the foreign eating habits as, apparently, a symbol of prestige.[166] This change of attitude appears to generally coincide with the same post-1777 period during which acceptance of European clothing became a part of the Tahitian way of life. And as with the change of clothing, the new attitude in dining habits seems to have been precipitated by the chiefly class. This was understandable, since they had the closest contact with Europeans and were under far fewer secular constraints than the common Tahitian. In fact, so great was their effort that by 1789 the Tahitian taboo forbidding men and women to eat together had been broken by Tu, the paramount chief.[167] This change resulted no doubt because the English had long explained that in their country it was most proper for the two sexes to share a common meal, and certainly Omai had confirmed this story after his visit abroad. By 1792 this breakdown of the eating taboo had extended to include at least one other chief, though Vancouver explained that such a practice was by no means common among the bulk of the population.[168] However, the trend undoubtedly continued, for, although Ellis gave the missionaries full credit for the breakdown of this taboo,[169] and they obviously aided its dissolution, the example had already been set by the chiefs well before these pious Christians had arrived on the island. Unfortunately, European eating habits also included the drinking of alcoholic beverages, both light and strong, and, although Tahitians were slow to accept this element of a proper meal,[170] when they did come to appreciate it, they did so with gusto.[171]

There were other aspects of European culture that appealed to Tahitians. During their numerous visits to the great ships they must have noted the convenient seaman's chests in which officers and crew stored that which was valuable to them, while the tent encampment on shore introduced them to the raised wooden bedstead. Although traditional chiefly custom had been to disburse material wealth as a gesture of greatness, it is possible that the European attitude of protective custody of one's personal wealth began to cause a change of chiefly attitudes in this regard. Or perhaps the sheer quantity of enticing trade material had developed a sense of covetousness. However, such goods were so readily available that this latter idea seems an unlikely possibility. Regardless, what we do know is that by 1777 paramount chief Tu found it necessary to ask Cook if he would have a chest made for him in which he could safely store all the trade goods and gifts he had accumulated. As if such would not be secure enough, he further asked that a bed be built into it so that he might sleep upon his treasures.[172] The same kind of a request was made to Bligh in 1788,[173] and in 1792 Vancouver was stuck with having to direct his carpenters to make another large chest for Pomare, then regent, who refused to settle for the smaller one originally planned for him.[174] However, by then Tahitian carpenters had become highly adept at using iron tools, one man surprising Bligh by exhibiting his wooden copy of a sailor's chest. It must have been a remarkable piece of craftsmanship, for the sides were dove-tailed together, and the hinges and even the lock with bolt were expertly worked from wood. Only the key was made from iron.[175] By 1797 a large chest, often used to sleep upon, was common in the houses of Tahiti.[176]

As for the independent bedstead, the first request for such was recorded in 1788.[177] Others may have been brought, or made, by later ship's companies, but the fact that by 1797 they were not uncommon in ordinary houses suggests that many, if not most, had been made locally. Although the normal sleeping habit of the Tahitian was to roll up in tapa cloth on the floor of his house, the practice of some of the islanders of sleeping on boards placed over an indoor pigpen made the transition to a bedstead not too great a change from traditional custom. Getting off the damp ground may well have been an inducement toward using the European bedstead, but the missionaries suggested an even stronger reason: it seems that the flea had been included among the faunal introductions of the Europeans, and it quickly found a warm and comfortable abode in the grass-covered floors of Tahitian houses. A raised bed thus kept all but the most athletic of these creatures from disturbing the sleep of the rightful lords of the Tahitian household.[178]

What other duplicates of European household effects may have been made we do not know, though, as has been mentioned earlier, the historic development of a rectangular dwelling in place of the traditional parallel-sided one with round ends was almost certainly the result of European influence. While it was almost inevitable that sooner or later the Tahitians would attempt to copy a European sailing vessel, which they did in 1797,[179] it is somewhat disconcerting to learn that by 1789 simple, long box coffins were occasionally being constructed. However, since the custom of body exposure of the chiefly dead was still strongly adhered to, the function of the European-derived coffin had been modified by the Tahitians to the role of a convenient container in which to carry the dead from the dwelling to the drying rack. It was, apparently, a prestige symbol, for boards were hard to split and trim, and thus a coffin was only occasionally employed.[180]

With the Tahitians' love of dance and sports, it took little time before they had added to their repertoire the sailor's hornpipe as well as various versions of English folk dances. As for music, in 1791 Edwards and George Hamilton were the surprised witnesses to the arrival of Tahiti's paramount chief and his retinue, preceded by no less a European feature than a band of musicians![181] While many of the sports maintained their traditional forms, the Tahitian technique of boxing gradually began to take on the characteristics of the English boxing of the period. No doubt this was the result of watching sailors exhibiting their own version of the sport. As for cockfighting, long presumed to have been a common pre-contact sport indulged in throughout Tahiti, I have made the case for its probable introduction by the English in 1773 in a previous chapter. That it became an overwhelming success in the years that followed was clearly attested to by the missionary Ellis who, it would appear, accepted without question the legend of the sport's prehistoric introduction to the island.[182]

Of all of the choices of European traits made by the Tahitians, the gun and the change from the old attitude of war for prestige to the idea of war for land acquisition and control were, perhaps, the most significant. That the gun was adopted can be readily understood, for Wallis had used it effectively against a numerically superior force of Tahitians. Even as early as 1769, a native had taken Banks' gun from his hands and fired it to show that he knew how. The fact that it accidentally flashed in the pan was unimportant in the light of the islander's ability, based only on observation, to cock and fire the musket.[183]

Although Bligh had the dubious honor of having been the first to leave guns on the island of Tahiti, it must have been Cook's gift of three or four guns to Omai to protect himself on Huahine Island that got the chiefs thinking that if one Polynesian could obtain muskets from the English, so could they. At least the record shows that the first formal request that the British bring out guns and ammunition was made to Cook that same year.[184] As Bligh later found out, Omai showed all of the Society Islanders exactly what a handful of guns could do in one of their battles. His island of Huahine had proceeded to conduct a war against the neighboring islands of Raiatea and Borabora, using Omai and his paltry armament as the critical factor. Although the locks on the muskets were no longer functional, Omai and his men devastated the enemy: after loading his gun, each man aimed while another stood by his side and set fire to the priming with nothing more than a glowing stick. Thus, even with something less than completely workable flintlocks, an inter-island battle was won with few difficulties. Little wonder that Bligh was pressured into leaving guns on Tahiti, and for the same avowed reason that Omai had gotten his muskets from Cook—that is, for personal defense.

Bligh's 1798 contribution to eventual mayhem consisted of nothing more than two muskets and a pair of pistols, along with suitable ammunition. Even then he could report that no less a person than the wife of the paramount chief was already an excellent shot, as was Odiddy, who had traveled with Cook in 1773–74.[185] Two years later the Tahitians had acquired twenty guns and two hundred rounds of ammunition,[186] much of which appears to have been given them by the mutineers of the *Bounty.*[187] The following year, 1792, Bligh returned to the island and attempted a precise count of their accumulated weaponry. He now found that they had no fewer than twenty-seven muskets, twenty-one pistols, and even a swivel gun.[188] Such were not idle curiosities either, for the Tahitians were capable of taking the guns apart and putting them together again. Even more important, they were fully cognizant of the advantage this armament gave them over the other islands in the Society group.[189]

A superior weapon of battle was rapidly becoming a part of Tahitian culture and with it, as noted earlier, was coming a change in the purpose of warfare. The drive for acquisition of land and the political and military force to hold it was rapidly replacing the old attitude that victory should be accompanied by only a short-lived attempt to devastate the economic base of the enemy, but not to dominate that base. The European touch was becoming evident, and, as if to complete the picture, Pomare, after victoriously gaining the entire island for himself in 1790 or 1791, grandiously revealed his personal flag, which consisted of a Union Jack decorated with patterns of pearls and red feathers. This newly developed emblem was carried to all of the conquered districts as his symbol of political domination.[190] Was this, perhaps, the original Union Jack that Cook had given Tu, then paramount chief, in 1774, and which was still preserved in 1777?[191] Or was it, in fact, simply the Jack from a passing ship, as the missionaries claimed it to be?[192] I rather suspect it was the former, for it had originally been presented by Cook with the idea that it be flown on a great war canoe then being built for Tu.

There is no doubt that European culture, through direct contact, was by far the strongest force in precipitating change among the Tahitians. However, there were other sources which, though not European, were instigated by Europeans. The results from these particular sources have never really been investigated, nor can this be readily accomplished with the data on hand. One source of change was the Tahitians who voyaged out across the Pacific in European ships, some to return to their homeland, others to die on strange, foreign soil. Of those that returned, there were the two brought back from Lima by the Spaniards in 1774,[193] and Odiddy, with his servant,[194] whom Cook took with him in 1773 into the cold seas of Antarctica. Here Odiddy not only cast eyes on hardened water, or ice, but in the course of the voyage became personally acquainted with such Polynesian islands as New Zealand, Tonga, Easter, and the Marquesas. Not only must he have broadened the geographic knowledge of his countrymen upon his return, but his accounts of religion and other customs of the people he had seen and talked to may have affected, if not Tahitian cultural structure, perhaps the content of its orally transmitted legends. Then, too, there was Omai with his much longer two-way voyage with Cook plus his extended stay in England which, potentially, had even more to offer his fellow islanders.[195]

Reversing this view for a moment, one must also wonder what influence these men had on the Polynesians whose islands they visited during their historic voyages. In addition to the above, there was also the native Ahutoru, whom Bougainville took back with him to France but who died on the return trip,[196] and the great chief and priest Tupaia and his native assistant, whom Cook attempted to take to England in 1769 but who died enroute,[197] all of whom must also have left some kind of mark on the islands they visited. All of these men could, after all, talk with the people of other Polynesian islands, although there were occasional difficulties because of dialectic differences. Nonetheless, it is possible that Tupaia's, Odiddy's, and Omai's discussions with the Maori of the glories of their Tahitian homeland may have given rise to the latter's eventual legend of fleets of Society Islanders immigrating to New Zealand. And what stories might have been injected into later legendary accounts by the Hawaiian whom Vancouver had with him in Tahiti in 1792, and who was returned to his homeland in the north, though very much against his will?[198] We shall probably never know for certain. However, the potential for native-to-native early historic diffusion of island culture traits was present and, it might be added, was greatly increased during the first half of the following century when Polynesians shipped out on whaling and trading vessels. Here, then, might be the source for some of the apparent cultural similarities between distant islands which have previously been thought to be of prehistoric origin. Here also might be the source for the building of, or adding to, the content of migration legends based upon newly acquired, but historic, geographic knowledge of distant Polynesian lands.

A far less important source of cultural change, if not just contamination, was the artifacts picked up by sailors and their officers from various islands and left in the hands of Tahitians. Cook, for example, having learned of the high value placed upon red feathers by the Tahitians, imported quantities of these from the Tongan islands, most of them glued to pieces of tapa cloth or forming decorations on coconut fiber materials. However, also included were such things as baskets, clubs, painted tapa, and Tongan mats. In fact, as a result of listening to Odiddy's accounts of the islands he had visited with Cook, the Tahitian chiefs began requesting artifacts not only from Tonga, but also from Easter Island and the Marquesas.[199] In 1777 Cook and his men brought more items from Tonga, including feather head-pieces.[200] It would also appear that on this occasion even Omai had brought back a Maori canoe. At least John Rickman reported that the high chief of Tahiti was so intrigued by Omai's tales of his travels that he gave him a fine double canoe to take the place of the one Omai had purchased in New Zealand.[201]

Other items must have been brought to Tahiti as well, for George Mortimer mentioned seeing a fine Tongan spear on the island in 1789,[202] and two years later Hamilton found panpipes, a west Polynesian musical instrument, being played in Tahiti.[203] Even the *Bounty* mutineers played a part in this transfer of native goods, for Bligh was shown a large drum which Fletcher Christian had brought back from Tubuai.[204] Again, as late as 1797 an entire Tongan canoe brought back by Wilson was presented as a gift to the paramount chief of Tahiti.[205] Quite probably such artifact dispersals had no great effect on the lives of Tahitians. However, they are almost certain to cause havoc in the work of some unknowing anthropologist studying early Tahitian artifacts in the sacred halls of great museums where a Tongan club or other item may be very honestly labeled as having been obtained in Tahiti.

For thirty years, from 1767 to 1797, the Tahitians had hosted their foreign visitors. At first it was done from fear of their dreaded guns, but this soon changed to an attitude of joyful expectancy as each new vessel brought more interesting exotics from the outside world. Before the end of the century, anticipation had become tempered with need, as the culture became progressively more dependent upon such things as textiles and iron. However, this dependence had not been forced upon them, for no one had demanded that they accept this or that object or conduct their lives in other than their traditional manner. True, stealing had always been a problem, but it was almost the only situation in which the two cultures clashed for brief periods before things were smoothed over by an exchange of gifts. In the meantime, the Tahitians continued to choose freely those material things and lifeways of their guests that appeared to be most desirable. That not all of their original choices were best suited to them seems clear, since some were quickly abandoned and others might have eventually been discarded had freedom of choice been given more time in which to operate. Unfortunately, the time factor was against this. In 1797 the good ship *Duff* brought with her the viable seeds of ethnocentrism with all of its biases and patronizing aspects, neatly packed in humanitarian wrappings which could have borne the label, "Protestantism of the Eighteenth Century."

The missionaries were the first to bring forced culture change to the island of Tahiti. Although they were the smallest of minorities, they were strong of will, and they knew what was right and good for Tahitians. With the best of Tahitian manners, the island's women indicated their pleasure at seeing these visitors by puncturing their heads with a shark's tooth and symbolically weeping, only to be told to stop such absurd actions immediately and simply shake hands or smile as any proper European might do.[206] Pridefully, the missionaries accepted without question the Tahitian claim that they had been responsible for stopping the traditional, but immodest, uncovering of the upper body as a gesture of respect for chiefs, pointing out that this applied only to those appropriately dressed in European clothing.[207] Learning that such undraping had actually been discontinued some years earlier because of the difficulty of lowering a European, tailored jacket rather than because of any missionary-induced sense of modesty would have been a disillusionment. Apparently, the Tahitians did not want to impose such an embarrassment upon their new guests.

It was not too many months after their landing that the missionaries reported on their progress toward native acculturation in the direction of Protestant codes of conduct. This included having restrained the Tahitians' "natural levity," and having driven them to conduct their favorite recreational heiva at some distance from missionary eyes and ears. By then, too, either the Christians had unknowingly become somewhat accustomed to the casual dress of Tahitians or they had, in fact, done what they claimed and enforced a greater sense of modesty in native accoutrement.[208] As for the Tahitian women, they played their part well by convincing these pious souls that all of their sexually flagrant acts of the past were completely the fault of the British "brutes."[209] One wonders just how many sailors must have raised their eyebrows in surprise when that dastardly observation was first published in England.

Thus was born in Tahiti the acculturative process in which the islanders became successively more limited in their freedom of choice in modifying their cultural ways and

The paramount chief of Tahiti (still under taboos requiring him and his wife to be carried) ceding land to Captain James Wilson for the missionaries. Engraving from a painting by R. Smirke.

increasingly forced into new and often nonintegrating patterns of European lifestyles. The "do's and don't's" of
eighteenth-century Protestantism were eventually to be replaced by those of Catholicism and finally by the political
hegemony of France.

Some two hundred years after Wallis's discovery, the
ways of early Tahiti no longer exist, and the bustling, teeming streets of its little capital city of Papeete presage a growing competition with Honolulu. New mini-highrises jut,
derrick-like, into the sky, and black volcanic scrapings on
smoothly rolling foothills mark ugly terrace sites for new
homes or apartments for the well-to-do. The people are
called native Tahitians, but their dress and manner, the cars
they drive, and much of the obvious about them is European. However, in the upper levels of the business world
they disappear. Tahitians have been acculturated into a
world of French colonials, but they have not been allowed to
fully integrate into the French economic life, except at the
lower levels. Nonetheless, change is an on-going phenome-
non, and, along the roads of the narrow, twisting coastland
on the far side of the island, a few flags of horizontal red and
white bands can be seen in the front yards of plain little
houses. They symbolize a restive desire of the Tahitians to
regain their old freedom of choice, to control their own des-
tiny. The abrasiveness of nearly two hundred years of
forced culture change has worn away much that was good in
Tahitian living without replacing it with a satisfactory substitute. The past cannot be relived, but the freedom of choice
that was once their mainstay might yet be recoverable.

Glossary

'ahia: The fruit tree *Syzygium malaccense* (L.) Merr. and Perr., sometimes called the Tahitian apple.

ahu: The raised masonry platform at one end of a marae court. Large ahu were often terraced, or stepped.

amo'a: A series of ceremonies performed to remove certain religious taboos which a newborn child was thought to possess when first brought into the world.

ari'i: A chief, or member of the chiefly class.

'arioi: A society of entertainers all of whom appear to have belonged to the chiefly class.

fe'i: A banana plant, *Musa troglodytarum* L., noted for its yellowish-orange fruit which grows on an erect stem.

heiva: A form of public entertainment consisting of dances or plays, some of which were formal, others high-spirited or farcial.

'ie'ie: A vine, *Freycinetia demissa,* used in making baskets.

mahi: Breadfruit preserved by allowing it to ferment in a covered pit.

manahune: Originally the class name for landowning commoners on Tahiti nui, but later used in the same region to designate landless laborers and farmers.

marae: An open-air religious structure for formalized worship. They varied greatly in size, but the basic components consisted of a court with a raised masonry platform, or ahu, at one end.

maro: A breechclout, made of tapa or fine matting.

maro 'ura: The sacred and profusely ornamented breechclout worn on ceremonial occasions by the paramount chief of Tahiti nui.

mata'eina'a: One of the smaller subdivisions of a district, including the people therein, which was under the immediate control of a subordinate chief, probably a to'ofa.

mati: The fig tree *Ficus tinctoria* Forst.

metua: A subchief, usually a relative, who acted as the representative of a paramount or district chief on land owned by such a superior chief but located outside his district or immediate area of personal control.

miri: Mortuary specialists who undertook the preservation of the chiefly dead by oiling and drying the corpses.

'opio: An exceptionally large pit oven used for the communal cooking of breadfruit.

ora: The fig tree *Ficus prolixa* Forst. Also the name of a tapa cloth made from the inner bark of the fig tree.

pahi: A type of canoe hull with raised prow and stern having a cross-section resembling an inverted spade symbol in a deck of cards. Such hulls were always lashed a few feet apart in parallel alighment to form double canoes.

patu: A major subdivision of a large district.

pia: The Polynesian arrowroot *Tacca leontopetaloides* (L.) Kuntze.

pipi: Theherbaceous plant *Phaseolus truxillensis* MBK.

popoi: Any plant food beaten into an edible paste.

purau: *Hibiscus tiliaceus* L., whose bark and soft wood were used for a variety of purposes.

ra'a: Anything sacred.

ra'atira: The name for landowning commoners on Tahiti iti, or Taiarapu.

rahui: A taboo, or restriction, placed against the harvesting of certain crops, the killing of particular domestic animals, or fishing in certain waters of the lagoon.

roava: An apparent alternate name for the tamanu tree, *Calophyllum inophyllum* L., when planted in a marae.

ta'ata 'orero: The spokesman for a paramount chief on all formal occasions. In addition he was required to memorize and recite, as needed, the chief's lineage and gods, as well as certain historical happenings. He also served as teacher of the young of chiefly status.

tahu'a: A religious priest and teacher.

taio: A formally adopted friend

tamanu: The tree *Calophyllum inophyllum* L.

teuteu: The landless, lowest class of people who worked as skilled and unskilled laborers, or as servants. Near the close of the eighteenth century the term came to designate only servants.

teve: The aroid *Amorphophallus campanulatus* (Roxburgh) Blume, no longer used as food in Polynesia.

ti: The plant *Cordyline terminales* (L.) Kunth, whose sweet roots were used as food.

ti'i: An apparent term for a commoner's individual landholding within the small subdivision of a district known as a mata'eina'a.

tiputa: A poncho of tapa or matting with a hole or slit in the middle through which to pass one's head.

toa: The tree *Casuarina equisetifolia* J. R. and G. Forster.

to'ofa: A subordinate, and usually a relative, of a district chief, whose duties were to assure that the chief's wishes were carried out.

va'a: A type of canoe hull with raised stern and a horizontal, flat board extending forward of the cutwater to form a prow. Such hulls were either squared or rounded, their bottom portion being adzed out of a log. Such vessels were used singly with outrigger, or lashed a few feet apart in parallel alighment to form double canoes.

vi: The so-called Polynesian plum *Spondias dulcis* Forst.

Notes to the Chapters

Landfall Tahiti

1. Samuel Wallis, "An Account of a Voyage Round the World in the Years 1766, 1767, and 1768," p. 435.
2. For observations on the physical features of the Tahitians see *A Journal of a Voyage Round the World, in His Majesty's Ship Endeavour, In the Years 1768, 1769, 1770, and 1771...*, p. 43; Fr. José Amich, "An Account of the First Voyage of the *Aguila* under Captain Don Domingo de Boenechea to Tahiti: 1772–73," p. 79; José de Andia y Varela, "Narrative of a Voyage Performed to the Island of Amat, Otherwise by Name Otahiti,... in the Years 1774 and 1775," pp. 257, 265; William Bligh, "A Voyage to the South Sea ... in His Majesty's Ship the Bounty ...," p. 66; Domingo Boenechea, "Narrative of the Voyage performed by Don Domingo Boenechea,... in the Frigate *Santa María Magdalena* (alias *el Aguila*)..., pp. 319, 330; Louis Antoine de Bougainville, *A Voyage Round the World... in the Years 1766, 1767, 1768 and 1769*, p. 249; James Cook, *The Journals of Captain James Cook*, vol. 1, pp. 123–24, and vol. 3, p. 1343; Bolton G. Corney, ed., *The Quest and Occupation of Tahiti by Emissaries of Spain in the Years 1772–76*, vol. 2, p. 459; George Forster, *Voyage Round the World ... During the Years 1772, 3, 4, and 5*, vol. 1, pp. 255, 259, 265, 305, 326–27, and vol. 2, p. 100; John R. Forster, *Observations Made During a Voyage Round the World ...*, p. 593; John Ledyard, *Journal of Captain Cook's Last Voyage*, pp. 48–49; Sydney Parkinson, *A Journal of a Voyage to the South Seas, in His Majesty's Ship the Endeavour: Faithfully Transcribed From the Papers of the Late Sydney Parkinson...*, pp. 13–14, 18, 22; George Robertson, "A Journal of the Second Voyage of H.M.S. *Dolphin* ... in the Years 1766, 1767, and 1768," pp. 148, 179, 229; Máximo Rodríguez, "Daily Narrative Kept by the Interpreter Máximo Rodríguez at the Island of Amat, Otherwise Otahiti, in the year 1774," p. 193; Anders Sparrman, *A Voyage Round the World With Captain James Cook in H.M.S. Resolution*, pp. 49, 53, 62, 70; Wallis, p. 480; James Wilson, *A Missionary Voyage to the Southern Pacific Ocean, Performed in the Years 1796, 1797, 1798 in the Ship Duff...*, pp. 336–37.

3. For observations on the treatment of body hair see *Journal of a Voyage*, p. 44; Amich, p. 79; Andia y Varela, p. 257; Boenechea, p. 330; Bougainville, p. 250; Cook, vol. 1, pp. 123–24; Corney, vol. 2, p. 459; George Forster, vol. 1, pp. 259, 327; John R. Forster, p. 443; Ledyard, p. 49; Parkinson, pp. 22, 25; Sparrman, p. 66.

4. George Forster, vol. 1, pp. 283, 291; John R. Forster, p. 593; Sparrman, p. 58.

5. John R. Forster, p. 593.

6. John R. Forster, p. 513.

7. J. C. Beaglehole, *The Exploration of the Pacific*, p. 183; Andrew Sharp, *The Discovery of the Pacific Islands*, p. 60.

8. For observations on tattooing see Joseph Banks, *The Endeavour Journal of Joseph Banks*, vol. 1, p. 309; Boenechea, p. 330; Cook, vol. 1, p. 125; Corney, vol. 2, p. 471; Parkinson, p. 44; Wilson, p. 339.

9. Cook, vol. 3, pp. 202–3, 980.

10. For references to Tahitian dress and ornament see *Journal of a Voyage*, pp. 43–44; Amich, pp. 79–80, 83; Andia y Varela, pp. 258, 277, 300; Boenechea, pp. 317, 330–31; Bougainville, pp. 246, 250–52; Cook, vol. 1, pp. 90, 125–26; Corney, vol. 2, pp. 459, 472–73; George Forster, vol. 1, pp. 254–55, 327, 361–62; John R. Forster, pp. 397, 448; Ledyard, pp. 49–50; Parkinson, pp. 18, 24, 26, 40–43, 46, 49; Robertson, pp. 172, 174, 206, 228; Rodríguez, pp. 98, 111; Sparrman, pp. 50–51, 54; Wallis, pp. 468, 481–82; Wilson, p. 395.

Law and Order

1. José de Andia y Varela, "Narrative of a Voyage Performed to the Island of Amat, Otherwise by Name Otahiti, . . . in the Years 1774 and 1775," p. 265; James Cook, *The Journals of Captain James Cook*, vol. 2, p. 396; John Ledyard, *Journal of Captain Cook's Last Voyage*, pp. 57–58.

2. George Vancouver, *A Voyage of Discovery in the North Pacific Ocean, and Round the World . . .*, vol. 1, pp. 323–24.

3. For social stratification and restrictions see *A Journal of a Voyage Round the World, in His Majesty's Ship Endeavour, in the Years 1768, 1769, 1770, and 1771 . . .*, pp. 48–49; William Bligh, *A Voyage to the South Sea . . . in His Majesty's Ship the Bounty . . .*, p. 81; Cook, vol 1, p. 134, and vol. 2, p. 411; George Forster, *Voyage Round the World . . . during the Years 1772, 3, 4, and 5*, vol. 1, pp. 365–66; John R. Forster, *Observations Made During a Voyage Round the World, . . .*, p. 354; Ledyard, pp. 57–58; John Rickman, *Journal of Captain Cook's Last Voyage . . . in the Years 1776, 1777, 1778, 1779 . . .*, pp. 138–39; James Wilson, *A Missionary Voyage to the Southern Pacific Ocean, performed in the Years 1796, 1797, 1798, in the Ship Duff . . .*, pp. 218, 333–34.

4. Fr. José Amich, "An Account of the First Voyage of the *Aguila* under Captain Don Domingo de Boenechea to Tahiti: 1772–73," p. 79; Raimundo Bonacorsi, "Voyage to the Island of Otayty performed by Don Domingo Boenechea . . . Commanding the Frigate . . . *La Aguila*, . . . 26th September, 1772," p. 58; Wilson, pp. 325, 329.

5. Bligh, p. 55; Ida Lee, *Captain Bligh's Second Voyage to the South Seas*, p. 92.

6. Fr. Geronimo Clota and Fr. Narciso González, "Diary of Things Noteworthy That Occurred at Amat's Island (Alias Otagiti) Between the 28th Day of January, 1775 ... and the 12th of November in the Same Year ...," pp. 343–44; George Forster, vol. 1, p. 301, and vol. 2, p. 96.

7. John R. Forster, p. 354; Edward Edwards and George Hamilton, *Voyage of H.M.S. "Pandora" ... in the South Seas, 1790–91*, p. 104; Juan de Hervé, "Information Acquired from the Natives of the Island of Amat (by Them Called Otajiti) During the Voyage After Leaving the Port of Valparaiso ...," p. 357; Ledyard, p. 57.

8. Lee, p. 117, n. 1.

9. Wilson, pp. 202, 210, 215, 330.

10. Wilson, p. 330.

11. Wilson, pp. 330, 364.

12. John R. Forster, p. 354; Ledyard, p. 57.

13. For references to the power of a chief over his district see Andia y Varela, pp. 264, 266; Cook, vol. 3, pp. 1315–16; Máximo Rodríguez, "Daily Narrative Kept by the Interpreter Máximo Rodríguez at the Island of Amat, Otherwise Otahiti, in the Year 1774," pp. 23, 27, 44, 54, 55; Anders Sparrman, *A Voyage Round the World with Captain James Cook in H.M.S. Resolution*, p. 54; Wilson, pp. 331, 339.

14. Wilson, p. 331.

15. Cook, vol 1, p. 92; George Forster, vol. 2, p. 100; Wilson, p. 217.

16. For references to the to'ofa see Rodríguez, pp. 26, 64, 73, 97, 105, 131, 143; Wilson, p. 331.

17. Lee, p. 117 n. 1; Wilson, p. 186.

18. George Forster, vol. 1, p. 357; Wilson, p. 330.

19. Wilson, pp. 392–93. The *amae*, or, as it was named when planted in a marae, the roava, may represent other, or later, names for the *tamanu* (*Calophyllum inophyllum* L.) which according to Sydney Parkinson, *A Journal of a Voyage to the South Seas, in His Majesty's Ship the Endeavour: Faithfully Transcribed from the Papers of the Late Sydney Parkinson ...*, p. 41, was planted in marae as sacred to the god Tane. As claimed for roava, its wood was used for canoes and handles for tools. All botanical identifications of Polynesian plants are based upon Jacques Barrau, *Subsistence Agriculture in Polynesia and Micronesia*, and Elmer D. Merrill, *The Botany of Cook's Voyages and Its Unexpected Significance in Relation to Anthropology, Biogeography and History*.

20. For references to hova and fana, or as Cook called them, *hoa* and *whanno*, see Andia y Varela, p. 264; Joseph Banks, *The Endeavour Journal of Joseph Banks*, vol. 1, p. 271; Domingo Boenechea, "Narrative of a Voyage Performed by Don Domingo Boenechea, ... in the Frigate *Santa María Magdalena* (Alias *el Aguila*)... to Explore the Island Called by Navigators after King George or Saint George, and by the Natives Otacite, ... ," pp. 316–17; Cook, vol. 2, pp. 396, 410; George Forster, vol. 1, pp. 304, 307, 325–26, 328, 334, 346, 355; Tomás Gayangos, "The Official Journal of the Second Voyage of the Frigate *Aguila* from El Callao to Tahiti...," p. 146; Hervé, p. 357; Rodríguez, pp. 7, 73–74, 103, 140; Sparrman, pp. 54, 65.

21. For references to the ta'ata 'orero see Clota and González, pp. 340–41; Cook, vol. 3, p. 217; Rodríguez, p. 179; Vancouver, vol. 1, p. 256; Wilson, pp. 76–77, 328.
22. Andia y Varela, p. 265.
23. For observations of councils and council meetings see Louis Antoine de Bougainville, *A Voyage Round the World ... in the Years 1766, 1767, 1768, and 1769*, pp. 223–24, 254; Cook, vol. 1, p. 90, and vol. 2, pp. 204, 210, 213–15; George Forster, vol. 1, p. 325; George Robertson, "A Journal of the Second Voyage of H.M.S. *Dolphin* ... in the Years 1766, 1767, and 1768," p. 212; Rodríguez, p. 189.
24. Andia y Varela, p. 265.
25. William Ellis, *Polynesian Researches: Society Islands, Tubuai Islands, and New Zealand*, pp. 101–2; Irving Goldman, Ancient Polynesian Society, pp. 180–81; E. S. C. Handy, *History and Culture in the Society Islands*, p. 36; Marshall D. Sahlins, *Social Stratification in Polynesia*, p. 44.
26. For references to chiefly succession see Bligh, pp. 65, 102, 122; Clota and González, pp. 343–44, 347–48; Bolton G. Corney, ed., *The Quest and Occupation of Tahiti by Emissaries of Spain in the Years 1772–76*, vol. 2, pp. 470, 472; Edwards and Hamilton, p. 110; George Forster, vol. 2, p. 96; Hervé, p. 357; Rodríguez, pp. 124, 204–5; Wilson, pp. 52–53, 192.
27. For the observations and references upon which this analysis of the youthful sanctity and restrictions of the Tahiti nui paramount chief are based, as well as the process of their removal, see Andia y Varela, p. 265; Banks, vol. 1, p. 293; Bligh, pp. 65, 66, 74; Cook, vol. 2, pp. 206–8, 382, 387–88, and vol. 3, pp. 192–93, 206, 213; George Forster, vol. 1, pp. 325–26, and vol. 2, p. 107; Lee, pp. 72, 80, 83, 110; John Turnbull, *A Voyage Round the World, in the Years 1800, 1801, 1802, 1803, and 1804*, pp. 131, 139, 279; Vancouver, vol. 1, pp. 253, 255, 269, 273, 336; George Vason, *An Authentic Narrative of Four Years Residence at Tongataboo ...*, pp. 51–52; Wilson, pp. 52, 62–64, 67, 69, 75, 81, 158, 217, 330.
28. For references to taboos regarding use of chiefly paraphernalia see Cook, vol. 2, p. 394; Rodríguez, pp. 72, 122, 200.
29. G. Forster, vol. 1, p. 327.
30. References to signs of respect for the paramount chief are as follows: Banks, vol. 1, p. 293; Bligh, p. 74; Cook, vol. 1, p. 103; Edwards and Hamilton, p. 116; George Forster, vol. 1, pp. 304, 327, 338; John R. Forster, p. 361; George Mortimer, *Observations and Remarks made during a Voyage to the Islands .... in the Brig Mercury ...*, p. 47; Rodríguez, pp. 51–52; Sparrman, p. 68; Vancouver, vol. 1, p. 285; Wilson, pp. 184, 190, 329, 338.

    References to historical changes in the sign of respect are Bligh, p. 74; Sparrman, p. 68; Wilson, p. 366.
31. Lee, pp. 122–24; Vancouver, vol. 1, p. 255.
32. Cook, vol. 3, pp. 202–3.
33. Wilson, p. 328.
34. Wilson, p. 328.
35. Clota and González, pp. 347–48; Rodríguez, pp. 204–05.
36. Cook, vol. 3, pp. 193, 204.
37. Cook, vol. 1, p. 134; George Forster, vol. 1, pp. 259, 365; John R. Forster, p. 354.

38. For references to the work of teuteu see Bligh, p. 97; Clota and González, p. 344; Cook, vol. 2, pp. 387, 398, and vol. 3, p. 1065; George Forster, vol. 1, pp. 295, 315, 329; John R. Forster, pp. 356, 370–71, 376; Parkinson, p. 66; Vancouver, vol. 1, p. 277; Wilson, pp. 186, 192, 342.
39. Rodríguez, pp. 105–6.
40. References to historic changes and additions to social class nomenclature are William Ellis, *Polynesian Researches: Polynesia,* pp. 256, 259; William Ellis, *Polynesian Researches: Society Islands, Tubuai,* p. 95; George Forster, vol. 2, p. 90; John R. Forster, p. 371; Sahlins, pp. 37–38; Vancouver, vol. 1, pp. 316–17; Wilson, p. 331.
41. John R. Forster, pp. 358–59.
42. Wilson, pp. 332–33.
43. R. C. Green, "The Immediate Origins of the Polynesians."
44. For references to crime and punishment see Andia y Varela, pp. 259, 264–65; Bligh, p. 115; Clota and González, p. 331; Edwards and Hamilton, pp. 30, 110; John R. Forster, pp. 364, 407; Hervé, pp. 356–57; Lee, p. 105; Mortimer, p. 72; Rodríguez, pp. 87–88, 101, 155, 159, 191, 195–96, 203; Wilson, pp. 184, 351.

The Supernatural World

1. James Wilson, *A Missionary Voyage to the Southern Pacific Ocean, Performed in the Years 1796, 1797, 1798 in the Ship Duff . . .*, p. 343.
2. For references to the god Tane see Louis Antoine de Bougainville, *A Voyage Round the World . . . in the Years 1766, 1767, 1768, and 1769,* p. 255; James Cook, *The Journals of Captain James Cook,* vol. 1, p. 134; Wilson, pp. 107, 343.

For the god Oro see William Bligh, *A Voyage to the South Sea . . . in His Majesty's Ship the Bounty . . .*, p. 87; Cook, vol. 3, p. 981; Máximo Rodríguez, "Daily Narrative Kept by the Interpreter Máximo Rodríguez at the Island of Amat, Otherwise Otahiti, in the Year 1774," p. 170; Wilson, pp. 107, 343.

For the god Maui see *A Journal of a Voyage Round the World, in His Majesty's Ship Endeavour, In the Years 1768, 1769, 1770, and 1771 . . .*, p. 48; John R. Forster, *Observations Made During a Voyage Round the World, . . .*, p. 430; Wilson, p. 167.

For the god Opuna see Rodríguez, pp. 15, 205. For the god Ta'aroa, or Tangaroa, see Wilson, p. 343.
3. Wilson, pp. 343–44.
4. For references to the lesser deities see *A Journal of a Voyage,* p. 48; José de Andia y Varela, "Narrative of a Voyage Performed to the Island of Amat, Otherwise by Name Otahiti, . . . in the Years 1774 and 1775," p. 259; John Ledyard, *Journal of Captain Cook's Last Voyage,* p. 57; Wilson, p. 344.
5. Bougainville, p. 267.
6. For references to the materialistic symbol for the god Oro see Bougainville, p. 221; Cook, vol. 3, pp. 203, 216, 981; Ida Lee, *Captain Bligh's Second Voyage to the South Seas,* p. 91; Wilson, pp. 211–12.
7. *A Journal of a Voyage,* pp. 48–49; John R. Forster, p. 430; Wilson, p. 167.
8. Joseph Banks, *The Endeavour Journal of Joseph Banks,* vol. 1, p. 302; Cook, vol. 1, pp. 111–12.

9. Domingo Boenechea, "Narrative of the Voyage Performed by Don Domingo Boenechea, . . . in the Frigate *Santa María Magdalena* (Alias *el Aguila*) . . . to Explore the Island Called by Navigators after King George or Saint George, and by the Natives Otacite, . . . ," p. 334.

10. Lee, p. 113.

11. Cook, vol. 1, p. 113.

12. Kenneth Emory, *Stone Remains in the Society Islands*.

13. For references to ahu sizes and features see Fr. José Amich, "An Account of the First Voyage of the *Aguila* under Captain Don Domingo de Boenechea to Tahiti: 1772–73," p. 85; Boenechea, p. 316; Fr. Geronimo Clota and Fr. Narciso González, "Diary of Things Noteworthy that Occurred at Amat's Island (Alias Otagiti) Between the 28th Day of January, 1775 . . . and the 12th of November in the Same Year . . . ," pp. 327–28; Cook, vol. 1, p. 113; Emory, pp. 64–65 and figs. 31–34; George Forster, *Voyage Round the World . . . During the Years 1772, 3, 4, and 5*, vol. 1, pp. 293–94; George Robertson, "A Journal of the Second Voyage of H.M.S. *Dolphin* . . . in the Years 1766, 1767, and 1768," p. 178.

14. For references to marae courts and their seating stones see Andia y Varela, p. 260; Banks, vol. 1, pp. 294, 298, 303–4; Cook, vol. 3, p. 982; Samuel Wallis, "An Account of a Voyage Round the World in the Years 1766, 1767, and 1768," pp. 485–86.

15. For references to marae offertories and their content see Bligh, p. 106; Cook, vol. 1, pp. 113, 134–35, and vol. 3, pp. 204, 984, and pl. 24; George Forster, vol. 1, pp. 267–68; Lee, p. 91; Rodríguez, p. 176; Wilson, p. 211.

16. Sydney Parkinson, *A Journal of a Voyage to the South Seas, in His Majesty's Ship the Endeavour: Faithfully Transcribed From the Papers of the Late Sydney Parkinson*, pp. 40–42, reported the tamanu, or *Calophyllum inophyllum* L.; the *miru*, or *Thespesia populnea* Sol.; and the *auariiroa*, or *Terminalia glabrata* Forst., as trees growing in marae, the first two being sacred to Tane. Anders Sparrman, *A Voyage Round the World with Captain James Cook in H.M.S. Resolution*, p. 64; Banks, vol. 1, p. 303; Cook, vol. 1, p. 113; and George Forster, vol. 1, p. 294, included the ironwood, or *toa* tree, *Casuarina equisetifolia* J. R. and G. Forster, as yet another to be found in these sacred structures, while Cook included *Musa* sp. and George Forster the coconut palm, *Cocos nucifera* L.

17. Cook, vol. 3, pl. 24; Rodríguez, p. 172; Wilson, p. 211.

18. Andia y Varela, p. 260; Wilson, p. 351.

19. Banks, vol. 1, p. 297; Cook, vol. 1, p. 108; George Forster, vol. 1, pp. 267, 293; Robertson, p. 178; Wilson, p. 211.

20. Cook, vol. 3, pp. 199–200; Rodríguez, pp. 148, 196; Wilson, pp. 339, 351, 361.

21. Boenechea, p. 335.

22. Wilson, p. 186.

23. Wilson, pp. 332–33.

24. Andia y Varela, p. 259; Wilson, pp. 353–54.

25. Parkinson, pp. 39–40, called it *pouraoo* and named it *Crataeva-frondosa.* Elmer D. Merrill, *The Botany of Cook's Voyages and Its Unexpected Significance in Relation to Anthropology, Biogeography and History,* p. 350, identified it as *Crataeva religiosa* Forst., now called *puaveoveo* in Tahiti.
26. Andia y Varela, p. 260.
27. Rodríguez, p. 141; Wallis, pp. 485–86.
28. Tomás Gayangos, "The Official Journal of the Second Voyage of the Frigate *Aguila* from El Callao to Tahiti . . . ," pp. 140–41; Rodríguez, p. 30.
29. Rodriguez, pp. 100, 103.
30. Bligh, pp. 114–15.
31. Rodríguez, pp. 66, 109.
32. Banks, vol. 1, p. 292.
33. Andia y Varela, pp. 260–61; Raimundo Bonacorsi, "Voyage to the Island of Otayty performed by Don Domingo Boenechea ... Commanding the Frigate ... *La Aguila,* ... 26th September, 1772," p. 57.
34. Gayangos, pp. 142–43; Rodríguez, p. 31.
35. Wilson, p. 349.
36. For references to the range of religious functionaries see Clota and González, p. 328; Ledyard, p. 58; Wilson, pp. 347, 350.
37. Bligh, p. 104.
38. Bolton G. Corney, ed., *The Quest and Occupation of Tahiti by Emissaries of Spain in the Years 1772–76,* vol. 2, p. 472; John R. Forster, pp. 494–95; Rodríguez, pp. 57, 136–37, 151.
39. *A Journal of a Voyage,* p. 48; Andia y Varela, p. 262; Rodríguez, p. 186; Wilson, p. 364.
40. Andia y Varela, p. 263; Clota and González, p. 332; Wilson, p. 344.
41. Rodríguez, p. 33; Wilson, p. 348.
42. For references to inspirational priests see Cook, vol. 3, pp. 191, 200–1; Ledyard, p. 54; Rodríguez, pp. 148–49; Wilson, pp. 348–50.
43. Banks, vol. 1, p. 303; Cook, vol. 1, pp. 111, 113.
44. Cook, vol. 2, p. 411; Sparrman, p. 55.
45. John R. Forster, pp. 207, 367.
46. John R. Forster, pp. 207, 367.
47. For references to some of the deific uses of red feathers see Cook, vol. 2, p. 411; John R. Forster, pp. 207, 366; Sparrman, pp. 55, 70.
48. For references to the obtaining of human sacrificial victims and the means of putting them to death see Clota and González, p. 336; Corney, vol. 2, p. 472; Rodríguez, pp. 151, 178, 180, 189; Wilson, pp. 350–51.
49. Wilson, p. 351.
50. Rodríguez, pp. 181, 189.
51. Lee, pp. 90–91.
52. Edward Dodd, *Polynesian Seafaring,* p. 98.
53. William Ellis, *Polynesian Researches: Polynesia,* p. 348.
54. Clota and González, p. 342; Wilson, p. 351.
55. Dodd, p. 98.
56. Lee, pp. 122–23.

57. Wilson, p. 399.
58. Lee, pp. 115, 122.
59. Rodríguez, pp. 125, 171.
60. Edward Edwards and George Hamilton, *Voyage of H.M.S. "Pandora" ... in the South Seas, 1790–91*, p. 113.

Daily Life

1. John R. Forster, *Observations Made During a Voyage Round the World ...*, p. 404.
2. Louis Antoine de Bougainville, *A Voyage Round the World ... in the Years 1766, 1767, 1768, and 1769*, p. 252; James Cook, *The Journals of Captain James Cook*, vol. 1, p. 124; George Forster, *Voyage Round the World ... during the Years 1772, 3, 4, and 5*, vol. 1, p. 339; John R. Forster, p. 397; Ida Lee, *Captain Bligh's Second Voyage to the South Seas*, p. 111; Sydney Parkinson, *A Journal of a Voyage to the South Seas, on His Majesty's Ship the Endeavour: Faithfully Transcribed From the Papers of the Late Sydney Parkinson ...*, p. 26; James Wilson, *A Missionary Voyage to the Southern Pacific Ocean, Performed in the Years 1796, 1797, 1798 in the Ship Duff ...*, p. 357.
3. George Forster, vol. 2, p. 111; Wilson, p. 356.
4. For references to the number and times of meals see José de Andia y Varela, "Narrative of a Voyage Performed to the Island of Amat, Otherwise by Name Otahiti, ... in the Years 1774 and 1775," p. 380; Bougainville, p. 270; George Forster, vol. 2, pp. 111–12; John R. Forster, p. 405; Wilson, p. 380.
5. For references to the dispersed settlement pattern see Fr. José Amich, "An Account of the First Voyage of the *Aguila* under Captain Don Domingo de Boenechea to Tahiti: 1772–73," pp. 78–79; Domingo Boenechea, "Narrative of the Voyage Performed by Don Domingo Boenechea, ... in the Frigate *Santa María Magdalena* (Alias *el Aguila*) ... to Explore the Island Called by Navigators After King George or Saint George, and by the Natives Otaciti, ...," p. 337; Bougainville, p. 244; Cook, vol. 1, pp. 120, 128; George Forster, vol. 1, p. 268; Parkinson, p. 23; Anders Sparrman, *A Voyage Round the World With Captain James Cook in H.M.S. Resolution*, p. 57
    For clustering on the Taiarapu Peninsula see Tomás Gayangos, "The Official Journal of the Second Voyage of the Frigate *Aguila* from El Callao to Tahiti ...: 1774–75," pp. 126, 129; John Ledyard, *Journal of Captain Cook's Last Voyage*, p. 45.
6. Cook, vol. 1, p. 128; Ledyard, p. 50; Wilson, pp. 60, 341.
7. Boenechea, p. 337
8. Boenechea, p. 319; John R. Forster, p. 456.
9. Peter H. Buck (Te Rangi Hiroa), *Samoan Material Culture*, p. 666; Edwin N. Ferdon, Jr., "Sites E-4 and E-5," pp. 306–8, fig. 83.
10. Albert B. Lewis, *The Melanesians: People of the South Pacific*, pp. 58–59.
11. Edwin G. Burrows, *Western Polynesian: A Study in Cultural Differentiation*, pp. 32–33.
12. E. S. C. Handy, *History and Culture in the Society Islands*, p. 9.
13. William Ellis, *Polynesian Researches: Polynesia*, p. 175.
14. For references to house dimensions see Cook, vol. 1, pp. 128–29; John R. Forster, p. 456; Ledyard, p. 50.

15. For references to portable canoe deck houses see Amich, pp. 81–82; Joseph Banks, *The Endeavour Journal of Joseph Banks*, vol. 1, p. 259; Cook, vol. 1, pp. 129, 131; Edward Dodd, *Polynesian Seafaring*, pp. 89, 92, 98; Wilson, pp. 199, 400.

16. Bougainville, p. 221; Máximo Rodríguez, "Daily Narrative Kept by the Interpreter Máximo Rodríguez at the Island of Amat, Otherwise Otahiti, in the year 1774," p. 171; Samuel Wallis, "An Account of a Voyage Round the World in the Years 1766, 1767, and 1768," p. 462; Wilson, pp. 195, 209.

17. For references to house post contruction see Cook, vol. 1, p. 128; John R. Forster, p. 456; Ledyard, p. 50; Wilson, p. 60. Sparrman, pp. 57–58, and Wilson, pp. 373–74, mentioned use of breadfruit *Artocarpus altilis* (Parkinson) Fosberg, for house posts, while the use of hibiscus, or what is now identified as *Hibiscus tiliaceus* L. was reported by Parkinson, p. 42.

18. John R. Forster, p. 456; Wilson, p. 60.

19. Ellis, *Polynesian Researches: Polynesia*, pp. 171–72; John R. Forster, p. 456; Rodríguez, p. 30; Wilson, p. 393.

20. Burrows, pp. 32–33.

21. Ellis, *Polynesian Researches: Polynesia*, pp. 171–72; Wilson, pp. 395–96. The 'ie'ie vine is probably the same as the *yei yei* mentioned by Parkinson, p. 49, used in making baskets. Its botanical identity is uncertain, but is probably *Freycinetia demissa*.

22. This was probably the grass *Miscanthus japonicus* Anders., also used, according to Andia y Varela, p. 278, to occasionally wall in a house.

23. For references to the technique of thatching a roof see Andia y Varela, p. 278; Ellis, *Polynesian Researches: Polynesia*, pp. 172–74; George Forster, vol. 1, pp. 270–71; John R. Forster, pp. 442–43, 457; Parkinson, p. 46; Rodríguez, p. 39; Sparrman, p. 57; Wilson, pp. 394–95.

24. Andia y Varela, p. 278; Bonechea, p. 336; Raimundo Bonacorsi, "Voyage to the Island of Otayty Performed by Don Domingo Boenechea ... Commanding the Frigate ... *La Aguila*, ... 26th September, 1772," p. 56; Cook, vol. 1, p. 129; Ledyard, p. 50; Rodríguez, p. 206; Sparrman, p. 58.

25. Ellis, *Polynesian Researches: Polynesia*, p. 176; George Forster, vol. 1, pp. 278, 287, 298; Wilson, p. 185.

26. Andia y Varela, pp. 277–78; George Forster, vol. 1, pp. 271, 352; John R. Forster, p. 456; Parkinson, p. 23; Sparrman, p. 57.

27. Amich, p. 83; John R. Forster, p. 457.

28. Bonacorsi, p. 56; John R. Forster, p. 457.

29. For references to treatment of house beams see Bonacorsi, p. 56; Ellis, *Polynesian Researches: Polynesia*, p. 173; George Forster, vol. 2, p. 61; Parkinson, p. 26; Wilson, p. 60.

30. For references to temporary houses and the moving of dwellings see Bonechea, p. 9; Rodríguez, pp. 20, 71, 72; Wilson, pp. 354, 376, 377.

31. Andia y Varela, p. 278.

32. John R. Forster, p. 449; Parkinson, pp. 19, 46. The rush was not identified botanically by Forster, but the pandanus was probably *Pandanus tectorius* (Solander) Parkinson, while the hibiscus bark came from *Hibiscus tiliaceus* L.

33. Boenechea, p. 336; Bonacorsi, p. 56; Cook, vol. 2, p. 204; George Forster, vol. 1, pp. 278, 304; Parkinson, pp. 40, 41, 42; George

Robertson, "A Journal of the Second Voyage of H.M.S. *Dolphin* ... in the Years 1766, 1767, and 1768," p. 173; Sparrman, p. 54. Woods employed in making stools were breadfruit, or *Artocarpus altilis* (Parkinson) Fosb.; hibiscus, or *Hibiscus tiliaceus* L.; tamanu, or *Calophyllum inophyllum* L.; and what Parkinson called *aowiree*, or *Terminalia glabrata* Forst.

34. Boenechea, p. 336; Bonacorsi, p. 56.
35. For references to basketry containers see Andia y Varela, p. 278; Boenechea, pp. 319, 336; George Forster, vol. 1, p. 332; Parkinson, pp. 18, 46, 47, 49; Rodríguez, p. 59; Wilson, p. 377.
36. Andia y Varela, p. 278.
37. Bonacorsi, p. 56; George Forster, vol. 1, p. 295; Parkinson, pp. 41, 45; Robertson, p. 191; Wilson, p. 392.
38. George Forster, vol 1, p. 295; Parkinson, p. 45.
39. For references to coconut shell containers see Andia y Varela, p. 280; Cook, vol. 1, pp. 110, 122; George Forster, vol. 1, pp. 278, 288; Parkinson, pp. 17, 49; Robertson, pp. 191, 222; Rodríguez, p. 151.

    For containers made from the gourd *Lagenaria siceraria* (Mol.) Standl. see Andia y Varela, p. 279; Elmer D. Merrill, *The Botany of Cook's Voyages and Its Unexpected Significance in Relation to Anthropology, Biogeography and History*, pp. 350–51; Parkinson, p. 49; Robertson, pp. 147, 191; and for bamboo sections used for liquids see Andia y Varela, p. 281; Parkinson, pp. 19, 39; Robertson, pp. 147, 191; Wilson, pp. 331, 332, 394.

40. Parkinson, p. 39; Wilson, pp. 355, 379.
41. Boenechea, p. 337; Parkinson, p. 49; Wilson, p. 341.
42. For references to land ownership and boundary markings see William Bligh, *A Voyage to the South Sea ... in His Majesty's Ship the Bounty ...*, p. 75; George Forster, vol. 2, p. 103; Gayangos, pp. 126–27; Wilson, pp. 177; 334–35.
43. Banks, vol. 1, pp. 299, 306; Boenechea, p. 307; Cook, vol. 1, p. 109.
44. Cook, vol. 2, pp. 201, 212.
45. Wilson, p. 331.
46. Andia y Varela, p. 264; Rodríguez, pp. 27, 44; Sparrman, p. 54.
47. For references to men's work see Boenechea, p. 334; John R. Forster, p. 404; Parkinson, p. 49.
48. For references to women's work see Amich, p. 83; Andia y Varela, p. 258; Boenechea, p. 334.
49. Wilson, p. 214.
50. Fr. Geronimo Clota and Fr. Narciso González, "Diary of Things Noteworthy that Occurred at Amat's Island (Alias Otagiti) between the 28th Day of January, 1775 ... and the 12th of November in the Same Year ...," p. 341; Cook, vol. 1, p. 124, and vol. 3, p. 1063.
51. John R. Forster, p. 398.
52. For references to the use and making of mono'i, or scented coconut oil, see Amich, p. 79; Boenechea, pp. 305, 330; Bougainville, p. 250; Cook, vol. 1, p. 124; George Forster, vol. 2, p. 83; John R. Forster, pp. 365; 482, 594; Parkinson, pp. 22, 38, 40, 41, 44, 49, 50; Wilson, pp. 56, 322, 356, 379, 389, 393, 395.
53. Cook, vol. 1, p. 124.
54. John R. Forster, pp. 583–84; Wilson, pp. 386–87.
55. Andia y Varela, p. 258; Wilson, pp. 354, 361.

56. Andia y Varela, p. 258; Banks, vol. 1, p. 266; Bonacorsi, p. 55; Bougainville, p. 270; Cook, vol. 1, p. 123, and vol. 2, p. 410; Bolton G. Corney, ed., *The Quest and Occupation of Tahiti by Emissaries of Spain in the Years 1772–76*, vol. 2, p. 471; George Forster, vol. 1, p. 283; John R. Forster, pp. 405, 423; Ledyard, p. 51; Parkinson, p. 17; Wilson, p. 361.
57. Wilson, p. 354.
58. Cook, vol. 1, p. 123.
59. Wilson, pp. 364–65.
60. Corney, vol. 2, p. 471; Rodríguez, pp. 111–12.
61. *A Journal of a Voyage Round the World, in His Majesty's Ship Endeavour, In the Years 1768, 1769, 1770, and 1771 . . .*, pp. 47–48; Bligh, p. 66; Cook, vol. 1, p. 86; Wilson, pp. 74, 81.
62. Wilson, p. 380.
63. Banks, vol. 1, pp. 292–93; Cook, vol. 1, p. 103.
64. William R. Broughton, *A Voyage of Discovery to the North Pacific Ocean . . . in the Years 1795, 1796, 1797, 1798*, p. 27.
65. For references to the popoi mixtures see *A Journal of a Voyage*, p. 52; Boenechea, p. 327; Cook, vol. 1, pp. 110, 122; George Forster, vol. 1, p. 295, and vol. 2, p. 56; Parkinson, p. 17; Wilson, pp. 378–79. The taro mentioned is *Colocasia esculenta* (L.) Schott.; the pia, or Polynesian arrowroot, is *Tacca leontopetaloides* (L.) Kuntze.
66. Parkinson, pp. 19, 45.
67. For references to stone-cooked puddings see Bligh, p. 130; Cook, vol. 3, pp. 206–7; Parkinson, pp. 17, 47; Wilson, pp. 376, 378. Teve, or *Amorphophallus campanulatus* (Roxburgh) Blume, is no longer used in Polynesia.
68. *A Journal of a Voyage*, p. 51; Amich, p. 84; Andia y Varela, p. 280; Bligh, p. 94; Bougainville, p. 222; Cook, vol. 1, pp. 78, 121–22; George Forster, vol. 1, p. 288; Ledyard, p. 51; Parkinson, pp. 19–20; Wilson, p. 380.
69. For references to the construction and use of the fire plow see Parkinson, pp. 17, 42; Wilson, p. 357.
70. Ferdon, "Sites E-4 and E-5," fig. 83.
71. Sparrman, p. 57.
72. Cook, vol. 1, p. 122.
73. For references to the construction of pit ovens see *A Journal of a Voyage*, p. 51; Amich, pp. 83–84; Andia y Varela, pp. 279–80; Clota and González, p. 348; Cook, vol. 1, p. 103; Ledyard, p. 50; Parkinson, p. 17.
74. Banks, vol. 1, p. 292; Cook, vol. 1, p. 103; Ledyard, p. 54; Wilson, p. 379.
75. For references to the preparation and cooking of animals in a pit oven see Andia y Varela, pp. 279–80; Banks, vol. 1, pp. 292–93; Clota and González, p. 348; Cook, vol. 1, p. 103; Ledyard, pp. 50–51; Parkinson, pp. 17, 20, 46; Wilson, pp. 379–80.
76. Amich, pp. 83–84.
77. Bonacorsi, p. 50; Rodríguez, pp. 23, 154.
78. Wilson, pp. 382–83.
79. Amich, p. 81; Wilson, pp. 373, 382.
80. Amich, p. 81; Samuel Wallis, "An Account of a Voyage Round the World in the Years 1766, 1767, and 1768," p. 488.
81. The name 'ape is the Tahitian word for *Alocasia macrorrhiza* (L.) Schott.

82. Andia y Varela, p. 280; George Forster, vol. 1, p. 298; Lee, p. 93; Parkinson, pp. 43, 47; Robertson, p. 203; Wilson, p. 381.
83. Corney, vol. 2, p. 460; Robertson, p. 204.
84. Clota and González, p. 349; Cook, vol. 1, pp. 122–23; Corney, vol. 2, p. 460; George Forster, vol. 1, p. 343.
85. Andia y Varela, p. 281; Parkinson, p. 19.
86. Parkinson, p. 16; Wilson, pp. 357–58.
87. Wilson, pp. 357–58.
88. Andia y Varela, p. 280.
89. Ledyard, p. 51; Robertson, pp. 204, 210; Wilson, pp. 350, 380.
90. For references to the eating habits of Tahitians see *A Journal of a Voyage*, p. 51; Amich, p. 84; Boenechea, p. 333; Bonacorsi, p. 55; George Forster, vol. 1, pp. 295–96; John R. Forster, p. 480; Ledyard, p. 51; George Mortimer, *Observations and Remarks Made During a Voyage to the Islands . . . in the Brig Mercury . . .*, p. 37; Wilson, pp. 362, 380.
91. Andia y Varela, p. 281; Rodríguez, p. 80; Wilson, pp. 402–3.
92. John R. Forster, p. 377.
93. Wilson, p. 204.
94. George Vason, *An Authentic Narrative of Four Years Residence in Tongataboo . . .*, p. 56; Wilson, pp. 189, 365.
95. John Rickman, *Journal of Captain Cook's Last Voyage . . . in the Years 1776, 1777, 1778, 1779 . . .*, pp. 141–42.
96. Robertson, pp. 203–4; Wallis, p. 464.
97. Bligh, p. 121; John R. Forster, p. 87; Sparrman, p. 58.
98. John R. Forster, p. 405.
99. For references to nose flutes see Amich, p. 80; Andia y Varela, p. 289; Cook, vol. 1, p. 127; George Forster, vol. 1, p. 29; John R. Forster, pp. 467–68; Parkinson, pp. 39, 49.
100. For references to drums see Andia y Varela, p. 289; Cook, vol. 1, p. 127; Rodríguez, p. 182. According to Parkinson, pp. 38, 40, 41, woods used in making drums were, in present botanical nomenclature, *Ochrosia parviflora* (Forst. f.) Henslow, *Terminalia glabrata* Forst., and *Fragraea berteriana* A. Gray ex Benth.
101. Andia y Varela, p. 289; Clota and González, p. 329.
102. Bougainville, p. 247; Parkinson, p. 24.
103. John R. Forster, pp. 466, 467.
104. George Forster, vol. 2, p. 81; John R. Forster, p. 405.
105. Cook, vol. 1, p. 136; George Forster, vol. 1, p. 319; John R. Forster, pp. 528–29; Wilson, p. 341.
106. Cook, vol. 1, p. 136; Lee, p. 93; Rodríguez, p. 209; Wilson, p. 188.
107. Wilson, p. 341.
108. Robertson, p. 199.
109. Andia y Varela, p. 287; Cook, vol. 1, p. 136; John R. Forster, p. 509; Wilson, p. 341.
110. Cook, vol. 1, p. 136.
111. John R. Forster, pp. 505, 507; Wilson, p. 341.
112. John R. Forster, p. 505.
113. Andia y Varela, p. 287.
114. Edwin N. Ferdon, Jr., "The Ceremonial Site of Orongo," pp. 228–29 and fig. 61.
115. Bligh, p. 109; John R. Forster, p. 504.

116. Ellis, *Polynesian Researches: Polynesia,* pp. 351–52.
117. George C. Vaillant, *The Aztecs of Mexico,* pp. 187–201.
118. Andia y Varela, p. 287.
119. John R. Forster, p. 500.
120. Robertson, pp. 137, 160, 212, 213, 215, 223, 225, 227; Wallis, p. 465.
121. Mortimer, p. 43.
122. Wallis, p. 478.
123. Boenechea, pp. 300, 311, 319; Bonacorsi, p. 51; Cook, vol. 3, p. 190; Corney, vol. 2, pp. 470, 471.
124. Cook, vol. 3, p. 1344; Rodríguez, p. 4.
125. Gayangos, p. 133; Rodríguez, pp. 6, 8.
126. George Forster, vol. 1, p. 271.
127. Cook, vol. 3, pp. 69–70, 239.
128. Bligh, p. 65.
129. Mortimer, p. 43; George Vancouver, *A Voyage of Discovery in the North Pacific Ocean, and Round the World . . . ,* vol. 1, p. 256.
130. Wilson, pp. 67, 78, 159, 200, 363. Here it should be noted that no less an observer than Sparrman, p. 74, writing at the beginning of the nineteenth century, commented about the introduction to Tahiti of the Maori and Tongan method of greeting since his visit to the island with Cook in 1773.
131. Wilson, p. 363.
132. Banks, vol. 1, p. 255; Bougainville, p. 220; Parkinson, p. 15.
133. Wilson, p. 365.
134. Cook, vol. 3, pp. 207–8; Rodríguez, p. 43.
135. Rodríguez, p. 52.
136. Banks, vol. 1, pp. 275–76.
137. Wilson, p. 365.
138. Cook, vol. 3, pp. 214–15; George Forster, vol. 1, pp. 352–53; Mortimer, p. 44; Vancouver, vol. 1, p. 264; Wilson, p. 159.
139. Bligh, p. 123
140. Parkinson, p. 44; Wilson, p. 392.

Tapa: The Gift of Value

1. Joseph Banks, *The Endeavour Journal of Joseph Banks,* vol. 1, p. 355; John Ledyard, *Journal of Captain Cook's Last Voyage,* p. 49; Anders Sparrman, *A Voyage Round the World with Captain James Cook in H.M.S. Resolution,* p. 50.
2. Ledyard, p. 49; Sydney Parkinson, *A Journal of a Voyage to the South Seas, in His Majesty's Ship the Endeavour: Faithfully Transcribed From the Papers of the Late Sydney Parkinson . . . ,* p. 19.
3. James Wilson, *A Missionary Voyage to the Southern Pacific Ocean, Performed in the Years 1796, 1797, 1798 in the Ship Duff . . . ,* p. 390.
4. For references to the use of paper mulberry, *Broussonetia papyrifera* (L.) Vent., see Banks, vol. 1, p. 353; George Forster, *Voyage Round the World . . . During the Years 1772, 3, 4, and 5,* vol. 1, p. 277; John R. Forster, *Observations Made During a Voyage Round the World . . . ,* p. 216; Parkinson, p. 44; Sparrman, p. 50.

For breadfruit, *Artocarpus altilis* (Parkinson) Fosberg, see Banks, vol. 1, p. 353; Bolton G. Corney, ed., *The Quest and Occupation of Tahiti* by *Emissaries of Spain in the Years 1772–76,* vol. 2, p. 472; John R. Forster, p. 126; Ledyard, p. 49; Parkinson, pp. 45–46; Sparrman, p. 50; Wilson, p. 373.

For the fig tree, called 'aoa or ora, *Ficus prolixa* Forst., see Banks, vol. 1, p. 353; John R. Forster, p. 447; Parkinson, p. 47. The second fig tree, which John R. Forster, p. 447, called *Ficus aspera,* was undoubtedly the *mati,* or *Ficus tinctoria* Forst., mentioned in Wilson, p. 394. as another source for bark cloth.

5. Banks, vol. 1, p. 353.
6. Banks, vol. 1, p. 353; John R. Forster, p. 447; Parkinson, p. 47.
7. Banks, vol. 1, p. 353; Parkinson, pp. 45–46.
8. Louis Antoine de Bougainville, *A Voyage Round the World . . . in the Years 1766, 1767, 1768 and 1769,* p. 261.
9. Banks, vol. 1, pp. 353, 354; James Cook, *The Journals of Captain James Cook,* vol. 1, p. 132; George Forster, vol. 1, p. 277; John R. Forster, p. 445.
10. George Vancouver, *A Voyage of Discovery in the North Pacific Ocean, and Round the World . . . ,* vol. 1, p. 333.
11. Edward Edwards and George Hamilton, *Voyage of H.M.S. "Pandora" . . . in the South Seas, 1790–91,* p. 115.
12. For references to cultivating and harvesting young paper mulberry see Banks, vol. 1, p. 354; Cook, vol. 1, p. 132; George Forster, vol. 1, p. 277; John R. Forster, p. 445; Parkinson, p. 44; Wilson, p. 389.
13. Wilson, p. 389.
14. *A Journal of a Voyage Round the World, in His Majesty's Ship Endeavour, in the Years 1768, 1769, 1770, and 1771 . . . ,* p. 53; Banks, vol. 1, p. 354; John R. Forster, p. 446; Parkinson, p. 18.
15. José de Andia y Varela, "Narrative of a Voyage Performed to the Island of Amat, Otherwise by Name Otahiti, . . . in the Years 1774 and 1775," p. 258; Banks, vol. 1, p. 354; Cook, vol. 1, p. 133; Edwards and Hamilton, p. 115; George Forster, vol. 2, p. 110; Parkinson, p. 18; Wilson, p. 391.
16. Wilson, p. 381.
17. Banks, vol. 1, pp. 354–56.
18. For references to the preparation of bark for beating into tapa see *A Journal of a Voyage,* p. 53; Banks, vol. 1, p. 354; Domingo Boenechea, "Narrative of the Voyage Performed by Don Domingo Boenechea, . . . in the Frigate *Santa María Magdalena* (Alias *el Aguila*) . . . to Explore the Island called by Navigators After King George or Saint George, and by the Natives Otacite, . . . ," p. 332; Cook, vol. 1, pp. 132–33; John R. Forster, p. 446; Wilson, pp. 389, 393.
19. Fr. José Amich, "An Account of the First Voyage of the *Aguila* under Captain Don Domingo de Boenechea to Tahiti: 1772–73," p. 83; Banks, vol. 1, p. 253; Edwards and Hamilton, p. 115; George Robertson, "A Journal of the Second Voyage of H.M.S. *Dolphin* . . . in the Years 1766, 1767, and 1768," p. 214; Sparrman, p. 50; Wilson, pp. 204, 390.
20. Banks, vol. 1, p. 354; John R. Forster, p. 446.
21. Wilson, p. 389.
22. References to the wooden anvil upon which the bark was beaten are Boenechea, p. 332; Wilson, pp. 389, 391–92. For the two woods, toa, or *Casuarina equisetifolia* J. R. and G. Forster, and mara, or *Neonauclea*

forsteri (Seem.) Merr., used as anvils see Parkinson, pp. 37, 47.

23. Sparrman, p. 50; Wilson, p. 390.
24. Descriptive references to bark beaters are *A Journal of a Voyage*, pp. 53–54; Banks, vol. 1, p. 355; Cook, vol. 1, pp. 132–33; Wilson, pp. 391–92.
25. George Forster, vol. 1, p. 277.
26. *Pia*, botanically known as *Tacca leontopetaloides* (L.) Kuntze.
27. For reference to the beating, pasting, and patching of tapa cloth see Banks, vol. 1, pp. 355–56; Boenechea, p. 332; Bougainville, p. 261; Cook, vol. 1, pp. 132–33; George Forster, vol. 1, pp. 276–77; John R. Forster, p. 447; Wilson, p. 390.
28. For references to multilayered tapa cloth see *A Journal of a Voyage*, p. 54; Amich, p. 83; Cook, vol. 1, p. 133; John R. Forster, p. 447; Ledyard, p. 49; Sparrman, p. 50; Wilson, p. 204.
29. For references to original and recycled types of tapa see Banks, vol. 1, p. 355; John R. Forster, p. 447; Wilson, pp. 390–91.
30. Wilson, p. 390.
31. Boenechea, p. 332; John R. Forster, p. 447; Wilson, p. 389.
32. *A Journal of a Voyage*, p. 54; Banks, vol. 1, p. 355.
33. Nono, known botanically as *Morinda citrifolia* L.
34. Turmeric, known botanically as *Curcuma longa* L.
35. Tamanu, known botanically as *Calophyllum inophyllum* L.
36. Miro, known botanically as *Thespesia populnea* Sol.
37. Piripiri, known botanically as *Euphorbia atoto* Forst.
38. Parkinson, p. 49.
39. For references to dyeing and staining tapa cloth see Andia y Varela, p. 274; Banks, vol. 1, pp. 357–60; Boenechea, p. 332; George Forster, vol. 1, p. 354; John R. Forster, pp. 448–49; Parkinson, pp. 18, 38, 40, 41, 46; Wilson, pp. 390–91, 393, 394.
40. *Aleurites moluccana* Wildenow (*A. triloba* J. R. and G. Forster).
41. John R. Forster, p. 449; Parkinson, p. 44.
42. Fr. Geronimo Clota and Fr. Narciso González, "Diary of Things Noteworthy that Occurred at Amat's Island (Alias Otagiti) Between the 28th day of January, 1775 ... and the 12th of November in the Same Year ... ," p. 345; Wilson, p. 391.
43. George Forster, vol. 1, p. 354; John R. Forster, p. 448.
44. Cook, vol. 1, p. 118.
45. Edwards and Hamilton, p. 115; Wilson, p. 391.
46. Wilson, p. 391.
47. Parkinson, p. 42; Robertson, p. 222; Wilson, p. 211. The cotton was *Gossypium taitense* Parl.

Recreation

1. References to swimming are George Forster, *Voyage Round the World ... during the Years 1772, 3, 4, and 5*, vol. 1, pp. 265–66; Sydney Parkinson, *A Journal of a Voyage to the South Seas, in His Majesty's Ship the Endeavour: Faithfully Transcribed From the Papers of the Late Sydney Parkinson ...* , p. 19; George Robertson, "A Journal of the Second Voyage of H.M.S. *Dolphin* ... in the Years 1766, 1767, and 1768," p. 147; Anders Sparrman, *A Voyage Round the World with Captain James Cook in H.M.S. Resolution*, p. 60. For surfing see James Wilson, *A Missionary*

Voyage to the Southern Pacific Ocean, Performed in the Years 1796, 1797, 1798, in the Ship Duff ... , pp. 367–68.

2. George Forster, vol. 1, p. 265.

3. William Bligh, *A Voyage to the South Sea* ... *in His Majesty's Ship the Bounty* ..., p. 107; Domingo Boenechea, "Narrative of the Voyage performed by Don Domingo Boenechea, ... in the Frigate *Santa María Magdalena* (Alias *el Aguila*) ... to Explore the Island Called by Navigators After King George or Saint George, and by the Natives Otacite, ...," p. 324.

4. Bligh, p. 123; Boenechea, p. 333; Wilson, p. 368.

5. Wilson, pp. 369–70.

6. References to wrestling are Joseph Banks, *The Endeavour Journal of Joseph Banks,* vol. 1, p. 272; Bligh, pp. 89, 128–29; James Cook, *The Journals of Captain James Cook,* vol. 1, p. 91; Máximo Rodríguez, "Daily Narrative Kept by the Interpreter Máximo Rodríguez at the Island of Amat, Otherwise Otahiti, in the year 1774," p. 161; Wilson, pp. 66, 331, 369.

7. John Ledyard, *Journal of Captain Cook's Last Voyage,* p. 51.

8. Ida Lee, *Captain Bligh's Second Voyage to the South Seas,* p. 114; Wilson, p. 66.

9. William Ellis, *Polynesian Researches: Polynesia,* pp. 208–9.

10. Ellis, *Polynesian Researches: Polynesia,* p. 219.

11. Kenneth Emory, *Stone Remains in the Society Islands,* pp. 42–43.

12. For references to archery contests see José de Andia y Varela, "Narrative of a Voyage Performed to the Island of Amat, Otherwise by Name Otahiti, ... in the Years 1774 and 1775," p. 268; Rodríguez, p. 45; Wilson, p. 368.

13. Wilson, p. 368. Purau is known botanically as *Hibiscus tiliaceus* L., toa as *Casuarina equisetifolia* J. R. and G. Forster. As noted in Chapter 2, n. 19, roava was possibly *Calophyllum inophyllum* L.

14. Andia y Varela, p. 268.

15. E. S. C. Handy, *History and Culture in the Society Islands,* p. 59.

16. Ellis, *Polynesian Researches: Polynesia,* p. 220.

17. Peter H. Buck (Te Rangi Hiroa), *Ethnology of Mangareva,* p. 193.

18. Handy, p. 59.

19. Sparrman, p. 68.

20. For references to the variety of heiva observed see Bligh, pp. 76, 128; Fr. Geronimo Clota and Fr. Narciso González, "Diary of Things Noteworthy That Occurred at Amat's Island (Alias Otagiti) between the 28th Day of January, 1775 ... and the 12th of November in the Same Year ...," pp. 330–31; Cook, vol. 2, p. 209, and vol. 3, pp. 208, 985; Edward Edwards and George Hamilton, *Voyage of H.M.S. "Pandora"* ... *in the South Seas, 1790–91,* p. 108; John R. Forster, *Observations Made During a Voyage Round the World,* ..., pp. 471, 476; John Marra, *Journal of the Resolution's Voyage, in 1772, 1773, 1774, and 1775* ... *also a Journal of the Adventure's Voyage, in the Years 1772, 1773, and 1774* ..., p. 192; George Mortimer, *Observations and Remarks Made During a Voyage to the Islands* ... *in the Brig Mercury* ..., pp. 44–46; John Rickman, *Journal of Captain Cook's Last Voyage* ... *in the Years 1776, 1777, 1778, 1779* ..., pp. 142–43, 156–58; Rodríguez, pp. 90, 200; Sparrman, p. 68; Wilson, pp. 370–71.

21. Descriptive references to prepared heiva areas are John R. Forster, p.

450; Mortimer, pp. 44–45, 48; Sparrman, p. 58; George Vancouver, *A Voyage of Discovery in the North Pacific Ocean, and Round the World ...*, vol. 1, p. 289; Wilson, pp. 370–71, 395.

22. References to the dress and ornament of female heiva dancers are Fr. José Amich, "An Account of the First Voyage of the *Aguila* Under Captain Don Domingo de Boenechea to Tahiti: 1772–73," p. 80; Rickman, pp. 156–57; Wilson, p. 370.
23. John R. Forster, p. 467.
24. For references to body and facial movements of female heiva dancers see Amich, p. 80; John R. Forster, pp. 466–67; Parkinson, pp. 24, 25, and pl. 7, fig. 2.
25. John R. Forster, p. 465; Mortimer, p. 45; Parkinson, p. 24.
26. Andia y Varela, p. 289; Edwards and Hamilton, p. 108; John R. Forster, p. 467; Wilson, p. 370.
27. John R. Forster, p. 465.
28. George Forster, vol. 1, p. 337; Wilson, pp. 355–56, 371.
29. Bolton G. Corney, ed., *The Quest and Occupation of Tahiti by Emissaries of Spain in the Years 1772–76*, vol. 2, p. 472.
30. Edwards and Hamilton, p. 108.
31. Sparrman, p. 67.
32. Cook, vol. 3, p. 978.
33. Cook, vol. 2, p. 208.
34. Rickman, p. 143.
35. Mortimer, p. 45; Rickman, p. 143.
36. John R. Forster, p. 471.
37. John R. Forster, pp. 471–72.
38. Rickman, p. 157.
39. John R. Forster, pp. 472–74.
40. Wilson, p. 370.
41. Mortimer, p. 46; Wilson, p. 370.
42. Cook, vol. 1, p. 128; John R. Forster, p. 467; Wilson, pp. 65–66, 178.
43. Rickman, p. 162; Wilson, p. 65.
44. Banks, vol. 1, p. 290; Bligh, pp. 77, 129.
45. Sparrman, p. 123.
46. Bligh, p. 78; Cook, vol. 1, p. 128; Wilson, pp. 153, 360.
47. Ellis, *Polynesian Researches: Polynesia*, p. 233.
48. Cook, vol. 2, p. 411; Sparrman, p. 123; Wilson, pp. 174, 335.
49. Rickman, p. 162.
50. Bligh, pp. 78–79.
51. Wilson, p. 335.
52. Irving Goldman, *Ancient Polynesian Society*, pp. 192–93.
53. Goldman, p. 191.
54. Bligh, p. 79.

From Birth to Death

1. James Cook, *The Journals of Captain James Cook*, vol. 1, p. 128; James Wilson, *A Missionary Voyage to the Southern Pacific Ocean, Performed in the Years 1796, 1797, 1798 in the Ship Duff ...*, p. 194.
2. William Bligh, *A Voyage to the South Sea ... in His Majesty's Ship the Bounty ...*, p. 78; Cook, vol. 1, p. 128; Wilson, pp. 153, 360.
3. *A Journal of a Voyage Round the World, in His Majesty's Ship Endeavour, In*

the Years 1768, 1769, 1770, and 1771 ..., p. 47; Bligh, p. 81; Wilson, pp. 74, 218.

4. José de Andia y Varela, "Narrative of a Voyage Performed to the Island of Amat, Otherwise by Name Otahiti, ... in the Years 1774 and 1775," p. 263; John R. Forster, *Observations Made During a Voyage Round the World* ..., p. 392, 424; Wilson, p. 360.

5. Wilson, p. 194.

6. Bligh, p. 79.

7. Ida Lee, *Captain Bligh's Second Voyage to the South Seas,* p. 110; Wilson, pp. 337, 360.

8. Wilson, p. 339.

9. For references to postpartum taboos and rituals, including the series of amo'a ceremonies, see Wilson, pp. 339, 353–55, 366.

10. Wilson, p. 337.

11. *Operculina terpethum* (L.) S. Manso.

12. *Pandanus tectorius* (Solander) Parkinson.

13. Sydney Parkinson, *A Journal of the Voyage to the South Seas, in His Majesty's Ship the Endeavour: Faithfully Transcribed From the Papers of the Late Sydney Parkinson* ... , p. 33.

14. For references to the childhood of Tahitians see Bligh, p. 107; Edward Edwards and George Hamilton, *Voyage of H.M.S. "Pandora" ... in the South Seas, 1790–91,* p. 113; John R. Forster, pp. 441, 528–29; Wilson, pp. 339–40, 355, 359, 368–69.

15. Raimundo Bonacorsi, "Voyage to the Island of Otayty Performed by Don Domingo Boenechea ... Commanding the Frigate ... *La Aguila,* ... 26th September, 1772," pp. 57–58; George Robertson, "A Journal of the Second Voyage of H.M.S. *Dolphin* ... in the Years 1766, 1767, and 1768," p. 211; Wilson, p. 355.

16. Domingo Boenechea, "Narrative of the Voyage Performed by Don Domingo Boenechea, ... in the Frigate *Santa María Magdalena* (Alias *el Aguila*) ... to Explore the Island Called by Navigators After King George or Saint George, and by the Natives Otacite, ... ," p. 330.

17. Bonacorsi, pp. 57–58; John Ledyard, *Journal of Captain Cook's Last Voyage,* p. 56; Wilson, p. 355.

18. Wilson, p. 355.

19. *A Journal of a Voyage,* p. 47; John R. Forster, p. 432; John Marra, *Journal of the Resolution's Voyage, in 1772, 1773, 1774, and 1775 ... also a Journal of the Adventure's Voyage, in the Years 1772, 1773, and 1774* ..., p. 44.

20. Andia y Varela, p. 263; Wilson, p. 359.

21. Andia y Varela, p. 258.

22. Louis Antoine de Bougainville, *A Voyage Round the World ... in the Years 1766, 1767, 1768, and 1769,* p. 218.

23. Robertson, pp. 207–9.

24. Robertson, pp. 184–85.

25. George Forster, *Voyage Round the World ... During the Years 1772, 3, 4, and 5,* vol. 1, p. 284, and vol. 2, p. 54.

26. Cook, vol. 3, pp. 1059, 1343–44.

27. *A Journal of a Voyage,* p. 47; John R. Forster, p. 433.

28. Wilson, p. 205.

29. Andia y Varela, p. 262; Lee, p. 107.

30. George Forster, vol. 2, p. 89.

31. Lee, pp. 106–7.

32. Wilson, p. 353.
33. George Mortimer, *Observations and Remarks Made During a Voyage to the Islands ... in the Brig Mercury ...*, p. 76.
34. Edwards and Hamilton, p. 113.
35. Wilson, pp. 157, 200–1, 333.
36. Bengt Danielsson, *Love in the South Seas*, p. 149.
37. For references showing that polygamy was thought to have been practiced see Boenechea, p. 335; Bougainville, p. 256; Parkinson, p. 21; for those showing that it did not occur see *A Journal of a Voyage*, p. 47; Andia y Varela, p. 263.
38. Cook, vol. 1, p. 104; John R. Forster, p. 424; Juan de Hervé, "Information Acquired from the Natives of the Island of Amat (by Them Called Otajiti) During the Voyage After Leaving the Port of Valparaiso ...," p. 357
39. Boenechea, p. 335.
40. Bligh, p. 95; Edwards and Hamilton, p. 103; Wilson, p. 74.
41. Wilson, pp. 155–56.
42. Máximo Rodríguez, "Daily Narrative Kept by the Interpreter Máximo Rodríguez at the Island of Amat, Otherwise Otahiti, in the Year 1774," p. 201.
43. Andia y Varela, p. 263; Bligh, p. 116; Cook, vol. 1, p. 128.
44. George Forster, vol. 2, p. 94; John R. Forster, p. 365.
45. Bligh, p. 97.
46. Edwards and Hamilton, p. 109; Wilson, pp. 355–56.
47. Edwards and Hamilton, pp. 109–10.
48. Bligh, pp. 136–37; John R. Forster, p. 585; George Vancouver, *A Voyage of Discovery in the North Pacific Ocean, and Round the World ...*, vol. 1, pp. 270–71.
49. Wilson, pp. 214, 404–5.
50. John R. Forster, p. 491.
51. Bligh, p. 142.
52. Cook, vol. 1, pp. 124–25; John R. Forster, p. 485.
53. Rodríguez, p. 141.
54. Cook, vol. 2, p. 399; George Forster, vol. 2, p. 81; John R. Forster, p. 493.
55. Wilson, p. 404.
56. Andia y Varela, pp. 288–89; Parkinson, pp. 19–20; Wilson, p. 405.
57. Rodríguez, pp. 137–38, 192–93.
58. Wilson, p. 403.
59. Andia y Varela, p. 275; John R. Forster, p. 495; Parkinson, p. 43; Wilson, p. 165.
60. Wilson, p. 395.
61. For references to wounds and their treatment see Bligh, p. 63; George Forster, vol. 2, p. 85; John R. Forster, pp. 495–96; Parkinson, pp. 25, 41; Wilson, p. 392.
62. Bligh, p. 123; Wilson, p. 404.
63. Wilson, p. 337.
64. Wilson, p. 404.
65. Wilson, p. 404.
66. Joseph Banks, *The Endeavour Journal of Joseph Banks*, vol. 1, pp. 260–61.
67. Rodríguez, pp. 94–95.
68. Andia y Varela, p. 260; Wilson, p. 404.

69. Rodríguez, p. 50.
70. Fr. Geronimo Clota and Fr. Narciso González, "Diary of Things Noteworthy That Occurred at Amat's Island (Alias Otagiti) Between the 28th Day of January, 1775 ... and the 12th of November in the Same Year ...," p. 347; Bolton G. Corney, ed., *The Quest and Occupation of Tahiti by Emissaries of Spain in the Years 1772–76*, vol. 2, p. 472.
71. Rodríguez, p. 182.
72. Vancouver, vol. 1, pp. 280–81.
73. Bligh, p. 131.
74. Lee, p. 108.
75. *A Journal of a Voyage*, p. 50; Lee, p. 108; Vancouver, vol. 1, pp. 280–82.
76. Boenechea, pp. 337–38; Bonacorsi, p. 57.
77. Cook, vol. 3, pp. 201, 204–5; Rodríguez, p. 14; Wilson, p. 364.
78. Banks, vol. 1, p. 261; Rodríguez, p. 14; Wilson, p. 364.
79. At least one of the plants used to decorate the bier, according to Parkinson, pp. 39–40, was *Crataeva religiosa* Forst., which was said to be dedicated to the god Tane.
80. For references to the desiccation of a body and the miri who tended such corpses, see Bougainville, pp. 254–55; Cook, vol. 1, p. 83, and vol. 3, pp. 191, 208–9, 1060–61; Corney, vol. 2, p. 470; George Forster, vol. 1, p. 294; Lee, p. 108; Rodriguez, p. 14; Vancouver, vol. 1, pp. 288, 296–97; Wilson, pp. 161, 212–13, 363.
81. Andia y Varela, p. 262; Bligh, p. 137; Bougainville, p. 255; Rodríguez, p. 201; Wilson, pp. 339, 364.
82. Banks, vol. 1, p. 295.
83. Wilson, p. 198.
84. Edwards and Hamilton, p. 104.
85. Wilson, p. 364.
86. Vancouver, vol. 1, p. 297; Wilson, p. 364.
87. Lee, p. 108; Wilson, p. 364.
88. Andia y Varela, p. 262.
89. For Melanesia see Albert B. Lewis, *The Melanesians: People of the South Pacific*, p. 224; for New Zealand see Peter H. Buck, *The Coming of the Maori*, p. 426; and for Easter Island see William Mulloy, "The Ceremonial Center of Vinapu," p. 100.
90. Rodríguez, p. 31.
91. Andia y Varela, pp. 261–62.
92. Rodríguez, p. 34.
93. Vancouver, vol. 1, pp. 288–92.
94. Cook, vol. 3, pp. 191, 1061.
95. Banks, vol. 1, p. 286; Cook, vol. 3, p. 191; George Forster, vol. 1, p. 294.
96. Banks, vol. 1, p. 286; George Forster, vol. 1, p. 294.
97. *A Journal of a Voyage*, p. 50; Andia y Varela, pp. 261–62; John R. Forster, p. 588; Rodríguez, pp. 32, 178, 184, 186, 190; Vancouver, vol. 1, pp. 286–87; Wilson, p. 363.
98. George Forster, vol. 2, p. 74; Rodríguez, p. 93.
99. George Forster, vol. 2, p. 75.
100. *A Journal of a Voyage*, p. 50; Cook, vol. 1, p. 136.
101. Banks, vol. 1, pp. 288–89.
102. George Forster, vol. 2, p. 74; John R. Forster, p. 453.

103. Rodríguez, p. 205.
104. Wilson, p. 382.
105. The best early descriptions of this costume with its mask are to be found in George Forster, vol. 2, pp. 72–74, and John R. Forster, pp. 450–53. In this country, the Bernice P. Bishop Museum in Honolulu has an early specimen in its collections in a remarkably fine state of preservation.
106. John R. Forster, p. 452; Rodríguez, p. 93; Vancouver, vol. 1, p. 279.
107. Rodriguez, p. 190.
108. Corney, vol. 2, p. 471.
109. Rodríguez, pp. 184–86; Vancouver, vol. 1, pp. 280–90.
110. Vancouver, vol. 1, p. 281.
111. Rodríguez, p. 186.
112. Rodríguez, pp. 185–92.
113. Clota and González, p. 347; Rodríguez, p. 189.
114. Cook, vol. 2, p. 207; Parkinson, p. 21; Wilson, p. 67.
115. Banks, vol. 1, pp. 265–66; Parkinson, p. 21.
116. Banks, vol. 1, p. 265; Bligh, p. 116; Wilson, p. 67.
117. Parkinson, p. 21.
118. Parkinson, p. 25.
119. Parkinson, p. 25; Vancouver, vol. 1, p. 287; Wilson, pp. 352–53.
120. Lee, p. 120.
121. Ledyard, p. 54; Wilson, pp. 345–46.
122. John R. Forster, pp. 534–35.
123. *A Journal of a Voyage*, pp. 48–49.
124. Wilson, pp. 345–46.
125. Wilson, p. 213.

Food From the Land

1. Sydney Parkinson, *A Journal of a Voyage to the South Seas, in His Majesty's Ship the Endeavour: Faithfully Transcribed From the Papers of the Late Sydney Parkinson ...*, p. 41; James Wilson, *A Missionary Voyage to the Southern Pacific Ocean, Performed in the Years 1796, 1797, 1798 in the Ship Duff...*, p. 376.
2. José de Andia y Varela, "Narrative of a Voyage Performed to the Island of Amat, Otherwise by Name Otahiti, ... in the Years 1774 and 1775," p. 284; Juan de Hervé, "Information Acquired From the Natives of the Island of Amat (by Them Called Otajiti) During the Voyage After Leaving the Port of Valparaiso ...," p. 358; George Robertson, "A Journal of the Second Voyage of H.M.S. *Dolphin* ... in the Years 1766, 1767, and 1768," p. 178; Máximo Rodríguez, "Daily Narrative Kept by the Interpreter Máximo Rodríguez at the Island of Amat, Otherwise Otahiti, in the Year 1774," p. 11.
3. William Ellis, *Polynesian Researches: Polynesia*, p. 46.
4. Parkinson, p. 50, and Wilson, p. 375, mentioned the yam, *Dioscorea alata* L., while the latter author, p. 376, also added the *teve*, or *Amorphophallus campanulatus* (Roxburgh) Blume, as well as a plant called *mapura*, said to be a small, wild taro. However, this latter may have been more closely related to the teve, since both contained a hot, acid ingredient which was dispelled through cooking in a pit oven. The

most common upland edible plant was the fe'i banana, *Musa trog-lodytarum* L., which was well documented as a mountain grown plant by Joseph Banks, *The Endeavour Journal of Joseph Banks*, vol. 1, p. 307; George Forster, *Voyage Round the World ... During the Years 1772, 3, 4, and 5*, vol. 1, pp. 313, 343; John R. Forster, *Observations Made During a Voyage Round the World*, ..., p. 219; and Parkinson, p. 47.

5. For early descriptions of the landscape and soils see *A Journal of a Voyage Round the World, in His Majesty's Ship Endeavour, In the Years 1768, 1769, 1770, and 1771 ...*, p. 41; James Cook, *The Journals of Captain James Cook*, vol. 1, pp. 108, 128, and vol. 3, p. 1373; George Forster, vol. 1, pp. 270, 314, 341, 352; John R. Forster, p. 105; Robertson, p. 201.

6. Andia y Varela, p. 275; Banks, vol. 1, p. 297; Cook, vol. 1, p. 108.

7. George Forster, vol. 1, p. 270.

8. Cook, vol. 1, p. 128.

9. Louis Antoine de Bougainville, *A Voyage Round the World ... in the Years 1766, 1767, 1768, and 1769*, p. 229; George Forster, vol. 1, p. 274.

10. Wilson, p. 195.

11. This was the 'uru or *Artocarpus altilis* (Parkinson) Fosberg.

12. William Bligh, *A Voyage to the South Sea... in His Majesty's Ship the Bounty ...*, p. 109; John R. Forster, p. 441.

13. Ida Lee, *Captain Bligh's Second Voyage to the South Seas*, p. 105.

14. Not all taro, or *Colocasia esculenta* (L.) Schott., is grown in water, as witness its dry land cultivation in Fiji, Tongatapu, Samoa, and even Easter Island in the late twentieth century. Whether taro irrigation is a culturally determined trait or a requirement of particular varieties of the plant offers interesting potential as evidence in the study of inter-island contacts.

15. George Forster, vol. 1, p. 341.

16. Wilson, p. 375.

17. Andia y Varela, p. 271; John R. Forster, p. 442; John Ledyard, *Journal of Captain Cook's Last Voyage*, p. 48; Elmer D. Merrill, *The Botany of Cook's Voyages and Its Unexpected Significance in Relation to Anthropology, Biogeography, and History*, pp. 343–45; Parkinson, p. 47.

18. Of the lowland bananas, including plantains, Parkinson, p. 47, listed only *Musa paradisiaca* L. However, Merrill, pp. 343–44, stated that most "authors" now regard the numerous varieties as belonging to one or the other of the two species, *M. paradisiaca* L. and *M. sapientum* L. Although he did not explain why, Jacques Barrau, in *Subsistence Agriculture in Polynesia and Micronesia*, p. 48, appears to have taken the position that *M. paradisiaca* is a post-European introduction into Polynesia!

19. John R. Forster, p. 404.

20. *Musa troglodytarum* L., of which Solander, in Merrill, p. 344, listed five varieties.

21. Banks, vol. 1, pp. 299, 307; John R. Forster, p. 219; Wilson, p. 56.

22. Andia y Varela, p. 271; Wilson, p. 378.

23. For references to yams see Parkinson, p. 50; Wilson, p. 375. For the sweet potato, *Ipomoea batatas* (L.) Lamarck, see Andia y Varela, p. 275; Domingo Boenechea, "Narrative of the Voyage Performed by Don Domingo Boenechea, ... in the Frigate *Santa María Magdalena* (Alias *el Aguila*) ... to Explore the Island Called by Navigators After King

George or Saint George, and by the Natives Otacite, ... ," p. 55;
Raimundo Bonacorsi, "Voyage to the Island of Otayty Performed by
Don Domingo Boenechea ... Commanding the Frigate ... *La Aguila*,
... 26th September, 1772," p. 321; Wilson, p. 375. The early presence
of *Dioscoria alata* L. seems assured from Parkinson's listing of it.
Whether *D. nummularia* Lamarck was present and represented one of
the "several sorts" of yams mentioned by Parkinson is not known. Its
present distribution, according to Barrau, p. 46, is pan-Polynesian.

24. Bolton G. Corney, ed., *The Quest and Occupation of Tahiti by Emissaries
    of Spain in the Years 1772–76*, vol. 2, p. 472; Parkinson, p. 39; Anders
    Sparrman, *A Voyage Round the World With Captain James Cook in H.M.S.
    Resolution*, p. 57; Wilson, p. 377. This was the fruit tree *Spondias dulcis*
    Forst.
25. Andia y Varela, p. 273; Boenechea, p. 327; John R. Forster, p. 442;
    Parkinson, p. 40; Wilson, p. 377. Merrill, p. 335, identified this as
    Syzygium malaccense (L.) Merr. and Perr.
26. John R. Forster, p. 442; Parkinson, p. 46. This was *Pandanus tectorius*
    (Solander) Parkinson.
27. The 'ihi or *Inocarpus edulis* Forst., also known as *I. fagiferus* (Parkinson)
    Fosberg, was referred to in Banks, vol. 1, p. 298; Bligh, p. 139; John R.
    Forster, p. 442; Parkinson, p. 39. Reference to the south sea almond,
    Terminalia catappa L., may be found in Boenechea, p. 32; and Parkin-
    son, p. 40.
28. For reference to pia, or *Tacca leontopetaloides* (L.) Kuntze, see Bligh, p.
    139; John R. Forster, p. 443; Parkinson, p. 38; Wilson, p. 376. For
    references to teve, or *Amorphophallus campanulatus* (Roxburgh) Blume,
    see John R. Forster, p. 443; Parkinson, p. 47; Wilson, p. 376.
29. According to Parkinson, p. 38, there were five varieties of the ti plant,
    Cordyline terminales (L.) Kunth. For references to the use or plantings
    of the sugar cane *Saccharum officinarum* L., see Andia y Varela, p. 275;
    Bligh, pp. 85–86; Bougainville, p. 245; Parkinson, p. 37; Wilson, p.
    396.
30. Edmund Fanning, *Voyages and Discoveries in the South Seas, 1792–1832*,
    p. 51; Rodríguez, p. 122; Wilson, p. 396.
31. Parkinson, pp. 37, 42. The toxic kava was *Piper methysticum* Forst., the
    nontoxic, *P. latifolium* L.
32. John R. Forster, p. 481.
33. Tomás Gayangos, "The Official Journal of the Second Voyage of the
    Frigate *Aguila* from El Callao to Tahiti ...," p. 159.
34. Rodríguez, p. 52.
35. Cook, vol. 3, pp. 215, 1058, 1343, 1378.
36. Wilson, p. 195.
37. Cook, vol. 3, p. 612; George Forster, vol. 2, pp. 8, 28.
38. G. H. von Langsdorff, *Voyages and Travels ... During the Years 1803,
    1804, 1805, and 1807*, vol. 1, p. 126.
39. Peter H. Buck, *Ethnology of Mangareva*, p. 8.
40. Alfred Métraux, *Ethnology of Easter Island*, p. 159.
41. George Forster, vol. 1, p. 367; John R. Forster, pp. 370–71.
42. Bligh, p. 84; Gayangos, p. 129; Rodríguez, p. 75.
43. Lee, p. 101.
44. Ellis, *Polynesian Researches: Polynesia*, p. 137.

45. Robertson, pp. 231–32.
46. Barrau, p. 15; Kenneth P. Emory, *Material Culture of the Tuamoto Archipelago,* p. 36 and fig 13*a*.
47. Ellis, *Polynesian Researches: Polynesia,* pp. 137–38.
48. Barrau, p. 15.
49. Rodríguez, p. 98.
50. Parkinson, p. 45.
51. Rodríguez, pp. 96, 100.
52. Andia y Varela, p. 274. This was, of course, *Cocos nucifera* L.
53. George Forster, vol. 1, p. 348; Parkinson, p. 16.
54. For reference to the picking and husking of coconuts see Parkinson, p. 16.
55. Cook, vol. 1, p. 122; John R. Forster, p. 219.
56. Wilson, p. 323.
57. Cook, vol. 1, p. 114; John R. Forster, pp. 105, 504; Rodríguez, p. 105.
58. Banks, vol. 1, p. 288; Wilson, p. 175.
59. Banks, vol. 1, p. 306; John R. Forster, p. 504; Wilson, p. 323.
60. Cook, vol. 3, p. 975; John R. Forster, pp. 104–5.
61. Edwin N. Ferdon, Jr., "A Reconnaissance Survey of Three Fortified Hilltop Villages," pp. 9–12.
62. Gayangos, p. 137; Rodríguez, pp. 27, 50.
63. Parkinson, p. 22.
64. Rodríguez, pp. 150–51; Wilson, pp. 331–32.
65. Cook, vol. 1, p. 122.
66. Rodríguez, p. 56; Wilson, p. 374.
67. For this technique of making and using mahi see Cook, vol. 1, p. 122.
68. Wilson, p. 374.
69. Parkinson, pp. 45–46.
70. This was probably the *peereeperee* noted by Parkinson, p. 42, and since identified as *Urena lobata* L.
71. Wilson, pp. 374–75.
72. Ellis, *Polynesian Researches: Polynesia,* p. 42.
73. George Forster, vol. 1, pp. 314–15; Robertson, p. 179; Sparrman, p. 61.
74. Helmut Epstein, *Domestic Animals of China,* pp. 70–71.
75. Epstein, pp. 92–93.
76. Friedrich E. Zeuner, *A History of Domestic Animals,* p. 257.
77. George Forster, vol. 1, p. 315.
78. George Forster, vol. 1, p. 281; John R. Forster, p. 457.
79. Cook, vol. 3, p. 202.
80. John R. Forster, pp. 583–84.
81. Bougainville, p. 247; George Forster, vol. 1, p. 342; Rodríguez, p. 152.
82. Bonacorsi, p. 55.
83. Wilson, pp. 360–61.
84. Andia y Varela, p. 287; George Forster, vol. 1, p. 378.
85. Margaret Titcomb, *Dog and Man in the Ancient Pacific,* pp. 76–80.
86. Epstein, pp. 125–27.
87. Cook, vol. 1, p. 122.
88. John R. Forster, pp. 185, 215–16.
89. Banks, vol. 1, p. 293.
90. Parkinson, pp. 20–21.
91. Bonacorsi, p. 55.

92. George Forster, vol. 1, p. 28; John R. Forster, p. 187; Sparrman, pp. 58, 119.
93. Bligh, p. 121.
94. *A Journal of a Voyage*, p. 247; Boenechea, p. 328; Bonacorsi, p. 55; George Forster, vol. 1, p. 280; John Marra, *Journal of the Resolution's Voyage, in 1772, 1773, 1774, and 1775 ... Also a Journal of the Adventure's Voyage, in the Years 1772, 1773, and 1774 ...*, p. 47; Sparrman, p. 58; Wilson, p. 372.
95. Carl O. Sauer, *Agricultural Origins and Dispersals*, pp. 28–33.
96. Andia y Varela, p. 28; Corney, vol. 2, p. 472; Robertson, p. 179.
97. John R. Forster, p. 185.
98. John R. Forster, p. 215.
99. Ellis, *Polynesian Researches: Polynesia*, pp. 221–23.
100. E. S. C. Handy, *History and Culture in the Society Islands*, p. 65.
101. George Forster, vol. 1, pp. 458–59.
102. Rodríguez, pp. 189, 197.

Food From the Sea

1. James Wilson, *A Missionary Voyage to the Southern Pacific Ocean, Performed in the Years 1796, 1797, 1798 in the Ship Duff ...*, p. 386–87.
2. José de Andia y Varela, "Narrative of a Voyage Performed to the Island of Amat, Otherwise by Name Otahiti, ... in the Years 1774 and 1775," p. 273; Wilson, p. 387.
3. Wilson, pp. 386–87.
4. John R. Forster, *Observations Made During a Voyage Round the World, ...*, p. 441.
5. Fr. José Amich, "An Account of the First Voyage of the *Aguila* under Captain Don Domingo de Boenechea to Tahiti: 1772–73," p. 81; Domingo Boenechea, "Narrative of the Voyage Performed by Don Domingo Boenechea, ... in the Frigate *Santa María Magdalena* (Alias *el Aguila*) ... to Explore the Island Called by Navigators After King George or Saint George, and by the Natives Otaciti, ...," p. 334; John R. Forster, p. 404; Anders Sparrman, *A Voyage Round the World With Captain James Cook in H.M.S. Resolution*, p. 58; Wilson, p. 386.
6. Wilson, p. 387.
7. Amich, p. 81.
8. Boenechea, p. 328.
9. Andia y Varela, p. 272.
10. Wilson, pp. 385–86.
11. Wilson, p. 386.
12. Wilson, p. 385.
13. Wilson, p. 385.
14. Sydney Parkinson, *A Journal of a Voyage to the South Seas, in His Majesty's Ship the Endeavour: Faithfully Transcribed From the Papers of the Late Sydney Parkinson ...*, p. 39; Wilson, p. 393.
15. Wilson, p. 388.
16. The three plants listed by both Parkinson, pp. 39, 41, 43, and John R. Forster, p. 463, have been identified by Elmer D. Merrill, *The Botany of Cook's Voyages and Its Unexpected Significance in Relation to Anthropology, Biogeography and History*, pp. 348, 351, and 353 as *Barringtonia asiatica*

(L.) Kurz; *Wikstroemia foetida* (L.) A. Gray; and *Tephrosia purpurea* (L.) Pers. The fourth plant, whose proper botanical name I have failed to determine, was designated *Lepidium piscidium* by John R. Forster.

17. John R. Forster, p. 463. This was the tree *Barringtonia asiatica* (L.) Kurz.

18. Wilson, pp. 385, 395. Parkinson, p. 49, referred to it as *yeiyei* and mentioned its use in making baskets. It was probably the 'ie'ie, or *Freycinetea demissa.*

19. Ida Lee, *Captain Bligh's Second Voyage to the South Seas,* p. 113.

20. William Ellis, *Polynesian Researches: Polynesia,* pp. 138–39.

21. Ellis, *Polynesian Researches: Polynesia,* p. 139.

22. Parkinson, p. 41. This was the grass *Miscanthus japonicus* Anders., found widely scattered in Polynesia.

23. George Robertson, "A Journal of the Second Voyage of H.M.S. *Dolphin* . . . in the Years 1766, 1767, and 1768," p. 177.

24. Parkinson, p. 42, referred to the peeled wood of *Hibiscus tiliaceus* L. as being used for fish spears, while Wilson, p. 386, mentioned the hard wood of toa, or *Casuarina equisetifolia* J. R. and G. Forster, as used for the same purpose. The reed shafts mentioned by John R. Forster, pp. 461–62, are not identifiable botanically.

25. John R. Forster, pp. 461–62, specifically used the term *harpoon* to describe this weapon and he may be correct, though I have found no other early reference to such a device. While Bengt Anell, *Contributions to the History of Fishing in the Southern Seas,* p. 66, says the harpoon was known in Polynesia only in New Zealand, the Chathams, and Marquesas Islands, the bilateral barbs, or arrow shape, of John R. Forster's Tahitian specimen would seem to match the harpoon heads of those used in the Marquesas, as described by Anell.

26. Wilson, p. 386.

27. Wilson, p. 386.

28. Andia y Varela, p. 282; William Bligh, *A Voyage to the South Sea . . . in His Majesty's Ship the Bounty . . .*, p. 112; Wilson, p. 383.

29. Wilson, p. 383.

30. Máximo Rodríguez, "Daily Narrative Kept by the Interpreter Máximo Rodríguez at the Island of Amat, otherwise Otahiti, in the year 1774," p. 101.

31. Anell, p. 21.

32. James Cook, *The Journals of Captain James Cook,* vol. 1, p. 133.

33. Cook, vol. 1, p. 133 n. 5.

34. Parkinson, p. 19.

35. Merrill, p. 333; Parkinson, p. 38.

36. Andia y Varela, p. 282.

37. Cook, vol. 3, p. 208 n. 2; Wilson, p. 386.

38. Rodríguez, pp. 73–74, 143.

39. Parkinson, pp. 43, 46; Wilson, p. 384. For modern identification of Parkinson's plants see Merrill, pp. 352, 356.

40. Andia y Varela, p. 282 n. 1; Bolton G. Corney, ed., *The Quest and Occupation of Tahiti by Emissaries of Spain in the Years 1772–76,* vol. 2, p. 459 n. 2.

41. John R. Forster, p. 462; Parkinson, p. 42.

42. John R. Forster, p. 462; Parkinson, p. 44; Merrill, p. 362.

43. Wilson, p. 383.
44. Cook, vol. 3, p. 28; Rodríguez, p. 78.
45. Wilson, p. 385.
46. Wilson, p. 386.
47. For reference to bag nets see Wilson, p. 387.
48. Rodríguez, p. 114.
49. Rodríguez, p. 115.
50. Rodríguez, p. 143.
51. Ellis, *Polynesian Researches: Polynesia*, pp. 144–45.
52. Wilson, pp. 383–84.
53. John R. Forster, p. 462. All but mohu have been previously identified. Unfortunately, neither John R. Forster nor Parkinson described this plant, so its botanical identity is unknown, even though Parkinson, p. 37, gave it the name *Cyperus alatus*.
54. Amich, p. 81.
55. Andia y Varela, p. 281; Wilson, p. 386.
56. Joseph Banks, *The Endeavour Journal of Joseph Banks*, vol. 1, pp. 362–63.
57. Andia y Varela, pp. 281–82.
58. John R. Forster, p. 462.
59. Parkinson, p. 19.
60. *A Journal of a Voyage Round the World, in His Majesty's Ship Endeavour, in the Years 1768, 1769, 1770, and 1771*, pp. 52–53; Boenechea, p. 328; John R. Forster, p. 462; Parkinson, p. 19; Wilson, p. 386.
61. *A Journal of a Voyage*, p. 52.
62. Ellis, *Polynesian Researches: Polynesia*, pp. 145–46.
63. Amich, p. 81.
64. John R. Forster, p. 462.
65. Bligh, p. 112.
66. Wilson, p. 387.
67. Bligh, p. 112; John R. Forster, p. 463.
68. Wilson, pp. 383, 387.
69. Wilson, pp. 383–84.
70. Edward Dodd, *Polynesian Seafaring*, p. 50.
71. Bligh, p. 112.
72. Ellis, *Polynesian Researches: Polynesia*, p. 148.
73. Ellis, *Polynesian Researches: Polynesia*, pp. 147–48; Wilson, p. 384.
74. Ellis, *Polynesian Researches: Polynesia*, pp. 147–48; George Forster, *Voyage Round the World ... During the Years 1772, 3, 4, and 5*, vol. 2, pp. 51–52.
75. Ellis, *Polynesian Researches: Polynesia*, p. 147.
76. Wilson, p. 384.
77. *A Journal of a Voyage*, p. 52; Ellis, *Polynesian Researches: Polynesia*, p. 146.
78. Anell, p. 234.

Trade and Transportation

1. Edward Edwards and George Hamilton, *Voyage of H.M.S. "Pandora" ... in the South Seas, 1790–91*, p. 109; James Wilson, *A Missionary Voyage to the Southern Pacific Ocean, Performed in the Years 1796, 1797, 1798 in the Ship Duff ...*, pp. 225, 364–65.

2. Edwin N. Ferdon, Jr., "Easter Island Exchange Systems," pp. 140–43.
3. Anders Sparrman, *A Voyage Round the World With Captain James Cook in H.M.S. Resolution,* p. 56.
4. Ferdon, "Easter Island Exchange Systems," pp. 139–40; Raymond Firth, *Primitive Polynesian Economy,* pp. 316–20.
5. James Cook, *The Journals of Captain James Cook,* vol. 3, pp. 210, 211. Máximo Rodríguez, "Daily Narrative Kept by the Interpreter Máximo Rodríguez at the Island of Amat, Otherwise Otahiti, in the Year 1774," has so many references to welcoming and departing gifts for chiefs, which he observed during his year-long stay on the island, that his report alone is sufficient reference to this custom.
6. John Marra, *Journal of the Resolution's Voyage, in 1772, 1773, 1774, and 1775 ... Also a Journal of the Adventure's Voyage, in the Years 1772, 1773, and 1774 ...,* p. 177.
7. Cook, vol. 3, p. 221.
8. William Bligh, *A Voyage to the South Sea ... in His Majesty's Ship the Bounty ...,* pp. 69–70; Cook, vol. 3, p. 192.
9. Sydney Parkinson, *A Journal of a Voyage to the South Seas, in His Majesty's Ship the Endeavour: Faithfully Transcribed From the Papers of the Late Sydney Parkinson ...,* p. 22.
10. Rodríguez, p. 151; Wilson, pp. 331–32.
11. Wilson, p. 200.
12. Rodríguez, pp. 133–34.
13. Joseph Banks, *The Endeavour Journal of Joseph Banks,* vol. 1, p. 290; Wilson, p. 402.
14. Tomás Gayangos, "The Official Journal of the Second Voyage of the Frigate *Aguila* from El Callao to Tahiti ...: 1774–75," pp. 143, 151; Juan de Hervé, "Information Acquired from the Natives of the Island of Amat (by Them Called Otajiti) During the Voyage After Leaving the Port of Valparaiso ...," p. 359; Rodríguez, p. 40.
15. John R. Forster, *Observations Made During a Voyage Round the World ...,* pp. 365–67.
16. Rodríguez, p. 198; Wilson, p. 403.
17. *A Journal of a Voyage Round the World, in His Majesty's Ship Endeavour, in the Years 1768, 1769, 1770, and 1771 ...,* p. 56; José de Andia y Varela, "Narrative of a Voyage Performed to the Island of Amat, Otherwise by Name Otahiti, ... in the Years 1774 and 1775," p. 300; John R. Forster, p. 366.
18. Wilson, p. 403.
19. Bligh, p. 90; Ida Lee, *Captain Bligh's Second Voyage to the South Seas,* pp. 41–42; Rodríguez, pp. 133–34, 198.
20. Gayangos, pp. 133–35; Rodríguez, pp. 24–25, 190.
21. A Journal of a Voyage, pp. 41–42; Andia y Varela, p. 259.
22. George Robertson, "A Journal of the Second Voyage of H.M.S. *Dolphin* ... in the Years 1766, 1767, and 1768," pp. 154–56.
23. Only a few of the numerous references to such stealing activity are Banks, vol. 1, p. 263; Domingo Boenechea, "Narrative of the Voyage Performed by Don Domingo Boenechea, ... in the Frigate *Santa María Magdalena* (Alias *el Aguila*) ... to Explore the Island Called by Navigators After King George or Saint George, and by the Natives Otacite, ...," p. 333; Raimundo Bonacorsi, "Voyages to the Island of

Otayty Performed by Don Domingo Boenechea ... Commanding the
Frigate ... La Aguila, ... 26th September 1772," p. 57; George Forster,
Voyage Round the World ... During the Years 1772, 3, 4, and 5, vol. 1, p.
97; Lee, p. 120.

24. Banks, vol. 1, p. 267; Louis Antoine de Bougainville, *A Voyage Round
the World ... in the Years 1766, 1767, 1768, and 1769,* pp. 252–53;
Sparrman, p. 123.
25. John R. Forster, p. 370; Rodríguez, p. 111; Sparrman, p. 123.
26. *A Journal of a Voyage,* p. 46; George Forster, vol. 1, p. 344; Sparrman,
p. 59.
27. George Forster, vol. 1, p. 344; Sparrman, p. 59.
28. For references to trails and trail conditions see Banks, vol. 1, pp. 261,
279; Bougainville, p. 245; Cook, vol. 1, p. 128; George Forster, vol. 1,
pp. 279, 293, and vol. 2, p. 81; Wilson, pp. 188, 195–96, 198.
29. Wilson, p. 332.
30. Banks, vol. 1, p. 307.
31. Banks, vol. 1, p. 306; Bligh, p. 136; George Forster, vol. 1, p. 341;
Wilson, p. 171.
32. For references to human carriers see Bligh, p. 105; Boenechea, p. 316;
George Forster, vol. 1, pp. 267, 352; John R. Forster, p. 387; Rodríguez, pp. 36, 62; Sparrman, p. 59.
    For references to the use of a litter see Fr. Geronimo Clota and Fr.
Narciso González, "Diary of Things Noteworthy That Occurred at
Amat's Island (Alias Otagiti) between the 28th Day of January, 1775
... and the 12th of November in the Same Year ...," p. 340; Cook,
vol. 3, pp. 188, 190; George Vancouver, *A Voyage of Discovery in the
North Pacific Ocean, and Round the World ...,* vol. 1, p. 267.
33. Edward Dodd, *Polynesian Seafaring,* p. 84.
34. Dodd, pp. 86–87.
35. A. C. Haddon and James Hornell, *Canoes of Oceania,* vol. 1, p. 143.
36. Banks, vol. 1, p. 366.
37. Bougainville, p. 259.
38. Dodd, pp. 86–87.
39. Dodd, pp. 84–88.
40. Early illustrations of this feature are to be found in Dodd, pp. 91,
94–95.
41. Descriptive accounts of the va'a type canoe hull may be found in
Banks, vol. 1, pp. 364–67; Bougainville, pp. 258–59; Cook, vol. 1, pp.
129–30; Samuel Wallis, "An Account of a Voyage Round the World in
the Years 1766, 1767, and 1768," p. 486; Wilson, pp. 190, 400.
42. Descriptive accounts of the features of the more common pahi type
canoe hull may be found in Banks, vol. 1, pp. 319, 364–65; Cook, vol.
1, p. 131; John R. Forster, pp. 458–59; Hervé, p. 358. Excellent repro-
ductions of pahi illustrations by Parkinson and Webber are to be
found in Dodd, pp. 85, 93, and 96.
43. Cook, vol. 1, p. 131.
44. Dodd, p. 96; Haddon and Hornell, vol. 1, pp. 122–24, fig. 82.
45. Cook, vol. 1, p. 131.
46. Banks, vol. 1, p. 364.
47. Banks, vol. 1, p. 297.
48. Boenechea, p. 334.

49. Hervé, p. 358.
50. That some Tahitian pahi did originate in Raiatea is evidenced by the Raiatean gift of a large pahi filled with tapa cloth sent to the about-to-be-invested paramount chief of Tahiti iti, as recorded by Rodríguez, p. 188. However, it is difficult to imagine that such traffic accounted for all such canoes on the peninsula.
51. Cook, vol. 2, p. 402; Haddon and Hornell, vol. 1, p. 136, fig. 89.
52. E. S. C. Handy, *History and Culture in the Society Islands*, pp. 19–20.
53. Haddon and Hornell, vol. 1, pp. 138–39.
54. Cook, vol. 1, p. 130; John R. Forster, p. 460; Wilson, p. 401. For illustrations of such early outriggers see Dodd, pp. 91–92.
55. Banks, vol. 1, p. 366.
56. Banks, vol. 1, p. 365.
57. References to the paraphernalia needed to fit an outrigger canoe with sail are Fr. José Amich, "An Account of the First Voyage of the *Aguila* Under Captain Don Domingo de Boenechea to Tahiti: 1772–73," p. 82; Banks, vol. 1, p. 365; Bougainville, p. 259; Cook, vol. 1, p. 130; John R. Forster, p. 460; Wilson, p. 401.
58. Amich, p. 82; Andia y Varela, p. 283; Bougainville, p. 258; Dodd, p. 91; John R. Forster, p. 460.
59. References to the Tahitian sprit sail and masthead devices are Andia y Varela, p. 286; Banks, vol. 1, p. 367; Cook, vol. 1, p. 132; George Forster, vol. 1, p. 316; John R. Forster, pp. 450, 460; Wilson, p. 401. For good illustrations of early sails see Dodd, pp. 84–88, 92.
60. Andia y Varela, p. 286.
61. Dodd, pp. 84–85.
62. Dodd, p. 95.
63. Amich, p. 81.
64. Amich, p. 81; Boenechea, p. 334; Bougainville, p. 260; Cook, vol. 1, p. 130.
65 .Amich, p. 81; Boenechea, p. 334; Dodd, p. 89.
66. Dodd, pp. 84–88.
67. Dodd, pp. 84–85.
68. Dodd, pp. 85–87; Hervé, p. 358.
69. Andia y Varela, p. 284; Wilson, p. 401.
70. Dodd, pp. 85–87.
71. Dodd, pp. 94–95.
72. Boenechea, p. 334.
73. Cook, vol. 2, p. 396; Wilson, p. 386.
74. Wilson, p. 192.
75. Parkinson, pp. 37, 39–41, and 44–45, listed six trees whose wood was employed in making the larger sizes of canoes. Their modern botanical identifications are *Neonauclea forsteri* (Seem.) Merr., *Guettarda speciosa* L., *Spondius dulcis* Forst., *Terminalia glabrata* Forst., *Calophylum inophyllum* L., and *Artocarpus altilis* (Parkinson) Fosb. The same author, pp. 41–44, listed four other trees used only for small canoes. Botanically these are *Barringtonia asiatica* (L.) Kurz., *Hibiscus tiliaceus* L., *H. tiliaceus* L. var. *hastatus* (L.f.), and *Hernandia ovigera* L., the latter being used to construct what Parkinson termed "very small" canoes. He further noted, p. 41, the specialized use of certain trees, such as *Fragraea berteriana* A. Gray for making canoe thwarts and, p. 47, the use of the wood from *Rhamnus zizyphoides* Soland., ex Forst. f. in forming the

sterns of canoes. Perhaps here he was referring to the tall, carved stern posts often found on va'a type canoes. Of the three trees noted by the missionaries in Wilson, pp. 392–93, but not found in Parkinson's ethnobotanical list, none are botanically identifiable. One was used in building canoes, another was said to be used in many parts of a canoe, while the hard, white wood of yet another was said to be employed in outrigger construction.

76. Wilson, pp. 399–400.
77. Banks, vol. 1, p. 363.
78. Wallis, p. 487.
79. Banks, vol. 1, p. 320.
80. Banks, vol. 1, pp. 363–64.
81. Wilson, p. 398.
82. Wallis, p. 487.
83. Wallis, p. 487.
84. Banks, vol. 1, p. 320.
85. Banks, vol. 1, p. 364.
86. Banks, vol. 1, p. 320; Wilson, p. 400.
87. Parkinson, p. 26; Wilson, p. 400.
88. Banks, vol. 1, p. 364.
89. Evidence for the different patterns of lashing holes found on va'a and pahi canoes is based upon early paintings reproduced in Dodd, pp. 89, 91, 93, and 94–96.
90. Banks, vol. 1, p. 320; Wilson, p. 400.
91. Banks, vol. 1, p. 320.
92. Banks, vol. 1, pp. 367–68.
93. Amich, p. 82; Bonacorsi, p. 56; Wilson, p. 398.
94. Wilson, pp. 373, 377.
95. Wilson, pp. 398–99.
96. Andia y Varela, p. 284.
97. John R. Forster, p. 461.
98. Banks, vol. 1, p. 368.
99. Boenechea, p. 334; Bonacorsi, p. 56.
100. Banks, vol. 1, p. 368; John R. Forster, p. 458.
101. Wilson, p. 192.
102. Andia y Varela, p. 284.
103. Andia y Varela, p. 282; Wilson, p. 401.
104. Wilson, p. 401.
105. Wilson, p. 402.
106. Andia y Varela, pp. 286–87; Wilson, p. 340.
107. Andia y Varela, p. 286.
108. Andia y Varela, p. 286; John R. Forster, pp. 509–11; Wilson, p. 340.
109. David Lewis, "Hokule'a Follows the Stars to Tahiti," p. 517.
110. George Forster, vol. 2, p. 105.
111. Banks, vol. 1, pp. 320, 366.
112. Bougainville, p. 269.
113. Banks, vol. 1, p. 312.
114. John R. Forster, p. 511.
115. Cook, vol. 1, pp. 291–93.
116. Bligh, p. 122; Wilson, p. 203.
117. Jack Golson, ed., *Polynesian Navigation: A Symposium on Andrew Sharp's Theory of Accidental Voyages*, pp. 138–49.

118. Gayangos, pp. 187–94.
119. Cook, vol. 1, p. 293 n. 1.
120. Andia y Varela, p. 300; Boenechea, p. 306; Cook, vol. 1, p. 293; Gayangos, p. 193.
121. Boenechea, p. 306.
122. Gayangos, p. 194.
123. Cook, vol. 1, p. 293; Gayangos, p. 193.
124. Cook, vol. 1, p. 292; John R. Forster, p. 522.
125. Andia y Varela, p. 300; John R. Forster, p. 522; Gayangos, p. 193.
126. Cook, vol. 1, p. 291.
127. Wilson, pp. 203, 359.
128. Cook, vol. 1, pp. 292–93.
129. Cook, vol. 3, p. 256.

Warfare

1. James Cook, *The Journals of Captain James Cook*, vol. 2, pp. 405–6.
2. Ida Lee, *Captain Bligh's Second Voyage to the South Seas*, pp. 38–39.
3. Anders Sparrman, *A Voyage Round the World With Captain James Cook in H.M.S. Resolution*, p. 69.
4. James Wilson, *A Missionary Voyage to the Southern Pacific Ocean, Performed in the Years 1796, 1797, 1798 in the Ship Duff . . .*, p. 363.
5. Lee, pp. 73–74.
6. William Bligh, *A Voyage to the South Sea . . . in His Majesty's Ship the Bounty*, p. 98.
7. George Forster, *Voyage Round the World . . . During the Years 1772, 3, 4, and 5*, vol. 2, p. 94.
8. Domingo Boenechea, "Narrative of the Voyage Performed by Don Domingo Boenechea, . . . in the Frigate *Santa María Magdalena* (Alias *el Aguila*) . . . to Explore the Island Called by Navigators After King George or Saint George, and by the Natives Otaciti, . . . ," p. 307; Edward Edwards and George Hamilton, *Voyage of H.M.S. "Pandora" . . . in the South Seas, 1790–91*, pp. 102, 104.
9. Lee, p. 85; Wilson, p. 183.
10. Cook, vol. 1, p. 76; George Forster, vol. 2, p. 93.
11. Wilson, pp. 182–83.
12. Wilson, p. 185.
13. John Rickman, *Journal of Captain Cook's Last Voyage . . . in the Years 1776, 1777, 1778, 1779 . . .*, p. 159.
14. Cook, vol. 2, p. 405.
15. Cook, vol. 2, p. 401.
16. Lee, p. 84.
17. This composite view of the Tahitian war council and ceremonies which preceded the actual naval engagement between Tahiti and Moorea derives from observations recorded by James Cook, William Anderson, Charles Clerke, and James King in Cook, vol. 3, pp. 197–204, 210–14, 977–82, 1315–16, and 1376–77.
18. Cook, vol. 2, p. 386; John R. Forster, *Observations Made During a Voyage Round the World, . . .*, p. 217.
19. Cook, vol. 2, p. 385; George Forster, vol. 2, pp. 64–65.
20. Cook, vol. 2, p. 401; George Forster, vol. 2, p. 65.
21. Cook, vol. 2, p. 408.

22. Cook, vol. 2, pp. 385–86; George Forster, vol. 2, p. 65.
23. Edward Dodd, *Polynesian Seafaring,* pp. 104–5.
24. A few war canoes were even longer than the figure given. Dodd, pp. 140–41, has illustrated the detailed draft of a 108-foot-long pahi war canoe drawn by Cook in Tahiti in 1777, while John R. Forster, p. 218, mentioned one on the island of Huahine which may have been of equal size.
25. Dodd, pp. 104–5; George Forster, vol. 2, p. 62.
26. Dodd, pp. 104–5; 140–41; George Forster, vol. 2, pp. 61–62.
27. Cook, vol. 1, p. 130; Dodd, pp. 104–5, 140–41; George Forster, vol. 2, p. 62.
28. George Forster, vol. 2, pp. 61–62.
29. John Marra, *Journal of the Resolution's Voyage, in 1772, 1773, 1774, and 1775 . . . Also a Journal of the Adventure's Voyage, in the Years 1772, 1773, and 1774 . . .* , p. 179.
30. Whereas the wood of the toa, or *Casuarina equisetifolia* J. R. and G. Forster was, according to Sydney Parkinson, *A Journal of a Voyage to the South Seas, in His Majesty's Ship the Endeavour: Faithfully Transcribed From the Papers of the Late Sydney Parkinson,* p. 44, used to make a wide variety of items, including spears and clubs, it is perhaps significant to note that the same author, p. 40, reported that the wood of the *ararua,* or *Decaspermum fruticosum* J. R. and G. Forster was uniquely employed in making lances and clubs.
31. This was the plant *Hibiscus rosa-sinensis* L.
32. For references to spears and lances see *A Journal of a Voyage Round the World, in His Majesty's Ship Endeavour, In the Years 1768, 1769, 1770, and 1771 . . .* , p. 55; Cook, vol. 1, p. 132; John R. Forster, p. 208; Wilson, pp. 368, 392.
33. For references to fighting clubs see Cook, vol. 1, p. 132; George Forster, vol. 2, p. 104; Rickman, p. 157; Wilson, p. 392. Two long clubs may be seen in the Hodge illustration of war canoes reproduced in Dodd, pp. 104–5.
34. Cook, vol. 2, p. 406.
35. George Forster, vol. 2, p. 63.
36. Cook, vol. 2, pp. 390, 391.
37. Cook, vol. 2, p. 390.
38. Cook, vol. 2, p. 391.
39. John R. Forster, p. 455.
40. John R. Forster, p. 404.
41. George Forster, vol. 2, p. 64; John R. Forster, p. 454.
42. José de Andia y Varela, "Narrative of a Voyage Performed to the Island of Amat, Otherwise by Name Otahiti, . . . in the Years 1774 and 1775," p. 271.
43. Cook, vol. 2, pp. 406–7.
44. Cook, vol. 2, p. 407 n. 3.
45. Cook, vol. 3, pp. 212–13.
46. This view of the events and ceremonies of truce after the 1777 war between Tahiti and Moorea derives from Cook and, especially, King in Cook, vol. 3, pp. 214, 1379–80.
47. George Forster, vol. 2, p. 93.
48. Cook, vol. 2, p. 401; George Forster, vol. 2, p. 104.
49. George Forster, vol. 2, pp. 94–95; John R. Forster, p. 407.

50. Cook, vol. 2, p. 383; George Forster, vol. 2, p. 58.
51. Cook, vol. 3, p. 194 n. 1.
52. Bligh, pp. 72–73.
53. Edwards and Hamilton, pp. 112–13.
54. John R. Forster, p. 407.
55. Lee, p. 84.
56. Joseph Banks, *The Endeavour Journal of Joseph Banks*, vol. 1, p. 300; Cook, vol. 1, p. 110; Máximo Rodríguez, "Daily Narrative Kept by the Interpreter Máximo Rodríguez at the Island of Amat, Otherwise Otahiti, in the year 1774," p. 121.
57. Cook, vol. 3, pp. 204–5.
58. Anderson in Cook, vol. 3, p. 983.
59. Banks, vol. 1, p. 305.
60. Cook, vol. 3, p. 205.
61. Andia y Varela, p. 266; Tomás Gayangos, "The Official Journal of the Second Voyage of the Frigate *Aguila* from El Callao to Tahiti ...: 1774–75," p. 138; Rodríguez, pp. 27–28.
62. Gayangos, p. 138.
63. Andia y Varela, p. 266.
64. Samuel Wallis, "An Account of a Voyage Round the World in the Years 1766, 1767, and 1768," pp. 444, 448.
65. Wallis, p. 65.
66. William Ellis, *Polynesian Researches: Polynesia*, pp. 196–97.
67. Ellis, *Polynesian Researches: Polynesia*, p. 297.
68. George Vancouver, *A Voyage of Discovery in the North Pacific Ocean, and Round the World ...*, vol. 1, pp. 334–35; Wilson, pp. 397–98.
69. Fr. Geronimo Clota and Fr. Narciso González, "Diary of Things Noteworthy That Occurred at Amat's Island (Alias Otagiti) Between the 28th Day of January, 1775 ... and the 12th of November in the Same Year ...," p. 349.

To Accept or Reject

1. Anders Sparrman, *A Voyage Round the World With Captain James Cook in H.M.S. Resolution*, p. 67.
2. George Robertson, "A Journal of the Second Voyage of H.M.S. *Dolphin* ... in the Years 1766, 1767, and 1768," pp. 137, 139, 143, 147, 154, 160, 166, 172, 177, 179, 183, 210.
3. Louis Antoine de Bougainville, *A Voyage Round the World ... in the Years 1766, 1767, 1768, and 1769*, p. 225; Sydney Parkinson, *A Journal of a Voyage to the South Seas, in His Majesty's Ship the Endeavour: Faithfully Transcribed From the Papers of the Late Sydney Parkinson*, p. 13.
4. John Marra, *Journal of the Resolution's Voyage, in 1772, 1773, 1774, and 1775 ... Also a Journal of the Adventure's Voyage, in the Years 1772, 1773, and 1774 ...*, p. 47.
5. Robertson, pp. 137, 172, 177, 179.
6. James Cook, *The Journals of Captain James Cook*, vol. 1, pp. 82, 118, and vol. 2, p. 411; Marra, p. 47.
7. Cook, vol. 3, p. 187.
8. Cook, vol. 1, p. 118, and vol. 2, p. 411; Marra, p. 47; George Vancouver, *A Voyage of Discovery in the North Pacific Ocean, and Round the World ...*, vol. 1, p. 332.

9. Marra, p. 47; Robertson, p. 137.

10. Vancouver, vol. 1, p. 332.

11. Bolton G. Corney, ed., *The Quest and Occupation of Tahiti by Emissaries of Spain in the Years 1772–76*, vol. 1, p. 248; Marra, p. 47; Samuel Wallis, "An Account of a Voyage Round the World in the Years 1766, 1767, and 1768," p. 480.

12. John R. Forster, *Observations Made During a Voyage Round the World . . .*, p. 398.

13. Cook, vol. 1, p. 118.

14. Vancouver, vol. 1, p. 332.

15. Cook, vol. 2, p. 411.

16. Máximo Rodríguez, "Daily Narrative Kept by the Interpreter Máximo Rodríguez at the Island of Amat, Otherwise Otahiti, in the year 1774," pp. 93–94.

17. Corney, vol. 1, p. 249.

18. Wallis, p. 409.

19. Raimundo Bonacorsi, "Voyage to the Island of Otayty Performed by Don Domingo Boenechea . . . Commanding the Frigate . . . *La Aguila,* . . . 26th September, 1772," p. 50.

20. Cook, vol. 1, p. 411; Marra, p. 47.

21. Cook, vol. 3, p. 1059.

22. Cook, vol. 3, pp. 192, 195.

23. Cook, vol. 3, p. 1056.

24. Ida Lee, *Captain Bligh's Second Voyage to the South Seas*, p. 87.

25. James Wilson, *A Missionary Voyage to the Southern Pacific Ocean, Performed in the Years 1796, 1797, 1798 in the Ship Duff . . .*, p. 176.

26. Lee, p. 80; Wilson, p. 68.

27. Robertson, p. 183.

28. Andrew Sharp, *The Discovery of the Pacific Islands*, p. 97.

29. Cook, vol. 3, p. 285.

30. Bonacorsi, pp. 50, 58; Cook, vol. 1, p. 131; Rodríguez, p. 98; Wallis, p. 487.

31. Cook, vol. 1, p. 118.

32. Corney, vol. 1, pp. 248–49.

33. John R. Forster, p. 368.

34. Cook, vol. 3, p. 187.

35. William Bligh, *A Voyage to the South Sea . . . in His Majesty's Ship the Bounty . . .*, p. 65; Marra, p. 192.

36. Wilson, p. 192.

37. Vancouver, vol. 1, p. 332.

38. Corney, vol. 1, p. 248.

39. Marra, p. 47.

40. Wilson, p. 79.

41. Wallis, p. 484.

42. Wilson, p. 79.

43. Vancouver, vol. 1, pp. 333–34.

44. Wallis, p. 476.

45. Rodríguez, p. 79.

46. Joseph Banks, *The Endeavour Journal of Joseph Banks*, vol. 1, p. 308.

47. Bligh, p. 86.

48. Edward Edwards and George Hamilton, *Voyage of H.M.S. "Pandora" . . . in the South Seas, 1790–91*, p. 112.

49. Wilson, p. 378.
50. Lee, pp. 83, 107.
51. Rodríguez, p. 79.
52. Lee, p. 83.
53. Cook, vol. 3, p. 195.
54. Bligh, p. 121; Lee, pp. 84–85.
55. Cook, vol. 3, p. 1057.
56. Cook, vol. 3, p. 1371; Wilson, p. 373.
57. Bligh, p. 86; Vancouver, vol. 1, p. 338.
58. Bligh, p. 121.
59. Lee, p. 83.
60. References to the early introduction of the pineapple are Bligh, p. 86; Cook, vol. 1, p. 137, and vol. 3, p. 195; Edwards and Hamilton, p. 112; Lee, p. 107.
61. Wilson, p. 166.
62. Bougainville, p. 229.
63. Cook, vol. 1, p. 137.
64. Domingo Boenechea, "Narrative of the Voyage Performed by Don Domingo Boenechea, ... in the Frigate *Santa María Magdalena* (Alias *el Aguila*) ... to Explore the Island Called by Navigators After King George or Saint George, and by the Natives Otacite, ...," p. 309; Rodríguez, pp. 64, 78, 153.
65. Edwards and Hamilton, p. 113.
66. Boenechea, p. 309; Corney, vol. 1, p. 248; Rodríguez, p. 78.
67. Rodríguez, p. 97.
68. Bligh, pp. 130, 132.
69. Edwards and Hamilton, pp. 111–12; Vancouver, vol. 1, 339; Wilson, p. 378.
70. Elmer D. Merrill, *The Botany of Cook's Voyages and Its Unexpected Significance in Relation to Anthropology, Biogeography and History,* p. 218.
71. Cook, vol. 1, pp. 136–37.
72. Merrill, p. 218.
73. Wallis, p. 469.
74. Margaret Towle, *The Ethnobotany of Pre-Columbian Peru,* pp. 90–92.
75. Merrill, pp. 264–65.
76. Merrill, p. 350.
77. Merrill, pp. 255–56.
78. Robertson, p. 147.
79. Boenechea, p. 309; Corney, vol. 1, p. 248.
80. Towle, p. 90.
81. Bligh, pp. 64, 69.
82. William Ellis, *Polynesian Researches: Polynesia,* p. 65.
83. Boenechea, p. 309; Corney, vol. 1, p. 248.
84. Cook, vol. 3, p. 195.
85. Ellis, *Polynesian Researches: Polynesia,* p. 66.
86. Cook, vol. 1, p. 137.
87. Bligh, p. 86.
88. Tomás Gayangos, "The Official Journal of the Second Voyage of the Frigate *Aguila* from El Callao to Tahiti ...: 1774–75," p. 174.
89. For references to onions see Boenechea, p. 309; Bougainville, p. 229; Corney, vol. 1, p. 248; Edwards and Hamilton, p. 112; Rodríguez, p. 123. For garlic see Boenechea, p. 309; Rodríguez, pp. 64, 95. For

turnips, tomatoes, parsley, broccoli, endives, and chili peppers see Rodríguez, pp. 61–62, 78, 107, 123, 140, 175. For cucumbers and okra see Bligh, pp. 68, 121. For mustard see Banks, vol. 1, p. 308; Cook, vol. 1, p. 137. For lettuce see Corney, vol. 1, p. 248; Edwards and Hamilton, p. 112; Rodríguez, p. 61. For cabbages see Edwards and Hamilton, p. 112; Rodríguez, pp. 79, 175.

90. Rodríguez, p. 191.
91. Cook, vol. 3, p. 1371.
92. Bligh, p. 64.
93. Wilson, p. 394.
94. Rodríguez, p. 64.
95. Banks, vol. 1, p. 268.
96. Bligh, p. 69; Wilson, p. 389.
97. Wilson, p. 389.
98. Wilson, p. 167.
99. Bligh, p. 86.
100. Lee, p. 83.
101. Cook, vol. 3, p. 195.
102. Bligh, p. 86.
103. George Mortimer, *Observations and Remarks Made During a Voyage to the Islands . . . in the Brig Mercury . . .* , p. 41.
104. Lee, p. 83.
105. Vancouver, vol. 1, p. 339.
106. Bougainville, p. 229; Robertson, p. 206; Wallis, p. 469.
107. Banks, vol. 1, p. 300.
108. Rodríguez, p. 168.
109. Cook, vol. 3, p. 194.
110. Rodríguez, p. 209.
111. Cook, vol. 3, pp. 193–94.
112. Bligh, p. 72; Cook, vol. 3, p. 194 n. 1.
113. Edwards and Hamilton, p. 118; Vancouver, vol. 1, p. 338.
114. William R. Broughton, *A Voyage of Discovery to the North Pacific Ocean . . . in the Years 1795, 1796, 1797, 1798*, p. 27.
115. Wilson, p. 372.
116. José de Andia y Varela, "Narrative of a Voyage Performed to the Island of Amat, Otherwise by Name Otahiti, . . . in the Years 1774 and 1775," pp. 298–99.
117. Cook, vol. 2, pp. 207, 411–12.
118. Cook, vol. 3, p. 223.
119. Cook, vol. 3, p. 219.
120. Edwards and Hamilton, p. 35.
121. Vancouver, vol. 1, pp. 339–40.
122. Bligh, p. 133; Wilson, p. 372.
123. Edwards and Hamilton, p. 118; Lee, p. 81; Vancouver, vol. 1, p. 339.
124. Wilson, p. 372.
125. For references to the early introduction of sheep and their eventual destruction, see Andia y Varela, p. 299; Bligh, p. 72; Cook, vol. 3, pp. 194 n. 1, 211; George Forster, *Voyage Round the World . . . During the Years 1772, 3, 4, and 5*, vol. 1, p. 356.
126. Wilson, p. 372.
127. Wilson, pp. 162, 222.
128. Gayangos, p. 174.

129. Rodríguez, pp. 46, 209.
130. Cook, vol. 3, p. 194.
131. Charles Clerke in Cook, vol. 3, p. 1314.
132. Cook, vol. 3, pp. 194, 211.
133. Bligh, p. 72.
134. Bligh, pp. 93–96, 117, 121.
135. Edwards and Hamilton, pp. 35–36.
136. Vancouver, vol. 1, p. 320.
137. Wilson, p. 372.
138. Wilson, p. 372.
139. Gayangos, p. 174; Rodríguez, pp. 59, 84, 157, 209.
140. William Anderson in Cook, vol. 3, p. 973.
141. David Samwell in Cook, vol. 3, p. 1057.
142. Bligh, p. 70.
143. Wilson, p. 61.
144. For references to these early introductions of cats see Cook, vol. 2, p. 412; Rodríguez, p. 209; Wallis, p. 469.
145. Cook, vol. 3, pp. 973, 1371.
146. Bligh, p. 121.
147. Wilson, p. 152.
148. Broughton, p. 27.
149. Rodríguez, p. 149.
150. Sparrman, p. 66.
151. Rodríguez, p. 168.
152. Rodríguez, pp. 196, 209.
153. Cook, vol. 3, p. 1371.
154. Cook, vol. 3, p. 223.
155. Mortimer, p. 40.
156. Wilson, p. 177.
157. Ellis, *Polynesian Researches: Polynesia,* p. 72.
158. George Forster, vol. 1, p. 333; Marra, p. 188.
159. Bligh, pp. 76, 83.
160. Wilson, p. 341.
161. Cook, vol. 3, p. 1065; Wilson, p. 205.
162. Wallis, p. 482.
163. George Forster, vol. 1, pp. 333–34.
164. George Forster, vol. 2, p. 80.
165. Samwell in Cook, vol. 3, p. 1065.
166. Edwards and Hamilton, p. 103; Vancouver, vol. 1, p. 264.
167. Mortimer, p. 50.
168. Vancouver, vol. 1, pp. 263–64.
169. William Ellis, *Polynesian Researches: Society Islands,* pp. 123–24.
170. John Rickman, *Journal of Captain Cook's Last Voyage . . . in the Years 1776, 1777, 1778, 1779 . . . ,* p. 145.
171. Lee, p. 86; Mortimer, p. 73; Vancouver, vol. 1, p. 265.
172. Rickman, p. 159.
173. Bligh, p. 96.
174. Vancouver, vol. 1, p. 267.
175. Lee, pp. 114–15.
176. Wilson, p. 341.

177. Bligh, pp. 76, 83.
178. Wilson, p. 342.
179. Wilson, pp. 70, 224.
180. Bligh, p. 131.
181. Edwards and Hamilton, p. 107.
182. Ellis, *Polynesian Researches: Polynesia*, pp. 221–25.
183. Banks, vol. 1, p. 276.
184. Cook, vol. 3, p. 221.
185. Bligh, p. 140.
186. Edwards and Hamilton, p. 115.
187. Wilson, p. 164.
188. Lee, pp. 81–82.
189. Edwards and Hamilton, p. 115.
190. Wilson, p. 327.
191. Cook, vol. 3, p. 220.
192. Wilson, p. 327.
193. Gayangos, pp. 118–19, 128.
194. Cook, vol. 2, pp. ixxiii, 230.
195. Cook, vol. 2, p. ixxiii, and vol. 3, pp. 185–89.
196. Bougainville, p. 263; Sparrman, p. 63.
197. Cook, vol. 1, p. 117; Sparrman, p. 63.
198. Vancouver, vol. 1, p. 303.
199. George Forster, vol. 2, p. 75.
200. Cook, vol. 3, pp. 192, 1053.
201. Rickman, p. 161.
202. Mortimer, pp. 52–53.
203. Edwards and Hamilton, p. 116.
204. Lee, pp. 93–94.
205. Wilson, p. 217.
206. Wilson, p. 362.
207. Wilson, p. 366.
208. Wilson, pp. 150–51.
209. Wilson, p. 342.

Bibliography

Amich, Fr. José. "An Account of the First Voyage of the *Aguila* Under Captain Don Domingo de Boenechea to Tahiti: 1772–73." In: Corney, Bolton G., *The Quest and Occupation of Taniti by Emissaries of Spain in the Years 1772–76.* (Hakluyt Soceity, 2nd Series, Vol. 36, pp. 65–89.) London, 1815.

Andia y Varela, José de "Narrative of a Voyage Performed to the Island of Amat, Otherwise by Name Otahiti, ... in the Years 1774 and 1775." In: Corney, Bolton G., *The Quest and Occupation of Tahiti by Emissaries of Spain in the Years 1772–76.* (Hakluyt Society, 2nd Series, Vol. 36, pp. 221–317.) London, 1915.

Andrews, Edmund, and Andrews, Irene D. *A Comparative Dictionary of the Tahitian Language.* (Special Publication No. 6, Chicago Academy of Sciences.) Chicago, 1944.

Anell, Bengt. *Contributions to the History of Fishing in the Southern Seas.* (Studia Ethnographica Upsaliensia, 9.) Uppsala, 1955.

Banks, Joseph. *The Endeavour Journal of Joseph Banks.* Edited by J. C. Beaglehole, 2 vols. Sydney: Angus and Robertson, 2nd ed., 1963.

Barrau, Jacques. *Subsistence Agriculture in Polynesia and Micronesia.* (Bernice P. Bishop Museum, Bulletin 223.) Honolulu, 1961.

Beaglehole, J. C. *The Exploration of the Pacific.* Stanford: Stanford University Press, 1966.

Bligh, William. *A Voyage to the South Sea ... in His Majesty's Ship the Bounty ... 1792.* Facsimile reprint. Honolulu: Rare Books, Ltd., n.d.

Boenechea, Domingo. "Narrative of the Voyagle Performed by Don Domingo Boenechea, ... in the Frigate *Santa María Magdalena* (Alias *el Aguila*) ... to Explore the Island Called by Navigators After King George or Saint George, and by the Natives Otacite, ..." In: Corney, Bolton G., *The Quest and Occupation of Tahiti by Emissaries of Spain in the Years 1772–76.* (Hakluyt Society, 2nd Series, Vol. 32, pp. 284–345.) London, 1913.

Bonacorsi, Raimundo. "Voyage to the Island of Otayty Performed by Don Domingo Boenechea ... Commanding the Frigate ... *La Aguila,* ... 26th September, 1772.' In: Corney, BoltonG., *The Quest and Occupation of Tahiti by Emissaries of Spain in the Years 1772–77.* (Hakluyt Society, 2nd Series, Vol. 36, pp. 29–63.) London, 1915.

Bougainville, Louis Antoine. *A Voyage Round the World ... in the Years 1766, 1767, 1768, and 1769.* Translated by J. R. Forster. (Facsimile reprint, Bibliotheca Australiana, No. 12.) Amsterdam: N. Israel, 1967.

Broughton, William R. *A Voyage of Discovery to the North Pacific Ocean ... in the Years 1795, 1796, 1797, 1798.* (Facsimile reprint, Bibliotheca Australiana, No. 13.) Amsterdam: N. Israel, 1967.

Buck, Peter H. (Te Rangi Hiroa). *Samoan Material Culture.* (Bernice P. Bishop Museum, Bulletin 75.) Honolulu, 1930.

————. *Ethnology of Mangareva.* (Bernice P. Bishop Museum, Bulletin 157.) Honolulu, 1938.

————. *The Coming of the Maori.* Wellington, New Zealand: Whitcombe and Tombs, Ltd., 1950.

Burrows, Edwin G. *Western Polynesia: A Study in Cultural Differentiation.* (Etnologiska Estudier, No. 7, pp. 1–192.) Göteborg, 1938.

Clota, Fr. Geronimo, and González, Fr. Narciso. "Diary of Things Noteworthy That Occurred at Amat's Island (Alias Otagiti) Between the 28th Day of January, 1775 ... and the 12th of November in the Same Year ...." In: Corney, Bolton G., c*The Quest and Occupation of Tahiti by Emissaries of Spain in the Years 1772–76. (Hakluyt Society, 2nd Series, Vol. 36, pp. 319–49.)* London, 1915.

Cook, James. *The Journals of Captain James Cook.* Edited by J. C. Beaglehole. 3 vols. (Hakluyt Society, Extra Series, Nos. 34, 35, 36.) Cambridge, 1955–67.

Corney, Bolton G., ed., *The Quest and Occupation of Tahiti by Emissaries of Spain in the Years 1772–76.* 3 vols. (Hakluyt Society, 2nd Series, Vols. 32, 36, 43.) London, 1913–19.

Danielsson, Bent. *Love in the South Seas.* New York: Reynal, 1956.

Dodd, Edward. *Polynesian Seafaring.* New York: Dodd, Mead, 1972.

Edwards, Edward, and Hamilton, George. *Voyage of H.M.S. ''Pandora''... in the South Seas, 1790–91.* Introduction and notes by Basil Thomson. London: Francis Edwards, 1915.

Ellis, William. *Polynesian Researches: Polynesia.* Rutland and Tokyo: Tuttle, 1969.

————. *Polynesian Researches: Society Islands.* Rutland and Tokyo: Tuttle, 1969.

————. *Polynesian Researches: Society Islands, Tubuai Islands, and New Zealand.* Rutland and Tokyo: Tuttle, 1969.

Emory, Kenneth P. *Stone Remains in the Society Islands.* (Bernice P. Bishop Museum, Bulletin 116.) Honolulu, 1933.

————. *Material Culture of the Tuamotu Archipelago.* (Bernice P. Bishop Museum, Pacific Anthropological Records No. 22.) Honolulu, 1975.

Epstein, Helmut. *Domestic Animals of China*. Farnham Royal, Bucks.: Commonwealth Agricultural Bureaux, 1969.

Fanning, Edmund. *Voyages and Discoveries in the South Seas, 1792–1832.* (Marine Research Society, Publication No. 6.) Salem, 1924.

Ferdon, Edwin N., Fr. "Easter Island Exchange Systems," *Southwestern Journal of Anthropology*, Vol. 14, No. 2, pp. 136–51.

_____. "Sites E-4 and E-5." In: *The Norwegian Archaeological Expedition to Easter Island and the East Pacific*. Vol. 1: *Archaeology of Easter Island*. Edited by T. Heyerdahl and E. N. Ferdon, Jr. (School of American Research and Museum of New Mexico, Monograph No. 24, pt. 1, pp. 305–11.) Santa Fe, 1961.

_____. "The Ceremonial Site of Orongo." In: *The Norwegian Archaeological Expecition to Easter Island and the East Pacific*. Vol. 1: *Archaeology of Easter Island*. Edited by T. Heyerdahl and E. N. Ferdon, Jr. (School of American Research and Museum of New Mexico, Monograph No. 24, pt. 1, pp. 221–55.) Santa Fe, 1961.

_____. "A Reconnaissance Survey of Three Fortified Hilltop Villages." In: *The Norwegian Archaeological Expedition to Easter Island and the East Pacific*. Vol. 2: *Miscellaneous Papers*. Edited by T. Heyerdahl and E. N. Ferdon, Jr. (School of American Research and Kon Tiki Museum [Oslo], Monograph No. 24, pt. 2, pp. 9–21.) Santa Fe, 1965.

Firth, Raymond. *Primitive Polynesian Economy*. London: George Routledge and Sons, 1939.

Forster, George . *Voyage Round the World … During the Years 1772, 3, 4, and 5*. 2 vols. London: White, Robson, Elmsly and Ribonson, 1777.

Forster, John R. *Observations Made During a Voyage Round the World, …*. London: Robinson, 1778.

Gayangos, Tomás. "The Official Journal of the Second Voyage of the Frigate *Aguila* from El Callao to Tahibit …: 1774–75." In: Corney, Bolton G., *The Quest and Occupation of Tahiti by Emissaries of Spain in the Years 1772–76*. (Hakluyt Society, 2nd Series, Vol. 36, pp. 103–86.) London, 1915.

Goldman, Irving. *Ancient Polynesian Society*. Chicago: University of Chicago Press, 1970.

Golson, Jack, ed. *Polynesian Navigation: A Symposium on Andrew Sharp's Theory of Accidental Voyages*. (The Polynesian Society, Memoir No. 34.) Wellington, New Zealand, 1963.

Green, R. C. "The Imeediate Origins of the Polynesians." In: Highland, G. A., R. W. Force, A. Howard, M. Kelly, Y. H. Sinoto, eds., *Polynesian Culture History*. (Bernice P. Bishop Museum, Special Publication 56, pp. 215–40.) Honolulu, 1967.

Haddon, A. C., and Hornell, James. *Canoes of Oceania*. 3 vols., 1935. Reprint. (Bernice P. Bishop Museum, Special Publication 27, 28, and 29.) Honolulu, 1975.

Handy, E. S. C. *History and Culture in the Society Islands*. (Bernice P. Bishop Museum, Bulletin 79.) Honolulu, 1930.

Hervé, Juan de. "Information Acquired From the Natives of the Island of Amat (by Them Called Otajiti) During the Voyage After Leaving the Port of Valparaiso ...." In: Corney, Bolton G., *The Quest and Occupation of Tahiti by Emissaries of Spain in the Years 1772–76*. (Hakluyt Society, 2nd Series, Vol. 32, pp. 351–59.) London, 1913.

A Journal of a Voyage Round the World, in His Majesty's Ship Endeavour, In the Years 1768, 1769, 1770, and 1771 ... (Facsimile reprint, Bibliotheca Australiana, No. 14.) Amsterdam: N. Israel, 1967.

Langsdorff, G. H. von. *Voyages and Travels ... during the Years 1803, 1804, 1805, and 1807*. 2 vols. (Facsimile reprint, Bibliotheca Australiana, No. 40.) Amsterdam: N. Israel, 1967.

Ledyard, John. *Journal of Captain Cook's Last Voyage*. (Oregon State Monographs: Studies in History, No. 3.) Corvallis: State University Press, 1964.

Lee, Ida. *Captain Bligh's Second Voyage to the South Seas*. London: Longmans, Green, 1920.

Lewis, Albert B. *The Melanesians: People of the South Pacific*. Chicago: Chicago Natural History Museum, 1951.

Lewis, David. "Hokule'a Follows the Stars to Thaiti." *National Geographic*, Vol. 150, No. 4, pp. 512–37.

Marra, John. *Journal of the Resolution's Voyage, in 1772, 1773, 1774, and 1775 ... Also a Journal of the Adventure's Voyage, in the Years 1772, 1773, and 1774* .... (Facsimile Reprint, Bibliotheca Australiana, No. 15.) Amsterdam: N. Israel, 1967.

Merrill, Elmer D. *The Botany of Cook's Voyages and Its Unexpected Significance in Relation to Anthropology, Biogeography and History*. (Chronica Botanica, Vol. 14, pp. 161–384.) Waltham: Chrinca Botanica Co., 1954.

Métraux, Alfred. *Ethnology of Easter Island*. (Bernice P.Bishop Museum, Bulletin 160.) Honolulu, 1940.

Mortimer, George. *Observations and Remarks Made During a Voyage to the Islands ... in the Brig Mercury* .... Dublin: Byrne, Moore, Grueder, Jones, and White, 1791.

Mulloy, William. "The Ceremonial Center of Vinapu." In: *The Norwegian Archaeological Expeditions to Easter Island and the East Pacific*. Vol. 1: *Archaeology of Easter Island*. Edited by T. Heyerdahl and E. N. Ferdon, Jr. (School of American Research and Museum of New Mexico, Monograph No. 24, pt. 1, pp. 93–180.) Santa Fe, 1961.

Oliver, Douglas. *Ancient Tahitian Society*. 3 vols. Honolulu: University Press of Hawaii, 1975.

Parkinson, Sydney. *A Journal of a Voyage to the South Seas, in His Majesty's Ship the Endeavour: Faithfully Transcribed From the Papers of the Late Sydney Parkinson* .... London: Dilly and Phillips, 1784.

Rickman, John. *Journal of Captain Cook's Last Voyage ... in the Years 1776, 1777, 1778, 1779* .... (Facsimile reprint, Bibliotheca Australiana, No. 16.) Amsterdam: N. Israel, 1967.

Robertson, George. "A Journal of the Second Voyage of H.M.S. *Dolphin* ... in the Years 1766, 1767, and 1768." In: Carrington, H., ed., *The Discovery of Tahiti.* (Hakluyt Society, 2nd Series, Vol. 98, pp. 3–255.) London, 1948.

Rodríguez, Máximo. "Daily Narrative Kept by the Interpreter Máximo Rodríguez at the Island of Amat, Otherwise Otahiti, in the Year 1774." In: Corney, Bolton G., *The Quest and Occupation of Tahiti by Emissaries of Spain in the Years 1772–76.* (Hakluyt Society, 2nd Series, Vol. 43, pp. 109210.) London, 1919.

Sahlins, Marshall D. *Social Stratification in Polynesia.* Seattle: University of Washington Press, 1958.

Sauer, Carl O. *Agricultural Origins and Dispersals.* (The American Geographical Society, Bowman Memorial Lectures, Series 2.) New York, 1952.

Sharp, Andrew. *The Discovery of the Pacific Islands.* London: Oxford University Press, 1962.

Sparrman, Anders. *A Voyage Round the World With Captain James Cook in H.M.S. Resolution.* London: Robert Hale, 1953.

Titcomb, Margaret. *Dog and Man in the Ancient Pacific.* (Bernice P. Bishop Museum, Special Publication 59.) Honolulu, 1969.

Towle, Margaret. *The Ethnobotany of Pre-Columbian Peru.* Chicago: Aldine, 1961.

Turnbull, John. *A Voyage Round the World, in the Years 1800, 1801, 1802, 1803, and 1804 ....* 2nd edition. London: A. Maxwell, 1813.

Vaillant, George C. *The Aztecs of Mexico.* New York: Doubleday, 1947.

Vancouver, George. *A Voyage of Discovery in the North Pacific Ocean, Round the World, ...* 6 vols. London: J. Stockdale, 1801.

Vason, George. *An Authentic Narrative of Four Years Residence at Tongataboo ....* London: Longman, 1810.

Wallis, Samuel. "An Account of a Voyage Round the World in the Years 1766, 1767, and 1768." In: Hawkesworth, J., ed., *An Account of the Voyages Undertaken by Order of His Present Majesty for Making Discoveries in the Southern Hemisphere,* Vol. 1, pp. 363–522. London: Strahan and Cadell, 1773.

Wilson, James. *A Missionary Voyage to the Southern Pacific Ocean, Performed in the Years 1796, 1797, 1798 in the Ship Duff ....* London: Chapman, 1799.

Zeuner, Friedrich E. *A History of Domestic Animals.* New York: Harper and Row, 1963.

Index

Adultery, 154–155
Adzes, 241, 242
Afterlife, 174–175
'Ahia, 183, 186, 189
Ahu, 42, 54–55, 259
Albacore, 211, 214, 215, 217; restrictions on eating of, 199
Alcoholic beverages, European introduction of, 304
Amo'a, ceremonies of, 37, 146; general restrictions prior to, 37–38, 86–87, 146; restrictions of Tahiti nui paramount chief prior to termination of, 35, 36–40; sacredness of child before, 145
Anvil, *tapa*-beating, 113
'Aoa, use of bark of, 109
'Ape, use of leaves of, 95
Ararua, use of, in spears, 262
Ari'i, 44, 197, 236
'Arioi, 71, 117, 122, 130, 143, 144, 223, 224; function of, 140–141; membership limitation in, 139
Arrowroot, Polynesian, 90, 183, 220; preparation of, 90–91; use of, as paste, 116
Atiu, 252
Australs, 249, 252
'Aute. See Mulberry, paper
Aviti fishhook, 213, 214

Bamboo, use of, 99, 128, 186, 214; as container, 81, 86, 95, 223; as knife, 93, 116
Bananas, 56, 88, 89, 91, 182, 187, 189; as offering to deity, 55, 145, 260; ritual use of shoots and leaves of, 59, 82, 165, 267, 268, 272; secular use of leaves of, 89–90, 94, 95, 112, 119. See also *Fe'i* banana
Banquets, 97–99
Bark cloth, 79, 84, 105, 124, 132, 144, 162, 167, 264; as extra-island trade item, 225; as gift, 43, 44, 83, 138, 222, 223; as offering, 165, 173; as payment for services, 69, 145, 150, 210; fabrication of, 111–117, 118, 121, 122
Barter, 183, 221
Baskets, 80–81, 94, 192, 217
Bedsteads, 305
Birds, 94; hunting of, 94–95, 170; sacred, 63, 259
Bloodletting, 82, 164, 166, 172, 173
Bone, human, use of, 242
Bonito, 211, 214, 215, 217
Borabora, trade with, 226
Bows and arrows: use of, in contests, 127–128; use of, in hunting, 94–95

Boxing, 306
Breadfruit, 88, 89, 90, 91, 92, 94, 187–189; as offering to deity, 55, 260; mass baking of, 103, 191–193; use of bark of, 109, 117; use of resin of, 94, 128, 243; use of wood of, 76, 80, 240. See also *Mahi*
Breastplates, 195, 225, 264–265
Broiling, 91
Burial, 159–160, 163, 165; of sacrificial victims, 69

Candlenut, 22–23, 59, 107, 121, 243
Canoes, 75, 178, 223, 238–239, 261; *pahi*, 230, 232, 234–236, 261; raiding of, 226; sacred, 68–69, 260; *va'a*, 230, 232, 236, 261. *See also* Outriggers; Rafts; Sails: War canoes
Casuarina: root of, as fishhook, 213–214
Cats; as food, 89; European introduction of, 300
Cattle, European introduction of, 298–299
Chenopodium quinoa Willd., 289
Chestnut, Tahitian, 189
Chickens, 43, 88, 91, 197, 223; as offering to deity, 145, 146; introduction of European, 296
Chiefs, 29, 35–36, 75, 223; as priests, 60; signs of respect for, 32, 41–42, 82; subordinate, 31, 32, 33–34; taboos surrounding, 40–41. See also *Fana; Hova; 'Iatoai; Metua; Ta'ata 'orero; To'ofa*
Chisels, 242
Circumcision, 150
Clappers, shell, 100, 134
Classes, social, 27–29
Cleanliness, 72, 80, 95, 96, 99, 107
Clothing, 23–24, 109, 167
Clubs, fighting, 262, 264
Cockfighting, 197–198, 306–307
Coconuts, 88, 89, 90, 178, 183, 186–187, 189; as offerings to deity, 55, 260; cream of, 89, 90, 91; milk of, 89; use of husk of, 79, 82, 84, 119, 209, 242, 243; use of shells of, 81, 93, 95, 114, 118, 167

Coconut palms, 56; use of leaves of, 78, 79, 80, 94, 192, 206
Coffins, historic appearance of, 306
Construction, house, 76, 78–79
Convolvulus brasiliensis. See *Ipomoea pes-caprae* (L.) R.
Cooking, hot-stone, 90, 91, 93
Cooks, Southern, 249, 252
Coral, use of, 79, 81, 89, 90, 203, 213, 242
Cotton, wild, 122
Councils, 34–35; of war, 258
Counting, 100–101
Crane, fishing by, 215–217
Cremation, 163–164
Cucurbita lagenaria L. See *Lagenaria siceraria*
Culture change, European-inspired, 41–42, 46, 72, 74, 104, 110–111, 117, 121–122, 126–127, 136, 154, 180, 193, 273, 304. *See also* Boxing; Cockfighting

Dances, 132–136, 148; European-introduced, 306; master of, 134
Day, division of the, 101
Dogs, 93, 195–196, 220; as food, 88–89, 91; as offering to deity, 55, 259; introduction of European and South American, 300–301; restrictions on eating of, 195; use of hair of, 195, 225, 249, 265
Dolphin, 211, 214, 215; restrictions on eating of, 199
Drills, 213, 242
Drums, 99, 134
Dyes, sources of, 118–119, 120–121, 262

Ears, decoration of, 25
Earth ovens, 89, 91, 93–94, 191; construction of, 92–93
Easter Island, 74, 92, 102, 164, 185, 221, 222, 309, 310
Eating, 72, 96; restrictions pertaining to, 86–88
Elephantiasis, 156
Embalming, 160, 161, 166
Enemy dead, disposal of, 271
Exchange, systems of, 221–222

Fana, 32–33

Fatu Hiva, 252

Feathers, 42, 51, 52, 94, 132, 162, 167, 170–171, 172, 264, 266; religious importance of red, 42, 159, 167, 258, 259

Fe'i banana, 88, 89, 182–183, 189, 193–194, 220–221; use of rind of, 81; use of sap of, 120

Fenua ura, 225

Ferns, use of, 78, 176, 194

Ficus tinctoria Forst. See *Mati*

Fig trees. See *'Aoa; Mati; Ora*

Fiji, 129, 178

Firearms, European introduction of, 307–308

Fire making, 91–92

Fish, 43, 88; as offering to deity, 55, 260; restrictions on eating of, 199

Fishhooks, 84, 212; types of, 213–214, 217

Fishing, sex restrictions on, 200

Fleas, European introduction of, 305–306

Flies, abhorrence of, 95–96

Float lines, 214

Flute, nose, 99

Fly flap, 95

Flying fish, 208, 214

Food: restrictions pertaining to, 81, 86; sharing of, 97

Formal friendship. See *Taio*

Fowl, European-introduced, 295–296

Fruit, European-introduced, 287–289

Furnishings, house, 79, 80–81

Gardening, 180, 185–186

Gift-giving, 105–107

Goats, European introduction of, 111, 296–297

Gods, 50–52; means of descent of, 63, 158, 259; unexplained illnesses caused by, 61, 158; unexplained natural phenomena caused by, 70. *See also* Maui; Opunua; Oro; Ta'aroa; Tane

Gongs, slit, 100

Gorgets. *See* Breastplates

Gourds, 81

Grains, European introduction of, 289–290

Guardian spirits, 51

Hair, human, 20–21; decoration of, 25; plaited cords of, 132, 212

Hawaii, 185, 253

Headress. *See* Helmet

Heiva, 130, 136, 148

Helmet, 265–266

Hibiscus: use of bark of, 80, 208, 212; use of wood of, 76, 80, 91, 128, 205, 208

Hibiscus esculentus L., 114

Hibiscus tiliaceus L. *See* Hibiscus

Hivaoa, 253

Hobu, 116

Homosexuals, 153–154

Hopa, 117

Hospitality, 107

House construction, 76, 78–79

Hova, 32–33

Huahine, 184, 198, 234

Human bone, use of, 242

'Iatoai, 34

'Ie'ie, 78; use of vines of, 81, 203

'Ihi. See Chestnut, Tahitian

Infanticide, 154; among *'arioi*, 138, 140; reasons for, 29, 143–144

Ipomoea pes-caprae (L.) R., use of, in seines, 205

Iron, European introduction of, 123, 281–285

Irrigation, 182

Kauai, 282

Kava, 58, 99, 184–185, 258

Kites, 124, 147, 230

Lagenaria siceraria, 291

Lances, 262

Landholdings, boundary markers of, 82

Language change, 45–46

Lice, 85

Lying in state, 159–160

Mackerel, 208

Mahi, 89, 188; as sea ration, 191; pits for storage of, 191, 193; preparation of, 190–191

Maho. See Hibiscus
Mahu. See Homosexuals
Makemo, 252
Manahune, 44, 185; change in meaning of term, 45
Mangaia, 252
Mangareva, 128, 185, 249
Manuae, 252
Maori, 103, 104
Mape. See Chestnut, Tahitian
Mara, use of wood of, 113
Mara (as name for type of bark cloth), 117
Marae, 42, 44, 99, 203; basic features of, 54–55; ceremonies for men and women in, 56–57; ceremonies in, of *mata'eina'a,* 57–58; family, 58, 72, 102, 144; restrictions pertaining to chiefly, 56, 59–60; sacrificial, 66–67
Maro. See Clothing
Maro 'ura. See Sacred loincloth
Marquesas, 154, 185, 252–253, 309, 310
Marriage, 29, 152
Mashed food preparations. See *Popoi*
Masks, 52, 64, 84, 170–172, 272
Massage, 107
Mata'eina'a, 30, 57; control of, by *to'ofa,* 31
Mati: use of bark of, 109, 208, 212; use of, for dye, 118–119, 120
Mats, 75, 79, 80, 130, 144, 237, 249; as clothing, 109, 164, 167
Maui, 50, 70; wickerwork figure of, 51–52
Measuring, 101
Mehetia: subject to Taiarapu, 49, 225; trade with, 225
Melanesia, 74, 164
Metua, 32, 140
Micronesia, 185
Miri, 160–161, 166
Miro, use of, for dye, 120
Miru, as tree dedicated to Tane, 56
Mnemonic devices, 101
Mohu, use of bark of, 212
Mono'i, 85–86, 162, 223; as payment for services, 69; as trade item from other islands, 225

Moorea, 224, 225, 255; wars with Tahiti, 254, 257–261, 269, 270, 296, 297, 299
Motu one. *See* Fenua ura
Mo'u grass, 12
Mourner's costume, 64, 167, 170–172
Mourning: rites of, 164–165, 166–167; symbols of, 173–174
Mulberry, paper: as source of medicament, 157; flowers of, as dye, 262; plantations of, 109, 111; use of bark of, 109
Mullet, 214
Mururoa, 249

Navigation, 245–246
Nets, 82; for fishing, 205–209; restrictions on use of, 210
New Zealand, 164, 309
Nono, use of bark of, for dye, 120
Nose, deformation of, 20

Octopus lure, 210–211
Offertories, 55
Oil, coconut. See *Mono'i*
Omai, 86, 97, 104, 267, 280, 307, 309, 310
'Opio. See Breadfruit, mass baking of
Opunua, 50
Ora, use of bark of, 109
Ora (as name of type of bark cloth), 109
Oro, 50, 56, 259; symbol of, 51, 66, 68, 259–260, 268
Outriggers, 237

Pandanus, 86, 124, 183; fruit of, as food, 91, 147; use of leaves of, 78, 80, 81, 130
Parae. See Mourner's costume
Pareu. See Clothing
Patu, 30, 57
Peace, ceremony of, 267–269
Pearls, 25, 225, 249
Perepeere, 192
Pestle. *See* Poi pounder
Phaseolus truxillensis MBK. See *Pipi*
Pia. See Arrowroot, Polynesian

Pigs, 43, 88, 91, 194–195, 220; as gifts, 44, 223; as offering to deity, 55, 57, 58, 145, 146, 259, 260; as payment for services, 145, 150, 210; cooking of, 93–94; introduction of European varieties of, 299; restrictions on eating of, 195
Pipi, 208, 211
Pipturus argenteus (Forst. f.) Wedd. See *Roa*
Piripiri, 120
Pit oven. *See* Earth ovens
Pitcairn, 249
Planking, manufacture of, 241–242
Plantains. *See* Bananas
Plays, 136–138
Plum, Polynesian, 88, 183, 189; use of resin of, 243; use of wood of, 240
Poi pounder, 81, 191
Poison, fish, 202–203
Pomare, 45, 96, 224, 256, 257; conquest of Taiarapu by, 308
Popoi, 81, 88, 89–90
Porpoise, restriction on eating of, 199
Priests, 32, 44, 57, 58, 60–61, 65, 158, 168, 268; as historians, 61–62; inspirational, 62–63; payment for services of, 145; as sorcerers, 62; women as, 61
Prisoners of war, 46, 270–271. See also *Titi*
Puberty, 148–149
Puddings, 90–91, 93
Purau. *See* Hibiscus

Ra'a, 47, 58
Ra'atira, 45, 46, 57; change in meaning of term, 46
Rabbits, European introduction of, 301
Rafts, 299–230
Rahui, 31, 83, 223
Raiatea, 184, 225, 234, 235, 249, 252, 297
Raivavae, 249, 252
Rapa, 189
Rarotonga, 252
Rata. *See* Chestnut, Tahitian
Rats, 81, 196–197; guards against, 82

Rattus exulans, 196
Rattus norvegicus, 196
Ray, use of skin of, 79, 242
Redistribution of food or goods, formalized, 190, 222–224
Relics, human, 162–163, 271
Rimatara, 252
Roa, 208
Roasting, 93
Roava, 33; branch of, as symbol of paramount chief, 32–33
Root crops, European introduction of, 292
Rotuma, 253
Rumi. *See* Massage
Rurutu, 249, 252

Sacred loincloth, 23, 42–43, 45, 66, 259, 268
Sacrifice, human, 43, 65–66, 68–69, 173, 270–271; as aid in deific curing, 158; disposal of bodies of, 43, 259, 271; for divine aid in warfare, 258; sanctuaries for potential victims of, 49, 56
Sails, 237–238, 244
Salt. *See* Sea water, as condiment
Samoa, 74, 178, 184
Sandalwood, 86, 162
Sauce, fish, 96, 225
Scad, 206, 208
Sea chubb, 214
Seafood: range of, 199–200, 201, 202, 206, 208, 211, 214, 215, 217; restrictions on eating of, 199
Sea water, as condiment, 95
Self-feeding, restrictions against, 37, 88, 98, 145–146, 162
Settlement pattern, 72
Sexual license, 150–152, 155
Shark, 202, 217; restrictions on eating, 199; use of skin of, 79, 99; use of teeth of, 21, 82, 132, 164, 166, 174, 265
Sheds, canoe, 243–244
Sheep, European introduction of, 297–298
Shells: as cutting tools, 21, 81, 93; as scrapers, 91, 112; for decoration, 25, 132; use of, for fishhooks, 213; use of, for masks, 170–172

Sling, 124, 262
Society Islands, 15, 21, 178, 184, 248
Spears, 107, 124, 262; for fish-
    ing, 205
Squashes, European-introduced,
    291–292
Stealing: from Europeans, 226–227;
    punishment for, 48
Stilts, 147
Stingray, 262
Storage chests, 304–305
Sugar cane, 183–184
Surfing, 123
Sweat lodge, 144
Sweet potatoes, 88, 183, 187, 189;
    historic reintroduction of, from
    Peru, 292
Swimming, 123
Swordfish, 201

Ta'aroa, 50
Ta'ata 'orero, 33, 42, 268; as teacher,
    148
Taha, trade with, 225
Tahiti: migration of endemic plants
    to, 16; volcanic origin of, 15–16
Tahiti iti. *See* Taiarapu
Tahiti nui, 27, 40; division of land
    in, 30; investiture of paramount
    chief of, 42–43; restrictions of
    paramount chief of, during his
    early years, 36–40
Tahu'a. See Priests
Tahu'a ma'i. See Wound dresser
Taiarapu, 27, 35, 40, 72, 180, 198,
    235, 249, 261, 266; divisions of
    land in, 30; investiture of
    paramount chief of, 43–44; wars
    with Tahiti nui, 269–270, 308
Taio, 36, 104, 105, 150, 155
Takapoto, 282
Talking chief. See *Ta'ata 'orero*
Tamanu: uses of, 81, 120, 128, 157;
    as tree dedicated to Tane, 56, 120
Tane, 50, 51, 56
Tangaroa. *See* Ta'aroa
Tapa. See Bark cloth
Tapa beater, 114
Taputapu, 66, 68
Taputapuatea. See *Marae*, sacrificial

Taro, 88, 89, 90, 91, 182, 187, 189; as
    offering to deity, 203; leaves of,
    as food, 90
Tattooing, 22–23, 140, 147, 148–150
Tawa, 102
Taxation in kind, 83–84, 224;
    banishment for not paying
    271–727
Tetiaroa, trade with, 225
Teuteu, 44–45, 46, 47, 75, 98, 183,
    185; change in meaning of the
    term, 45
Teve, 90–91, 183
Textiles, European introduction
    of, 278–281
Ti, 183, 193–194; use of leaves of,
    80, 91
Ti'i, 30, 31; as term for sacred
    carved board or figure, 57
Tikopia, 222
Timoe, 249
Tinah (early name of Pomare),
    37, 47
Tiputa. See Clothing
Titi, 46
Toa: use of bark of, 120; use of
    leaves of, 118–119; use of wood
    of, 113, 114, 128, 205, 262
Tobacco, European introduction of,
    293–294
Tonga, 178, 184, 309, 310
Tongatapu, 198
To'ofa, 31, 40, 69, 139, 140
Torch fishing, 107, 204, 205, 209
Towha, 258, 260–261, 266, 267, 268
Trade, external, 224–226
Trade goods, European, 276–
    278, 279
Trails, 228–229
Transvestites. *See* Homosexuals
Traps, fishing, 201, 203–204
Tree-gourd, 85
Tropic bird, 170, 171
Trumpets, shell, 272–273
Tu (name of paramount chiefs of
    Tahiti nui and their family line),
    20, 21, 29, 37, 39, 42, 45–46, 74,
    155, 184, 256, 258, 259, 267, 268,
    269, 296, 301, 304
Tuamotus, 185, 239, 249, 252; Tahi-
    tian trade with atolls of, 225, 226

Tubuai, 252, 297, 298, 311
Tupaia (chief and navigator), 21,
 266, 309; islands known to,
 247 passim
Turmeric, 120
Turtle, 43, 199–200, 213, 214; as
 offering to deity, 55; restrictions
 on eating of, 199
Tuteha, 34, 270, 271
Tuti, 45
Tutui. See Candlenut
Tutuila, 253

Upolu, 253
'Ura. See Feathers, religious importance of red

Vegetables, European introduction
 of, 293
Vehiatua (name of paramount
 chiefs of Taiarapu and their family line), 29, 34, 36, 40, 49, 59,
172, 184, 210, 270, 271, 272; death
 of, 65–66, 158–159
Venereal disease, European introduction of, 156
Vi. See Plum, Polynesian

War canoes, 261–262, 269
Warfare, 255–256; historic changes
 in goals of, 256–257, 308; rituals
 prior to, 258–260; techniques of,
 at sea, 264, 266–267
Warriors, dress of, 64, 264–265
Whales, 201; restrictions on eating
 of, 199
Wound dresser, 157–158
Wrestling, 124–126

Yams, 88, 89, 183, 187, 189, 193–194,
 220; as sea ration, 178–179
Yaws, 156
Year, divisions of the, 101–102

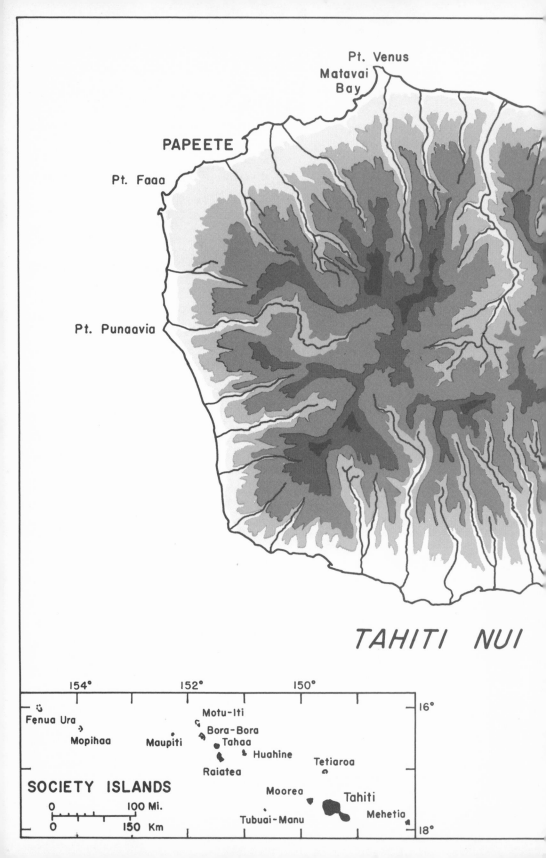

Pt. Venus
Matavai
Bay

PAPEETE

Pt. Faaa

Pt. Punaavia

TAHITI NUI

154°   152°   150°

· ·   16°
Fenua Ura   Motu-Iti
  ·   Mopihaa   ·   Bora-Bora
              Maupiti   Tahaa
                      ·   · Huahine
                    Raiatea   Tetiaroa
SOCIETY ISLANDS
                      Moorea   Tahiti
0   100 Mi.
                  Tubuai-Manu   Mehetia
0   150 Km   18°